ENGLISH PREACHERS
AND PREACHING
1640–1670

THE MACMILLAN COMPANY
NEW YORK · BOSTON · CHICAGO · DALLAS
ATLANTA · SAN FRANCISCO

MACMILLAN & CO., LIMITED
LONDON · BOMBAY · CALCUTTA
MELBOURNE

THE MACMILLAN CO. OF CANADA, LTD.
TORONTO

ENGLISH PREACHERS
AND PREACHING
1640-1670

BY

CAROLINE FRANCIS RICHARDSON

New York
THE MACMILLAN COMPANY
1928

Printed in the United States of America by
J. J. LITTLE AND IVES COMPANY, NEW YORK

To

JOSEPHINE MOORE RICHARDSON

INTRODUCTION

THIS study of Preaching and Preachers has been made with a view to presenting, from another angle than that of theology or politics, a large number of English clergymen who lived during a part of the seventeenth century when parties and individuals are not easily dissociated from sectarian preferences and prejudices. So firm is this impression of the preachers who were active during a part or all of the years from 1640 to 1670 that the human, everyday side of these men is obscured. We are prone to think of Laud, Calamy, or Fox as types: churchmen, nonconformist, quaker; but their own generation found them and their fellows to be endowed with secular as well as spiritual ambitions, with an appreciation of earthly as well as heavenly delights.

After the long parliament seated itself firmly in 1642, we might naturally expect that sermons of an acutely religious nature and preachers of unleavened orthodoxy would be much in evidence for years to come. In evidence, they undoubtedly were, but neither the man in the pulpit nor the man in the pew regarded the sermon from just the angle that would be taken for granted. Ostensibly, the two decades from 1640 to 1660 were intensely religious in thought and behavior. Convenience, if not safety, made all sectarian groups religious perforce. It is evident, however, that neither groups nor individuals could have lived at high pressure for twenty years, nor for one year; everyday habits will persist, everyday points of view quickly reassert themselves after a great experience. Consequently, we find, during the very time when dogmas and doctrines were at extreme tension, that there was a commonplace attitude toward the preacher and his preaching, an attitude that took the minister and his sermon as part of the weekly routine, giving them no special reverence, but, instead, much genuine and friendly interest. Ostensibly, again, the ten years succeeding the Commonwealth would show, it might be supposed, little concern with religious services, but there is proof through diaries, letters, and essays that worldly as well as devout persons went voluntarily to church.

It is entirely reasonable that the average parson of the seventeenth century, a man educated and formally ordained, should be neither unconventional nor unsophisticated; quite naturally he followed fashions that the poet and the playwright found useful. For example, the published sermon generally carried with it a flattering dedication to an influential man or generous woman, and a collection of memorial verses often included poems written by admiring or grateful clergymen. There is, of course, nothing extraordinary about all this. It is not argued that these preachers or those who judged them are a peculiar people; rather is this study intended to emphasize the fact that they are typical of any time; it is a sort of *Defensio pro Clerico Anglicano,* an effort to give the human side of a group that is neither so dull nor so doctrinal as tradition stamps it.

The discussion of men and matters in the chapters which follow is limited to about thirty years, from a decade before the death of Charles I to a decade after the crowning of Charles II. An exhaustive examination of this period has been made by Masson in his *Life of Milton,* and historians and essayists have also found the Commonwealth and Restoration times rich in material for studies in politics, philosophy, and economics. These topics are therefore omitted from this inquiry into secular activities. Omitted, too, are many famous quarrels between scholars, as, for instance, the Smectymnuan controversy; Chillingworth's exchange of argument with the Jesuit, Edward Knott; Laud *versus* Fisher; and Thomas Fuller *versus* Peter Heylin. Quarrels sound a-religious but most of the differences of opinion among the seventeenth-century clergy were connected with doctrinal belief or sectarian behavior. Those that reached the dignity of publication fail to offer anything more humanly interesting than analysis, proofs, and most logical deduction. There was probably no lack of pride, anger, and one or two other deadly sins in these intellectual charges and counter charges; but the stout folios and slender quartos are as impersonally assertive as the Thirty-nine Articles or the Westminster Confession.

In the pages which follow, a generation of English preachers is shown as interested in many subjects, some being an outgrowth of theological scholarship, others having no connection with religion. No one of the avocations that attracted clergymen is presented in complete detail, nor is any one influence or condition discussed to the fullest extent. The intention has been to give an impression of the intellectual and social background of the educated clergy during a particular period, not to write a history of medicine or mathematics, of education or fine arts, as developed under the Commonwealth and Restoration.

The most important sources for this study were found in the Library of Union Theological Seminary, New York City. I am grateful for the generous hospitality which permitted a stranger to handle freely the rare and valuable works in the McAlpin Collection.

My heaviest personal obligation is to Professor George

Philip Krapp of Columbia University. The subject and plan of the book are my own; but I have had the benefit of Professor Krapp's exact knowledge, his critical judgment, and, too, the encouragement of his unfailing kindness. He has read the book in its first draft, in completed form, and in proof. It has also been 'read by Professor Charles Sears Baldwin and Professor Frank A. Patterson, to both of whom I am indebted for corrections and suggestions.

CAROLINE FRANCIS RICHARDSON.

Newcomb College (Tulane University),
New Orleans, Louisiana.

CONTENTS

PAGE

INTRODUCTION   vii

CHAPTER I. THE TRAINING OF A PULPIT SPEAKER .   3

Grammar-school disputations and orations.—
Phrase-books, commonplace-books, rhetorics.—
University disputations.—*Terrae filius.*—Criticism of university education as a preparation for
the ministry.—Wright's *Five Sermons.*

CHAPTER II. THE PREACHER AND HIS PUBLIC . .   21

General interest in church-going.—Extraordinarily popular preachers.—The preacher's enjoyment of preaching.—The preacher's objections to preaching.—Instructions on preaching.
—Criticism of public performances, voice, mannerisms, gestures.—Pulpit extravagances compared with stage affectations.—The preacher's
memory.

CHAPTER III. THE SERMON AND THE PUBLIC . .   70

Formal construction of the sermon.—Custom of
taking down sermon-heads, or of taking copious
notes of the entire sermon.—Use of shorthand.
—Literary manner and matter in sermons.—Few
exempla.—Euphuistic phrasing.—Essay-sermons.
—Occasional sermons—Popularity of funeral
sermons.—Sermon-helps.—Sermon-length.—Sermon-borrowing.—The printed sermon.—Sermon
dedications.

PAGE

CHAPTER IV. THE SECULAR INTERESTS OF THE
CLERGY 137

I. Learned Avocations 138

Antiquities (chronology, coins, heraldry).—Astrology.— Chemistry.— Law.— Languages (ancient, oriental, the *Polyglot Bible,* Anglo-Saxon,
Welsh, Irish, modern tongues, translations, philology).—General learning (the Royal Society,
private libraries).—Mathematics.—Medicine.—
Teaching (textbooks, methods).

II. The Clergy and the Fine Arts . . 213

Drama. — Drawing. — Music. — Poetry. — Romances.—Pre-*Gothic* description.—Travel records.—Personal essays.—Miscellaneous avocations: secular reading.—Sports, games.—Mechanics.—Outdoor interests.—Farming.—Fishing.

CHAPTER V. THE PREACHER AND THE SOCIAL ORDER 260

Importance of good birth and breeding.—Cri-
ticism of typical candidates for the ministry.—
The university and the graduate in divinity.—
The private chaplain, at home, abroad.—The
court chaplain.—Pepys's attitude to the clergy.
—Salaries and fees paid clergymen.

CHAPTER VI. THE CHARACTER OF A PREACHER . . 282

Popularity of *Character*-writing; its influence
on personal descriptions.—Cheerful clergymen.
—Morose clergymen.—Baxter's comments on the
Anglican clergy at the Savoy Conference.—Ret-
ribution.—Peculiarly disagreeable divines.—
Idiosyncrasies.—*Characters* in verse, anagrams.
—Physical appearance.

BIBLIOGRAPHY 305

INDEX 331

ENGLISH PREACHERS
AND PREACHING
1640–1670

CHAPTER I

THE TRAINING OF A PULPIT SPEAKER

I F a young man went to Oxford or Cambridge in the seventeenth century, there was more than a possibility that he expected to enter the ministry. There were, of course, students at both universities who had no thought of taking a degree in divinity; and there were students outside the universities who worked under private teachers, planning to present themselves eventually before the proper authorities for examination and ordination. But the majority of intending divines matriculated at one of the two great institutions of learning, knowing well that through them ran the best as well as the easiest road to the pulpit. Having determined upon his profession, the ambitious youth would apply himself assiduously to his studies. Among these, a course in elocution would not be included; for there was no provision for formal training in preaching as an art, although there had been a professorship of Divinity at Cambridge and Oxford since Henry VIII's time. In spite of the omission of a subject of vital interest to a future preacher, the young bachelor of divinity would, because of the prevailing method of instruction both in grammar school and in the university, have had fairly regular practice in public speaking from his early boyhood.

Disputations were a common exercise in the grammar school,[1] but special emphasis was laid on the declamation

---

[1] Brinsley, John : *A Consolation for Our Grammar Schools, etc.*, p. 70. He recommends "disputing scholar-like of Grammar Questions, and to prepare for more learned Disputations in the Universities"; also, *Ludus Literarius,* Ch. XVII, p. 205.

or oration. The composing of a theme, as the oration was usually called, required much preliminary drilling, not only in the proper way to develop a subject but also in the selection of appropriate illustrations and figures of speech. As part of the preparation, every boy was expected to keep a notebook into which he wrote down forceful or fanciful phrases from the authors he read, historical and mythological references, anecdotes from good story-tellers like Plutarch, and Natural History from equally good story-tellers like Pliny. Natural History books were deliberately studied for the express purpose of finding startling similes, for the trail of John Lyly was still as conspicuous in rhetoric as was that of William Lily in grammar.[2]

Charles Hoole, in his *New Discovery of the Old Art of Teaching School*, said that a commonplace book should have these heads:

> Short Histories
> Apologues and Fables
> Adages
> Hieroglyphics
> Emblems and Symbols
> Ancient Laws and Customs
> Witty Sentences
> Rhetorical Exortations

[2] Hoole, Charles: *A New Discovery of the Old Art of Teaching School*, p. 281ff.

Watson, Foster: *The Curriculum and Textbooks of English Schools in the First Half of the 17th Century* (Tr. of the Bibliog. Soc. VI, 221-224).

Leach, A. K.: *Ed. Charters*, p. 451 (shows Eton time-table, 1530; cf. 17th cent. Curriculum).

When Francis Cheynell preached on *The Man of Honour* before the House of Lords, he compared unworthy men to beasts. He did this briefly, saying: "But I intend not to run over Aristotle, or Elians History of Animals; nor will I open Gesners Library, or tell you any strange stories out of Dresserus, Comerarius, or Gonlartius, of men turned into the shape of Beasts; I might as well turn Ovid his Metamorphosis into Prose; nor will I stand to dispute, whether Nebuchadnezzar was turned into a beastlike shape in respect of his body . . . nor will I trouble you with a comment on the Beasts at Ephesus . . ." (p. 24).

Topical Places
Description of things natural and artificial [3]

Under each head the schoolboy was expected to supply an ever-increasing number of examples. A phrase book was another necessity.[4] The selections copied into it might be original, adapted, or quoted; they might be disconnected, or designed to develop one topic, as follows:

Festina lente

1. Propositio: Damnosa est in gerendis rebus nimia festinatio.
2. Ratio: Nihil enim concilio tam inimicum est, quam temeraria negotii praecipitatio.
3. Confirmatio: Sine concilio autem quicquid fit, recte fieri non potest.
4. Similitudo: Ut aestas frugibus, ita deliberandi spatium maturandis negotiis necessarium.
5. Exemplum: Fabius Maximus, ut ferunt, Romanam cunctando restituit rem.
6. Vet. Test.: Noverat enim verum esse vetus illud verbum omnia fieri sat cito si sat bene.
7. Conclusio: Bene igitur videtur consulere, qui lente monet festinare.[5]

Hoole also advised that boys should "exercise themselves in Anagrams, Epigrams, Epitaphs, Epithalamias, Eclogues, and Acrosticks, English, Latine, Greek and Hebrew." In his childhood, therefore, a youth was specifically trained toward the acquirement of a dexterity in

[3] Hoole; *op. cit.*, p. 208.
[4] *Ibid.*, p. 209.
Barker, G. F. R.: *Memoir of Richard Busby; and School Life at Westminster in the 17th Century*, p. 80.
Watson, Foster: *The Curriculum, etc.*, p. 219.
See Rhetorics of the time, as Farnaby's *Index rhetoricus* which devotes many pages to Phrases, listing them under heads, as *Laudandi, Vituperandi*, etc.; or John Smith's *Mysterie of Rhetorique Unveil'd*, which generously provides tropes, figures, "lively Definitions," and scriptural examples.
[5] Watson, Foster: *The Curriculum, etc.*, p. 244 (Appendix).
Cf. Bacon (*Works*, VI, 118-120) on the causes of "an affectionate study of eloquence, and copie of speech." (Quoted, with discussion, in George Philip Krapp: *The Rise of Eng. Lit. Prose*, pp. x-xii.)

vocabulary and the use of a variety of illustration. It is
evident that a dull or lazy preacher could find much assistance in his own or anyone else's grammar school exercise
books, for there ready to his hand would be a wealth of
imagery and philosophy.

There were many works on Rhetoric which would aid the
teacher or the more advanced student in planning a theme
and constructing it according to the preferred pattern. The
authors of such textbooks frequently recommend other
Rhetorics by contemporary or nearly contemporary writers.[6]
John Brinsley, in his *Consolation,* expresses approval of
"Maister Farnabee, Mr. Butler's Rhetorick of Magdalen
College in Oxford, Maister Vicars *Manu ductio ad artem
Rhetoricam* (of Queens College, Oxford); Maister John
Stockwood." Hoole's *New Discovery* mentions: "William
Dugard's *Elementa Rhetorices,* Charles Butler's *Rhetoric,*
Thomas Farnaby's *Index Rhetoricus,* T. Horne's *Compen-
dium Rhetorices;* and for older pupils, Vossius's *Partitiones
Oratoriae,* the *Orator Extemporaneous, Tesuari Exercita-
tiones Rhetoricae,* Nic. Caussinus, Paiot, *de Eloquentia.*"
Farnaby filled the margins of his *Index Rhetoricus* with
authorities, modern as well as ancient.[7] The *Elementa
Rhetorica,* by the elder Vossius, is very simple compared
with Farnaby's book. Under *De Pronunciatione* there is
some comment on voice and gesture, but fourteen lines suffice
for the reminder that a natural tone and manner is most
successful in securing the approval of an audience.[8] John
Smith boldly writes in English. He thinks Rhetoric should
be divided into two parts:

[6] Aristotle, Cicero, Quintilian and Horace are inevitable authorities
that are cited by all these writers on rhetoric. For a detailed study
of classical theories, see Charles Sears Baldwin: *Ancient Rhetoric
and Poetic.*

[7] Farnaby's book is a duodecimo volume of only 103 pages, but it
is packed with information. The *Index Poeticus* would be valuable
to a sermon writer, as it offers an extraordinary assemblage of
heads, one of which is *Oratores inepti.*

Watson, Foster, in *The Curriculum,* names fourteen Rhetorics
printed from 1524 (Leonard Cox's) to 1657 (John Smith's).

[8] Vossius, G. J.: p. 47.

1. Garnishing of speech, called Elocution.
2. Garnishing of the manner of utterance, called Pronunciation (which in this Treatise is not principally aimed at).[9]

Thomas Hobbes also writes in English, presenting "an abridgement of the most useful parts of Aristotle's Rhetoric." Hobbes's illustrations are usually his own, as when he explains fallacious reasoning by means of the following:

> If every Minister were put out of the Church, and a
>   Preacher in his place, we should have good order,
> But we have good order, Therefore
> Every ignorant Minister is put out of the Church, and
>   a Preacher in his place.[10]

The subject of an oration might be any standard proposition. John Clarke's *Formulae Oratoriae in usum Scholarum concinnatae, una cum multis Orationibus, Declamationibus* . . . suggests fifty subjects for school orations. These are representative:

> Poetae nascantur, non fiant?
> Praestat aquam, an vinum bibere?
> Lucretia bene fecit quando seipsam interfecit?
> Praestet inopem esse quam impium?
> Nihil scire sit vita jucundissima?
> Liceat foeminis imperare? [11]

Having selected his topic and consulted his commonplace book and his phrase book, the school boy would develop his

---

[9] *The Mysterie of Rhetorique Unveil'd*, p. 15. (Opposite the title page is an indorsement of the book by the eminent divine, Joseph Caryl.)

[10] *The Art of Rhetorick*, p. 168. (In the Preface, Hobbes explains that he had written this work "some thirty years since" although the edition bears the date of 1681.)

[11] Quoted by Foster Watson in *The Curriculum*, pp. 266-7. In the same article is another extract from Clark's *Formulae:* a model oration having the conventional *Exordium, Propositio*, etc., p. 252. See also, Watson's *The English Grammar School to 1660*, Ch. XXVIII (The School Oration).

theme by sections: *Exordium, Narratio, Confirmatio, Confutatio, Conclusio.* Most probably he would write in Latin, but he might use Greek, Hebrew, or Arabic.[12]   John Evelyn was much impressed by the exercises at Westminster School, during which boys of twelve or thirteen employed not only Latin, but Greek, Hebrew, and Arabic in themes and extempore verses. As further proof of the thoroughness of preparation required for the ordeal, he mentions the names of the "examinants, or posers," who were "Dr. Duport, Greek professor at Cambridge; Dr. Fell, Dean of Christ Church, Oxford; Dr. Pierson; Dr. Allestree, Dean of Westminster; and any that would." [13]   Characteristically, Samuel Pepys was not at all awed when he went on Opposition Day to "Paul's Schoole" and heard the head forms posed in Latin, Greek, and Hebrew; "but I think they do not answer in any as well as we did, only in geography they did pretty well. Dr. Wilkins and Outram were the examiners." [14]   When Pepys's younger brother, whom he destined for the ministry, was at St. Paul's (some two years before this occasion), Pepys had so little confidence in the quality of instruction provided, or in his brother's ability, that he records in the *Diary:* "I rose early this morning and looked over and corrected my brother John's speech which he is to speak at the next opposition." [15]

Besides composing and declaiming his own speeches, the grammar school boy was required to learn the orations of Cicero and Demosthenes and other great speakers. Hoole states that, as part of the work of the Sixth Form, the boys must memorize "Plinie's Panegyricas, Quintilian's Declamations," in addition to "Tullie." These exercises were helpful both for performers and audience. When Dr. Roger Mainwaring (Lord Bishop of St. David's) was praised for

[12] Leach, A. F.: *Educational Charters and Documents, 598 to 1909,* p. 533.
Cook, A. K.: *About Winchester College,* pp. 311-314.
[13] *Diary,* May 13, 1661.
[14] *Diary,* Feb. 4, 1661/2.
[15] *Diary,* Jan. 9, 1559/60.

his ability as a pulpit orator, he "professed he owed his Elocution and Pronunciation to one of his Fellow Pupils gallant delivery of the Speeches of Ajax and Ulysses in Ovid for Poetry; and Cicero's Orations against Antony for Prose. . . ."[16]

From the point of view of a future pulpit career, all of these matters—the making of commonplace books and phrase books, the ordered arrangement of a theme, the study of ancient languages, the practice afforded by the disputation, the declamation, and the oration—would be of practical service. If a student had conscientiously compiled books full of answers to stock arguments, and of elaborate and startling figures of speech, if he had learned to construct themes with a beginning and an end, if he had accustomed himself to committing these themes—whether in Latin, Greek, Hebrew, or Arabic—to memory, and had declaimed them, then he had made, while still at Paul's or Westminster, a real beginning as a successful speaker.

At the university, students had further opportunity to practice public speaking, for declamations were a required exercise. They might be delivered before the tutor only [17] or before a large audience, they might be a frequent or rare experience; but even an onlooker at a declamation could not fail to get many working ideas in regard to elocution. Even more helpful would be attendance at the disputations whether the student were present as participant or audience. He would realize that theory must be supported by evidence, that statement must be made clear by illustration, that objection must be met by citation of authority, that, unless a man speaks clearly and distinctly, all his arguments will profit him nothing.[18]

---

[16] Lloyd : *Memoirs of the Lives, etc.*, p. 27.
[17] D'Ewes, Sir Simonds : *Autobiography*, I, 121. "My declamations . . . were very rarely performed, being but two in number; the first in my tutor's chamber, and the other in the college chapel."
[18] *Ibid.* "Nor was my increase of knowledge small, which I obtained by the ear as well as by the eye, by being present at the public commencements . . . at problems, sophisms, declamations."

Although disputations provided invaluable oral practice and illustration for the embryo divine, any student, obviously, would benefit by the experience. Quickness of thought, acuteness of argument, smoothness of phrase had long been thought of as part of a gentleman's training; the courtly-love analyzer, Castiglione's courtier, Sir Thomas Elyot's young reasoner all knew that the well-bred man must be prepared to answer objections swiftly and with at least an appearance of logic.

The dignity and seriousness of the disputations depended upon those who directed them. Some masters of colleges and other officers were most conscientious about attendance at ordinary sophister disputations and acts, as well as at the formal examinations for degrees. Dr. Edmund Staunton [19] was a model; Dr. Henry Hammond's high sense of duty led him "to interest himself not only in moderating at Divinity disputations . . . but in presiding at the more youthful Exercises of Sophistry, Themes and Declamations." [20]   Dr. Fell attended and presided over examinations, and if the examiners "would, or could, not do their duty he would do it himself to the pulling down of many. He did also sometimes repair to the ordinaries (commonly called wall-lectures from the paucity of auditors) and was frequently present at those exercises called disputations in Austins, where he would make the disputants begin precisely at one, and continue disputing till three." [21] Dr. Joseph Crowther "would often moderate in the public disputations within his own Hall at Oxford; but so fierce

[19] Clark, Samuel: *Eminent Lives*, p. 162.
[20] Fell: *Life of Hammond*, p. 48.
An exceptionally good student-disputant might preside over some undergraduate exercises, as did Matthew Robinson: "When senior sophister, he was appointed to be moderator of his year by his tutor Cawdrey then chosen proctor" (*Autobiography*, p. 23).
William Gouge went from Eton to "Kings College in Cambridge, where he was so Studious, and profited so much by his studies, that he was made moderator in the Sophisters Schools" (William Jenkyn: *A Shock of Corn Coming in Its Season*, p. 33).
[21] Wood: *Ath. Ox.*, IV, 195-6.
See Evelyn's account of a disputation at Oxford, *Diary*, July 9-10, 1669.

and passionate, that if the Opponent made a false syllogism, or the Respondent a wrong answer, he bade the next that sat by him kick their shins; and it became a proverb, Kick-shins Crowther." [22]

There was a good deal of worldly entertainment connected with the formal disputations, which were in reality tests of a young man's fitness to receive a degree; and many anecdotes are told of unhappy candidates, especially of those seeking a degree in divinity. Particularly unfortunate was Francis Potter: "In his younger years, he was very apt to fall into a swoune, and so he did in the Divinity-Schoole. . . ." [23] Dr. John Prideaux seems to have been noticeably humane in his dealings with nervous disputants —"so tender of young men's reputation that answered under him, unless they were self-conceited Paradox mongers (for then he would let them swoun before he gave them any hot water) that he was a staff to them, as that the standers by did not see but that they went upon their own legs. And when he pressed (a better Christian than a clerk) with an hard argument, and was answered, *Reverende Professor, ingenue confiteor me, non posse respondere huic argumento*, he replied kindly, *Recte respondes*." [24] It must have been a recollection of some such painful experience that led Archbishop Usher, in one of his sermons, to select an unusual comparison for the bar of judgment in heaven: ". . . he [the Saviour] is the common father of all mankind. . . . He shall present them to his father, as when one is presented to the University." [25]

Some clergymen could look back on their examination without embarrassment. When Peter Vinke took his degree, "the professor, having held his dispute with him

[22] Brydges: *Restituta*, I, 59 (Quoted from Kennett).
[23] Aubrey: *Brief Lives*, II, 163.
[24] Lloyd: *Memoirs, etc.*, p. 537. Fuller tells the same anecdote, but mentions no name, in The Controversial Divine (*The Holy and Profane State.*)
Wood shows Prideaux at the examination of Cornelius Burgess. *Ath. Ox.*, III, 681.
[25] Usher: *Eighteen Sermons* (fourth sermon, p. 67).

longer than ordinary (he continuing to answer in neat and
elegant Latin) . . . acknowledged that it was to entertain
the auditory." [26]   Dr. Edmund Staunton might have re-
called his experience with complacency, if he permitted
himself such an indulgence in self-approval. He appeared
as a candidate for a degree of doctor in divinity after he
had been suspended from his ministry (in 1635) for not
reading the Book of Sports. "When he answered in
Comitiis and opposed in *Vesperiis,* he was wonderfully
applauded by all that were present. There were several
Doctors in the University, whose fingers did itch to be
dealing with him, because he was a Country Minister and
a Puritan, among whom was a Doctor of great note among
them, who was so pittyfully Non-plust by Staunton, that
the Auditors hissed at him, and one called out for a Candle
that the Doctor might see his arguments." [27]   William
Gouge also won active approval from some of his hearers
when he made an impromptu speech during an act at Cambridge, overwhelming both the respondent and the moderator who took up the question. A sophister jeered, "whereupon the moderator rose up, and gave him a box on the ear,
then the school was all in a uproar; but the said William
Gouge was safely conveyed out from among them." [28]

The disputations, especially those concerned with theological questions, did not always satisfy the judgment or
taste of critics. Milton, in his *Means to remove Hirelings
out of the Church,* asserts: "Those theological disputations
there held in the University by Professors and Graduates
are such as tend least of all to the edification or capacity of
the people, but rather perplex and leaven pure doctrine with
scholastical trash than enable any minister to the better
preaching of the gospel." [29]   John Hall is more emphatic in

[26] Palmer: *Nonconformists Memorial,* I, 132.
[27] Clark, Samuel: *Eminent Lives,* p. 162.
[28] Clark, Samuel: *General Martyrology,* p. 491.
   See *The Flemings in Oxford,* 1650-1700, Appendix, p. 531ff, on The
Comitia or Act.
[29] *Prose Works,* III, 37.

An Humble Motion to the Parliament concerning the Advancement of Learning and Reformation in the Universities when he characterizes the disputations as "illiterate debates tossed to and fro among them without any delight to any but those who love brawling and canvassing such unlearned opinions which runne in this circle without end and contribute not the least to the promotion or discovery of Truth." [30]

A model disputant is offered by David Lloyd, the Memoir writer. He presents Dr. Daniel Featley (who sometimes spells his name Fairclough), as a man possessing "three things that would make a stupendious Disputant."

1. A calm Temper, injoying his adversaries frets, and advantage of his disorders.
2. A voluble tongue, used to discourse in the Club, that always attended Dr. Featley.
3. His rubbing over every year his Memory with Definitions, Divisions and Maxims, both in Philosophy and Divinity.[31]

The position of *jocoserius* or *terrae filius* gave a special opportunity to practice and display both quickness of wit and oratorical ability. No restrictions were placed on this speaker who might attack whom he would in language as coarse as his Latin vocabulary provided. A book published in the first part of the eighteenth century, *Terrae-Filius; Or, The Secret History of the University of Oxford,* announces in the Preface: "It has been our custom from time immemorial, for one of our family, to mount the Rostrum at Oxford at certain seasons and divert an innumerable crowd . . . with a merry oration in the Fescennine manner, interspersed with secret history, raillery and sarcasm. . . ." [32] The author gives examples of the free-

[30] *An Humble Motion,* etc., p. 30.
Thomas Hall, in his *Vind. Lit.,* p. 12, says Christ sat among the Doctors, "both hearing them, and asking them questions; and in his disputations he used Logicall consequences and reasonings from the Old Test. to the New." He also cites Paul as an excellent Disputant.
[31] Lloyd: *Memoirs,* p. 527.
[32] The book was printed anonymously, but the author is known to be Nicholas Amhurst.

dom with which the *terrae filius* would charge a venerable head of a college with immorality, or the wife of a dignitary with unbecoming conduct, or an unpopular tutor with any sin spectacular enough to startle the audience. Thomas Hearne relates that Lancelot Addison (long afterward, Dean of Lichfield), when filling the office of *terrae filius,* reflected so severely and insultingly on Dr. Robert South that the famous clergyman stood up and exclaimed: *"O monstrum horrendum, informe, ingens, cui lumen ademptum!"* [33] Dr. John Owen once warned the *terrae filius* to avoid profanity and obscenity and, his command being ignored, sent his beadles to pull down the young man. The scholars interposed; whereupon the Doctor seized the young man and sent him to the Bocardo, declaring: "I will not see the university so trampled on." [34] Evelyn, writing in 1669, laments that personal attacks have been substituted at Oxford for the old way of "rallying on the questions," and he remarks that the speech he has just heard from the *terrae filius* was a "tedious, abusive, sarcastical rhapsody. . . ." [35]

There were young men, however, who could fill the office of *terrae filius* and remain dignified while entertaining the company. Certain clergymen are remembered to have been particularly successful in this respect. Ralph Brownrig (afterwards Lord Bishop of Exeter) was a model *Jocoserius* in his student days, his "mirth married with that Modesty which became the Muses." [36] Martin Moreland "in his younger years . . . was *Terrae filius* in the Oxford act, as his brother . . . was Prevaricator in the Cambridge commencement. Both of them came off with honour and esteem for their ingenious performance, and their innocent and pleasant entertainment." [37]

[33] *Reliquae Hearnae,* I, 77-8.
[34] Burrows, Montagu: *The Register of the Visitors of . . . Oxford,* p. xli.
[35] *Diary,* July 9-10, 1669.
[36] Lloyd: *Memoirs,* p. 405.
[37] Palmer: *Nonconf. Mem.,* II, 28.

The ability to speak in public, intelligently and effectively, to bear himself easily when assaulted with arguments, was the most conspicuous good that a young preacher would have gained from his university experience, but his general education would also be valuable. The preacher must have something to say; he must know whether other men—scholars of all times, writing in many languages—had thought as he did.   Most subjects taught at the universities would, as a matter of fact, serve as preparation for preaching.[38]   The study of languages helped the future bachelor of divinity to appreciate the exact meaning of a word, the training in logic forced him to reason carefully, mathematics made him see the necessity of proof, and philosophy led him to inquiry.   In connection with his work in almost any field there would be much reading expected in ancient writings; and, as in his boyhood, he would keep a notebook for quotations, strange parallels, conceits, and sermon outlines.[39]   When he entered the church, all this would prove useful, whether "the church" meant, in his case, the organization recognized by the Stuart party, or a nonconforming body; because preach he must, be he established, or presbyterian, or independent, or baptist, or quaker.

It was expected that the man who was selected to preach religion, or doctrine, to a congregation must himself have been taught carefully and, if possible, according to the orthodox standards of those recognized as authorities in church affairs.   It was inevitable, therefore, that education in general and in the two universities in particular should be matters of interest to many of the clergy and laity of seventeenth-century England.   Each of the great parties wished to control the preparation of young men for life,

---

[38] Joseph Glanvill, in *An Essay on Preaching*, says the young Divine will need "the knowledge of Philosophy, Languages, History, and a competent Acquaintance with the most substantial writings of the Ancient and Modern Divines," p. 81.
[39] D'Ewes, Sir Simonds: *Autobiography*, I, 120.

especially for religious life; in consequence, Oxford and Cambridge were targets for criticism from both Royalists and Puritans. Hobbes declared with conviction: ". . . out of the Universities came all these Preachers that taught the contrary to the Rules of the Science of Just and Unjust. The Universities have been as mischievous to this Nation, as the Wooden Horse was to the Trojans." [40] And again: "For seeing the Universities are the Fountains of Civill, and Morall Doctrine, from whence the Preachers, and the Gentry, drawing such water as they find, use to sprinkle the same, (both from the Pulpit, and in their conversation) upon the People, there ought certainly to be great care taken, to have it pure, both from the Venime of Heathen Politicians, and from the Incantations of Deceiving Spirits." [41]

Another troubled and troubling person was William Dell. Bachelor and master of Cambridge though he was, he inveighed against an academic training as a necessary preliminary to a clergyman's career. "You will say . . . what need is there of our Philosophy, and of our Arts and Sciences to the Ministry of the New Testament? And what need is there of our Acts and Clerums? And what need is there of our Scarlet and Tippets? Answer, no need at all. . . . For it is one of the grossest errors that ever reigned under Antichrists Kingdom, to affirm that Universities are the foundation of the Ministers of the Gospel, which do only proceed out of Christ's flesh." [42] As Master of Caius College,[43] Dell did not condemn universities sweepingly; he felt they rendered genuine service "as Schools of good learning for the instruction and educating Youth in the knowledge of the Tongues and of the Liberal Arts and Sciences, thereby to make them useful and serv-

[40] Hobbes: *Behemoth*, p. 493.
[41] *Ibid., Leviathan*, p. 395.
[42] Dell: *A Stumbling Stone*, pp. 26-7.
[43] Appointed Apr. 15, 1649, following the ejectment of Dr. Batchcroft. Dell was himself ejected in 1660.

iceable to the Commonwealth. . . ." [44]   But he did not
believe that universities knew how to train preachers.

Dell was answering a sermon preached the year before
(1652) by Sydrach Simpson (Master of Pembroke) who
had stoutly maintained the contrary point of view; and
Dell's arguments were soon replied to by Joseph Sedgwick,
who, when his discourse was published, joined with it an
"Appendix or Postscript" of fifty-seven closely printed
objections to the *Stumbling Stone* (the title of Dell's sermon
when published), for Sedgwick felt keenly that only
through a classical education and general culture could a
young man be prepared to save souls, or himself be saved
intellectually or spiritually.[45]   Seth Ward also answered
Dell, even accusing him—a preacher—of ignorance of
Latin and of most university learning.[46]   A few years
earlier, in 1649, J. H. (John Hall) had published an elaborate study, entitled *An Humble Motion to the Parliament
of England Concerning the Advancement of Learning: and
Reformation of the Universities*.   He held that to advance
education is the great design of Religion and is the best
way to prepare young men to preach, but he believed the
sort of education provided by the universities only resulted
in filling the world "with detestable quacking Empiricks
. . . or ignorant, mercenary Divines." [47]

William Lilly, the astrologer, was interested in many
things besides the stars.   It is not surprising, therefore, to
find him criticizing the training given the clergy of his day.
He considers it inadequate, basing his objection entirely
on the shocking ignorance of Latin that he had found in
those with whom he had come in contact as a schoolboy.
Because of his own proficiency in speaking Latin, he had
always been summoned before visiting ministers.   "In the

[44] Dell: *A Stumbling Stone*, p. 27.
[45] *An Essay to the Discovery of the Spirit of Enthusiasm.*
[46] Ward: *Vindiciae Academiarum* (Appendix, pp. 62-65).   Ward's
pamphlet was written primarily as an answer to John Webster's *Acad.
Examen.*
[47] Hall: *An Humble Motion, etc.*, p. 24.

derivation of words, I found most of them defective, nor indeed were any of them good grammarians." [48]

It is to be expected that George Fox should feel that a university education is an unnecessary preliminary to a preacher's career. He says: "Now after I had received that opening from the Lord that to be at Oxford or Cambridge was not sufficient to fit a man to be a minister of Christ, I regarded the priests less, and looked more after the Dissenting people"; [49] again, he relates that "we came to Durham, where was a man come down from London to set up a college there to make men ministers of Christ, as they said. I went, with some others, to reason with him, and to let him see that to teach men Hebrew, Greek and Latin, and the seven arts, which were all but the teachings of the natural man, was not the way to make them ministers of Christ." [50]

On the other hand, Abraham Wright composed his *Five Sermons in five several styles or Waies of Preaching* with the definite purpose of showing the necessity of a university preparation for the preacher, whether he be established or nonconformist: "The chief thing that I drive at in printing these Sermons is to shew the difference betwixt Universitie and Citie breeding up of Preachers; and to let the people know that any one that hath been bred up a Scholar is able to preach any way to the capacitie and content of any Auditorie . . . all men will not be brought by the same way of preaching to heaven: some are well satisfied with the plaine easie way of Doctrine and Use; others are not taken with any Sermon, but what is fill'd with depth of Matter, height of Fancie, and good Language." Therefore, argues the Reverend Mr. Wright, a preacher must be so trained that he can dress his ideas according to taste, or order; and

---

[48] Lilly: *Hist. of His Life and Times*, p. 13. (Pepys complains of a navy chaplain who "preached a sad sermon, full of nonsense and false Latin," *Diary*, April 27, 1662.)
[49] Fox: *Journal*, p. 6ff.
[50] *Ibid.*, p. 164.

only a university can give such versatility based on sound
scholarship. To illustrate his contention, Wright composed
five sermons, each one in imitation of a popular preacher
or a popular manner:

Bishop Andrews his Way; before the late King on the first
day of Lent
Bishop Hall's Way; before the Clergie at the Author's own
Ordination in Christ-Church, Oxford
Dr. Maine's and Mr. Cartwright's Way; before the Universitie
of St. Marie's
The Presbyterian Way; before the citie at St. Paul's, London
The Independent Way; never preached

In writing these sermons, the author did not intend any
satirical presentation. All but one of the sermons were
literally preached, and each is sincere in its explanation of
some religious topic. No doctrines are emphasized, but
there is an evident intention to stress sectarian styles and
manners; all, however, are treated with dignity. The
author of the five sermons believed that mental activity was
necessary to a preacher, and he believed, too, that the training that could produce the ability to adjust and adapt
could be found only in the university.

Abraham Wright has another lesson to instill besides a
preacher's need of university training. "You are taught
from these leaves, that Secular Learning is not so heathenish
but it may be made Christian. Plato and Socrates, and
Seneca were not of such a reprobate sence, as to stand
wholly Excommunicate. The same man may be both a
poet, and a Prophet, a Philosopher and an Apostle. Ver-
gil's fancie was as high as the Magi's Star, and might lead
Wise Men in the West as clearly to their Saviour, as that
Light did those Eastern Sages. And so likewise Seneca's
positions may become St. Paul's text; Aristotle's Meta-
physicks convince an Atheist of God. . . ." These liberal
views are quoted from the Address to the Christian Reader

which introduces the *Five Sermons* and explains the author's intentions. The fact that most of the contents of the little book was spoken from a pulpit before being printed, helped in a practical and legitimate way to advertise it. It is interesting to realize that Abraham Wright felt sure that the best method of putting his ideas before the public was to preach a group of sermons and then print them. The *Five Sermons* was first published in 1656; in 1668 it was still so popular that Pepys felt he must read it. He enjoyed it immensely. He went through it one fine day on the river, and carefully compared the five styles, arriving at the conclusion "that contrary to the design of the book, the Presbyterian and the Independent are the best of the five sermons. . . ." [51]

There can be no doubt that all the young men who entered the ministry by way of school and the university had had some practice in public speaking. This fact did not automatically make them good preachers, as is shown by the frank disapproval of voice and manner that one may read in the writings of men and women who were competent judges of a pulpit performance. The following chapter will make clear the attitude of contemporaries toward the preacher as a public performer.

[51] Pepys: *Diary,* Sept. 6, 1668.

CHAPTER II

THE PREACHER AND HIS PUBLIC

GOING to church in the seventeenth century was, it would seem, a pleasantly automatic performance which might or might not be connected with conviction of sin and desire for spiritual development. Most people went to church, and they went after the Restoration hardly less than during the years of the Commonwealth. The thought naturally suggests itself that nonconformist congregations were stimulated after 1662 by a human and secular enjoyment of doing that which was forbidden; but Pepys tells of many a crowded church where the preacher was of a firmly Established variety. All sects plainly enjoyed themselves. "Tis most true," says Selden philosophically, "that all Men are equally given to their Pleasure, only thus, one Mans Pleasure lies one way, and anothers another . . . he that takes Pleasure to hear Sermons, enjoys himself as much as he that hears Plays,—and could he that loves Plays endeavour to love Sermons, possibly he might bring himself to it as well as to any other Pleasure." [1]

This habit of church attendance was not peculiar to any one class. Roger L'Estrange may be right in saying: ". . . for when people are Poor, they grow conscientious; and for want of money apply themselves to hearken after Religion." [2] But the writings of well-to-do, well-educated men and women offer evidence that the prosperous classes of L'Estrange's own generation went to church with regu-

[1] *Table Talk*, p. 122.
[2] L'Estrange, Roger: *A Memento*, p. 199.

21

larity and enjoyment. The mention of the preacher and a comment on his sermon appears frequently in diaries and letters, even though there may be no personal, political, or literary interest attaching to the man or his performance. It is evident that church news was welcome.

Edward Browne (the son of Sir Thomas Browne) rarely fails to record in his Journal the preacher at both the morning and the afternoon service. Sometimes he makes the entry include other matters: (Jan. 3, 1663/4) "I heard Mr. Johnson preach at Christchurch and Mr. Tenison at St. Luke's Chappell, and took notice that the sun rose in an eliptica, or oval figure, not round, the diameter was parallel to the horizon"; [3] or, (Feb. 14, .1663/4) "Mr. Hanner preached. A plaister for Mistress Bedingfield's back." [4] When young Browne is in France, he writes dutiful letters home mentioning services and preachers whenever he finds a Protestant congregation; in return, his father tells who has been preaching at Norwich.[5] The letters of Lady Brilliana Harley to her son contain many references to the preachers she has most recently heard, though no one of them was possessed of special powers. Churchgoing and sermons are a lively interest with her; she often makes a request such as, "If you have bine to heare the Scots ministers, send me word how you like them;" [6] or she despatches a sermon to her son, expressing the hope that "the publischers of such ventings of such matter . . . will be thought fite to be sencured . . ." [7]

Adam Eyre of Yorkshire found it quite possible to combine the exigencies of earth with those of heaven, and in consequence the Sabbath day entries in his *Diurnall* are rather mixed in subject matter. He does go to church, but the world is very much with him:

[3] Browne, Sir Thomas: *Works,* I, 44.
[4] *Ibid.,* I, 48.
[5] *Ibid.,* I, 7, 14, 16.
[6] Harley, Lady Brilliana: *Letters,* p. 118.
[7] *Ibid.,* p. 127; also, pp. 95, 97, 99.

April 18, 1646/7.   (Easter Day)   This morne I went to Cawthron, to church, where I heard Mr. Broadley preach in the fornoon; and after sermon, I gave Jo. Shirt a lettre and a book from Mr. Bosvile.   Then I went to dinner with Capt. Shirt; and, after, we went to Broadvats, and I spent 4d., and rid to Silkeston, where I heard Mr. Spoford preach, who labored mainly to uphold the excellency of the ministrey in the people's opinion. . . .

May 30, 1667.   This morne I went to Peniston, to church, on foote, and writ a note for Dr. Haigh, to be read in the church, for mending the way to Denby bridge.

Jan. 9, 1647/8.   This morne I purposed not to have gone to church, but James Marsden called on mee, and willed mee to meete Samuell Ramford at Peniston, so I went and heard Mr. West preach, and gave Samuell the leiftenants papers to give his brother.   I spoke to Wm. Pasley, promised to serve the proces when I should send them.   Hee reported yt Edmund Rogers was contused on New Yere's eve in the night when the great wind was; and after evening prayer I drunk at Ernshawe's with Richard Micklethwayte and Edward Huichcliffe; and so came home; in all 4 myle; as I went to church I found 7d.; spent it at Robuck's, and that was all I spent to-day.

Adam Eyre, like so many of his contemporaries, does not feel that a sermon must be received gratefully or humbly merely because it is a sermon.   This sort of entry is not infrequent:

May 23, 1647.   This day my wife, Ed. M[itchell] and I went to Homfrith, and heard Gam. Apleyard preach a very maliceful sermon.

July 25.   I went to Peniston to church, where Dr. Didsbury preached at random.

Oct. 12. . . . to Peniston to an exersyse, where Mr. Uxley and Mr. Clark preached and railed mightyly.

The godly Ralph Josselin records in his *Diary:* (April 3, 1670) "Cow calved; administered the sacrament, only 14 present."

The *Diary* of the Reverend Mr. Henry Newcome con-

tains only brief comments on the preachers he hears, with
no professional criticism of their technique:

> Jan. 11, 1662. Mr. Jackson preached on Mat. iii, 17, and
> preached pretty.
> Feb. 22. Mr. Browne's Curate preached twice this day.
> A yong raw man, the Lord helpe. Very confident and im-
> pertinent in his discourses.

John Evelyn's *Diary* shows him as much addicted to
churchgoing. He hated and scorned nonconformists as a
political party and religious sect combined, but he was not
altogether intolerant. "There was now and then an honest
orthodox man got into the pulpit," he records, "and, though
the present incumbent was somewhat of the Independent, yet
he ordinarily preached sound doctrine, and was a peaceable
man; which was extraordinary in this age." [8] Evelyn went
twice to London especially to hear Jeremy Taylor who, the
first time, preached on evangelical perfection; the second,
on the conditions of eternal life. [9] Other preachers Evelyn
mentions, whose sermons he heard during the 50's and 60's,
are: Richard Allestree, Isaac Basire, Robert Creighton,
John Earle, John Fell, Peter Gunning, John Hacket, Peter
Heylin, Thomas Manton, Richard Meggott, John Owen,
Richard Owen, Simon Patrick, Edward Rainbow, Ed.
Reynolds, William Sancroft, Robert Sanderson, John Tillotson, James Usher, Richard Wild, and John Wilkins. A
number of these men, it will be noticed, are nonconformists
of special prominence. Reynolds conformed after the
Restoration and was made Bishop of Norwich, but Evelyn
went to hear him preach in 1658 when he was still opposed
to an established church. John Wilkins also found it possible to conform after 1660, but he had won Evelyn's respect
long before that time. An entry in the *Diary*, February 10,
1656, mentions a sermon preached by Wilkins in St. Paul's,

[8] Evelyn: *Diary*, Jan. 30, 1652/3; also, Nov. 2, 1656.
[9] *Ibid.*, April 15, 1652/3; Feb. 18, 1655/6.

and there follows the comment: "He was a most obliging
person, who had married the Protector's sister, and took
great pains to preserve the Universities from the ignorant
sacrilegious commanders and soldiers, who would fain have
demolished all places and persons that pretended to
learning."

The man who made churchgoing an art and sermon-tast-
ing a science is Samuel Pepys. To go to church was to him
not a duty, but an active pleasure. His own church was
St. Olave's, Hart Street, but all churches in and about
London were Samuel Pepys's province. He went to any
place where a religious service promised entertainment; if
no particular man in the pulpit or handsome woman in the
congregation attracted him to a church, he might sample a
number of congregations:

> March 16, 1662. This morning, till churches were done, I
> spent going from one church to another, and hearing a bit
> here, and a bit there.
> May 25, 1662. Looked into many churches—among them,
> Mr. Baxter's, at Blackfryers.[10]

Pepys went to church when on shipboard and when
spending the day at Greenwich or at Oxford; he went to
Whitehall for the social opportunities; he went to Westminster Abbey and St. Paul's and the Temple Church. He
went to the French church at the Savoy; to hear a German preach ("in a tone hard to be understood"); to a
Portuguese sermon in the Queen's chapel; to a Dutch
sermon in the French church; to the Jewish Synagogue;
and a number of times to mass in the Queen's chapel.
After music returned to its place in religious services, Pepys
frequently selected his church because of a good choir or
organ. Of course he made a point of hearing Farewell
Sermons; and he even tried to attend a meeting of quakers,
"who, they say, do meet every Lord's day at the Mouth, at

[10] See also, May 29, 1663; June 26, 1664; Oct. 2, 1664.

Bishopsgate; but I could see none stirring, nor was it fit to ask for the place." [11]

Church congregations of that time probably included many persons who regarded religion as Pepys did. His own belief was of a comfortable, adjustable variety. He would never have died for a dogma nor would he have killed anybody else for holding to one. He would have given a practical interpretation to a sentence in one of Christopher Love's sermons: "God never did so order Religion that it should be a disadvantage to our particular callings in the world"; [12] and have felt entire sympathy with Joseph Glanvill's assertion: "Though Religion be difficult to prove, it is safer to have it." [13] The level-headed Mr. Pepys was well disposed to the Puritans and had no objections to the Church of England; it made him uncomfortable to see nonconformists ridiculed, and it made him uneasy to think that his old schoolfellow, Mr. Christmas, might remember certain approving remarks offered by him, Pepys, on the day King Charles was beheaded. A comment set down one Lord's day (August 7, 1664) reveals, fairly well, Mr. Pepys's attitude toward religious convictions: "I saw several poor creatures carried by, by constables, for being at a conventicle. They go like lambs, without any resistance. I would to God they would either conform, or be more wise, and not be catched."

There were many sources of entertainment at church, quite unconnected with the preacher or the service, that were enjoyed by Pepys and, no doubt, by his fellow churchgoers. First, in importance, was the matter of clothes. Seasons and fashions are marked by what Mr. and Mrs. Samuel Pepys wear to church. When Pepys heard Thomas Fuller preach, he prefaces the statement by an

[11] Pepys: *Diary*, Oct. 2, 1664.
[12] Love: *The Combat between Flesh and Spirit* (*Twenty-seven Sermons*), p. 52.
[13] Glanvill: *Sermon against Scoffing at Religion* (*Some Discourses*), p. 212.

equally noteworthy fact: "This day I first began to go forth in my coate and sword, as the manner now among gentlemen is." [14] On another Sunday, "To church with my wife, who this day put on her green petticoate of flowered sattin, with fine white and black gimp lace of her own putting on, which is very pretty." [15] There was a particularly self-conscious occasion when Pepys wore his new periwig to church: "I thought that all the church would presently have cast their eyes all upon me, but I found no such thing." [16]

Church was also a pleasant means of marking the social advance of the ambitious Clerk of the Acts. He is complacent when he and his wife are accompanied by his boy, "waiting on us with his sword, which this day he begins to wear, to outdo Sir W. Pen's boy. . . ." [17] But he fairly struts through the paragraph that begins: "Up, and to church in the best manner I have gone a good while—that is to say, with my wife, and her woman, Mercer, along with us, and Tom, my boy, waiting on us." [18] The acquisition of a pew is another milestone in the steady upward progress of Samuel Pepys, and constitutes an additional reason for going to church. He does enjoy that pew. For one thing, there is always the excitement of whether the joint owner will take up too much room, or be affronted if Mr. and Mrs. Pepys do not yield precedence in leaving the pew. One tense morning, ". . . I stood, in continual fear of Mrs. Markham's coming, and offering to come into our pew, to prevent which, soon as ever I heard the great door open, I did step back, and clap my breech to our pew-door, that she might be forced to shove me to come in; but as God would have it, she did not come." [19]

[14] *Diary*, Feb. 2, 1660.
[15] *Ibid.*, June 29, 1662.
[16] *Ibid.*, Nov. 8, 1663.
[17] *Ibid.*, May 4, 1662.
[18] *Ibid.*, Sept. 11, 1664; cf. William Lilly, when he is in service to Gilbert Wright: ". . . my work was to go before my master to church . . ." (*Hist. of His Life and Times*, p. 15).
[19] *Diary*, Sept. 15, 1667.

From January 1, 1659/60 to May 30, 1669, Pepys's *Diary* shows him attending church about 325 times. There were Sundays when he was ill, or had to work in the Admiralty office, or had other distractions; but there were also Sundays when he went twice and three times to church, listened to the sermon carefully, and at night wrote out the text and the heads in his *Diary*.

Samuel Pepys is more entertaining, and certainly more frank, than most people in his references to churchgoing and preachers, but many of his contemporaries show the same matter-of-course inclusion of services and sermons in their daily life.[20] Popular conduct books of the century make it plain that Religion is a genteel quality, although they do not insist that it be considered a necessary ingredient in a gentleman. *The Compleat Gentleman* advises the frequenting of learned sermons;[21] *The English Gentleman* vaguely recommends both professing and practicing religion, adding a caution in regard to discussions of religious questions;[22] *The Gentleman's Calling* (credited to a divine, Richard Allestree) says nothing directly about churchgoing, but asserts that a gentleman should not think the duty of exhorting belongs to the divines alone; he should give a like service to those needing it "and prepared to receive it," . . . "for what comes out of the pulpit passes for the foolishness of preaching, or for the discourses of those whose trade it is to inveigh against sin."[23] Joseph Glanvill, in a sermon on behavior, says that to ignore religion is open discourtesy: "'Tis to make Fopps of our Forefathers, and Idiots of the Founders of our Laws and Government. . . . Let such men quit all pretences to civility and breeding, they are ruder than . . . wild Americans; and were they treated according to their deserts from man-

[20] See quotations under *Popularity*, p. 29, and *Criticism*, p. 47.
[21] Henry Peacham. First published in 1622, reissued in 1634, 1661, etc.
[22] Richard Braithwaite. Published, 1641.
[23] Richard Allestree, 1660.

kind, they would meet everywhere with Chains and Strappadoes." [24]

The evidence of a widespread and genuine enjoyment of churchgoing in the seventeenth century is strong, but it cannot be denied that even in that heyday of preaching there was sometimes a difficulty in filling a church. Nicholas Ferrar was accustomed to give food and a piece of money to the poor who came to the church at Little Gidding,[25] Matthew Robinson also gave money to the humble members of his congregation,[26] Thomas Gouge, in his remote Welsh parish, secured a daily attendance at catechetical classes by distributing small coins among the aged poor, once a week, astutely varying the day,[27] and Peter Austin made a practice of dividing a shilling among six children every Sunday, taking successive groups, and when the last child had been reached, going back to the first.[28]

The Extraordinarily Popular Preacher

Although few preachers seem to have had difficulty in finding people to preach to, yet because one man differeth from another in glory there were individuals who were conspicuously popular as pulpit orators or as personalities, sometimes as both. Thomas Fuller was a man liked for himself and for his sermons. When he was Lecturer at the Savoy in the Strand, he "became so famous, and was thronged with such distant congregations, that those of his own cure were in a manner excommunicated from their own church, if they came not early enough to fill it, which, without conforming to his own habitual temperance, they could seldom do: tho' he had an audience without, and another within the pale, the windows and sextonry were so crowded as if bees had swarmed to his mellifluous discourse." [29]

[24] *Sermon against Scoffing at Religion*, p. 213.
[25] Mayor: *Nicholas Ferrar*.
[26] Mullinger: *Cambr. in the 17th Cent.*, p. 102ff.
[27] Palmer: *Nonconf. Mem.*, I, 144.
[28] *Ibid.*, II, 214.
[29] *Biog. Brit.*, III, 2051.

John Earle was a man of somewhat the same type as Fuller, though of less ability as a speaker. Evelyn says Earle was "a rare preacher," but it was to his social gifts that he owed his popularity. It is with considerable enthusiasm that Evelyn includes in his *Diary* an account of the Consecration dinner to which he was invited by the Dean of Westminster: ". . . on his being made Bishop of Worcester . . . one of the most plentiful and magnificent dinners that in my life I ever saw; it cost near £600 as I was informed. Here were the Judges, nobility, clergy, and gentlemen innumerable, this Bishop being universally beloved for his sweet and gentle disposition." [30]

A less cheerful but no doubt as sincere an expression of the liking of many people for a clergyman is shown in a letter which comments on the ejecting of Mr. John Clark: "His loss . . . was bitterly Lamented: So that if Lawn Sleeves of all the Bishops in England were cut into Handkerchiefs they would scarce have been sufficient to have wip'd away the Tears that were shed at his Farewell Sermon." [31] Dr. James Usher was a much liked and respected preacher, though the extremists of all parties thought that he too obviously endeavored to walk safely in the middle of the road. But he was so sincerely desirous of making it possible for theological lions and lambs to lie down together, so genuinely willing to aid scholars of any religious sect, that he won real regard from both Puritans and Royalists. He was permitted to preach regularly at Lincoln's Inn from 1647 until physical infirmities forced him to give up the work in 1655.[32] When he died, Cromwell insisted upon a public funeral in Westminster Abbey, some of the expense being borne by the government.[33] Usher's popularity may be explained in part by his conspicuous position, which

[30] Evelyn: *Diary*, Nov. 30, 1662.
[31] Calamy: *Account, etc.*, II, 90.
[32] Rushworth: *Hist. Coll.*, Dec. 30, 1647, VII, 937-8; Cary: *Mem.*, I, 374.
[33] Gardiner: *Hist. of the Com. and Protectorate*, III, 334. Walker: *Sufferings* . . . Pt. II, 9; Wood: *Ath. Ox.*, IV, 799.

brought him in contact with many people; but Dr. Thomas Manton the presbyterian, who had no extraordinary opportunities to impress the public, also won general approval and liking. When he died (Ralph Thoresby writes in his *Diary*), this preacher, "deservedly styled the King of Preachers," had a funeral "attended with the vastest number of ministers of all persuasions, etc., that ever I saw together in my life. And the Ministers walked in pairs, a Conformist and a Nonconformist." [34]   Five hundred persons, "amongst whom Dr. Tillotson and Stillingfleet and other conformable ministers were present," attested the popularity of Richard Fairclough by accompanying him to his grave; [35] and when "Mr. Ralphson," another nonconformist, was buried, Aubrey says "1000 persons were at his funerall." [36]   The three ministers just mentioned died in Restoration times, but their nonconformist principles and practices had evidently not militated against their ability to win friends and admirers.

All Pepys's preacher-criticisms are made after January 16, 1659/60; consequently the crowded churches and popular preachers that he mentions are not to be credited to Puritan insistence on churchgoing. It was on a spring day in 1663 that he went to Whitehall to hear "Dr. Creeton" (Robert Creighton), when the chapel was so "monstrous full" that Pepys could not get into his own pew—assigned him as Clerk of the Privy Seal—and he had to sit among the choir. A year later he again hears "Dr. Critton" at Whitehall and this time the chapel was "most infinite full." [37]   When the archbishop of York preached, Pepys could not get near enough to catch a word of the sermon, but "I had the pleasure once in my life, to see an Archbishop in a pulpit." [38]   When he tried to hear Edward Stillingfleet, there was not even standing-room and W. Batten and Pepys

[34] Thoresby : *Diary*, I, 7.   [36] Aubrey : II, 195.
[35] Wood : *Ath. Ox.*, I, xcvi.   [37] *Diary*, March 25, 1664.
[38] *Ibid.*, April 8, 1666. (This was Richard Sterne, great-grandfather of Lawrence Sterne.)

went "to eat herrings at the Dog Tavern; and then to
church again." They found another popular young man
was in the pulpit—Robert Frampton—and the crowd was
so great that Pepys gave up the attempt to hear the
sermon.[39]

The majority of these preachers are, to our thinking,
frankly dull, yet they were listened to eagerly. When Dr.
Ralph Brownrig preached before "the honourable society
of both the Temples . . . such as could hear him preach,
rejoiced at his gracious words, such as for the crowds could
not come nigh enough to hear him, had pleasure to stay and
behold him, conceiving they saw a sermon in his looks." [40]
John Shaw, writing in his Diary, mentions Trinity Church,
Hull, as the place where "I had usually preached to about
4000 hearers or more at once." [41] Lawrence Chadderton
once concluded a sermon which had lasted two hours at
least, with the courteous assurance that he did not wish to
trespass longer on the patience of the congregation:
"Whereupon all the auditory cried out . . . 'for God's sake,
sir, go on, go on.' " This he did satisfactorily though unprepared because, says Fuller who tells the anecdote in his
Worthies, "These constant preachers, like good house-
keepers, can never be taken so unprovided but that (though
they make not a plentiful feast) they can give wholesome
food at a short warning." [42]

[39] *Diary,* Oct. 10, 1666. (The occasion was a Fast Day for the Fire.
See, however, the reference to Frampton's preaching, Jan. 26, 1666/7,
"the church crammed by twice as many people as used to be.")
[40] Lloyd: *Memoirs,* p. 393.
[41] Shaw: *Diary,* p. 138; also, ". . . usually the churches were so
thronged by nine o'clock in the morning that I had much adoe to get
to the pulpit," p. 138. (This was in 1644.)
[42] Fuller: *The Hist. of the.Worthies of England,* II, 208-9.
Even a constant preacher might find a sudden demand disconcerting.
Dr. Juxton was sent for, at the request of Charles I, to prepare him
for death. The bishop, "being altogether unprepared for such a work,
broke out into these expressions, God save me, what a trick is this,
that I should have no more warning, and I have nothing ready! but
recollecting himself a little, he put on his scarf and his other furni-
ture, and went . . . to the King, where having read the Common
Prayer and one of his old sermons, he administered the sacrament to
him . . ." (Ludlow: *Memoirs,* I, 218-219). See also, Dr. Manton's
embarrassment, when called upon without warning to deliver the

Hugh Peters says of his own preaching at St. Sepulchre's: "At this lecture, the resort grew so great that it contracted envey and anger, though I believe 100 every week were persuaded from sin to Christ." [43]   There was too a Mr. Thomas Harrison who, Calamy observes, "was extreamly Popular, and this stirr'd up much Envy." [44] Mr. Harrison is not reported as struggling against his dangerous attractiveness, but Mr. Richard Holdsworth dealt sternly with his admirers.   "Once as he was preaching at Mercers-Chapel on the Acclamation made to Herod, the Auditory several times Hummed him in such a manner, that he could not be Heard; in so much that he was forced to call out to them once, I pray remember the Text.   Nor must it be omitted, that at another time, when he saw them thronge in Great Multitudes to Hear him Preach, he dismissed them with the Prayers and an Homily; endeavouring to persuade the Giddy People of those Times, not to have Mens Persons in Admiration, and to Prefer the Publick Offices of the Church to the Private Performances of any, the Best Man whatsoever." [45]   Calamy's week day lecture "was frequented by persons of the greatest quality, and that constantly for 20 years together; being seldom so few as 60 coaches." [46]   Nathaniel Vincent, in London after the fire, "preached to large multitudes: sometimes to thousands in the ruins."   He does not seem to have pleased everyone, as it is related that once he was pulled out of the pulpit by his hair.[47]

Excessive popularity was deplored by sensible men who realized that the emotional admiration aroused by a preacher of marked oratorical ability might mean little of sincere acceptance of the lesson taught; and furthermore that the

prayer upon the occasion of Cromwell's becoming Protector (Burton: Diary, II, 311).
[43] Peters: A Dying Father's Legacy, etc., p. 100 (Quoted in Dict. Natl. Biog.).
[44] Calamy: Account, etc., II, 122.
[45] Walker: Sufferings, etc., Pt. II, 79.
[46] Palmer: Nonconf. Mem., I, 74.
[47] Ibid., I, 239.

preacher himself might easily be the worse for too much and
too cheap applause.   The unassuming Bunyan discovered
"that gifts being alone, were dangerous, not in themselves,
but because of those evils that attend them that have them;
to wit, pride, desire of vain-glory, self conceit, etc., all
which are easily blown up at the appearance and commendation of ever unadvised Christians to the endangering of a
poor creature to fall into the condemnation of the devil." [48]
Henry Beesley was either unusually popular himself, or had
observed in others the lamentable result of exciting general
admiration, for he preached eight sermons on the subject,
publishing them under the general title: *The Soules Conflict with the Sins of Vain-glory, etc.*[49]   Thomas Fuller
denounces the preacher who obviously seeks popularity.[50]
Arthur Hildersham condemns the listener who praises one
minister at the expense of another—"there may be a difference in gifts in ministers, without any inequality"; [51] and
Christopher Love warns against overvaluing a minister's
gifts whatever their kind or degree.[52]

Preacher-worship was common enough to impel John
Tombes to deliver and publish an entire sermon on the subject.   As Tombes was himself a man not only of ability but
of much personal charm, it may be supposed that he spoke
in part from his own experience when he presents an exposition of *Anthropolatria: Or, The Sinne of Glorying in Men,
especially in Eminent Ministers of the Gospel.*   He specifically condemned: "disparaging some Preachers injuriously,
extolling others immoderately, disdainfully withdrawing

[48] Bunyan: *Grace Abounding, etc.*, p. 103.
[49] Beesley: *The Soules Conflict, etc.*, p. 108.
[50] Fuller: *Abel Redivivus*, p. 364.
[51] Hildersham: *CVIII Lectures, etc.*, pp. 37, 276.   Fénelon discusses
the too-popular preacher in his *Dialogues sur l'Eloquence*, p. 1.   The
reasonable arguer called *A* refuses to hear a certain divine recommended by the deprecatory *B*:   *Je me garderai donc bien de l'aller
entendre, car je ne veux point qu'un prédicateur me dégoûte des
autres; au contraire, je cherche un homme que me donne un tel goût
et une telle estime pour la parole de Dieu, que j'en sois plus disposé à
l'ecouter partout aileurs.*
[52] Love: *Grace: the Truth and Growth and Different Degrees
Thereof*, p. 87.

from some without just cause, inordinately running after others without sufficient reason; swallowing doune the dictates of some without chewing, loathing the wholesome food which others present, without tasting." "By such attitudes," declares Mr. Tombes in his fourth point (the sermon has thirteen sections), "the despised persons are often discouraged and disheartened, . . . the remembrance of contempt . . . benums a man's spirit, and enfeebles him in his work . . . and Teachers gloried in, are puffed up and perverted." [53]

The Preacher's Enjoyment of Preaching

A great deal might be said about the sheer joy that the preacher derived from what Dr. John Hacket called "the other wing of the cherubin [sic] which is preaching." [54] Neither he nor his fellows seems to have suspected that there might be a bit of sinful indulgence in what was quite clearly a delight to himself. Nothing could stop a determined preacher. Matthew Robinson always preached twice on Sundays and continued the practice when so ill "that he could not stand in the pulpit his last six years, yet would he sit in it upon an high stool." [55] We read of Robert Atkins that "towards the latter end of his Life, he was much afflicted with the Gout; yet would he not neglect his Work, often Preaching in his own House in his Chair, when he was not able to go or stand, or so much as use his Hands to turn his Notes." [56] Samuel Hierow also suffered from the gout, but "he hath often preached and prayed when he has not been able to stir out of his place, nor so much as hold a book in his hand; but he was eminent for his patience." [57] That mild and kindly soul, Joseph Alleine (author of *The Alarm to the Unconverted*), was physically frail, but he

[53] Tombes: *Anthropolatria*, pp. 16, 12.
[54] Fuller: *Church Hist.*, VI, 197.
[55] *Autobiography*, p. 43.
[56] Calamy: *Abridgement*, II, 217.
[57] Palmer: *Nonconf. Mem.*, I, 371.

ordinarily preached six or seven times a week, frequently ten times, once fourteen times in eight days. When he was sent to jail—for preaching—he arrived at the prison to find the jailer absent, and immediately seized the opportunity to preach outside while he waited to be incarcerated.[58] One of his severe illnesses was the result, his physician said, of preaching too soon after meals.[59] Nathaniel Ecles "was forced to preach sitting, which he did until about a fortnight before his death"; [60] Timothy Dod (son of Dr. John Dod) "in the latter part of his time was so very corpulent, that he could not get up into the pulpit, and therefore preached in a pew, or in the desk"; [61] and of Samuel Tapper we read: "The last year, his intellect was much impaired, and yet he could not without difficulty be with-held from his beloved work of praying and preaching." [62]

It is impossible not to respect the tremendous capacity for work that these men possessed. They did not believe in extempore preaching. The quaker did, and so did the tradesman whose spirit moved him to express himself on religious topics, but neither of these talkers was taken seriously by the critics of the day. The ordained minister was in nearly all cases a university man, and, conformist or otherwise, he had been trained to construct an argument, to offer examples, to cite authorities. The great majority must have found genuine pleasure in every step of the sermon process from the choice of a text to the final appearance in print, for an extraordinary number of sermons were printed. The thoroughness with which a text was expounded is appalling. Only a man who loved talking for its own sake would deliberately deliver one hundred and forty-five sermons on a single chapter, as Anthony Burgess did when he gradually presented the seventeenth chapter of the Gospel of John, *Explicated and both Practically and Polemically Improved.*[63] "Mr. Arthur Hildersham, minister

---

[58] *Life of Joseph Alleine,* p. 9.
[59] *Ibid.,* p. 68.
[60] Palmer: *Nonconf. Mem.,* II, 45.

[61] *Ibid.,* II, 218.
[62] *Ibid.,* I, 283.
[63] London, 1656.

in Ashby-de-la-Zouche for many years, preached and printed many sermons on the fourth of *John*," says William Lilly who liked to include items of general interest in his Life.[64] Joshua Hoyle, when divinity professor in the University of Dublin, "expounded the whole Bible through in daily lectures, and in the chiefest books ordinarily a verse a day; which work held him almost fifteen years." Then "he began the second exposition of the whole Bible in the church of Trinity College and within ten years he ended all the New Testament (excepting one book and a piece), all the prophets, all Solomon and Job. . . . He preached also and expounded thrice every Sabbath for the far greater part of the year, once every holyday, and sometimes twice. To these may be added his weekly lectures as professor in the controversies. . . ."[65] Thomas Lydyat, who accepted a rectory reluctantly (having once positively refused it), evidently became interested in his duties, because "he did not only go over the harmony of the gospels in less than 12 years, making thereon above 600 sermons, but wrote also several books."[66] Henry Newcome records in his *Diary:* "I preached on my old text, Mark X, and brought it nearer to a conclusion, but ended it not."[67] A posthumous work of Josias Shute bears the title: *Sarah and Hagar; Or, Genesis the sixteenth chapter opened, in XIX Sermons.* . . .[68] And G. W.[alker] "plainly opened and expounded in severall sermons" *The History of the Creation,* proving incidentally that the world began in March, not September.[69]

A man might cultivate a wide range of subject. Mr. William Bagshaw, " 'tho he preach'd so often (and seldom on the same Text in Two Auditories) yet he had laid in a Stock of several Hundreds of Sermons, which he liv'd not

[64] *Hist. of His Life,* p. 12 (*CVIII Lectures on the Fourth of John*).
[65] Wood: *Ath. Ox.,* I, 383. (Lord Falkland once said that Dr. Hoyle "was a person of some weak parts, but of many strong infirmities," *Ath. Ox.,* I, 384.)
[66] *Ibid.,* III, 186.
[67] Oct. 6, 1661.
[68] London, 1648.
[69] London, 1641.

to make use of." That these sermons were carefully prepared is proved by the statement that "at the end of every year, he usually repeated to his People the Substance of the Sermons he had preach'd on, all the Lord's Days in the Year: And in the beginning of the New Year, he went to the Houses of his Hearers, and preach'd a suitable sermon in each." [70]   Mr. Ephraim Udall had a similar intention, but his method was to impress rather than to repeat: "once a year [he] preached one sermon to teach his people to benefit by his former sermons. . . ." [71]

These genuinely good and faithful and hard working, and often suffering, preachers always feel that they are generously giving of their knowledge and experience, as in truth they are. But one wonders why there is no word from them of commendation for those who come to listen, only reproof for those who stay away. It must have been very inconvenient for working people to attend so many, and such long, sermons; it cannot always have been interesting material that was presented. Yet the congregations seem unfailing even at what would appear to be a difficult hour for an assembly to convene. Before one of his numerous departures for jail, for instance, Joseph Alleine wished to exhort his people, and "he appointed them to meet him about one or two o'clock in the night . . . there was of young and old many hundreds; he preached and prayed with them about three hours." [72]   Thomas Edge "commonly gather'd People together before their Neighbours were out of their Beds, and broke up a little before the Publick [Minister]." [73]   If no other congregation were available, a conscientious preacher frequently delivered a sermon to his own family.

A clergyman of bold and independent character found much enjoyment, one cannot doubt, in the plain speaking

[70] Calamy : *Abridgement, etc.*, II, 200, 203.
[71] Feltham : *A Brief Character of the Low Countries*, p. 507.
[72] Alleine : *Life, etc.*, p. 61.
[73] Calamy : *Account, etc.*, p. 129.

for which his office gave him opportunity. Such a man did not hesitate to interpret original sin in terms of contemporary conditions. Robert Wilde, in an Assize sermon, listed quite clearly the examples of wickedness and selfishness he had found common among men, such as those to whom he preached, whose derelictions were matters of law rather than of gospel: ". . . look to your Edicts, your Warrants, your Orders, your Licenses. . . . Take heed you trust not knowne Knaves, and wicked men in any place, or office, under you, for all the Evill which they doe, will be found lying at your doores." He tells of his experience in prison, and of the increased wickedness which prisoners learn from one another. And he risks unpopularity still further by declaring, "As much as men whine and complaine of Taxes, I doe believe that there is that drink needlessly, sinfully, and shamefully guzzled away in England, which would pay the tax thrice told, and no man feel it. . . ."[74] Another use of contemporaneous conditions as subject matter for a stirring sermon is a discourse by John Moore on the text: "This he said, not that he cared for the poor." It was published under the title, *The Crying Sin of England, of not caring for the Poor wherin Inclosure, viz., such as does unpeople Townes, and uncorn Fields, is Arraigned, Convicted and Condemned by the word of God.* The whole sermon is in reality a study in economics and sociology.[75]

Even those in high places might meet with rebuke from a fearless preacher, who, being human, could hardly fail to enjoy his own temerity. Once Calamy, shortly after the Restoration, was preaching before General Monk. "Some men," declared the nonconformist orator, "will betray their kingdoms for filthy lucre's sake"; and he threw his handkerchief (which he usually waved up and down while

---

[74] Wilde: *The Arraignment of a Sinner at the Bar of Divine Justice,* pp. 34-5.
[75] Moore. Preached in 1653.

preaching) directly at the pew in which the general sat.[76]
Francis Cheynell, when preaching before the Lords on *A
Man of Honour,* speaks plainly but is not abusive. He even
flatters them by telling them that he will not do so, "My
Lords, I dare not flatter you, there are enough to do that,
who are only men in black, and no divines." He does,
however, name their characteristic sins with freedom and
exactness.[77] John Shaw remarks (in his *Diary,* 1653) that,
when he was called to preach before Cromwell at Whitehall,
he did so "with the plainness of old Latimer." [78] Pepys was
in the chapel at Whitehall one Lord's day, "and there
though crowded, heard a very honest sermon before the
King by a Canon of Christ Church, upon these words,
'Having a form of godlinesse, but denying, etc.' Among
other things, he did much insist upon the sin of adultery:
which methought might touch the King, and the more because he forced it into his sermon, besides his text." [79]
And at another time, ". . . they told me of the strange,
bold sermon of Dr. Creeton yesterday before the King;
how he preached against the sins of the Court, and particularly against adultery, over and over instancing how for
that single sin in David, the nation was undone; and of our
negligence in having our Castles without ammunition and
powder when the Dutch came upon us; and how we have
no courage now-a-days, but let our ships be taken out of our
harbour." [80]

The Preacher's Objections to Preaching

When Parliament was in power, those clergymen of the
Church of England who did not sympathize with their con-

[76] Calamy : *Account, etc.,* p. 5ff ; also, *Continuation, etc.,* p. 8.
Calamy, when Cromwell tentatively brought up the question of a
kingship, frankly discouraged it, saying, "Oh, 'tis against the voice of
the nation ; there will be nine in ten against you" (Burton : *Diary,*
I, 321).
[77] Cheynell : *A Man of Honour,* p. 41.
[78] Shaw : *Diary,* p. 149.
[79] Pepys : *Diary,* April 6, 1662.
[80] *Ibid.,* July 29, 1667.

gregation's pleasure in sermons, found themselves in difficulties. They did not hesitate to protest. No. 21 in John
White's *Century of Scandalous Malignant Priests* is a
flippant Doctor of Divinity, Nicholas Andrews, "for that
he is not only negligent in preaching himselfe, but he hath
also expressed himselfe to be an enemy to frequent preaching, saying that Peters sword cutt off but one eare, but long
sermons like long swords, cutt off both at once . . . and that
the silliest creatures have longest eares, and that preaching was the worst part of God's worship, and that if he left
out anything, he would leave out that." [81]   Herbert Thorndike thinks preaching a matter of physical endurance: "If
he [a curate] be tied to preach as often as the Church door
opens, the Church door must be shut, because no sides can
hold out, so often as Christians ought to meet for God's
service. I call the World to witness; is it not a work as
much of lungs and sides, as an office of God's service, which
takes up the time of their Church Assemblies." [82]   But another divine who really liked to preach is listed by White
as scandalous and malignant, because in his sermons he
"introduces all private grievances, the widdows that will
not marry him, the brother-in-law that will not pay his
tithes, etc." [83]

[81] P. 8.
Skelton knew this type and this situation:
> The temporalyte say playne,
> Howe bysshoppes dysdayne
> Sermons for to make,
> Or such laboure to take;
> And for to say trouth,
> A great part is for slouth,
> But the greatest parte
> Is for the have but small **arte**
> And right sklender cunyng
> Within theyr heedes wonnying.
>   (Colin Clout, ll. 162ff.)

[82] *The Due Way of Composing, etc.*, p. 50.
See No. 24 in White's *Century*, for James Mountford who had
brazenly declared "that the Sabbath was made for ministers to rest in
as well as for the people."
[83] *Century*, p. 50.
Clarendon discusses the term "scandalous clergy," *Hist. of the Rebellion*, I, 263-4. For "malignant" and "plunder," see Fuller: *Church
Hist.*, VI, 241.

When Matthew Wren, Bishop of Ely, was impeached by
Parliament, it was clearly stated in Article XVI "that by
reason of the Bishop's superstitious practices and denying
of preaching . . . many of his majesty's subjects to the
number of three thousands, many of which used Trades,
Spinning, Weaving, Knitting, and making of Cloth, Stuffs,
Stockings and other manufactures of Wool [eleven prod-
ucts are specified] some of them setting an Hundred Poor
People on Work, have removed themselves, their Families
and Estates into Holland and other parts beyond the Seas,
and there set up and taught the Natives there, the said
Manufactures, to the great Hindrance of Trade in this
Kingdom." [84]   The flavor of Article XVI, it may be noticed,
is distinctly secular, the spiritual depression occasioned by
an insufficiency of preaching being forgotten in the deeper
gloom engendered by a loss of trade.

Instructions on Preaching

The interest in preaching which drew people to church as
to an entertainment, and the zeal of the preacher which
made him enjoy the preparation and delivery of sermons,
led to the writing of instructions on the Art of Preaching. [85]
Most of the authors understand "preaching" to mean ser-
mon-composition; only a few give real attention to the
spoken word.   Robert South devotes an entire sermon to
Preaching, discussing at considerable length natural ability,
judgment, memory, and invention.   He impartially condemns those who discredit the church by either light and

[84] Rushworth : IV, 353-4.
Wren, Sir Christopher: (*Parentalia*, p. 100) asserts that these
tradesfolk began to go in 1633 and 1636, the chief cause being the
low wages paid in England.
[85] Joseph Glanvill says in the Epis. Ded. to his *Essay concerning
preaching:* "Some learned men, I know, have written on the subject
(tho not so many as one would think should on an Argument of
such importance . . .)."
Dr. Thomas Barlow's *Genuine Remains* begins (pp. 1-121) with
"Directions to a young Divine for his Study of Divinity, and choice
of Books."

comical, or dull and heavy, discourses, and he allows himself the liberty of making veiled (and maliceful) allusions
to the rhetorical mannerisms of John Owen and Jeremy
Taylor.[86]   Bishop Taylor is entirely practical and unaffected in his own Rules and Advice to the Clergy of the
Diocese of Down and Connor.   He warns his subordinates
against too technical or too undignified language in the
pulpit, and in his conclusion reminds them that the approval
of the world is not the chief end of preaching: "Let no man
envy any man that hath a greater audience or more fame in
preaching than himself; let him not detract from him or
lessen his reputation directly or indirectly . . . no man is
the better for making his brother worser . . . if you cannot have the fame of a good preacher, yet you may have
the reward of being a good man; but it is hard to miss
both." [87]

In *Ichabod: or, Five Groans of the Church,* three founda-
tions of oratory are named but not discussed: Eloquence,
Persuasion, and Rhetoric;[88] a more thorough study is that
entitled: *The Preacher, or, The Art and Method of Preaching* by William Chappell (Bishop of Cork, sometime fellow
of Christ College, Cambridge).[89]   He offers, as a text, a
line from I Peter iv. 11 that would be likely to discourage
a modest clergyman: "If any man speak, let him speak as
the oracles of God."   The work is divided under many heads
with common-sense suggestions illustrating most of them;
but the bishop's predilection for scholarly terms, and his
determination to hide his brilliant ideas under bushels of
phrases and parentheses must have made an humble divine
feel helpless to acquire either a method or an art of presenting his sermon.   For example: "A text considered in
itself is either Axiomatical or Sylogistical. . . . Although

[86] South: *Works,* II, 337-60 ("The Scribe Instructed").
[87] Taylor: *Works,* III, 711-13.
[88] Anon., p. 22.
[89] First pub. 1663 anonymously.   John Wilkins includes it in his
list of authorities on preaching, in *Ecclesiastes,* adding, "said to be
by Bishop Chappell," p. 5.

when the word *Est* is merely Syncategorematical, and both parts, or the one in respect of the other, implies a negation to the real *esse*, as in feigned, some privative, and contradictory things, there neither part with *Est* categorematically taken, will make a divine axiome, and though when by reason of the nature of the parts, and affection of the one with the other, an axiome may be constituted, it seems to be there contained rather by deduction than expressly." [90] But here is an excerpt that can be understood at one reading: "*Crypsis*. It will not be advisedly done, to buzze many, especially subtile objections into the hearers Ears, which peradventure would not otherwise entre into their thought, and which it is not so easie to root out, and dangerous to have in their minds." [91]

Under "the Uses from the Hypothesis to the Thesis, or from the Species to the Genus," he presents: "the *consantaneum*, or what is agreeable, the *dissentaneum*, or what is dissenting, or disagreeable." [92] Dehortation might reasonably have been included under this latter head, but it appears sixty-two pages farther on: "Dehortation hath a relation to some future evil, to which the hearers are obnoxious: instigating the heart to avoid and fly it. The scope of this is to excite fear; and therefore it represents that, from which it doth dehort, under the formal reason of the objected fear, that it is a great evill, imminent, avoidable." [93]

These wordy passages do not give a fair idea of the book, which is a modest duodecimo volume, with most of its statements and recommendations stripped to bare outline form. The construction of the sermon interests Bishop Chappell more than its delivery, therefore he offers no

---

[90] Chappell: *The Preacher, etc.*, pp. 38-9. Lloyd testifies that Chappell was "famous for his many and eminent pupils; more for the eminent Preachers, made so by his admirable method for the theory, and Praxis . . . for the practice of Preaching." (Chappell, it will be remembered, is the tutor generally supposed to be responsible for Milton's being suspended from Cambridge.)

[91] *Ibid.*, p. 130.

[92] *Ibid.*, p. 137-8.

[93] *Ibid.*, p. 199.

definite suggestions in regard to a correct pulpit voice or manner.

Ecclesiastes: or a Discourse concerning the Gift of Preaching, as it falls under the Rules of Art is a "painful" work by Dr. John Wilkins. It is essentially a manual for sermon writing [94] and says little about how the sermon should be said or read, although in the first part of the volume the author refers scornfully to those who when they have "passed over their philosophical Studies, and made some little entrance on Divinity, they think themselves fit for the pulpit, without any farther inquiry; as if the gift of Preaching and sacred Oratory, were not a distinct Art in itself." [95]   In "the Art of Preaching, or making Sermons," says Dr. Wilkins, ". . . the chief helps are these three: Method, Matter, Expression." He reaches Expression at page 199 (the book ends at the top of page 204) where he divides the subject into Phrase and Elocution.   Elocution is disposed of in a few lines: "there are two extremities to be avoided, too much Boldness, and Fear." Nothing is said about tone or gesture, but both may be understood as included in the final pronouncement: "In brief, the most proper manner of elocution, is to speak with modesty and gravity, which will best suit with our calling and business." [96]   How far Dr. Wilkins preached according to the practice he enjoined one cannot say; but something may be inferred as to his delivery from the comment of Mr. Pepys whose private judgment is never disturbed by public opinion: "Up and to church to St. Lawrence to hear Dr. Wilkins, the great scholar, for curiosity, I having never heard him; but was not satisfied with him at all, only a gentleman sat in the pew I by chance sat in, that sang most excellently." [97]

[94] See *Sermon-helps,* p. 107.   In 1669, the book could be bought for 1s. 4d.   *The Flemings at Ox.,* p. 452.
[95] Wilkins: *Ecclesiastes,* p. 3.
[96] *Ibid.,* p. 204.
[97] Pepys: *Diary,* Feb. 12, 1664/5.

Joseph Glanvill, like his fellows, is primarily interested in the sermon, but he does give some practical suggestions as to the way to make the sermon effective when used in the pulpit. Hearers vary, he observes in his *Essay concerning Preaching,* "Some are for the taking phrases, and passionate out-cryes; for loudness and vehemence, for action and imitation, and this, with them, is powerful Preaching. . . ." Others think, "The Preacher must speak in one key, and tenour of voice, and stand as unmoveable as a Statue: He must speak as if he said a lesson." [98] Toward the end of the *Essay,* Glanvill returns to the same subject: "The Voice should be lively and earnest, but without any set or affected tone. . . . You should avoid a droning dulness of speech on the one hand, which shews unconcernment, and want of zeal; and a boisterous noise on the other, which argues rudeness, and want of modesty and manners." [99]

Richard Baxter, in the Appendix to *The Reformed Pastor,* reproves a certain type of preacher, thereby giving broad hints as to the proper way to address a congregation. "Few ministers," says the author, "will so much as exert their voice and stir themselves up to an earnest delivery. Or if they speak loud and earnestly, oftentimes do not answer it with earnestness of manner; and then the voice does but little good. The people will estime it but mere bawling, if the matter does not correspond." [100] Again he says, "The best matter will not move them [the hearers] unless it be movingly delivered. When a man has a reading or declaiming tone, and speaks like a school boy saying a lesson, or pronouncing an oration, few are much affected with anything he says." [101]

William Price published a detailed study of preaching, *Ars concionandi,* but fills only a page and a half with advice

[98] Glanvill: *An Essay Concerning, etc.,* p. 7.
[99] *Ibid.,* pp. 78, 79.
[100] Baxter: *The Reformed Pastor,* p. 34.
[101] *Ibid.,* p. 37.

on how to speak the paragraphs that should be built according to a generally accepted law and order. He urges simplicity, telling the preacher to avoid a loud voice, a pedantic manner, and meaningless words.[102]   John Alsted devotes a brief chapter of his *Theologia Prophetica* to remarks *de elocutione ecclesiastica.* He feels that some rules for speaking concern the intelligence and the affections, others belong to rhetoric, still others to morals. He presents his recommendations under nine heads, most of which have to do with style, as figures, verbosity, artificiality. Above all, he concludes, the preacher must deliver his sermon: *"Ita enim est, ut ille ait, Oratorio dum scribitur, mortua est, dum bene recitatur, vitam accipit."* [103]

The most practical of clergymen-advisers was Dr. Lawrence Chadderton: "After he was master of Emmanuel, his manner was, not to suffer any young scholars to go into the country to preach, till he had heard them first in the college chapel." [104]

General Criticism of Preaching

The critics of preaching as an art were sometimes preachers themselves, and sometimes laymen; but all those that sat in judgment seem to have been actuated by the same standards. The delivery of a sermon must be a finished performance. The critics may differ as to what constitutes a correct pulpit manner or a proper elocution, but neither ecclesiastic nor worldly wiseman ever feels, apparently, that there is any sacrosanct quality about a clergyman's way of expressing his ideas. When he delivers a sermon, he is a public performer and is judged as such.

In the middle of the seventeenth century, pulpit oratory reached a remarkably high level both in France and Eng-

[102] Price : *Ars concionandi,* p. 319.
[103] Alstedius, Joh. : *Theo. Proph.,* p. 80-1.
[104] Clarke : *General Martyrology,* p. 460.

land. It does not seem probable that the one inspired the other, but rather that each was influenced by the same canons of literary taste which were reflected in many forms of contemporary literature. Bossuet and Bourdaloue are often given credit for the excellence of seventeenth-century English sermons; but a number of conspicuously successful English preachers had made their reputations sometime before the French orators had won their deservedly great renown.[105]

For many years, no occupation in England could compete with preaching in arousing interest. Through a generation—from 1640 to 1670—preaching filled an important place in men's thoughts. Religion was then, as always, a popular and controversial subject; to preach or not to preach was an extremely serious question when Laud was in power, and again at the Restoration. Even under the Commonwealth, Acts of Parliament were necessary to protect the ordained minister from the competition of the lay preacher who earnestly (and obstinately) desired to exhort sinners when and where he felt disposed. Moreover, during these three decades, there was the constant excitement of listening to pulpit speakers to whom something dramatic might happen the next day. There were sequestrations and ejectments; there were fines and pillory sentences; there was imprisonment for many eminent clergymen; there was beheading for Archbishop Laud; there was hanging, drawing and quartering for Hugh Peters. Undeniably, such occurrences must give emphasis to the sufferer's profession. Men and women of the generation that lived under Charles I and Cromwell and Charles II went to church, listened to the preacher, talked about him, and (for our learning) wrote down what they thought of him, of what he said, and of how he said it.

If a reader of the twentieth century wonders at the fre-

[105] Bossuet was born in 1627, Bourdaloue and Fléchier in 1632. Andrews was born in 1555; Donne, in 1573; Calamy, in 1600; Thomas Adams, about 1612; Jeremy Taylor, in 1613.

quency with which sermon-criticisms are recorded in the
seventeenth century and the definiteness of the judgments
pronounced, he should remember that the congregations of
that day were not amateur listeners. Established or nonconformist, independent or Brownist, baptist or quaker,
whatever sect they might uphold (and there was no lack
of variety to choose among), they were accustomed to sermons at any hour and in virtually any place. The average
person in England had, by the middle of the century, acquired a nice taste in sermons that made him listen attentively or read critically; both these habits rendering him
a competent judge of the sermon proper, though not, perhaps, of the learning displayed or the subtle interpretation
devised. There is a sweeping denunciation of contemporaneous criticism in Joseph Glanvill's satirical continuation
of Bacon's *New Atlantis:* "And indeed things had come to
that pass in Berusalem [the governor of Solomon's House
is explaining the religious situation] that there was scarce
any other use made of Preaching, but to pass judgments
on the Preacher and the Sermon; which was not only undertaken by People of Age and Experience, or by those of
better education and advanced knowledge, but every Age
was thought fit to judge here . . . every Rustick and
Mechanick would pass absolute and definitive sentence in
this matter." [106]

Bishop Glanvill speaks scornfully, but his profession
made it impossible for him to realize that any fairly regular church-goer has heard far more sermons than the
preacher can possibly have listened to, and is a better authority on the practical, working value of a pulpit discourse
than is the man who delivers it. Edmund Calamy said
once (in the prayer before his Farewell Sermon): "We
confess many of us have grown sermon proof; we know
how to scoff and mock at sermons, but we know not how

---

[106] *Essays on Several Subjects in Philosophy and Religion.*, Lond.,
1676, pp. 41-2.

to live sermons"; [107] yet he himself could have heard few sermons; he was far too busy preaching them. And the same objection applies to Jeremy Taylor's reproof: "We sit as unconcerned as the pillars of a church, and hear the sermons as the Athenians did a story, or as we read a gazette." [108]

The Preacher's Voice

However respectful and appreciative of a sermon a seventeenth-century writer may be, he seldom fails to note the possession or the lack of a good voice in the man to whose pulpit performance he has given attention. A clear and pleasant voice is an important factor in elocution, especially in what Matthew Robinson's biographer calls "concionalary elocution," but not all the preachers were so fortunate as to possess one. Richard Baxter did not hesitate to judge his own manner of speaking in his later years. He says that, in youth, "by the advantage of affection, and a very familiar moving voice and utterance, my preaching then did more affect the auditory. . . ." [109] George Bull's voice "was always exerted with some Vehemency, whereby he kept the Audience awake, and raised their attention to what he delivered." [110] The best Calamy can say for Mr. Robert Constantine's oratorical ability is that he had "an audible Voice, good method and very taking." [111] Mr. John Fairfax "was to his Hearers as a very lovely Song, of one that had a pleasant Voice." [112] Robert Frampton completely satisfied the judgment, based on much experience, of that expert in sermons, Mr. Samuel Pepys who records in his Diary: "the best sermon, for goodness and oratory, without affectation or study, that ever I heard in my life.

[107] *An Exact Collection of Farewell Sermons* (Sermon delivered Aug. 17, 1662).
[108] *Works*, I, 760.   See Dedicatory letter to Richard, Lord Vaughn.
[109] Baxter : *Autobiography*, p. 102.
[110] Nelson : *Life of Bull*, p. 60.
[111] Calamy : *Abridgement, etc.*, II, 398.
[112] *Ibid.*, 642.

The truth is, he preaches the most like an apostle that ever
I heard. . . ." [113]   Richard Gilpin "had a Voice strong
enough to Command the most Publick Places of Divine
Worship.   It was Piercing and Sweet, and naturally well
Model'd.   He had the true Skill of fixing an Accent upon
particular Words, where the matter needed it." [114]   John
Owen had a "good elocution, graceful and affectionate." [115]
Pepys thought that Dr. Pierce had "as much of natural
eloquence as most men that ever I heard in my life, mixed
with so much learning." [116]   Mr. Starkey, one of the ejected
nonconformists, possessed a delivery that "was graceful,
but not noisy; and it appeared by him that there is a mildness in speaking that is as powerful as force." [117]   Benjamin Woodbridge was an unusually effective preacher,
"having a commanding Voice and Air." [118]   The danger
arising from an especially finished and elegant delivery is
obvious.   Samuel Shaw expresses his feeling in regard to
this matter by declaring in his sermon, *A Voice Crying in
the Wilderness,* "Thus did they in Ezekiel 33, 32, who
delighted in the Prophet's eloquence, and in the Rhetorick
of his Sermons as much as in a well tuned voice, and harmonious musick; and so do thousands in England, who read
the Bible for the stories sake, and love to sit under learned
and elegant discourses, more for accomplishment, than for
conversion. . . ." [119]

The statement that a man's voice is inaudible or disagreeable is usually combined with the assurance that his
divinity is sound or his learning extraordinary.   That important scholar, Thomas Greaves, for example, who was
at one time deputy professor of the Arabic lecture in the
absence of Edward Pocock, was at a later day rector of

[113] *Diary,* Jan. 20, 1666/7.
[114] Calamy: *op. cit.,* II, 155.
[115] Owen: *Sermons* (Prefatory Memoir), **p. xxxiv.**
[116] Pepys: *Diary,* April 8, 1663.
[117] Palmer: *Nonconf. Mem., Etc.,* II, 145.
[118] Calamy: *Abridgement, etc.,* II, 96.
[119] Shaw: *A Voice Crying, etc.,* p. 198.

Buryfield in Northamptonshire, "which last he resigned
some years before his death, through trouble from his parishioners, who, because of his slowness of speech and bad
utterance, held them insufficient for them and it, notwithstanding he was a man of great learning." [120] Mr. Richard
Capel "excelled in all that ever he would set his hand to,
unless it were his utterance in the public congregation, and
therein indeed he had a great defectiveness." [121] Mr.
Samuel Coates "had an unacceptable kind of Stammering
in his Delivery," which comment suggests that he, too, had
a congregation that demanded a professional excellence of
speech in addition to "Substantial Divinity," which Calamy
says he possessed.[122] Mr. Malthurst was "of great Eloquence and Fervour: only Defective in Elocution." [123]
Mr. Henry Wilkinson "was a good scholar, always a close
student, an excellent preacher (tho' his voice was shrill
and whining)." [124]

Pepys felt that his brother's voice was a serious draw-
back to his chance of success in the church. "I made my
brother, in his cassock, to say grace this day, but I like
his voice so ill, that I begin to be sorry he hath taken
orders." [125] Ten days later, Pepys has his first private talk
with his brother, "and find he hath preached but twice in
his life. I did give him some advice to study pronunciation, but I do fear he will never make a good speaker, nor, I
fear, any general good scholar; for I do not see that he
minds optiques or mathematiques of any sort, nor anything else that I can find. I know not what he may be at
divinity or ordinary school learning. However, he seems

---

[120] Wood: *Ath. Ox.*, III, 1061.
[121] Clarke: *General Martyrology*, p. 531.
[122] Calamy: *Abridgement, etc.*, II, 530.
[123] *Ibid.*, p. 467.
[124] Wood: *Ath. Ox.*, III, 1039. See, also: John French, "very Defective in his Delivery" (Calamy: *Abridg.*, II, 731) ; Robert Bath,
"no very ready Utterance" (*Ibid.*, p. 399) ; John Knight, "such an
impediment in his speech, as not to be acceptable in his preaching"
(Palmer: *Nonconf. Mem.*, I, 372) ; Samuel Sprint, "his preaching was
very instructive, but his delivery was not popular" (*Ibid.*, II, 24).
[125] Pepys: *Diary*, Oct. 7, 1666.

sober, and that pleases me." [126] Robert Creighton's voice
jarred on the sensitive ear of Mr. Pepys, and though the
Scotchman had great repute as a preacher, Pepys, after
once listening critically to a sermon by him, deliberately
slept on other occasions when he found Dr. Creighton in
the pulpit.[127] Perhaps Fuller saw him do it: "It is a
shame," one may read in "The Good Parishioner," "when
the church itself is a caemeterium wherein the living sleep
above ground as the dead do beneath." [128] As a general
thing, the preacher wins some measure of serious attention
from Mr. Pepys. He may drop asleep, and he is easily
diverted by pew neighbors, but he usually makes note of
the text, he watches the development of the "heads," and
he judges the preacher's delivery. If he is wakeful and the
sermon is not worth listening to, he has resources: "At
church . . . where in the pew both Sir William Pen and
I had much talk . . ."; [129] or, "we, in spite to one another,
kept one another awake; and sometimes I read in my book
of Latin plays, which I kept in my pocket . . ."; adding
by way of explanation, not apology, "an old doting parson
preached." [130]

A too low voice was as irritating to a sermon listener of
Puritan proclivities as it would be to a professedly worldly
minded person. The godliness of the preacher and the
orthodox matter of the sermon did not excuse a man who
bent his head and read his discourse indistinctly. An
argument such as the following, which Thomas Burton
records in his *Diary,* represents a frequent protest against
indistinct speech in the pulpit:

July 19, 1656/7

Alderman Foot desired Mr. Reynolds to preach.
Exceptions were taken to his too low voice. . . .

[126] *Ibid.,* Oct. 17, 1666.
[127] *Ibid.,* March 7, 1661; April 19, June 21, 1663.
[128] *Holy and Profane State,* p. 72.
[129] *Diary,* Oct. 27, 1661.
[130] *Ibid.,* July 5, 1663.

> Mr. Wardstone and Major Haines moved, that Mr. Warren
> might be the one to preach, for Dr. Reynold's voice is
> too low, and so is Mr. Caryl's.
>
> Lord Strickland. It is strange we should not hear as well
> now as we did fourteen years ago.
>
> Mr. Robinson. Ministers tell us our faults. It is fit we
> should tell them theirs. Their reading of sermons makes
> their voices lower.[131]

Pepys makes much the same comment on "one Dr. Lewes,
said heretofore to have been a great witt; but he read his
sermon every word, and that so brokenly and so low, that
nobody could hear at any distance, nor I any thing worth
hearing that sat near." [132]

To some people, an ordinary tone of voice was not desirable in the pulpit. John Selden inclined to that opinion
although he did not of course recommend extravagance in
intonation. "The tone in preaching," he writes, "does much
in working upon the People's Affections. If a Man should
make Love in an ordinary Tone, his Mistress would not
regard him; and therefore he must whine. If a man should
cry Fire, or Murther in an ordinary Voice, nobody would
come out to help him." [133] Robert Fish felt the same way.
He, though physically frail, "used to speak in the pulpit
with vehemence. Some friends attempting to dissuade him
from it, he replied, 'If persons cry, Fire, fire, in an unconcerned manner, who will take notice of it?' " [134] Richard
Northam's preaching "was affecting and aweful; for he
delivered his sermons with a thundering voice." [135]

Evelyn, though he does not express approval, writes
tolerantly: "Dr. Fell, Canon of Christ Church, preached
before the King . . . a formal discourse, and in blank
verse, according to his manner; however, he is a good

[131] *Op. cit.*, I, 359.
[132] *Diary*, March 1, 1662/3 ; also an unnamed bishop: May 29, 1664.
See Calamy, of Mr. Michael Briscoe (*Account, etc.*, II, 407).
[133] *Table Talk*, p. 38.
[134] Palmer: *Nonconf. Mem.*, II, 466.
[135] *Ibid.*, p. 148.

man." [136]   John Fell undoubtedly had a liking for regular cadences:

> The dying miser may as well hope for life, by applying a bag of money to his heart, as a sick state expect a remedy from pecuniary supplies. A clock whose movements are decaied, will not go well though the weights hung at it are of Gold.[137]

Or:

> . . . the strong depends upon the weak, as much as the weak do's on the strong: the rich is assisted by the poor, as the poor is by the rich: the wise is aided by the ignorant, as the ignorant is by the wise. The Sceptre rests on the mattock and the spade, and the Throne on the Plough.[138]

Probably Fell spoke in a sing-song fashion, observing regular pauses. It would be almost impossible to avoid doing so in reading such definitely separated clauses as are in the examples just quoted.

One of the many clerical affectations that annoyed John Fry was the fashion of mumbling prayers, and then, "when Artificially they have raised their voices, what a puling do some make!" [139]   Samuel Butler through one of his *Characters* ("An hypocritical nonconformist") scorns the preacher who "uses more artificial Tricks to improve his Spirit of Utterance either into Volubility of Dullness, that it may seem to go of itself, without his Study or Direction, than the old Heathen Orators knew, that used to liquor their throats, and Harangue to Pipes. For he has fantastic and extravagant Tones, as well as Phrases, that are no less agreeable to the Sense . . . a Kind of *stilo recitatio* between singing and braying." [140]

Robert South condemned "rhyming cadencies of similary

[136] Evelyn: *Diary*, Feb. 24, 1665.
[137] Fell: *A Sermon preached before the House of Peers*, p. 9.
[138] *Ibid.*, p. 2. (For an example of the same rhythm, see his *Last Daies* sermon, pp. 23-24.)
[139] Fry: *The Clergy in their Colours*, p. 35.
[140] Butler: *Remains*, p. 42ff.

words" which, he said, "are such pitiful embellishments of speech, as serve for nothing but to embase divinity; and the use of them but like the plastering of marble, or the painting of gold, the glory of which is to be seen, and to shine by no other lustre, but their own." [141]   Especially does Dr. South condemn "speaking through the nose, which I think cannot so properly be called preaching, as toning of a sermon." [142]

There were also curious practices to emphasize special points; for example, the "spitting pauses" should be long enough to produce an effect,[143] and coughing and hemming intervals were planned for.[144]   Weeping was considered a legitimate elocutionary aid to impressiveness.   Calamy observes that Mr. William Smith "seldom pray'd or preach'd without Tears"; [145] and he refers to James Nalten as the Weeping Prophet because "his seriousness oft express'd itself by Tears." [146]   Thomas Westfield was extremely emotional: "his lips and eyes," says Lloyd in his usual decorative phrasing, "by a strange Metathasis changing their offices, these outdid the oratory of those (for tears are very vocal), he in the Prophets phrase dropping his words (though soft and silent, yet warm and melting ones), and his doctrine (not in a Metaphor) distilling like Rain, and descending on his people like Dew. . . ." [147]   Dr. Thomas Comber did not actually shed tears, but he was "a melting Preacher, preaching as much by his silent and grave gesture, composed to a smiling sweetness, as by his learned and honest Sermons." [148]

[141] South :   *Sermons*, II, 359.
[142] *Ibid.*, p. 362.   See Glanvill : *Essays, etc.* (Essay VII), 42.
[143] Fuller :   *Worthies, etc.*, II, 482.
[144] Butler :   *Hudibras,* p. 31.   (A note refers to a sermon of Olivier Maillard's printed in Brussels, 1500, on the margin of which places are marked where the preacher hummed once or twice, or coughed.)
[145] Calamy :   *Account, etc.*, II, 541 ; also, Stephen Hughes (Palmer : II, 621).
[146] *Ibid.*, p. 2 ; also, John Wilkins (not the famous Wilkins), Palmer : I, 347.
[147] Lloyd, p. 300 ; see, too, Mr. Gilpin who "generally melted into tears" (Palmer : II, 482).
[148] *Ibid.*, p. 448.

The Dr. Westfield referred to above was a person of such admirable modesty that he fainted away when he mounted the pulpit to preach before the king at Oxford, but "that excellent Prince was contented to wait till he had Recovered himself, and then had from him a Sermon which abundantly Rewarded such a Royal and Christian Condescension." [149]   Robert South had the same embarrassing experience, though shyness was certainly not one of his characteristics; he had, as a matter of fact, experienced an attack of the same nature a few months before the unfortunate seizure which caused him to fall unconscious while preaching before Charles II.   Pepys, who hated to miss anything, planned to go to Whitehall the very next Sunday (April 20, 1662) to hear Dr. South (hoping, one suspects, that he would collapse again) but it was a rainy, windy day and no coach nor boat could be found to convey Mr. Pepys to the King's Chapel.[150]   Baxter tells a similar story about Dr. Creighton: "the most famous, loquacious, ready-tongued preacher of the court, who was ready to preach Calvin to hell, and the Calvinists to the gallows, and by his scornful revilings and jests to set the court on a laughter, was suddenly, in the pulpit (without any sickness) surprised with astonishment, worse than Dr. South, the Oxford orator, had been before him; and when he had repeated a sentence over and over, and was so confounded that he could go no further at all, he was fain, to all men's wonder, to come down.   And his case was more wonderful than almost any other man's, being not only a fluent extempore speaker, but one that was never known to want words, especially to express his satirical or bloody thoughts. . . ." [151]   There is no mystery about William Sancroft's failure to preach one day.   He writes the painful details to his father and does not lay any of the blame on nervousness where, no doubt, some of it properly be-

[149] Walker: Pt. II, 3.
[150] See Wood's account: *Ath. Ox.*, IV, 635-6.
[151] Baxter: *Autobiography*, pp. 201-2.

longed. "I was yesterday to have preached the afternoon lecture . . . and had accordingly provided for it; and though I found not myself well the day before, hoped, with God's assistance, to have performed it: but just when the bell was ringing, and when I was now come to Mrs. Bainbrigg's house, just by the church door, I was there surprised (besides my former feverish distemper and a dizziness in my head) with such a fulness of stomach and vomiting, that I was forced to lay down all thoughts of preaching, it being now grown impossible; and my cousin Barker, upon notice, stepped up at that short warning, and supplied the vacuity." And he adds his suspicion that he had eaten too freely of the fat of a rabbit on Friday night.[152]

Mannerisms

Some preachers must have been naturally awkward in gesture and harsh of voice; others were unattractive in appearance, or cursed with timidity; but there were still others who apparently cultivated eccentricity when in the pulpit and planned to startle and amuse. Of Christopher Fowler, Anthony à Wood says severely, "by his very many odd gestures and antic behaviour (unbecoming the serious gravity to be used in the pulpit) he drew constantly to his congregation a numerous crowd of silly women and young people who seemed to be hugely taken and enamour'd with his obstreperousness and indecent cants."[153] Wood, usually sharp-tongued, was likely to be especially so when identifying an Oxford man who did not conform, and Edmund Hall fared no better than Fowler though the former's nonconformity had mitigating circumstances in that he was opposed to Cromwell; but Wood sees no good in Hall's sermons which "had in them many odd, light and whimsical passages, altogether unbecoming the gravity of

[152] Cary: *Memorials, etc.,* II, 64.
[153] Wood: *Ath. Ox.,* III, 1098.

the pulpit: and his gestures being very antic and mimical, did usually excite somewhat of laughter in the more youthful part of the auditory." [154]

Evelyn satirizes the undignified preacher who has the action rather of a thrasher than a divine, "thus encouraging every pert mechanick to out-preach them. . . ." [155] John Fry exclaims: "What wry mouths, squint-eyes and scru'd faces do they make. . . ." [156] And the author of *Ichabod,* "Oh, the pride . . . that formeth your countenances, that putteth the Accents and Emphases on your Words, that ordereth your Habit, modelleth your Gestures. . . ." [157] South also objects to "strange new gestures . . . such as shutting the eyes, distorting the face. . . ." [158] John Taylor put a person of this sort into verse:

> He did address himselfe in such a fashion
> As well befitted such a Congregation.
> He made some faces, with his hands erected,
> His eyes (most whitest white) to heaven directed:
> His lims, his stroking of the beard, his spitting,
> His postures, and impostures, done most fitting. [159]

Certain mannerisms became identified with particular religious groups, as is plain from Aubrey's admiring comment on Sir William Petty's powers of mimicry: "He can be an excellent droll (if he haz a mind to it) and will preach extempore incomparably either the Presbyterian way, Independent, Cappuchin frier, or Jesuite." [160] On a certain glorious occasion Pepys, bursting with pride, had dined with the archbishop of Canterbury and was about to leave, when "I heard by a gentleman of a sermon that

[154] *Ibid.,* IV, 213.
[155] *Character of England,* p. 153.
[156] *The Clergy in their Colours,* p. 35.
[157] *Ichabod,* p. 34.
[158] *Sermons,* II, 362. Shutting the eyes was practiced by some preachers as a means of aiding the memory. Fénelon discusses the subject at some length in connection with Bourdaloue who was much criticized for this mannerism (*Dialogues, etc.,* pp. 39, 45).
[159] *A Swarm of Sectaries and Schismatiques, etc.,* London, 1641, p. 10.
[160] Aubrey, II, 143.

was to be there; and so I staid to hear it, thinking it serious,
till by and by the gentleman told me it was a mockery, by
one Cornet Bolton . . . that behind a chair did pray and
preach like a Presbyter Scot that ever I heard in my life,
with all the possible imitation in grimaces and voice. And
. . . a serious good sermon, too, exclaiming against Bishops . . . but I did wonder to have the Bishop at this
time to make himself sport with things of this kind, but
I perceive it was shown him as a rarity; and he was
careful to have the room door shut. . . ." [161]

Stephen Marshall had strong lungs and used them freely.
In one of his poems, John Cleveland offers a comparison:

> Or roar like Marshall, that Geneva bull,
> Hell and Damnation a pulpit full. . . . [162]

It was Marshall who nearly made Dorothy Osborne laugh
aloud in church. She writes all about it to Sir William
Temple: "Would you believe that I had the grace to go
to hear a sermon upon a week day? In earnest, 'tis true;
a Mr. Marshall was the man that preached, but never anybody was so defeated. He is so famed that I expected rare
things of him, and seriously I listened to him as if he had
been St. Paul; and what do you think he told us? Why,
that if there were no kings, no queens, no gentlemen, nor
gentlewomen, in the world, 'twould be no loss to God
Almighty at all. . . . I had the most ado to look soberly
enough for the place I was in that ever I did in my life.
He does not preach so, always, sure? If he does, I cannot
believe his sermons will do much towards bringing anybody to heaven more than by exercising their patience." [163]

That contradictory dramatic person, Hugh Peters, was,

---

[161] *Diary*, May 14, 1669.
[162] *Poems*, p. 147 ("The Rebel Scot").
[163] *Love Letters of Dorothy Osborne to Sir William Temple*, p. 202-3.
There is an interesting tradition that Marshall's two daughters in-
herited their father's elocutionary powers and became famous actresses
in Killigrew's company. Pepys believed this, and so did Dryden;
Genest repeats the story. For arguments against its authenticity,
see H. B. Wheatley: *Samuel Pepys and the World He Lived In*, pp.
220-1.

as might be supposed, an extravagant pulpit performer. Wood calls him "the theological buffoon"; and Pepys uses him as a measure of eccentric and undignified delivery. When he wishes to dispose of "Dr. Creeton," he says, "the most comical man that ever I heard in my life. Just such a man as Hugh Peters." [164] Any reference to Peters was understood to be humorous and more or less insulting; for example, when Robert Wilde, the presbyterian poet, was preaching before John Owen (then Vice-chancellor of Oxford), Owen said "that he knew not the man, but by his preaching he guess'd him to have been begotten by Hugh Peters in his younger yeares"; [165] and Colybute Downing (a chaplain in Essex's army) "preached so seditiously that he was commonly called Young Peters, or Hugh Peters the Second." [166]

Robert Mossum was a preacher Pepys heard frequently with approval, but one Sunday, though the sermon was good, it was "only too eloquent for the pulpit," which comment hints that the conservative Clerk of the Acts objected to a display of oratory in a sermon; however, he approved entirely of a Portuguese "fryer" he heard in the Queen's chapel: "He was full of action, but very good and decent, I thought, and his manner of delivery very good." [167] Alexander Morus, the great Scotch-French clergyman, also had an energetic delivery. Evelyn, having just heard him, notes briefly: "At St. James's chapel preached, or rather harangued, the famous orator, Monsieur Morus, in French." [168]

The whole question of manner is a difficult one, Baxter thinks: "If Ministers deal plainly with you, you say they rail. If they speak gently or coldly, you either sleep under them or are little more affected than the seats you sit

[164] March 7, 1661/2; also, April 3, 1663.
[165] Wood: *Ath. Ox.*, III, 35 (note).
[166] *Ibid.*, 107. An example of a political sermon by Peters, is *God's Doings and Man's Duty* (1646).
[167] *Diary*, March 17, 1666/7.
[168] *Diary*. Jan. 12, 1661/2.

upon." [169]   But a Mr. Mason of St. Andrews Undershaft had a mannerism of speech different from anyone that has been mentioned: ". . . he dispersed, rather than spake his words; pausing with a reflection upon what he had said, before he said any more; a way of three advantages to him, 1. Because so he might correct the error of a former word, 2. He might take occasion, and matter for a following word: and 3. Likewise observing by the looks and carriage of him he spoke with, frame his speech accordingly." [170]

Artificial tones and studied or exaggerated gestures naturally suggested the stage. The acts of parliament which put an end to public performances of plays could not, of course, wipe out vocabulary of terms and comparisons that were a part of everyday speech. Moreover, although formal dramatic presentations were not permitted, there were wandering actors who risked arrest now and then by giving an entertainment, there were old plays in libraries, and new plays being published. The comparisons, therefore, which clergymen or their critics borrow from the theater, are not strained, half-forgotten expressions; they are, on the contrary, lively figures and references that would bring a man or his manner clearly before a reader or a listener.

"An unprofitable man, whilst living, is dead," cried the preacher in his funeral sermon for Sir Thomas Lucy. "Live, Live, Live quickly, Live much, Live long. So you are welcome to the world: els, you are but Hissed and Kickt off this Stage of the World. . . ." [171] An unsigned tribute to Richard Vines names a number of clergymen who died shortly before him. Among these, says the anonymous poet:

> Their only strife,
> Hath been (of late) who should first part with Life.
> Those few who yet survive, sick of this Age,
> Long to have done their Parts, and leave the Stage. [172]

[169] A Call to the Unconverted, p. 103.
[170] Lloyd: Memoirs, p. 506.
[171] Harris: Abner's Funeral, p. 24.
[172] Clark, S.: Eminent Lives, p. 53.

Chillingworth knows he will be readily understood when, wishing to show that the clergy themselves are sometimes to blame for the disapproving attitude of some congregations, he says: ". . . we make the church a stage whereon to act our parts, and play our pageantry. . . ."[173] The writer of the Epistle to the Reader, which is prefixed to the collection of eighteen sermons by Usher, complains that "our pulpits turn'd as it were into stages; and sadly prostituted to froth and jerks at godlinesse. . . ." This critic in writing in 1659, the end of the Puritan régime; in 1633, William Prynne had written his famous diatribe, *Histrio-Mastix*, in which he declared ". . . hee is the best Minister who is most unlike a player both in his gesture, habit, speech and elocution, and as Theatricall gestures are altogether unseemly for a minister . . . so likewise are all poeticall Playhouse phrases, Clinches and strong lines . . . too frequent in our Sermons, which in respect of their Divisions, language, action, stile and subject matter, consisting either of wanton flashes of luxurious wits, or meere quotations of humane Authors, Poets, Orators, Histories, Philosophers and Popish Schoole-men; or sesquipedalia verbs, great empty swelling words of vanity and estimation more fitter for the Stage, from whence they are oftimes borrowed, (then the pulpit) unsuitable for ministers."[174] Owen Feltham, in 1640, insisted that the pulpit had much to learn from the stage. "We complain of drowsiness at a sermon, when a play of doubled length leads us on still with alacrity. But the fault is not all in ourselves. If we saw Divinity acted, the gesture and variety would as much invigelate. . . . A

---

[173] *Sermons*, I, 532. See in the same sermon, p. 536: ". . . the chief actors in this bloody tragedy which is now upon the stage." (Chillingworth died in the beginning of the civil war, in 1643.)

[174] Prynne: *Hist.-Mas.* (Prefatory Epistle).

Erasmus had said all this, a hundred years before: "All their preaching is mere stage playing, and their delivery the very transports of ridicule and drollery. Good Lord! how mimical are their gestures? what heights and falls in their voices? what toning, what bawling, what singing, what squeaking, what grimaces, working of mouths, Apes faces, and distorting of their countenance. . . ." (*In Praise of Folly*, p. 143.)

good Orator should pierce the ear, allure the eye, and invade the mind of his hearer. . . . A kemb'd Oration will cost both sweat and the rubbing of the brain. And kem'd I wish it, not frizzled, nor curl'd. Divinity should not lasciviate. . . . Words are not all, nor matter is not all: nor gesture; yet together they are." [175]

Hobbes was convinced that it was "by a long practiced Histrionic Faculty" that the presbyterian clergy "preached up the Rebellion powerfully . . . they so framed their countenance and gesture at their entrance into the pulpit, and their pronunciation both in their prayer and sermon, and used the Scripture phrase (whether understood by the people or not) as that no tragedian in the world could have acted the part of a right godly man better than these did. . . ." [176] Selden thinks the success of a sermon has little to do with the clearness of the exposition. " 'Tis with a Sermon as 'tis with a Play; many come to see it, which do not understand it; and yet hearing it cried up by one whose judgement they cast themselves upon . . . they swear and will die in it, that 'tis a very good Play." [177] John Fry does not know whether actors or preachers are to blame for the manner that is common to both: "Whether the fools and knaves in Stage Plays, took their pattern from these men, or these from them, I cannot determine; but sure one is a Brat of the other, they are so well alike." [178] Calamy says they were sometimes one and the same: "The clergy of these Parts where Baxter lived as a boy were (generally speaking) Lazy and Vitious. Some by forging Orders, had compass'd a Translation even from the Stage

---

[175] *Resolves: Divine, Moral, and Political*, p. 36 (Pub. before the *Histrio-Mastix*. Seven editions before 1670).
Cf. Erasmus: ". . . if what is delivered from the pulpit be grave, solid, rational discourse, all the congregation grow weary, and fall asleep . . . whereas if the preacher (pardon the impropriety of the word, the prater I would have said) be zealous in the thumps of the cushion, antic gestures, and spend his glass in the telling of pleasant stories, his beloved shall then stand up, tuck their hair behind their ears, and be very devoutly attentive," *op. cit.*, p. 92.
[176] *Behemoth*, p. 483.
[177] *Table Talk*, 140.
[178] *The Clergy in their Colours*, p. 34.

to the Pulpit." [179]   And the serious-minded Mrs. Lucy Hutchinson quotes "a gentleman of as exquisite breeding and parts as England's court ever enjoyed," who ridiculed and disparaged the clergy: "some young preachers he would make stage-players in their pulpits." [180]

It was not easy to find an acceptable mean. If a preacher of no special oratorical gift did permit himself to use even the most dignified of stage tactics, he would be reproved: "If a man have emphasis, whose conceptions and delivery receive spirit and lustre from each other, whose gesture breathes out living passions . . . his classical friend will cry out he is a dramatist, fitter to personate upon a theatre a Cassius or a Catiline." [181]

Memory

Seventeenth-century congregations, established or non-conformist, had a distinct preference for sermons that were delivered, not read. A good memory was almost a necessity to a preacher who hoped for popular approval. Fortunately, memory training was a part of grammar school experience; fortunately, too, sermons were used for practice work in oral repetition. The Rules for Eton Scholars (1646) require "that those who can write take notes of sermons and those under the Master render them to him and those under the Usher render to him. . . ." [182] Charles Hoole's *New Discovery of the Old Art of Teaching School* gives elaborate directions for taking sermon notes; the "four middlemost forms" for instance, "should mind to write the text, doctrines, reasons, uses, motives, derivations, with the quotations of scripture-places as they are best able." [183] Accustomed, then, from boyhood to concentrat-

---

[179] Calamy : *Abridgement, etc.,* I, p. 5.
[180] *Memoirs of the Life of Col. Hutchinson,* p. 52.
[181] *Reliq. Hearnae,* III, 253 (Appendix IX).
[182] Watson, Foster : *Eng. Grammar Schools, etc.,* p. 44.
[183] Hoole :   *New Dis.,* pp. 289-90 ; Brinsley :   *Ludus Literarius* (1612) recommended copying sermon notes into commonplace-books, pp. 196-7, 198-9 ; also, D'Ewes, I, 61-2 ; 95, 104.

ing on sermons, a man with merely a normal memory would find it easy to remember the heads and divisions of his pulpit discourses; but a man with an unusual memory could do astonishing things.

Dr. William Bates, at seventy-four, delivered his sermons from memory and, says the preacher of Dr. Bates's funeral sermon, "hath some time told me, with an amiable freedom, that he partly did it to teach some that were younger to preach without notes." [184] George Bull was quite capable of preaching without notes, but he did like to have them within reach. Once they flew out of his Bible, and the congregation, "consisting of wild Seafaring Persons," laughed. But a few respectful persons gathered up the notes and took them to Dr. Bull who received them, put them back in the Bible, closed the book—ostentatiously, probably—and finished the sermon without their aid. [185] Samuel Clifford was "noted for his extraordinary memory," but Calamy gives no details; [186] Fuller, by all accounts, really was exceptional, being able to repeat five hundred strange words after hearing them twice, and a sermon if he read or heard it, and "he would repeat to you forwards and backwards all the signs from Ludgate to Charing-crosse." [187] Fuller himself speaks scornfully of "artificial rules which at this day are delivered by memory-mountebanks. . . . Adventure not all thy learning in one bottom, but divide it between thy memory and thy notebooks." [188] Richard Gilpin was a popular preacher who did not use notes; [189] Bishop Joseph Hall conscientiously memorized his sermons: "he preached thrice a week in constant course. Yet (as he himself witnessed) never durst climb up on the Pulpit to preach any Sermon, whereof he had not before

[184] Bates : *Spiritual Perfection*, p. xviii.
[185] Nelson : *Life of George Bull*, p. 301.
[186] Calamy : *Abridgement, etc.*, II, 764.
[187] Lloyd, 523 ; Aubrey, I. See Pepys on Fuller's memory, *Diary,* Jan. 22, 1660/1.
[188] *The Holy and Profane State*, pp. 180-1.
[189] Calamy : *op. cit.*, 155.

penn'd every word in the same Order, wherein he hoped
to deliver it; although in his expressions hee was no slave
to syllables, neither made use of his Notes." [190]

Henry Hammond's memory "was a sign of his good
judgment, that is, it was serviceable but not officious;
faithful in things and business, but unwillingly retaining
the contexture and punctualities of words." [191] Mr. Thomas
Harrison first wrote and then learned his sermons; [192] Peter
Heylin, Wood declares, "had a tenacious memory to a
miracle"; [193] Henry Jessey "was so great a scripturist, that
if one began to rehearse any passage, he could go on with
it, and name the book, chapter, and verse where it might
be found." [194] Dr. Williams had a like ability; he had the
words and phrases of the Scriptures in "the most perfect
concordance in his memory, and had it the readiest about
him, of all men that ever I saw," says Gilbert Burnet.[195]
Thomas Lydyat once gave up the idea of entering the
ministry because of "a great defect in his memory and
utterance," [196] but he later took orders, and in less than
twelve years produced above six hundred sermons. Dr.
Roger Mainwaring (Lord Bishop of St. David's) is quoted
as saying that he "had a good Memory if he did not
trust it. . . ." [197]

Mr. Ferdinand Nichols, like Dr. Bull, was uneasy unless
his notes were within reach. "Being to preach before the
Judges, he put his Notes into his Wife's Bible, as being
finer than his own, and so fitter for that Occasion: But
being call'd away on a sudden, he snatch'd up his own old
Bible, and went to Church without his Notes. Perceiving
his mistake before he began, he pray'd the Congregation

---

[190] Whitefoot's *Funeral Sermon* for Hall, pp. 67-8.
[191] Fell: *Life of Henry Hammond*, p. 45.
[192] Calamy: *op. cit.*, 122.
[193] Wood: *Ath. Ox.*, III, 186.
[194] Crosby: Hist. of the Baptists, I, 307ff. Also, Dr. Ball, Howe's
Funeral Ser. for Ball, p. 72; Thomas Wilson, *Eminent Lives*, p. 37.
[195] Burnet, *Hist. of his own Times*, p. 130.
[196] Wood: *Ath. Ox.*, III, 557.
[197] Lloyd: 271.

to sing a Psalm, and told them what had happened to him. He soon return'd, and he preach'd with great Freedom, without once looking upon his Notes all the while." [198] John Owen was able "on a sudden without any premeditation" to express himself "well and pertinently on any subject; yet were his sermons mostly studied and digested; nor did he generally use notes in the pulpit." [199] Dr. Robert Sanderson learned an Art of Memory in his younger days, and Isaac Walton says that Sanderson's memory was "so matchless and firm, as it was only overcome by his bashfulness; for he alone to a friend, could repeat all the Odes of Horace, all Tully's Offices, and much of Juvenal and Persius without book." [200] But Aubrey insists that Sanderson "had no great memory," and says he himself heard the Doctor when he was "out" in the Lord's Prayer.[201]

Joseph Trueman, "by meer Strength of Memory when he had read a Book once over, he would pertinently and faithfully recite what his Author had said"; [202] Usher "had in readinesse in his head all he had read"; [203] and John Wallis "when he was fourscore years of age, or near it, could, purely by the help of his memory, multiply twenty numbers by twenty, and then extract the cube root, which as well as his art of decyphering, is an instance of his extraordinary parts." [204] But it was all hard work for Thomas Westfield: "It cost him much pains to set his sermons on his heart . . . as it did to get them into his head." [205]

There was, of course, a difference of opinion about the

[198] Calamy: *Abridgement, etc.*, II, 218. Also Samuel Fairclough (*Em. Lives*, p. 163).

[199] *Sermons* (Memoir prefixed), p. xxxiv. See Calamy's tolerant comment on John Lomax: ". . . and tho' he used notes . . . that did not at all hinder his being universally respected" (Palmer: *Nonconf. Mem.*, I, 274).

[200] *Life of Sanderson*, p. 43.

[201] Aubrey: II, 212. (Pepys heard one of the King's chaplains, "one Mr. Floyd," when he "was out two or three times in his prayer, and as many times in his sermon, but yet he made a most excellent sermon," Nov. 25, 1666.)

[202] Calamy: *op. cit.*, II, 527.

[203] Bernard's *Funeral Sermon* for Usher (Eighteen Sermons), p. 44.

[204] *Reliq. Hearnae*, I, 73-4.

[205] Lloyd: 304. Also John Dod (Clark, S.: *Gen. Mar.*, p. 469).

way a sermon should be presented; Baxter remarks that
"one will not hear a Minister, because he readeth his Sermons, and another will not hear him, because he doth not
read 'em." [206]   A very different person, the Duchess of
Newcastle, scouts the idea that anyone should be expected
to remember what he had written.   "Indeed, it's against
nature for natural wits to remember; for it is impossible
that the brain should retain and create. . . ." [207]   Jeremy
Taylor thinks "an ill memory" has compensations.   In a
sermon, "On the Good and Evil Tongue," he says that a
man with a poor memory is secured against malice and
ambition, because his anger or aspiration disappears rapidly.
Such a man, furthermore, could read books again as if new;
and he would tell the truth because he would not remember
a lie." [208]   Robert South discusses memory in one of his
sermons, but he has no doubt that, whether blessed or not
with a good memory, a minister should try to learn his
sermons by heart: "There being, in the esteem of many,
but little difference between sermons read, and homilies,
save only this, that homilies are much better." [209]

[206] *A Call to the Unconverted,* p. 104.
[207] *Life of the Duke of Newcastle,* p. 268.
[208] *Works,* I, 734.
[209] *Sermons,* II, 345.

CHAPTER III

THE SERMON AND THE PUBLIC

THE sermon is an adaptable form of composition. Theoretically, it is a combination of exposition and argument on a religious subject, said or read by a clergyman to a group of listeners. In actuality, however, the sermon may be an essay, a story, a political harangue, a complimentary address to the living or on the dead, a news-sheet, an apologia, a valedictory—anything, in fact, that a preacher or patron may desire or circumstances suggest. Its identification as a sermon lies in the vocation of the author and the occasion of the delivery.

It is perhaps the adaptable quality of the sermon and its possibilities of variation in content and purpose that have given it recurrent popularity. There has always been, apparently, a steady, respectful interest in going to church and listening to sermons, but every now and then there seems to be an abandonment to sermon-attendance that is difficult of explanation. Persecution may be a factor, curiosity plays a part, and the personality of the preacher undoubtedly is a reason for filling a church. In the middle of the seventeenth century, people not only sat in pews and stood in aisles to hear sermons, but they bought sermons to read at home, they borrowed them, they stole them, they took them down in shorthand and then printed them with or without the preacher's permission.

The Construction of the Sermon

The sermons that were preached and heard and read with such general satisfaction were all built on virtually the same pattern. A typical seventeenth-century sermon, constructed à la mode, had in the first place as striking a text as the writer could find in holy Scripture. The selection was a matter of grave concern, the preacher knowing well that his audience would make mental, if not literal, note of it. Pepys frequently records the exact text even if he does not intend to comment on its appropriateness to the occasion or to the discourse. As a source for texts, the more excitable and oratorical clergy preferred the Old Testament because it offers many varieties of denunciation and retributive justice.[1] Some men selected a text for the opportunity it afforded to play with words: "In choosing your Text," warns Glanvill, "you should take care that you discover not any conceitedness, or lightness of phancy; for that is one way of abusing the Word of God; which should never be plaid or trifled with. . . ."[2]

The text being decided upon, the preacher would set about building his sermon. The framework of a technically correct sermon was an elaborate arrangement of main topics, sub-topics, illustrations, authorities, "uses" and applications, the whole held together by formal transition words, phrases, even sentences, in order that no hearer could fail to know which thought developed from which.

Calamy's explanation of Richard Gilpin's method would serve for that of many other pulpit speakers: "He usually proposed some Subject, and pursu'd it on various Texts. Every Head with its enlargements was closely Studied, and his particulars under each general, were admirably chosen.

---

[1] An anonymous writer tells of a preacher "supposed by his externall gesture to be some Scholler" (though he was proved later to be a Brownist), who spoke on the text, "For the fire of Hell is ordained from the beginning, yea even for the King it is prepared" (*The Cobblers End*).

[2] Glanvill: *Essay Concerning Preaching*, p. 41.
See Fénelon, *Dialogues sur l'eloquence*, p. 230, for the original use of the text.
See J. M. Neale, *Mediaeval Preachers and Mediaeval Preaching*, p. xlii, for examples of texts taken from an Antiphon, the verse of a hymn, and from the Catechism. Latimer is said to have taken Henry VIII's song, "Pastyme with good Company," as a text for a sermon before Edward VI (Besant: *Tudor London*, pp. 21-22).

. . . In the Handling of any Subject, after he had explain'd and prov'd what he had undertaken with a great deal of Clearness and Affection, he was most plain, familiar, and moving in his Applications." [3] Gilpin was a nonconformist, and so was Peter Sterry, who sometimes is very wordy ("that high flown blasphemer," says Wood) and sometimes strips his sermon down to divisions, subdivisions, questions, objections, answers, until it looks like a bare outline. [4] One of his popular sermons, *The Clouds in which Christ Comes*, is developed from four divisions of the text (Rev. i. 7):

1. A Show
2. A Shout
3. Spectators
4. Their Passions

Matthew Robinson, of the established church, is equally careful to follow the popular arrangement. His method was: "Exposition of the text, then a doctrinal observation, confirmed by reasons and demonstrations, next particular applications, as to conviction, refutation, exhortation, motives and incitation. . . ." [5] William Chillingworth, of the same faction, is just as precise; but his sermons read more smoothly because he uses many connectives and frequently reminds his hearer, or reader, of what has been said earlier in the discourse.

Although Richard Baxter was a man of distinct individuality, he held strictly to the analytical form of developing a topic. When, as one of the King's chaplains in 1660, he preached once (and he preached only once) at Whitehall, he took for his text the verse from the eleventh chapter of Hebrews which seeks to define Faith. Baxter must have felt the beauty of the words and rhythm, for he was himself a poet, though one of modest pretensions; but his sermon shows no inspiration of thought or fineness of style.

[3] Calamy: *Abridg.*, II, 156.
[4] E.g., *Before Parl. Nov.* 1, 1649.
[5] *Autobiography*, p. 70.

It is a formal, dignified exposition: eight suppositions are
stated, ten questions based on these suppositions are asked
and answered.[6] John Tillotson built his sermons in so precise and obvious a manner that he was the admiration of his
own day and of the generation that followed. His arrangement is without a flaw. Divisions are named, points
under each are numbered, objections presented and answered, first, secondly, thirdly. His arguments may not
always seem convincing to a present-day reader; but probably there was little dissatisfaction in his own time when
he offered proof as follows:

> Atheism, as it is absurd, so it is an imprudent Opinion
>> First, It is against mens present Interest
>> Secondly, Atheism is imprudent because it is unsafe in
>> the issue [7]

John Simpson's group of sermons published under the
deceivingly attractive title, *The Herbal of Divinity,* represents the extent to which subdivision can go. The sixth
point in the section, which argues that the spiritual man
born of God doth not, cannot, sin, presents twenty-eight
numbered arguments, each contention being established
by means of answers to a variety of objections.[8] It is not
surprising that John Brinsley, the rhetorician, should utilize
a framework prescribed by generations of logicians,[9] but

---

[6] In *The Reformed Pastor,* Baxter does not recommend the analytical
presentation which he himself usually employs (p. 38).

The presentation of opposing ideas through questions and answers
is an old literary device which had not lost its popularity in the
seventeenth century ; see, besides sermons, the controversies of Joseph
Hall and Milton, Fuller and Heylin, Chillingworth and Hobbes, and
also the writings of Baxter, Bunyan, Burnet, Henry More, Isaac
Walton.

[7] Sermon (*The Wisdom of being Religious*) preached at St. Paul's
in 1664, when Tillotson was "preacher to the Honorable Society of
Lincolns-Inn."

[8] Like the man in *Hudibras:*

> Profoundly skill'd in Analytick ;
> He could distinguish, and divide
> A hair 'twixt south and south-west side ;
> On either which he would dispute,
> Confute, change hands, and still confute (l. 65ff.).

[9] E.g., *The Saints Solemne Covenant with their God,* preached 1644.

it is far from being a matter of course that Bunyan should do the same thing. Take, for example, a sermon of his, published in 1658: *A Few Sighs from Hell; or, The Groans of a Damned Soul*. The text covers half of the sixteenth chapter of Luke, and the sermon follows the order of the verses, progressing steadily through the story of the rich man and Lazarus. The arguments in favor of a righteous life appear in numbered succession, a conclusion being reached by way of five Uses. The sermon has no flavor; Brinsley or Simpson might be the author as far as the plan and rhetorical proprieties are concerned. It is hard to believe that Bunyan did not preach informally, with colloquialisms of style, with homely illustrations drawn from his own experience. What probably happened was that after taking down the sermons by shorthand, a devoted follower transcribed his notes with an eye to dignifying the work of a man who was scorned by the educated clergy. The preferred method of sermon-construction was considered an evidence of scholarly training; sectarian preferences did not alter a well-informed man's conviction that the proper way to present an argument was through a succession of statements, supported by proofs, and reënforced by the citation of authorities. Reasonably, then, an admirer of Bunyan would wish him to appear in print not in his habit as he lived, but to some degree according to the manner of those preachers whose work and persons won respectful attention.

Christopher Love, in his sermon, *Grace: the Truth and Growth and Different Degrees thereof,* recognizes the danger that lies in too close an adherence to a model. He warns his fellows against imitating the Schoolmen's "sublime notions, Seraphical speculations, curious distinctions, subtile objections, and elaborate answers to them, grave and weighty sentences." [10] Most of the manuals on sermon-construction [11] recommend a precise method of developing a

[10] P. 88.   [11] See *Sermon-helps,* p. 107.

text, though they may differ as to whether the framework should be always in evidence. Wilkins thought Alsted (famous as an authority on sermon-writing) gravely at fault in asserting that the preacher should conceal, even alter, his method for variety's sake; [12] Henry Hammond hid his own plan; Ralph Brownrig made his conspicuous.

One of the advantages of the carefully constructed, logically divided sermon was that the auditors remembered it more easily. "Preaching," says Glanvill, "should be Methodical. Method is necessary both for the understandings, and memories of the hearers. . . ." [13] Matthew Robinson's "divisions . . . were neat and his method so exact, that any ordinary memory, from the heads and parts might easily carry away his whole sermon." [14] A preacher could always test the plan and clearness of his sermon by questioning his hearers as Thomas Wilson used to do: "After the publick Duties were ended, many of his neighbours came to his House, where he called his Family together, required of them, and of others present, an account of his Sermons preached that day; and most of those that were present would tell him somewhat; one what the text was, another the Division of it, another the Doctrine, another the Reasons, and others the Explications and Uses, methodically as he had delivered them. . . . Hereby their Understandings and Memories were much improved. . . . Children and Servants (who naturally have an averseness to, and hatred of all that is good) are usually heedless in hearing, and mindless both in public and private of what they hear." [15]

The ability to repeat a sermon after once hearing it was considered a genteel accomplishment. Schoolboys were trained in memorizing the heads and subdivisions of the

---

[12] *Ecclesiastes*, p. 6.
[13] *Essay on Preaching*, p. 38.
[14] *Autobiography*, p. 70.
See Fénelon, *Dial. sur l'Eloquence,* pp. 11-12, on division aiding the memory.
[15] Clark, S. : *Em. Lives,* p. 24.

Sunday sermons and of any week day lecture they might hear. When George Davenport is writing to his tutor, William Sancroft, the boy apologizes for not remembering all the sermon he had heard the Friday before; but he manages to give the text, the preface, and the substance.[16] In a young girl, the faculty of repeating a sermon was considered particularly elegant, and she was sure of being praised for her performance. Mistress Lucy Hutchinson says in witness to her own prococity: "By the time I was four I read English perfectly; having a great memory, I was carried to sermons; and while I was very young could remember and repeat them exactly, and being caressed, the love of praise tickled me, and made me attend more heedfully." [17]   The Matchless Orinda was, as a child, notably clever in remembering sermons.[18] The funeral sermon preached by Calamy for Lady Anne Walker mentions her habit of taking sermon-notes, as one of her twelve points of virtue; [19] and the same appreciation is manifested by John Bacchiler in his sermon, *The Virgin's Pattern: in the Exemplary Life, and Lamented Death of Mrs. Susanna Perwick*, when he speaks of her sermon-notes. Pepys says with approval (and surprise) that "my Lady Paulina . . . hath left many good notes of sermons and religion, wrote with her own hand, which nobody ever heard of; which I am glad of: but she was always a peevish lady." [20]   Edward Davenant would not let his children take notes because "it jaded their memories."   They must repeat the sermon without any aid.[21] Sir Ralph Verney advised against permitting a girl to learn shorthand; she would be sure to take

[16] Cary's *Mem.*, II, 371.
See Brinsley: *Ludus Lit.*, pp. 188-9; Hoole: *New Dis.*, p. 172; D'Ewes: *Jour.*, I, 61-2, 95, 104.
[17] *Memoirs*, 117.
[18] Aubrey, II, 153.
[19] *The Happiness of those who Sleep in Jesus*, p. 28. Calamy says that this sermon, because it testifies to Lady Anne's virtues, may be called a *Looking-Glasse for Ladies to dress themselves by every Morning*.
[20] *Diary*, April 14, 1669.
[21] Aubrey, I, 500.

down sermons and learn them, by which display, he said, she could hardly escape self-glorification.[22]

Teachers of shorthand made use of sermons for practice work. The directions given show how unvarying was the plan of the majority of sermons, a student being advised to go to any church and take note of Interpretation, Proof, Example, Instance, Reason, Use, Motive, Metaphor, Collusion, Similitude, Comparison. Jeremiah Rich's textbook has for title: *Charactery, or, A Most Easie and Exact Method of Short and Swift Writing whereby Sermons and Speeches may be exactly taken.* All the examples in the work are religious in tone. Certain phrases that were nearly inevitable in sermons, were each represented by a character, making it possible for the shorthand writer to express by a pothook, *abound in grace, increase in knowledge, wide is the way to Hell.*[23] The instructions are given through questions and answers which are so briefly definite that the twenty pages of the little book could be learned in a short time. Many a sermon reached the public by way of shorthand notes, taken legitimately, or otherwise. "The Art of Short-Writing," says the publisher of Richard Holdsworth's *Twenty Sermons,* is "the only way to retrieve winged words, and fix them to stay amongst us."

Literary Matter and Manner

The average preacher gave much thought not only to logical development but to what Dr. Wilkins (in *Ecclesiastes*) calls Confirmation. This he divides into Divine and Humane; the first, he explains, is concerned with the claims made by upholders of different faiths; the second

---

[22] *Verney Memoirs,* I, 123.
[23] P. 6. Rich's system was published in 1646; it reached its twentieth edition in 1792.
See Preface to the *Diary of Th. Cartwright,* p. xv, on shorthand; also the article on shorthand in the *Ency. Brit.,* Ninth Edition; and Foster Watson: *The Eng. Grammar Schools, etc.,* p. 67.
Dr. John Wilkins wrote a book on shorthand: *Mercury: or the Secret and Swift Messenger.*

varies with the taste, temper and ability of the preacher. Because of the temptations that lurk in the choice of phrase and of illustration, Dr. Wilkins issues a warning: "But in the managing of this part, care is to be taken (according to the allusions of the Ancients) that Hagar the Handmaid do not out-brave her Mistress Sarah; that blear-eyed Leah, be not preferred before beautiful Rachel. To stuff a sermon with citations of Authors, and the witty sayings of others, is to make a feast of vinegar and pepper; which are healthful and delightful being used moderately as sauces, but must needs be very improper and offensive to be fed on as diet." [24] Thomas Jacombe (in his Epistle Dedicatory to his sermon *Holy Dedication*) says much the same thing through a succession of denials: "here's no high strains of Rhetorick or humane eloquence, no fine and curious Metaphors, no compt and florid expressions to gratifie your fancy . . . here's no New notions or Novel matter to satisfie such as like nothing but what is so; here's something, which may suit the humble, serious, hungry Christian." The publisher of Mr. Josias Shute's serial group of sermons (*Sarah and Hagar: Or, Genesis the sixteenth chapter opened, in XIX Sermons*) also testifies, by negation, to the prevalent use of "Humane Confirmation": " 'Tis true, these are no strawberry-sermons, pick'd and culled out with long vagaries . . . but they are wholesome Food, and healthy Medicine, prepared and administered in due season. Not Almanack-discourses, calculated for any singular Meridian of Persons, Ends, or Humours; but for the General Elevation of the Pole of Virtue; for the common good of Christian Conversation." [25]

Richard Baxter thought it a mistake to make everything too clear: ". . . he usually put something into his Sermons that was above their [his auditors] Discovery, and which

---

[24] P. 24.
[25] *Op. cit.*, Epis. Ded. Latimer uses the expression "strawberry sermon"—meaning preaching once a year—two or three times. See *Sermons,* vol. 20, p. 33. Parker Society.

they had not known before, that they might be kept Humble, still perceive their Ignorance, and be willing to remain in a Learning State; and to increase their Knowledge, and make Religion pleasant to them by a daily Addition to their former Light. . . . For when Ministers tell their people of no more than they know, and do not show that they excell them in Knowledge and Abilities, they will be tempted to turn preacher themselves." [26] Calamy highly commends Mr. Luke Ogle for his tactful presentation of the points and illustrations in his sermons: "He well understood the Art of Preaching to all sorts of Hearers. When he would inform the more Judicious, he did it after a manner that rais'd the Attention, but no way rack'd the Understandings of the less Knowing: and when he would teach the Ignorant, he did it to the Edification and Satisfaction of the more Intelligent." [27]

Most of the sermons that Pepys heard were expositions of texts which counseled good behavior, or which admitted of learned interpretations. Certainly, he preferred those varieties and was distinctly irritated by a doctrinal discourse whether for or against a religious dogma.

(April 24, 1662) To church again, where Mr. Mills making a sermon on confession, he did endeavor to pull down auricular confession, but did set it up, by his bad arguments against it. . . .

(May 13, 1666) To Westminster, and into St. Margett's Church, where I heard a young man play the fool upon the doctrine of Purgatory.

(Feb. 10, 1667) To church, where Mr. Mills made an unnecessary sermon upon Original Sin, neither understood by himself nor the people.

(March 29, 1668) . . . and then a stranger preached, a seeming able man; but said in his pulpit that God did a greater work in raising an oake tree from an acorn, than a man's body raising it, at the last day, from his dust, showing the possibility of the Ressurrection: which was methought a strange saying.

[26] Calamy: *Abridg.*, I, 33. (Samuel Johnson quotes this approvingly to Sir Joshua Reynolds. Boswell: *Life*, IV, 185.)
[27] Calamy: *Account*, II, 503.

His attitude is not to be understood, of course, as general, or even as invariably characteristic of Mr. Pepys. He went "one afternoon, to the French church here in the city, and stood in the aisle all the sermon, with great delight hearing a very admirable sermon from a young man, upon that article of our creed, in order of catechism, upon resurrection." [28] Pepys was not a pious person, the preacher was unknown, the subject of the sermon unexciting, yet every seat was filled, and the occasion had been one of real enjoyment.

In the matter of illustration, it is noticeable that, compared with the English sermons of preceding centuries, the seventeenth-century pulpit discourse made little use of "exempla." There are many brief quotations from classical authorities, there are definite citations of writers who do or do not agree with the preacher, but the informal, colloquial "I knew a man who . . ." or "There was a woman that . . ." is strikingly rare. If the speaker does offer a man or woman as illustrative material, one usually lived in ancient Rome, and the other in more ancient Athens.[29] There are no "good stories" of timely interest and pleasantly personal as may be read on page after page of sixteenth-century sermons (especially those delivered at Paul's Cross) and in the collections of tales that cheered the pulpit in medieval times. Except in the Occasional Sermon, the preacher makes little use of background. He is likely to mention his appreciation of an invitation to preach before parliament or an assize gathering, but the sermon could usually have been delivered as easily in one environment as in the other; he does not say: "In this hall which recalls such and such an event," or, "In this country where this or that has happened."

---

[28] Nov. 30, 1662.
[29] These illustrations are usually of the established variety, as "Zeuxis and his lively Grapes" (Th. Pierce: *A Seasonable Caveat*, p. 25); or, the story of Aeschylus, the eagle and the oyster (Th. Jacombe: *Holy Ded.*, p. 56).

Even Bible stories are not a matter of course with the seventeenth-century preacher. He employs many Bible references and makes many assertions that "Esay" or Ezekiel or an Apostle will support the pulpit argument, but he introduces few narratives. Mr. Joshua Kirby's congregation complained "of his citing too many Scriptures in his Sermons: his Answer was, that it was as if the Baker complain'd that the Miller brought him too fine Flower to make Bread of: Can we speak more properly than in God's language?" [30] Although Bible stories were not plentiful, Bible information was conscientiously supplied. Evelyn heard a sermon on the text "whose shoe-lachet I am not worthy to unloose," and the preacher described "the various fashions of shoes, or sandals, worn by the Jews, and other nations: of the ornaments of the feet. . . ." [31] John Gauden, in his sermon at the funeral of Dr. Brownrig, said, "Elisha rent his garments in to pieces," and then added explanatorily, "not that the Jews were such ill husbands in their grief, as to tear their clothes inconveniently; but at the bottom of their Garments was a seam lightly sewed, which they easily rent in sunder, and mended afterwards again." [32]

The excision of anecdote is not to be explained by the austerity of the froward generation that argued and scolded from 1640 to 1670, but instead by the fact that the literary fashion of the day emphasized not narration, but analysis and unexpected figures. From the viewpoint of the twentieth century with its preference for simplicity, the seventeenth-century taste in sermons is difficult to understand. It approved verbosity; it encouraged pedantic references, strained metaphors and startling similes; it accepted long sentences complicated with clauses and entangled with parentheses; it enjoyed puns; [33] it applauded Wit. But,

[30] Calamy: *Account, etc.,* II, 794.
[31] Feb. 6, 1669.   [32] P. 128.
[33] As Joshua Bonhame: ". . . the best of all I can do being justly due, and devoted to your Honour as a small discharge of my Duty," *A New Constellation.,* Epis. Ded.

says D'Avenant in the Preface to *Gondibert*, "Wit is not only the luck and the labour, but also the dexterity of thought, rounding the world, like the Sun with unimaginable motion. . . . It is in Divines, Humility, Exemplarinesse and Moderation." Glanvill attacks the popular sermon-phraseology by praising the imaginary preachers in the imaginary country of Berusalem: "They affected not to ostentate learning, by high-flown expressions, or ends of Greek and Latine: They did not stiff their sermons with numerous needless quotations. . . . They us'd no jingling of words, nor inventions of sentences, no odd fetches of observation, or niceness in labour'd periods. . . ." [34] *Hudibras* characterizes the prevalent style as:

> A Babylonish dialect
> Which learned pedants much affect.
> It was a parti-colour'd dress
> Of patch'd and piebald languages;
> Like fustian heretofore on satin.[35]

Jeremy Taylor advised his clergy, when preaching, to use "primitive, known, and accustomed words, and affect not the new, fantastical, or schismatical terms." [36] But as far as known and accustomed words are concerned, Taylor in himself offered a dreadful warning: his *House of Feasting* sermon has ninety-five quotations in Greek and Latin. Perhaps he felt as did Joseph Sedgwick who in a sermon (preached in reply to William Dell's *Stumbling Stone* sermon) declared his approval of the use in a pulpit discourse, of Hebrew, Greek or Latin because "a great part of the hearers understand it." [37] Gilbert Burnet, on the other hand, condemns Dr. Peter Gunning as being "a dark and perplexed preacher. His sermons were full of Greek and Hebrew, and of the opinions of the fathers. Yet many of the ladies of a high form loved to hear him preach; which

[34] Essays on Several Subjects, p. 44.   [36] *Works*, III, 713.
[35] Line 93ff.   [37] P. 6.

the king used to say, was because they did not understand
him." [38]

Another warning given by the bishop of Down and
Conor was against any expressions except such as are
"wise, grave, useful, and for edification." In White's
Century of Scandalous, Malignant Priests, a parson is listed
who "in his Catechising and Preaching, calls his parishioners, Black mouthed Hell-hounds, Limmes of the Devill,
Fire-brands of Hell, Plow-joggers, Bawling doggs, Weav-
erly Jacks, and Church-Robbers, affirming that if he could
terme them worse he would." [39] Perhaps No. 94 had an
unusual vocabulary of abusive epithets, but judging by the
pamphlet literature of the day, and even by the titles of
published sermons, he possessed no extraordinary range in
untempered speech. John Ricraft, for example, called one
of his sermons: *A Nosegay of Rank-smelling Flowers, such
as grow in Mr. John Goodwin's Garden. Gathered upon
occasion of his late lying Libell against Mr. Thomas
Eduards which he himself fitly styled Cretensis, for the
foule lies therein contained, with sundry others, exactly
gathered and published;* and John Saltmarsh shows an
alliterative luxuriance: *Perfume against the Sulpherous
Stinke of the Snuffe of the light for Smoak, called Novello-
Mastix.*

What Jeremy Taylor was advising against was probably
the strained comparison and the euphuistic type of illustration and of sentence structure—"a disease of the time,"
says Howell, "affecting especially the preachers." [40] The
good bishop is guilty in some measure of most of the affectations he condemns, but because he is Jeremy Taylor, he
sins with a difference. A reader can drop in and out of
any of the Golden Grove series of sermons, and be sure of
finding a bookish comparison, a fanciful illustration, a
musical succession of rhythmic sentences wherever the eye

[38] *Hist. of his own Times,* p. 382.   [40] *Familiar Letters,* p. 437.
[39] P. 47.

may fall. Here are some lines that must have sounded even
better than they read:

> Aelian tells of the geese flying over the mountain Taurus;
> that for fear of eagles, nature hath taught them to carry
> stones in their mouths, till they be past their danger.[41]

Or:

> But falsely to accuse, is as spiteful as hell, and deadly as
> the blood of dragons.[42]

A lesser person will offer his natural history crudely, as
Nathaniel Hardy does:

> The Crocodiles about the Bankes of Nilus, if rub'd or but
> prickt with a Quill of Ibis, are so stupified that they cannot
> stirre. . . .[43]

Or Thomas Hall (in the Dedication to *The Pulpit
Guarded*):

> 'Tis a Proverb amongst the Naturalists, that except a
> Serpent do eat a Serpent, it cannot become a Dragon.

John Gauden prefers to give a literary dress to an item of
general information:

> Experience hath taught us that a dead hand is an excellent
> means by rubbing it on wens and tumours of the body to allay,
> disperse, and as it were mortifie that irregular and deformed
> excrescency.[44]

Another example of artificial style is quoted disapprov-
ingly by Mr. Pepys, bookish though it be. Usually Pepys
likes anything connected with books. When Nathaniel
Hardy was preaching in September, 1666, after the great
fire, he delivered "a bad, poor sermon, though proper for
the time; nor eloquent, in saying at this time that the City
is reduced from a large folio to a decimo-tertio." [45] Jeremy

---

[41] *Works*, I, 739-40.
[42] *Ibid.*, I, 747.
[43] *Justice Triumphing*, p. 30.
[44] *Funerals made Cordials*, p. 35.
[45] Sept. 9, 1666.

Taylor with all his love of metaphors would never have said that; he would have avoided the awkward comparison and the repetition of "o" sounds. Taylor always, one may imagine, had an ear as well as an eye to the effect of his sentences; and that is why his printed sermons are such pleasant reading. He would have been physically incapable of hissing a procession of words like this arrangement of Gauden's: "Darkness, disputes, division, distractions, dissatisfactions, and confusions must needs follow . . ." (any opposition to apostolic succession).[46] Bishop Taylor's consonants and vowels are kept in harmonious order.

A conscientious scholar, even though he preferred to express himself figuratively, was considerate of his hearers' ability to understand comparisons. Joshua Bonhame shows this thoughtfulness in his sermon on the text: "And he had in his right Hand seven Stars." Early in the discourse he explains: "As the words are spoken Mystically, and not Literally, we are not to conceive the Lord Jesus as really holding in his right hand seven of those Celestial lightsom Bodies which commonly we call Stars, for he might not have appeared on Earth with them, for many Reasons, but chiefly for this, That, if we do believe Astronomers, the least Star is Eighteen times bigger than the whole Earth, therefore we may safely conclude this Vision of St. John to have been nothing else but an Enigmatical and Mystical Representation of the Ministers Calling. . . ."[47]

Presumably, it was the preacher who did not help the congregation to interpret that John Wilkins had in mind when he remarks: "Besides these of positive Divinity, there are some other Writers that are stiled Mystical Divines, who pretend to some higher illumination . . . but they do, in the opinion of many sober and judicious men, deliver only a kind of Cabalistic or Chymical, Rosicrusian Theology, darkening wisdom with words; heaping together

[46] *Fun. Ser. for Dr. Brownrig*, p. 20.
[47] P. 88.

a farrago of obscure affected expressions, and wild Allegories. . . .[48]

The Essay-sermon

A distinctly literary variety of homiletic composition in the seventeenth century was what may be called the essay-sermon. Paragraphs and pages of the personal essay type may be found in scores of sermons; less common is it to read an entire sermon which, but for the grace of God, would go forth as an essay. It might or it might not be constructed with divisions and subdivisions; it might or it might not include something of religious quality; but essentially it was a secular work intended to appeal to the thoughtful, philosophical, well-educated person who recognized foibles and weaknesses in himself as quickly as in his fellows. There were sermons written in England during the 40's and 50's and 60's that belong as much to literature as to homiletics. That they are not popular reading today is immaterial; they have been read at various times by enough people who have earned the right to give judgment on literary work to assure them a respectable position in any library of dignity and a mention, however brief, in a history of English literature. "Why, Sir," Dr. Johnson once declared, "you are to consider that sermons make a considerable branch of English literature; so that a library must be very imperfect if it has not a numerous collection of sermons." [49] Take a dozen or more of Robert South's sermons, behead them of their texts, cut off their extremities of perfunctory reminder that souls should be saved, and what remains is a group of essays well worth reading. His *Scribe Instructed* is a practical treatise on English composition though it masquerades as a sermon. Here are a few titles of other sermons—and some of the texts are added

[48] *Ecclesiastes*, p. 6.   [49] Boswell: *Life*, IV, 105.

as a guarantee that the writings were intended for the
pulpit:

Of Teaching (Titus II, 15)   Of Friendship
Of Truth (John VIII, 17)   Of Words as Signs and Symbols
Of Chance (Prov. XVI)   Of Old Age
Of Lying (Prov. XII, 22)   Of Getting on with others
                             (includes War and Duelling)

Jeremy Taylor's most delightful essay-sermon is on Food,
a subject of abiding interest to mankind.[50] Under the title,
The House of Feasting; or, The Epicure's Measure, he de-
plores the existence of gourmands and gourmets, but his
illustrations are so specific and appetizing that the reader
feels no disapproval, only envy, of those who merrily eat
and drink to the confusion of their higher natures. Other
writings of this type are on Flattery, Talk and Talkers,
Memory, Superstition, and Women. Under this last topic,
he considers their ability, which he declares to be inferior
to that of men though a particular woman is sometimes
superior to a particular man; their capacity for friendship;
their right to be judged by a single moral standard for men
and women.

When Isaac Barrow wrote a sermon about *The Pleasantness of Religion,* he dwelt, quite untrammeled by any professional responsibility, on the joys of knowledge until he
reached Division XV, and Lastly, at which point he awk-
wardly introduced a few conventional exhortations. The
subjects of some of his sermons read like the table of contents in a volume of personal essays:

Of Industry in our Particular Calling as Gentlemen
Of Industry in our Particular Calling as Scholars
Of Self Confidence, Self Complacence, Self Will, and Self
  Interest
Of a Peaceable Temper and Carriage
Of Quietness and Doing our own Business
Of Contentment

[50] John Hales wrote a so-called sermon on Gluttony in which he
talks with informal intimacy about the indulgence which some permit
the ear, the nose and the eye, besides the usual failure to control the
taste or the touch (Works, III, 126).

The majority of Barrow's sermons, however, were written to be read, not to be preached; that fact will account for the especially strong essay quality in many of them. But the curious thing is that Barrow deliberately chose the sermon as the most popular, most alluring literary form he could employ to present his ideas to a reading public.

It is hardly necessary to say that Thomas Fuller was born an essayist though he was bred a preacher. There is no objection to pursuing both vocations simultaneously—many clergymen have done so—but in Fuller's case his active interest in church politics and church history interfered with the perfecting of his gift in literary expression. He wrote a great deal, and on many subjects which gave him an outlet for the generalizations and ironies which Taylor and Barrow put into sermons. Fuller's sermons could hardly be mistaken for what they are. An exception is his *Sermon of Assurance*. It has an informal, even jaunty opening sentence: "It is as natural for malicious men to backbite, as for dogs to bite, or Serpents to sting." That unpleasant truth is not the theme of the half-essay, half-sermon. The idea developed is contained in this sentence: "The Grecians had a three fold Song, the old men sung, we have beene, the middle-aged men, we are, the young men, we shall be."

The Occasional Sermon

The most conspicuous variety of sermon is, obviously, the occasional sermon. Such a discourse is carefully prepared for a particular purpose and delivered before a critical audience alert to judge the success of the effort. Sermons were preached by command, both before the king and before parliament; they were preached by request, before the universities, the assizes, the societies of the Temple, the church convocations, and at weddings, christenings, funerals, and at anniversaries such as that of November fifth and (after

the Restoration) of January thirtieth.   The Act of Uniformity, in 1662, was responsible for scores of Farewell
sermons, and the calamities of 1666 brought forth many
special discourses on battle and fire and plague.

In these occasional sermons, the subject is usually very
much after the fashion of this world.   That fact, however,
does not carry the implication that the preacher was trivial
or hypocritical, but only that his commanded or requested
sermon was less spiritual than timely.   When "George, lord
Bishop of Worcester" (George Morley, D. D.), preached
the coronation sermon for Charles II (April 23, 1660), he
devoted most of his remarks, logically enough, to matters
of government, reminding his audience how the people had
brought miseries on themselves by altering the government.
November-fifth sermons were inevitably concerned with
loyalty, and a hearty denunciation of conspirators.[51]   It
was, however, quite possible to ignore an occasion of the
first importance: John Owen preached before parliament
on January 31, 1648/9, and made no reference, only one
vague allusion, to the event of the day before.[52]

The wonderful year gave many opportunities to the man
who wished to preach and publish.   Hardy's *Lamentation,
Mourning and Woe, Sighed forth in a Sermon* was preached
"the next Lords-Day after the Dismal Fire in the City of
London."   He took his text, one may say of course, from
Lamentations i. 12:   "Is it nothing to you, all you that
pass by?   Behold and see if there be any sorrow like to my
sorrow."   Dr. Hardy's grief is real and personal, and
leaves little room for conventional sermon material.   He
has that curiously strong affection that some people have for
a city, a love jealous, capable of sacrifice, as absorbing as
for a human being.   He borrows the words of Isaiah, substituting London for Jerusalem: "Nay, if I forget thee

[51] E.g., Barrow: *Oratio habita quinto nov. anno 1651.*   Also,
William Jenkyn, same date; Nathaniel Hardy, 1546, at Pauls.
[52] In 1683, the Univ. of Ox. ordered that this sermon "be publicly
burnt by the hand of our marshal in the court of our Scholes" (*The
Judgment and Decree of, etc., Oxford*, p. 7).

(O London), let my right hand forget her cunning, let my tongue cleave to the roof of my mouth." His comparisons are not commonplace: "Some have enviously compared her (London) to the Spleen, whose high swelling made the rest of the body lean; but I doubt we shall find she may be more truly compared to the Stomach, and the Apologue made good, whil'st the stomach wants supply, the rest of the members cannot thrive. . . ."[53] William Sancroft, Dean of St. Paul's, preached before the king on a Fast Day for the Fire; the sermon was published with the title, *Lex Ignea: or The School of Righteousness.* The title page has a handsome inset which shows St. Paul's in wildly tossing flames.

"A Day of Thanksgiving for the late Victory at Sea" was the occasion of a sermon preached before the king by Dr. Dolben, the Dean of Westminster, on August 14, 1666. The theme is the glory of England, but the conclusion is "professional" in its insistence on the possibility of everyone's winning a victory over sin. On October third of the same year, the Bishop of Chester, George Hall, preached a rather perfunctory sermon before the Lords on "the Day of Solemn Humiliation for the continuing Pest." It is a fair example of many parliamentary sermons, having no special secular or spiritual interest, though the plague might well have stirred him to an expression of both. A less important person, Samuel Shaw (he puts his initials, only, on the title page), gives a much clearer idea of what the disease might mean to a family group. The cover of the quarto is crowded with information: *The Voice of one Crying in a Wilderness, Or, The Business of a Christian, both Antecedaneous to, Concomitant of, and Consequent upon a sore*

[53] Another good example is the sermon by Robert Elborough: *London's Calamity by Fire Bewailed and Improved in a Sermon.* He has a style: "I have seen the Plague . . . not leaving any Persons in Houses, and now this dreadful Judgment of Fire, not leaving Houses for Persons." Also, Thomas Jacombe: *Holy Dedication.* This sermon is on both Fire and Plague; it is even more rhetorical than Elborough's. London, 1668. (Pepys was very scornful of Elborough, *Diary,* January 6, 1662/3.)

*and heavy Visitation; Represented in several Sermons.
First Preached to his own Family, lying under such Visitation; and now made Publicke as a Thank-offering to the
Lord his Healer.* The Dedicatory letter tells briefly of
swift-descending tragedy borne without complaint, and
without a hint of resentment toward those who brought
death to the writer's home in the country, to which a minister and his family had come, fleeing from the Plague in
London. It is easy to understand how popular this little
sermon-book would be in the year 1666.

For a country congregation of the decent farming class,
Richard Steele preached twelve sermons on the *Husbandman's Calling.* As the series appears in print, it is divided
into ten chapters, not one of which wanders from the point.
Agriculture and Horticulture are leading topics, offering
an infinite variety of Lessons: the ground, fencing, grass,
stones, thorns, worms, ants. Steele's vocabulary is not of
the soil; he chooses his similes carefully and intelligently,
not spontaneously. He is always the M.A. of Cambridge.[54]

Weddings were occasions for special sermons. Nathaniel
Hardy preached a particularly successful one for Mr.
William Christmas and Mistress Elizabeth Adams, the bride
being the daughter of the Lord Mayor of London. The
title of the sermon is *Hope and Fear, the inseparable Twins
of a Blest Matrimony;* just below are printed three quotations: St. Paul in English, Chrysostom in Greek, Ambrosius in Latin. Every paragraph in the pamphlet is bul-
warked with marginal references and comments, usually
in Greek and Latin, but sometimes merely a citation of a
Bible chapter and verse in English. It is a publication of
which any young couple might be proud. Incidentally, it
sets forth the duties of husband and wife, particularly the
husband's because the wife must always be guided by him:

[54] Cf. Latimer's series of *Sermons on the Plough* which are Leicester-
shire in thought, figure of speech, and word, even dialect.
    For a brief study on Serial Preaching, see J. O. Murray, D.D.,
Hom. Rev., Nov., 1891.

"however superior soever she were before, yet by marriage she becomes his inferior. . . ." [55]

The farewell sermons were the most popular printed material of the year 1662. Tht Act of Uniformity was passed August 24, 1662, after which time any minister who refused to conform to the regulations of the Established church was automatically ejected from his living. Both the friends and enemies of these men wished, naturally enough, to know how they felt about the situation; thousands, therefore, packed the churches to hear the last sermons preached by those who were laying down their office, and thousands more read the sermons when printed. Some of the sermons were published separately; a good example is Thomas Watson's *The Righteous Man's Weal and the Wicked Man's Woe* which offers no special interest in subject matter—being largely concerned with hell fire—but which does show the ready sale on which the publisher counted. In the first place, the discourse, though dignified, is a defiant gesture, for it was preached on the Tuesday after Mr. Watson's official farewell sermon to his people. The publisher rushed the material through the press, haste being necessary because " 'tis more than suspected there is another impression of this sermon (taken by another hand) intended to be published." [56] The most successful publication of the group of valedictory addresses was the one called *An Exact Collection of Farewell Sermons, preached by the late London Ministers, viz. Mr. Calamy, Mr. Watson, Dr. Jacomb, Mr. Case, Mr. Schlater, Mr. Baxter, Mr. Jenkin, Dr. Manton, Mr. Lye, Mr. Collins.* Only two or three of these names are familiar knowledge today, but every name had advertising value in 1662, and the volumes sold as fast as a printing press could produce them. [57] Neither printer nor publisher

[55] Wesley says all this even more strongly in his sermon *Of a Wife's Duties*, Ch. 6 of Sermon LVII, *Works*, VI, 181.

[56] Another good example of a farewell sermon, published singly, is William Jenkins's *The Burning, yet un-consumed Bush: or, The Holiness of Places discuss'd.*

[57] See Th. Newcome: *Diary* (Oct. 11, 1662) ; Pepys, Aug. 17, 1662.

is named, not even an initial is ventured.[58] As a special
attraction, there is a frontispiece with twelve portraits of
the preachers represented in the collection, the two who
had preached funeral sermons being distinguished by a skull
placed just below the portrait. Additional sermons fill out
the book, and the (unsigned) preface which introduces them
all, announces pridefully: "Here lurks no Snake under
these Herbs, no poysonous Serpent under these fragrant
Flowers, no root of Errour, no slip of Schism, no fruit of
Disobedience." The next year, 1663, saw on the market
A Compleat Collection of Farewell Sermons, grown now to
forty-two in number but again warily published without the
name of the printer or the seller.

Other occasional sermons have already been mentioned in
connection with important clergymen. The occasion itself
does not always stir a man to the producing of something
worth reading though it is possible that his delivery made
it worth hearing. A sermon (*Great Actions*) preached in
1657 by Edward Reynolds before the East India Company
says nothing about India or the Company; Nathaniel Hardy
conducted the farewell service "at the departure of His
Majesty's Ambassador, the Hon. Sir Thomas Bendik for
Constantinople," and keeps his imagination within English
boundaries;[59] a Recantation sermon may read tamely in
spite of the dramatic fact that the cause of the recantation
has been publicly burnt by the common hangman;[60] Seth
Ward, preaching at Whitehall in 1661, could take as his
text, "And they that resist, shall receive to themselves
Damnation," and yet the result of his efforts was only a
remarkably dull sermon.

---

[58] ". . . when the censorship of the press was severe, printers and
publishers often contented themselves with placing their initials in
the imprints. . . ." See Henry R. Plomer: *A Dictionary of the
Booksellers and Printers . . . in England . . . 1641-1667*, p. viii.
[59] *The Safe Convoy*, etc.
[60] Rushworth: *Hist. Coll.*, IV, 208.

The Funeral Sermon

The funeral sermon is a recognized variety of discourse. It has an ancestry both honorable and ancient; it is twin brother to the Panegyric, and nearly related to the Story and the Essay; it may be seen in a highly developed form in Gregory of Nyssa's eulogy of Militius, Bishop of Antioch. Just as Gregory deprecates his own unworthiness and lack of ability to do justice to his great subject, so do the clergy of the Stuart and Cromwell eras apologize for their unworthiness to preach a sermon in honor of some man or woman; just as Gregory gave most of his space to a discourse, philosophical in tone and lofty in thought, passing thence to a brief character study, and finally to an exhortation, so proceeded the funeral preachers, hundreds of years later.[61] After all, a funeral sermon is not a form of composition that would allow much latitude. If it crystallized early, the reason is plain enough: there could be but one theme. However individual or important the person might have been for whom the sermon was preached, the quite ordinary but ever-astounding fact remained: he had lived, and was dead.

But though the plan of such a sermon can show little variation, the speaker has every opportunity to display his skill in phrasing, in selecting unusual metaphors, most of all in exerting his power of arousing emotion. A funeral sermon is, in the nature of things, an occasional sermon, and it is likely to be listened to more attentively than is the sermon

[61] For a brief account of the funeral oration in ancient Greece and Rome, see Preface to Vol. II of *The World's Orators.*
Gauden, in his funeral sermon on Robert Rich, gives a history of funeral sermons. Richard Meggott, in his funeral sermon on Nathaniel Hardy, does the same thing, and mentions a number of examples beginning with Nazienzen's eulogy of St. Bazil.
Howe, John: In *Real Comforts*, cites St. Chrysostom and St. Jerome as authorities on early funeral sermons.
Clark, S.: *Em. Lives.* See p. 129 for comment on funeral sermons.
Spurstow, W.: *Death and the Grave*, p. 45, for early funeral sermons.

of the every-Sunday variety. The preacher may well be inspired by the eager interest of many who are for the moment emotionally responsive to appeals to sentiment, to loyalty, to spiritual aspiration. If the man whom the sermon celebrates has been a great man, or nearly connected with great affairs, those who listen will thrill to the memory of the deeds that may have brought changes in their own lives and those of thousands besides; if the man be of importance only to his family and neighbors, then will they listen because one of themselves has gone away out of the pettiness and fret of nagging cares to a rest and a joy that, the preacher tells them, may be theirs, too, some day.[62]

Equally popular in England and France, it was in the latter country that the funeral sermon of the seventeenth century reached the perfection of eloquence. No contemporary English preacher can compare in the field of funeral orations with Bossuet or Bourdaloue or Fléchier. Of these three, Bossuet holds the highest rank; and a perfect example, from a literary point of view, of a funeral sermon is his oration on the Queen of England, Henriette-Marie, delivered November 16, 1669. The opening lines are often cited as an instance of inimitable rhetorical effect:

Monseigneur,

Celui qui règne dans les cieux, et de qui relèvent tous les empires, à qui seul appartient la gloire, la majesté et l'independance, est aussi le seul qui se glorifie de faire la loi aux rois, et de leur donner, quand il lui plaît, de grandes et de terribles leçons.

Soit qu'il élève les trônes, soit qu'il les abaisse, soit qu'il communique sa puissance aux princes, soit qu'il la retire a lui-même, et ne leur laisse que leur propre faiblesse, il leur apprend leurs devoirs d'une manière souveraigne et digne de lui.

---

[62] See Villemain in his essay preceding a collection of the funeral orations of Bossuet. He would not have an obscure man denied the dignity of a funeral sermon: *"Plus leur vie était obscure, plus leur mort devait être célébrée, et cette obscurité même, qui semble eloigner de la tombe d'un homme inconnu la publicité de l'eloge funèbre la rendait ici plus nécessaire et plus legitime,"* p. xxviii.

Almost as impressive and beautiful is his oration for Condé. But even if the English sermon does not equal the French "*oraison funèbre*" in soaring flights of rhetoric and profound depths of philosophy, it unquestionably serves many useful purposes and has, also, in many instances a real beauty and eloquence.

The funeral sermon seems to have been generally recognized in seventeenth-century England as authoritative source-material. Calamy in his account of the ejected and silenced ministers—nonconformists—says in his Preface that he has taken pains to consult the Funeral Sermons of the men whom he includes in his list,[63] and Walker who builds his book, *The Sufferings of the Clergy of the Church of England,* upon Calamy's—though from an opposite point of view—does the same thing.[64] Wood, Lloyd, Fuller, and Aubrey usually mention the preacher of the funeral sermon of the man under discussion, and often cite information from it. Bishop White Kennett is careful to include as an evidence of the kindness and courtesy of the established clergy who took the place of nonconformists ejected in 1662, that the new incumbents frequently preached the Funeral Sermons of the ministers whom they succeeded.[65] The preacher is often named in church records of burials.

Inevitably, a funeral sermon offered an opportunity for flattery and ostentation, and the religious element was often obscured if not lost. John Fry, who is so prodigal of condemnations, especially condemns those clergymen whose mouths may be so opened with a silver key that they will, in a funeral sermon, "canonize that man they could never speak well of whilst he lived, making merchandize of the word. . . ."[66] Robert Sanderson records his "utter dis-

---

[63] Vol. II, p. vii.
[64] See also where the *Biog. Brit.* (ed. 1750), in the notice of Thomas Adams, Lord Mayor of Lond., makes twelve references to N. Hardy's Fun. Ser. on Adams.   Neal (*Hist. of the Pur.*) usually names the preacher of a man's Fun. Ser., as Usher on Selden, p. 154; Calamy on Whitaker, p. 155.
[65] *Kennett's Register,* p. 897.
[66] *The Clergy in their Colours,* p. 44.

like of the flatteries used in funeral sermons"; [67] John Hales—the "ever memorable John Hales"—refused to have any sermon for himself.[68]   Mr. Richard Hawes also "desir'd that nothing might be said by way of Commendation of him, in his Funeral Sermon, and that if he were spoken of at all, it might be only as a great Sinner, which had obtain'd great mercy; which Request," continues Calamy who is identifying Mr. Hawes, "was scarce entirely complied with by the preacher, Mr. Jordan . . . who highly esteemed him, his text being Ps. xxxvii, 37." [69]   Even though a man should avoid flattery of the dead, there were yet many worldly opportunities that he could not be blind to in preaching the funeral sermon of a well-known person. There was, in the first place, the matter of payment for the services rendered.   Many wills of the time mention the amount that is to be paid for a funeral sermon.   Mistress Alice Thornton left five pounds to Mr. John Denton for the preaching of her funeral sermon, and even arranged that the same amount be given a substitute if Mr. Denton could not serve; [70] Dr. Robert Sanderson left five pounds for the speaker at his funeral, on the condition, however, "that he shall speak nothing at all concerning my person, either good or ill, other than I shall myself direct, only signifying to the auditory that it was my will to have it so"; [71] John Vaux, once Lord Mayor of York, in his will left twenty shillings to one Peter Calvert to preach his funeral sermon; [72] Ralph Josselin records: (Nov. 11, 1669) "Went to preach a funeral; I received 20 s., paire of gloves and blesse God."   George Verney left Mr. William Okley forty shillings for the same purpose.[73]   A charge frequently brought against clergymen was that of demanding high fees

[67] *Sermons*, p. 53 (his Will).
[68] *Works*, I, 205 (his Will).
[69] "Mark the perfect man. . . ."
[70] *Autobiography*, p. 338.
[71] *Sermons*, I, 52; also, Walton's *Life of Sanderson*, p. 52.
[72] *Life of Master John Shaw*, note, p. 129.
[73] *Verney Mem.*, II, 118.

for funeral sermons,[74] which custom added appreciably to the necessary expenses of a funeral of a person of quality. Lady Anne Fanshawe, in speaking of her mother's death, says: "Her funeral cost my father above a thousand pounds." [75] Calamy says of William Bagshaw: "Observing People to be more than ordinarily affected with Funeral sermons, he very willingly preach'd on such Occasions, even when he had no prospect of being in any way gratified for it." [76] Equally accommodating was Samuel Keene, royalist chaplain of a troop of horse, of whom it was said: "When any officer of the regiment was kill'd, he was ready to preach his funeral sermon . . . and was ready at all hours to do the like, provided the party died not a natural death." [77]

In the second place, a funeral sermon would almost always be delivered before a large auditory. Again, it would in most cases be printed, and the published work could be dedicated to someone who would appreciate the compliment. There might, indeed, be a series of dedications in particular, concluding with one to the Courteous Reader in general, and this prefatory matter could include the personal views that refused to fit into the sermon proper. Very often, too, the sermon was expanded far beyond its original proportions, and it would appear with a goodly title page, decorated with marginal cross-bones, skulls, or entire skeletons. Sometimes, a portrait was included, as in Gauden's funeral sermon for Dr. Brownrig. The late bishop of Exeter is represented as a dour, elderly gentleman, wearing a large Elizabethan ruff over his gown and surplice.[78] There were also prefixed, in the more elegant pamphlets, a number of eulogistic verses in Greek and Latin, occasionally in English. In outward appearance, the

[74] Wellington : *Hist. Notices*, p. 194ff.
[75] *Memoirs*, p. 50.
[76] *Abridg.*, II, 198.
[77] Wood : *Ath. Ox.*, II, 908.
[78] William Leo's sermon for Daniel Featley shows him in death, with a symbolic tree at his head and feet.

mound surmounted by a cross; above that, a crown held by
two stalwart angels. The bier is labeled "Ab Istac," the
cross "Per Hanc," the crown "Ad Illum."

A quarto that must have sold readily and profitably was
*The Archbishop of Canterbury's Speech, or, His Funeral
Sermon Preacht by himself on the Scaffold on Tower-Hill,
on Friday the 10 of January, 1644*. All faithfully written
by John Hinde, whom the Archbishop beseeched that he
would not let any wrong be done him by any phrase in false
copies. This publication, unlike the one last cited, was duly
"Licensed and Entred according to Order." Fuller omits
it in his *Church History* "because common as publicly
printed." [83]   The brief address begins:

> Good People,
>   You'll pardon my old Memory, and upon so sad an occasion
> as I am come to this place, to make use of my Papers, I dare
> not trust myself otherwise.

> Good People,
>   This is a very uncomfortable place to Preach in, and yet
> I shall begin with a Text of Scripture, in the twelfth of
> Hebrews. . . .

It is a pathetic introduction, and yet we read in Sir
Philip Warwick's *Memoirs:* "He appeared to make his own
Funeral Sermon with less passion, than he had in former
times made the like for a Friend." [84]   Fuller, too, who
describes the scene on the scaffold, comments on the Archbishop's calmness and normal appearance, mentioning especially that when the prelate's head was severed, "Instantly,
his face (ruddy in the last moment) turned white as ashes,
confuting their falsehoods, who gave it out that he had
purposely painted it, to fortify his cheeks against discovery
of fear in the paleness of his complexion." [85]

[83] Vol. IV, 293-4.
[84] *Memoirs*, p. 174.
[85] *Ch. Hist.*, IV, 294-5. See Heylin: *Cyprianus Anglicus*, p. 531ff.

The public funeral decreed by Parliament for the Earl of Essex was the occasion of an elaborate address by Richard Vines. The tone is moral, also mundane, being largely concerned with general and respectful comments on greatness and great men who, it was to be remembered, must die; and who must be reminded that "Sycophants and Flatterers lay their egges in your eares, and hatch monstrous opinions in you of your greatnesse. . . ." Parliament, well satisfied, ordered Mr. Richard Vines to print and publish this sermon, such an order being as great a compliment as an ambitious divine could ask. It was also stated that the sermon "is not to be Printed by any other but by Authority under his own hand, Jo. Browne Cleric. Parliamentorum"; the last clause and the signature of the clerk being necessary because of the sinful frequency with which popular reading matter was printed and sold without the author's permission. When Seth Ward, Lord Bishop of Sarum, preached the funeral sermon of the Duke of Albemarle, George Monk, on April 30, 1670, the order to print was issued, naturally enough, "by his Majesties special command."

John Owen preached the funeral sermon of Henry Ireton. It is an admiring character study, and is dedicated to Colonel Henry Cromwell, who was the dead man's brother-in-law.[86] For Cromwell, the Protector, no funeral sermon was preached at his burial because of quarrels in the *Corps Diplomatique* about precedence, and "there was not a single candle in Westminster Abbey . . . there were . . . neither prayers, nor sermon, nor funeral oration." [87] When Thomas Manton delivered the funeral sermon for Christopher Love (Aug. 25, 1651), he was showing respect to a man who had just been hanged for treason. The situation, for the preacher, was delicate, even dangerous; but the minister met it cleverly, knowing that Love's dramatic death would

[86] *Complete Coll.*
[87] *Verney Memoirs*, I, 131 (Entry of Nov. 11, 1658). Cf. Evelyn's account, *Diary:* Sept. 22, 1659. Peters preached a fun. ser. later.

give advertising to the sermon which would appear in print legitimately or otherwise, almost as soon as it was spoken. The published sermon is thirty-three pages in length; on the thirtieth is the first mention of Christopher Love, but the preacher explains that whatever he had advised as proper conduct, had been lived by Mr. Love, and "I shall not make any particular rehearsall of the passages of his exemplary life; I judge it not convenient." [88]   Calamy's sermon for Love, preached the Sunday after his execution, does not refer to Love except by implication, the topic being the death of St. Stephen.   There is, too, a suggestive observation on the first page: "the best of men are subject to violent and unnatural deaths."

Jeremy Taylor's funeral sermons, as all his sermons, are well known and easily accessible.   The funeral addresses are carefully built, even more carefully phrased; they are not guiltless of the conventional mannerisms that developed through the very popularity of this type of composition, but they are, because Jeremy Taylor wrote them, of a better literary style than similar writings by his contemporaries.   How he did enjoy words!   Not strange words, especially, or learned words—though he knew both sorts and made use of them on occasion; he loved words for their own sake.   In the funeral sermon for "John, late Lord Archbishop of Armagh and primate of all Ireland," Taylor sums up the subject of his discourse as "a wise prelate, a learned doctor, a just man, a true friend, a great benefactor to others, a thankful beneficiary when he was obliged himself. . . . For in him were visible the great lines of Hooker's judiciousness, of Jewel's learning, of the acuteness of bishop Andrews." [89]   Sometimes he employs the tricks of the professional conceit-maker even when he is sincerely moved, as he seems to have been by the death of his friend and patroness Lady Carbury.   In the dedicatory

[88] Sermon preached August 25, 1651.
[89] *Works*, II (Preached July 16, 1663).

letter prefixed to the sermon, he speaks of her as ". . . a woman fit to converse with angels and apostles, with saints and martyrs; give me leave to present you with her portrait drawn in little and in water colors. . . ." [90] It is to be hoped that the good Bishop of Down and Connor and Dromore (charmingly harmonious vowels) was permitted to hear his own funeral sermon as preached by Dr. Rust. Here is a sample sentence: "Had he lived among the ancient pagans, he had been ushered into the world with a miracle, and swans must have danced and sung at his birth; and he must have been a great hero, and no less than the son of Apollo, the god of wisdom and eloquence." [91] The sermon is nearly eight-five hundred words long.

Although funeral sermons may be constructed according to a conventional pattern, they are delightfully human in spots. If a reader will pass quickly through the opening paragraphs demanded by etiquette—the speaker's disapproval of laudatory funeral sermons, the speaker's regret that a more important person than himself had not been chosen to deliver this particular sermon—that reader will find himself gaining information of an unusual kind. He will learn some facts, undoubtedly, but he will learn even more of feelings, of the odds and ends that go to the making of a real human being. A few examples will show the sort of material that may be had for a glance.

Dr. James Usher is known to people interested in such mattrs as the author of a Chronology of the Bible that has attached itself so firmly to the Bible that it has become difficult to separate the two. But the preacher of the funeral sermon for the Bishop did not consider the Chronology as important as a number of other things. The reader learns that in Dr. Usher's childhood, "two of his Aunts who by reason of their blindnesse from their Cradles, never saw

[90] Works, II, 79-80. Another notable funeral sermon is that on Sir George Dalston (Vol. II, 130-42) whose love of sermons is commended highly: "he knew how to value that which was best, yet he was patient of that which was not so."
[91] Taylor's Works, I, xix.

letters, taught him first to read." It is said also that he gave up Cards; and Poetry lest it should have taken him off from more serious studies; that as a young man he joined Sir Thomas Bodley in buying rare books and manuscripts; that he "had in readinesse in his head all he had read"; that "no Spectacles could help him, onely when the Sun shined, he could see at a window, which he hourly followed from room to room." [92]

John Gauden reveals more of his own character than he does of Robert Rich's, whose funeral sermon Dr. Gauden is preaching. "I confess," he says toward the end of his address (page 102), "I unfeignedly deplore my loss of him, not that I either hoped or expected any secular advantages by his private or public station beyond those civil courtesies which I have often enjoyed from his other noble relatives. . . . As for publique favors obtainable by any mans mediation, I understand myself and the times so well in the point of preferment as not to look toward any, which are now rare to be seen in England for any Ecclesiastic of my proportions. . . ." He adds that he seeks only "an Evangelical and unenviable plow in a poor Country village." The sermon as published is impressive. There are six points in the introduction, fourteen in the body (with subheads), three *uses,* and a *lastly* that fills seventeen pages. A Prayer is added, after which follows the report in Latin of the six Physicians and two Surgeons who dissected young Rich. His death, at twenty-three, was due to "Struma, or Kings evil."

"It is a hard thing to funerall it well," sighs Robert Harris on the first page of his sermon for Sir Thomas Lucy, and his work proves it, being commonplace throughout. But the Dedicatory Epistle, addressed to "the Honorable and Vertuous, the Ladie Lucie of Charlcot," makes Sir Thomas a little more real. "It is confessed, Madam, That Sir Thomas and I were not alwaies of one minde. Dissent

[92] Pp. 22, 25, 42, 192 (Nicholas Bernard for Bishop Usher).

we did, in some things: But this I shall ever honour in Him,
That He was Himselfe, and his Friends too. Neither pros-
tituting his owne, nor ravishing another man's judgment;
Herein we concur'd, and for this I honoured him, and he
was pleased to owne me." [93]

Richard Meggott, D.D., Rector of St. Olave's, South-
werke, was an important clergyman and gentleman, and
when he was invited to preach the funeral sermon for
Nathaniel Hardy, who had himself preached many funeral
sermons for other men, he felt his responsibility. He
hurries as much as dignity permits through the necessary
preliminaries (objection to insincere praise of the dead,
regret that someone more worthy has not been chosen,
etc.) and then denounces Hardy's enemies with the vigor
of a loyal gentleman and the authority of a popular clergyman. He makes an effort to speak temperately: ". . . I
shall say no more than that there are such Things as Envy,
Pride, and Spight, which like Smoak always fly in the Faces
of the fairest." [94] David Clarkson, eulogizing John Owen,
disposes of Owen's enemies in a fashion that any
pamphleteer might well envy.[95]

Matthew Newcomen, when he is preaching at the funeral
of Mr. Samuel Collins, departs from precedent. So far
from deprecating the custom of eulogizing the dead, he
expresses himself as heartily in favor of it. "For why
should I not make a Speech in the praise of one deceased, as
well as another write a Poem in the praise of one deceased?
. . . I am sure this . . . hath precedent in Scripture; thus
Jeremy lamented for Josiah and made Poems, Verses in
memorial of him for the people to sing, as you may read
in 2 Chron. 35, 25. David wrote a poem in praise of Saul
and Jonathan, 2 Sam. 1." [96]

A funeral sermon was quite evidently a matter of bio-

[93] *Abners Funerall,* preached 1641. Sir Thomas was the grandson
of Shakespeare's Sir Thomas Lucy.
[94] *A Monitor of Mortalitie,* p. 40.
[95] *Sermons of John Owen* (Includes Clarkson's ser. on Owen).
[96] P. 6 (the sermon has no title).

graphical interest to be recorded by diarists. The mention of a death is almost invariably followed by the name of the preacher at the funeral, and usually some comment is made on the sermon as delivered. Both Evelyn and Pepys do this again and again; Lord Herbert of Cherbury, though writing many years after his mother's death (which had occurred in 1627), feels that he can best do her justice by concluding his praise of her with, "and briefly, was that woman Dr. Donne hath described in his funeral sermon of her printed." [97]

Sermon-helps

The dull or lazy preacher was not left unaided in the preparation of the sort of pulpit discourse that most congregations demanded. It was quite possible to stiffen a paragraph with references and figures of speech without exhausting labor, and even to construct an entire sermon on topics and outlines provided by successful and authoritative divines. Some of these works were published early in the seventeenth century; but through purchase or loan they would be accessible to a man who was struggling to compose sermons in the 40's, 50's, and 60's. A number of the books mentioned below are in Latin, a language that would present no difficulties to an educated man.

The *Theologia Prophetica* of John Henry Alsted (1622), besides being practically useful, is genuinely interesting. It has chapters on the usual topics that mark the development of the sermon from the text to the peroration; then follows *Tabula Mnemonica* which reduce each book of the Bible to brief statements. *Ruth* is digested to:

[97] *Autobiography,* p. 20.
See, too, references in Alice Thornton's *Autobiography,* pp. 25, 109, 151, 162, 166, 176, 218-9.
Verney Memoirs, I, 43, 440.
A handsomely bound collection (610 pages, folio) of 53 funeral sermons was published in 1661: *The House of Mourning, furnished with Directions for, Preparations to, Meditations on, Consolations at, the Hour of Death.*

Necessitudo Ruthae cum socru
Spicilegium Ruthae
Solicitatio Boasi ad conjugium cum Rutha
Conjugium Boasi cum Rutha

It is the sermon-outlines, however, that give the best suggestion as to how widely the preacher's information and imagination might travel:

I	Modus legendi librum naturae
II	Concio angelographica de Angelis
III	Concio Physiologica de proprietatibus corporum naturalium
IV	Concio Vranoscopica, de coelo
V	Concio Photoscopica, de luce
VI	Concio Astrographica, de Stellis
VII	Concio Heliographica, de Sole
VIII	Concio Chronographica, de quartuor anni temporibus hyeme videlicet, vere aestate et autumno
IX	Concio Selenographica, de Luna
X	Concio Pyrographica, de Igne
XI	Concio Aerographica, de Aere
XII	Concio Hydrographica, de Aqua
XIII	Concio Geographica, de Terra
XIV	Conciones meteorologicae de Meteoris ignitis, aeriis, aqueis, apparentibus
XV	Conciones Lithographicae, de Lapidus vulgarious, de lapidibus preciosis et de gemmis ignobilioribus
XVI	Concio Metallographica, de Metallis
XVII	Concio Oryctologica, de Mediis mineralibus
XVIII	Concio Botonologica, de Herbis
XIX	Concio de Fructicibus
XX	Conciones Dendrographice, de arboribus
XXI	Concio Theologica, de Bestiis
XXII	Concio Ornithologica de volatilibus
XXIII	Concio Ichthyologica, de Aquatilibus
XXIV	Concio Bucolica de bestiis terrestibus
XXV	Concio Anthropologica, de Homine
XXVI	Concio Oeconomica, de statu Scholastico
XXVII	Concio Ecclesiastica, de statu Ecclesiastico
XXVIII	Concio politica de statu politiae [98]

[98] Pp. 89-90.

A useful work of the same decade (1626) is that of Johanne Botsacco: *Promptuarium Allegoriarum et Similitudinum Theologicarum*. The suggestions are brief, sometimes being merely a text to illustrate a "head." The book has an especially well-arranged index which directs the reader to the figures of speech, all of which are listed in neat alphabetical order, making it easy to note, for instance, that the *diabolus* has many more entries than the *angeli boni*. *De Eloquentia sacra et humana* (1657) by Nicolas Caussinus is a work of more than a thousand pages. It has a chapter *De Pronuntiatione;* another, *De forma sacrae Eloquentiae*. A list of orators and of writers on rhetoric (all are Greek or Latin) is included, then a long list of figures, and at the end an index *"rerum et verbosum copiosus."* Another source of supply was a book by Robert Cowdrey, the lexicographer, who had published in 1609 *A Treasury, or Storehouse of Similes*. All are taken from the Bible, and a helpful interpretation is annexed to each example.

Bishop Chappell's *Art of Preaching* does not discuss figures beyond warning the preacher against "comparates, and semblables." He names many authors, tracts, sermons, and commentaries that might be of assistance, and presents a sample analytical outline on the subject of "The chief heads of the aggregations of sin." [99] Samuel Clark published a work that reached its second edition in 1654, entitled *A Mirrour or Looking-Glasse both for Saints and Sinners, Held forth in about two thousand Examples . . . collected out of the most Classique Authors both Ancient and Modern with some late Examples observed by myself. Whereunto are added, the Wonders of God in Nature . . . Art . . . Industry. As the most famous Cities, Structures, Statues, Cabinets of Rarities, etc. which have been, or are in the World*. It is a comprehensive work. No one, possess-

[99] Pp. 166-79.

ing it, need send forth his thoughts unsupported or un-adorned.

Thomas Hall printed in 1654 his *Centuria Sacra,* containing "About one hundred Rules for the expounding and clearer understanding of the Holy Scriptures. To which are added a Synopsis or Compendium of all the most materiall Tropes and Figures contained in the Scriptures." In this work, Hall explains the use of various words in the English translations, he gives the meaning of a number of Hebrew idioms, and suggests possible interpretations of vague terms such as St. Paul's "thorn in the flesh," which, Hall thinks, was neither a disease nor Alexander the Copper-smith, but a continuing spiritual struggle. He names thirty-three figures, shows the proper use of each one, and adds a variety of examples.

The *Allegoria profano-sacra* of Mollerus (1655) is entirely in German. The thick quarto—there are nearly four hundred and fifty pages—contains many little stories, each having its *Applicatio.* The narrative of the burning of the temple of Diana at Ephesus is followed by the assurance that the church of Christ will last always; the equally familiar anecdote of Titus and his exclamation, *Amici, diem perdidi,* inevitably brings the reminder that each moment should be well spent.

William Price wrote an *Ars concionandi* (1657) which has sections *de Applicatione, de Dehortatione, de Exhortatione,* etc. *De stylo concionum* fills only a page and a half. To sermon writers, the most helpful section must have been the long list of "heads," which are divided and sub-divided sometimes through two pages. *Voluptas* is analyzed at length, with its *qualitates,* as (1) *Licita,* (2) *Illicita.* Under Aegyptiorum Doctrina (Acts vii. 22) are: (1) *Mathematica,* (2) *Physica,* (3) *Theologica,* (4) *Moralis.* (5) *Magia.*

John Prideaux compiled a convenient reference book which he called *Conciliorum Synopsis.* The great Church

Synods are named and identified, making it possible for one who wished to include in his sermon a reference to a Judaical, Apostolical or Oecumenical assembly, or even a Controverted or Rejected one, to secure sufficient information to illustrate a point, or give support to an argument. Another work of Prideaux's, *Fasciculus Controversiarum Theologicarum,* has its material assembled under seven topics, as *De Scriptura, cognitione Dei, Peccato,* etc., with questions and objections at the end of each chapter, and finally an index to all Scripture references, and topics.   In 1658, John Spencer brought out a compilation of quotations, brief anecdotes and similes to the number of 2283. Thomas Fuller wrote a cheerful Preface for it, and under the vague but biblical title, *Things New and Old,* the book had a ready sale.   It is a compound of both old and new, Fuller assured the reader, and "like as changeable taffeta seemeth sundry stuffs to several standers-by, so will this book appear with wrinkles and grey headed to the lovers of antiquity, smooth and with down to such to whom novelty is most delightful."   Certainly no reader could fail to find something to his taste.   He may read from Pliny (noting in the margin that the quotation is from "lib. viii, cap. ii"): "The dragon wraps his tail around the elephant's legs and, causing him to fall, he bursteth himself and crusheth the dragon"; or from Ovid or Plutarch; from Holinshed; or from Dr. Featley, John Wall, Crashaw, Waterhouse, or Fuller himself.   "On the margin," says Fuller elegantly, "he hath entered the names of those at whose torch he hath lighted his taper."

A   work   of   Strada's   (*Societate   Jesu*),   *Eloquentia Bipartita,* differs from the other books of instruction mentioned, in that it gives extracts from seventy-four orations.

Still another practically helpful work would be *The Reconciler of the Bible: wherein Above Two Thousand seeming Contradictions throughout the Old and New Testament, are Fully and Plainly Reconciled.*   The author, J. T.

(possibly John Thaddeus), explains his intention in the prefatory letter: "though the Scriptures have no real contrarieties in its self . . . yet some apparent contrarieties there are in it, which cause some difficulty to the Reader. . . ."

Wilkins's *Ecclesiastes* has already been referred to in connection with the preacher's delivery, but the greater part of the book is devoted to the preparation of the sermon. It is essentially a reference book. It names authoritative writers of many faiths on each book of the Bible, and writers of sermons connected with doctrines, controversies, or "heads" in Divinity.

There were volumes of sermons that were probably as practically serviceable as the more formal books of instruction. Ralph Brownrig's *Fourty Sermons* are meticulously divided and subdivided with heads that could be adapted to the needs of any preacher. The sermon on Matthew xvii, is not only numbered but deeply indented and presented in comparatively brief paragraphs and sentences; it could easily be broadened or narrowed, shortened or lengthened. Arthur Hildersham's *CVIII Lectures* has a Table of twenty-five columns containing all the principal points handled, and eight columns of Scripture references. Richard Holdsworth's *Twenty Sermons* has much the same useful arrangement. Collections of Sermons by Luther were printed from time to time; and no doubt they furnished material to many a needy preacher. One volume which appeared in 1649 is called: *Thirtie Foure Special and Chosen Sermons of Martin Luther.* The translation is carefully made and the variety of topics would appeal to any hard-pressed gentleman from whom the dictates of fashion demanded assorted sermons.

Sermon Length

Having, by his own exertions or those of others, found the material for his sermon (which might be ordinary, or occasional) and arranged his "heads" in accordance with the popular taste in homiletics, the preacher would next consider whether that material should be expanded or contracted. Theoretically, the preacher's voice ceased with the last grain of sand in the hour-glass, but actually the time was often extended. If a great orator were in the pulpit, his audience approved his zeal when he turned the glass; if the average man did the same thing, the congregation became restless and noisy. There must have been some among the preachers to parliament who without the excuse of eloquence trespassed beyond the accepted time limit for sermons, for in the *Journal* of Guilon Goddard [100] may be found this suggestive entry:

> Ordered (Thursday, 18, 1656), that the lecturers who preach the morning lecture in the Abbey at Westminster, be desired to begin their sermon at seven of the clock, and to end at eight of the clock. ....

William Chillingworth tried to be conscientious about the length of his sermon, if one may judge by such remarks as: "In the prosecution of the former part (which may very well take up and spend this hour glass), I shall proceed thus. . . ." [101] and ". . . considered in general terms only (for so I shall only handle it in this hour's discourse)." [102] Of Matthew Robinson's preaching it is said approvingly: "Nor could they complain of the longness of his glass"; [103] and of Thomas Westfield's ". . . never standing above his glass . . . nor keeping a glass except upon an extraordinary occasion above a quarter of an hour. . . ." [104]

[100] Burton: *Diary,* I, clxxxix (Goddard is bound with Burton). Burton tells of a fast day (Friday, Feb. 4, 1658/9) when Owen, Reynolds, Calamy, and Manton all preached. "The exercises held from nine until six" (III, 6ff.). Note the argument in Commons, as to whether these sermons should be printed.
[101] *Works,* II, 551.
[102] *Ibid.,* IV, 583.
[103] *Autobiography,* p. 70.
[104] Lloyd, p. 303. The term *glass* was in general use. Dryden uses it matter of factly in his *Essay on Dramatic Poetry:* ". . . their actors speak by the hour glass, like our parsons" (*Works,* I, 89).

One of the many anecdotes connected with Hugh Peters plays on the word *glass*. The volume called *The Tales and Jests of Mr. Hugh Peters* includes various tales of the lustful friar and outwitted husband type, but also such innocuous inanities as this:

> #### How Mr. Peters preached for three Hours on a Fast Day
>
> Mr. Peters having on a fast day preached two long houres, and espying his glasse to be out after the second turning up, takes it in his hand, and having turned it, saith, Come my beloved, we will have the other glasse, and so we'll part.[105]

George Fox mentions that at Leominster he "stood up and declared about three hours"; [106] and he often mentions very lengthy exposition when the spirit was active within him. Edward Rainbow, Bishop of Carlisle, took nearly three hours to deliver the funeral sermon for Lady Anne Clifford.[107] One of the stories told of Barrow's long-windedness is of that occasion when only the blowing of the organ by a resourceful sexton brought him to a conclusion; and another, equally familiar, is that when a friend spoke sympathetically of the mental strain that must have accompanied the delivery of a particularly long sermon, Barrow disclaimed any fatigue in mind or voice, but admitted that, toward the end, his legs began to feel a little weary.

Cromwell once tested John Howe's staying powers by sending a note to the chancel, "while the psalm was singing," asking him to preach on a certain text. Howe preached on the text a full hour, turned the glass, "held on till it was run out, and was about to turn it a second time, when Cromwell gave him the sign to stop, and he broke off." [108]

---

[105] (Jest No. 50.) The same story is told of Daniel Burgess (*Bk. of Days*, II, 713).
[106] *Journal*, p. 145.
[107] *Life . . . of Lady Clifford*, p. 282.
[108] Palmer: *Nonconf. Mem.*, I, 351.

Sermon-borrowing

The great popularity of sermons, constructed with a special technique, and of approximately an hour's length, was an embarrassing fact to those divines who were unable or unwilling to perform what was thought by many to be the most important part of the pastoral duty. The necessity of having something to say from the pulpit led to the development of a special variety of clerical sinner, the sermon-borrower. Not always, however, was he denounced. Kindly Tom Fuller thinks the responsibility for the effect of a sermon lies entirely with the hearer, not the preacher of it. In one of his *Characters* (The Good Parishioner), Dr. Fuller says, ". . . and as it is no manners for him that hath good venison before him, to ask whence it came, but rather fairly to fall to it; so hearing an excellent sermon, he never inquires whence the preacher had it or whether it was not before in print, but falls aboard to practice it." [109] And, "The Good Minister preferreth rather to entertain his people with wholesome cold meat which was on the table before, than with that which is hot from the spit, raw and half roasted." [110]   Bunyan, too, is careful not to condemn the borrower: "I never endeavoured to, nor durst make use of other men's lines, Rom. xv, 18, (though I condemn not all that do.)" [111]   Henry Newcome makes an effort to be charitable, but is not especially successful when he writes in his *Diary* (Oct. 5, 1662): "Mr. Broune preached in the afternoon on Rom. xi, 30, on God's providence, very well. The confidence that the sermon was by him stolen, should make it never the less to me."   Bishop John Wilkins declares frankly that his *Gift of Prayer* "presents a copious Field of Matter, a regular Frame for Method, and Scripture-phrase for expression, which no man need be ashamed to imitate or borrow." [112]

[109] *Holy and Profane State*, p. 72.
[110] *Ibid.*, p. 65.
[111] *Grace Abounding, etc.*, p. 285.
[112] *Discourse concerning . . . Prayer* (Epis. Ded.).

When Adam Eyre and his fellow parishioners were try-ing to make their vicar leave and promising him £40 if he would do so, they drew up a certificate against him, the third article of which reads: "that during all the time of his being here, which is near 3 years, hee hath preached, though sometymes twice a day, yet either alto-gether or, for the most part, other men's works; and one thing 4 or 5 tymes, or oftener, repeated on so many several dayes, without any progresse at all, only tyreing the tyme with tautologies and vaine iteracions. . . ."[113] Edward Waterhouse, Esq., heartily denounces the lazy preachers—"they give God that which cost them nought, their sudden thoughts, immethodical discourses, and slovenly Sermocina-tions, that they Preach and Repreach the labours of other men new vamped. . . ."[114] But Selden says tolerantly, "'Tis good to preach the same thing again, for that's the way to have it learn'd. You see a Bird by often whistling to learn a Tune, and a Month after record it to her self."[115] Robert South evidently recognized that sermon-borrowing was a temptation frequently yielded to; for he is careful to include in his admonitory sermon, *The Scribe Instructed,* a reminder that "when Christ says that a scribe must be stocked with things new and old, we must not think that he meant that he should have an hoard of old sermons, (whoever made them) with a bundle of new opinions."[116] Bishop Sprat also felt that he must speak of what was plainly a common misdemeanor, and in a Visitation Sermon (first apologizing for mentioning the subject at all) he says emphatically "that every Person who undertakes this great employment preaching should make it a matter of Religion and Conscience, to preach nothing but what is the Product

---

[113] *Diurnall,* p. 20.
[114] *An Humble Apologie for Learning and Learned Men,* p. 157.
[115] *Table Talk,* p. 144.
[116] *Works,* II, 252. In the preface to a sermon never preached because of the death of Charles II, for whom it had been prepared, South says: "yet now it is printed, possibly some other may con-descend to do it, as before in several such cases the like has been too well known to have been done" (*Works,* II, 70).

of his own Study, and of his own Composing. . . . This sordid borrowing, this shameful, I had almost said sacrilegious purloining from other Mens Labours, is an utter irreconcilable Enemy to all Manner of Growth and Improvement in Divine Learning, or Eloquence." [117] A sermon-thief, Dr. Sprat concludes, rarely reforms.

The sermon-borrower is denounced in the Letter to the Reader which introduces Dr. Holdsworth's *Valley of Vision*. Some men, we read, "lazily imp their wings with other men's plumes, wherewith they soar high in common esteeme; yet have not the ingenuity with that son of the Prophet to confesse; Alasse! it was borrowed. (2. Kings 6.5.)" Richard Flecknoe includes among his *Sixtynine Enigmaticall Characters*, "A Pune Pragmatical Pulpit-filler": "His studies are as small as his brains, for its one of the torments of his life to think of his Sunday employment, and that makes him a speciall friend to the book-sellers old, obsolete and Noahcall sermons, and these are the parchments he especially takes care." [118]

So common was the practice of using another man's pulpit composition that Isaac Walton saw in it a neat way of illustrating a nice point in fishing. He tells of a sermon-borrower who complained because the reputedly successful work he had borrowed was, when he delivered it, a complete failure. The lender being reproached, answered, "I lent you, indeed, my fiddle, but not my fiddlestick; for you are to know that everyone cannot make music with my words. . . . And so, my scholar," warns Isaac, "you are to know that as the ill pronunciation or ill accenting of words in a sermon spoils it, so the ill carriage of your line, or not

[117] Sprat: *A Discourse, etc.*, pp. 22, 23 (Pub. in 1696, too late to apply directly to the period with which this study is concerned, but the Bishop of Rochester's injunctions are the result of years of experience, not of an end-of-the-century condition).

[118] Pp. 84-5 (cf. Fénelon's procrastinating prédicateur: *"Il se renferme dans son cabinet, il feuillette la Concordance, Combesix, Polianthea, quelques Sermonaires qu'il a achetez, et certaines collections qu'il a faites de passages détachez et trouvez comme par hazard"* (*Dialogues, etc.*, p. 80).

fishing ev.. to a foot in the right place, makes you lose your labor."

The Printed Sermon

The publishing of a sermon might come about in various ways. Many dull and commonplace discourses were printed because of a formal request from parliament, the king, or the family for whom a funeral or wedding sermon had been delivered. Such a request is always mentioned in the dedication. In the case of parliamentary sermons, a copy of the "order to print" is frequently reproduced; the following example is typical:

> Ordered by the Commons assembled in Parliament, that Mr. Popham doe from the House give Thanks unto Mr. Vines and Mr. Manton for the great pains they took in their Sermons preached on this day at Margarets Westminster, before the House of Commons: and that they be desired to print their Sermons, wherein they are to have the like priviledge of Printing of it, as others in like kinde usually have had.[119]
>
> H. Elsynge, Cler. Parl.

There is sometimes an addition:

> "and it is ordered, that none shall presume to Print their, or either of their Sermons, without first obtaining liberty under their handwriting."

Beneath this effort to protect the preacher's rights, it was customary to name the authorized printer or printers.

Often, a clergyman's friends would bring out a collection of his sermons shortly after his death, if his prominence (ecclesiastical, political, or literary) justified the venture. Again, a common explanation of an author's consent to print his sermon is that if he does not, some other man will. Equally common is the statement that modest reluctance has been overcome by the insistence of a patron

[119] These sermons were preached June 28, 1648.

or friends. There were men, of course, who were sincerely opposed to publishing anything they had prepared for the pulpit. Such a man was Richard Vines; his aversion to print was well known and the preacher of his funeral sermon made use of this characteristic to turn a phrase effectively when he published his tribute to Mr. Vines—for Thomas Jacombe did not share his friend's prejudice against publicity. In the Epistle Dedicatory, Dr. Jacombe laments the scarcity of printed sermons by the late divine, and then adds alertly: "do you live . . . so that we may see his sermons printed in your lives." [120]

Once printed, a discourse gained in dignity, and copies could be sent to friends in the same way that a modern student scatters scholarly reprints. The letters of Robert Baillie contain many entries illustrating this practice, as: "For my Lord Eglinton. I doe here present your Lordship with a copie of my poor sermon." "To Mr. William Spang. I sent you by Thomas Cunninghame my sermon before; but receave now another. . . . Mr. Samuell has sent you one of his sermons. . . . Mr. George also sends you his sermons." [121]

The appearance of the printed sermon could be enhanced in a number of ways borrowed from secular practices. Collected discourses appeared in well-bound folios with perhaps an emblematic design or a portrait of the author placed opposite the title page. It was common in humble as well as glorious publications to present a title page effectively by an arrangement of large and small type, long and short lines, which would attract the reader to the ingenious title and the appropriate quotations (often in three or four languages), and which would inform him as to the printer, publisher, place of selling, and date. A single sermon in quarto might have its title page set off by a small device, or a border broken at intervals with a skull, or other emblem.

---

[120] *Enochs Walk and Change.*
[121] *Letters,* II, 173-5 ; also, pp. 122, 310.

These decorative additions are rare in the quartos because they were published for quick selling, there being much of the timeliness of the newspaper *Extra* about some sermons, as those delivered at the funerals of prominent men, at important assemblies, at anniversaries of national interest, or by spectacular individuals.

The title of the printed sermon was the result of careful composition. It might be appropriate and specific, or intended to stir curiosity, to please the ear, to catch the eye, or to present a climax. For example:

> *The Penitent Death of a Woeful Sinner, Or, The Penitent Death of John Atherton, Late Bishop of Waterford in Ireland* [122]
>
> *A Sermon without a Text* [123]
>
> *The Valley of Vision, or, A Clear Sight of Sundry Sacred Truths* [124]
>
> *Fermentum Pharisaeorum, or, The Leaven of Pharisaicall Wil-Worship* [125]
>
> *An Arke for all Gods Noahs in a gloomy stormy day; Or, The best wine reserved till the last; Or, The transcendent Excellency of a believers portion above all earthly Portions whatsoever* [126]

A sermon when prepared for the press was likely to expand beyond its original limits. It is not unusual to read in the Dedicatory Epistle that the address now published has been preached "contractedly," or is printed "with some Additions and Enlargements." John Gauden in his funeral sermon for Robert Rich, *Funerals made Cordials,* explains his own method of revision. "The ensuing discourse is now much inlarged beyond the Horary limits of a Sermon, ex-

[122] Bernard, N.
[123] Freeman, J. He says the Printer phrased this title, "who thinks (that in these times), tis lawful for everyone to appear in his own humour."
[124] Holdsworth, R.
[125] Tombes, J.
[126] Brooks, T.

ceeding in length most of the ancient Orations. For in recollecting and ruminating my meditations they easily multiplied, and in transcribing my notes, as I had prepared them, I added with Baruch (Jer. 36, 32) many like words to what I had preached and penned, but omitted, being necessarily and so excusably contracted in the Pulpit, but now more dilated in the Presse, according to my own design and the desire of others, who have a great empire over me. . . ."

The *Six Sermons* of Edward Stillingfleet appeared in print "with a Discourse annexed concerning the true reason of the suffering of Christ wherein Crellius his Answer to Grotius is considered." Two of these sermons had been printed before; when the stationer asked that others be joined, the lavish clergyman offered enough extra material to fill six chapters. One hundred and nineteen pages were added to a group of sermons by J. Hughes, the published work being entitled: *"A Dry Rod Blooming and Fruit-Bearing; or a Treatise of the Pain, Gain and Use of Chastening.*[127] An extrordinarily modest addition to a published sermon was that made by Francis Riddington; it is only a Prayer and he says apologetically that it had been omitted when the sermon was delivered "because the glasse was run, and the Season then almost as hot as these eight years persecutions; but being it was really intended, it is therefore here verbatim inserted." The Prayer is a real addition to the commonplace sermon (*King Solomon's Directory*) because of its patriotic, and non-religious, fervor. Invocation gives place to fiery denunciation of those in civil authority at the time—1649—especially of the murderers of the king, the murder being a "Heinous, Treasonable, Damnable fact."

Brief additions could always be placed in the margins.

---

[127] See D'Avenant: *Gondibert* (Preface, p. 40). "Those that write by the command of conscience (thinking themselves able to instruct others, and consequently oblig'd to it) grow commonly the most voluminous."

Seldom were they allowed to stand empty, for not only did they offer a convenient location for "sources" and helpful bits of Hebrew, Greek, and Latin, but second thoughts could be added in fine print. Sometimes this practice resulted in an almost uninterrupted succession of reference and comment which, with the scholarly (or pedantic) citations, kept pace with the sermon proper like an attentive congregation. An honest man also found, in the convenient margin, an opportunity to prevent any misunderstanding. A certain Mr. Hughes, for instance, once quoted in his sermon: "Shall a nation be born at once?" and conscientiously inserted in the margin directly opposite the question, "Hyperbole." [128] Stephen Marshall is prone to utilize the scant space, left alongside his solid paragraphs, for an occasional digest of several pages of subject matter.[129] John Brinsley finds the margin a good place for a stimulating suggestion: "Enquire how our sins died, whether a naturall, or violent death." [130]

The copyright of a popular sermon was considered an asset. When James Allestry was ruined by the fire in London, Dr. Allestry gave him copies of eighteen sermons, the publication of which would restore some part of his losses. The printer Mariott was reckoned a fortunate man when he secured copyrights, or part copyrights, of the sermons of John Hales of Eton and of the works of Henry King and John Donne.[131]

Sometimes the preacher or the printer shows a delightfully worldly appreciation of the advantage of arousing

[128] *A Dry Rod Blooming and Fruit-Bearing, etc.*
[129] *A two-edged Sword out of the mouth of Babes, etc.*
[130] *Of Mystical Implantation,* p. 102 *(Two Treatises).*
In Hildersham's *CVIII Lectures,* the "godly Reader" is reminded of the value of the notes that "stand like Lights, or Goades, or Nailes, in the body of the discourse" (Preface).
[131] Masson: *Life of Milton,* VI, 403; also *Biog. Brit.,* III, p. 114.
The 1649 edition of Donne's sermons quotes the younger John Donne as follows: "The reward that many yeares since was proposed for the publishing of these Sermons, having been lately conferred upon me under the authority of the Great Seal, etc.," *N. and Q.,* VI, 77.

curiosity. John Eachard, in his foreword, gives good and interesting reasons for the publishing of his sermon, *The Axe against Sin and Error; and the Truth Conquering.* When it was delivered, we learn, a Christian desired it might be preached again at her funeral; but Satan hindered (we are not told how) and consequently it has been sent to the press "because the enemy hate it"; furthermore, it will serve as "a fore-runner to make way for a more excellent Work . . . wherein are showed the causes of the sword on England, and on the Lutherans, and the remedies that must be used, before the Judgements cease." Now that is a good piece of advertising. Anyone would wish to know what Satan objected to in the sermon; anyone would look forward to an explanation of how to remove danger from England, and also from the Lutherans.

The value of controversy as a means of advertising sermons was well understood by the bookseller Timothy Garthwaite, who when a nonconformist threatened him—this was in 1655—for selling a volume of Robert Sanderson's sermons in which there was "false divinity," declared boldly that "it was not his trade to judge of true and false divinity, but to print and sell books; and yet if any friend of his would write an answer to it, and owne it by setting his name to it, he would print the answer and provide the selling of it." [132] The publisher of Edmund Calamy's sermon, *Eli Trembling before the Ark,* is careful to remind the Reader in a foreword that this is the identical sermon that brought about the minister's imprisonment—he having preached it after he was "silenced." "We suppose you are desirous to see the Sermon, we have therefore gratified your desire." [133] When Dr. John Hewett was beheaded (June 8, 1658) on a charge of communicating treasonably with Charles II, the funeral sermon preached by that spe-

[132] Walton: *Life of Sanderson,* pp. 38-9.
[133] Equally well advertised is Zachary Crofton's *Hard Way to Heaven* (a Farewell Sermon), and John Ferriby's *The Lawful Preacher* (preached in 1652).

cialist in funeral sermons, Dr. Nathaniel Hardy, was promptly published along with Dr. Hewett's defense, the presentation of which had been denied him. The work was attractively entitled, *Beheaded John Hewett's Ghost crying for Justice.*[134] Sermons such as this last are much nearer the political pamphlet than the pulpit exposition. Among these compositions are many that probably owe their published existence to their controversial tone. *Satan the Leader in Chief to all who resist the Reparation of Sion* denounces *seriatim:* Arminians, Socinians, Popish Priests, and Bishops;[135] *Sheba's Head Cast over the Wall, Or, the Dead Scalp of Rebellion* attacks those who take up arms against their king;[136] *Jehoijdahs Justice* is an arraignment of Laud;[137] *Justice Triumphing, Or, The Spoylers Spoyled* is a November fifth sermon.[138] In these so-called sermons, there is no genuine religious element.[139] The sermon-vehicle was convenient for abuse, and was frankly utilized for that purpose just as in later times the novel has served as a means of presenting political and sociological problems.

Printed sermons of all natures were really in demand. Swollen with Dedicatory Epistles, additional discourses, explanatory notices, marginal references, they came swiftly from the press and were eagerly bought by readers whose intellectual appetite could be satisfied in no other way.[140] Edward Reynold's *Sinfulnesse of Sinne* (expanded from sermons preached at Lincoln's Inn) went through five editions by the year 1657; in the gayer days of the Restoration, Stillingfleet preached on a Fast Day for the Fire (Oct. 10, 1666), a sermon which reached a fourth edition in 1669.

---

[134] Neal: *Hist. of the Pur.*, II, 177. For Hewitt's complicity in the plot to restore "Cha. Stew.," see Thurloe: I, 707ff.

[135] Baillie, R.

[136] Reeve, T.

[137] Hoyle, J.

[138] Hardy, N.

[139] In these sermons, which represent a mass of similar works, there is complete intolerance of a differing point of view. "Tolerance," declared Edwards in *Gangraena,* "is very destructive to the glory of God, and the salvation of souls" (p. 92).

[140] Milton: *Areopagitica,* pp. 114-5, pp. 137-8.

The Farewell Sermons, Roger L'Estrange complains, had ten or twelve impressions, to the number of 30,000, since the Act of Conformity, yielding a return of £3300 to the (unlicensed) printers.[141]

An important feature of the printed sermon was the dedication. This was borrowed ready made from secular compositions, and, with no change of form and little of content, it was joined to almost every sermon that passed through the publishers' hands. But although a dedication owed its existence to a sermon, it had certain individual qualities which must be discussed at some length.

Sermon Dedications

The writing of a dedication for a printed book is a continuing fashion, one that, apparently, gives pleasure to him who phrases the foreword and to him for whom it is phrased. A dedication offers an opportunity to give and receive a compliment before witnesses. It offers, too, a range of courteous acknowledgment that stretches from an honest, grateful expression of obligation to an elaborate aggregation of flattering assertions.

The mid-seventeenth-century dedications are, for the most part, perfunctory compliments, automatic expressions of thanks for some opportunity or advancement given a man who was in need of such assistance. But the perfunctory, the automatic, quality is not in itself a sign of servility or of grasping ambition. A man wrote a dedication largely because his composition would have seemed crude and abrupt without a number of preliminary compliments to persons who might be concerned. Says Dr. Richard Meggot frankly in one of his sermon dedications: "When Epistles of this Nature are so much in Fashion, that all

---

[141] *Considerations and Proposals in order to the Regulation of the Press,* 1663 (Quoted in H. R. Plomer: *A Short Hist. of Eng. Pr., 1476-1898,* p. 202ff.).

Things in Print are thought undressed, if they are without them, I hope I shall not be censured. . . ." [142]

Again, a man wrote a dedication because he wanted his patron in particular and his readers in general to like his book, and to buy it. So popular did the eulogistic fore-word become, that it finally developed into a formula: introduction (deprecatory statement as to inability to produce anything worth the dedicatee's attention), discussion (the glorious attributes of the dedicatee), conclusion (the respectful affection of the author). The author who writes the prefatory letter may be of any literary variety: poet, playwright, preacher; but however he may differ from another man in profession or personality, he will resemble him in this habit of prefixing a dedication to any published work; furthermore, he will compose that dedication according to the prevailing fashion. We may be scornful of Dryden's excess flatteries which introduce his prose, poetry, and drama, we may wonder why John Evelyn thought it necessary to write Epistles Dedicatory, we may feel impatient at the same practice by Cowley, Etherege, and many others; but we realize how strong is this literary fashion, how inevitable is the inclusion of compliment to men and women of consequence, when we see that even the published sermon is padded with pretty speeches to someone who will like to read them.

There is a strong family resemblance between dedications written by men of the church and men of the world. Here are four examples that pair automatically:

   To his most honoured friend and patron
     Sir Roger Bourgoine
      Knight and Baronet

   Sir,
     It was the early felicity of Moses, when exposed in an ark of Nilotic papyre, to be adopted into the favour of so great a personage as the daughter of Pharaoh: such another ark

[142] *Fun. Ser.* for Dr. Hardy.

is this vindication of the writings of that divine and excellent person exposed to the world in; and the greatest ambition of the author of it is, to have it received into your patronage and protection.

(Edward Stillingfleet: *Originae sacrae*)

To the Rt. Hon. The Earl of Clarendon, Lord High Chancellor of England, etc.
My Lord,
  Though poems have lost much of their ancient value, yet I will presume to make this a present to your lordship; and the rather because poems (if they have anything precious in them) do, like jewels, attract a greater esteem when they come into possession of great persons, than when they are in ordinary hands.

(William D'Avenant: *The Siege of Rhodes*)

To the Earl of Huntingdon
  (The only reason the author yielded to the persuasions of "sundry" to publish his sermons was for the opportunity) "by the Dedication of them to give publick testimony unto the world of my duty and thankfulnesse unto your Honour, and unto your Noble House. . . ."

(Arthur Hildersham: *CVIII Lectures on the Fourth of John*)

To the Hon. Charles Lord Buckhurst
My Lord,
  I could not have wished myself more fortunate than I have been in the success of this poem. The writing of it was a means to make me known to your lordship; the acting of it has lost me no reputation; and the printing of it has now given me an opportunity to show how much I honour you.

(George Etherege: *The Comical Revenge, or, Love in a Tub*)

Naturally enough, the group dedication was popular. It was a thrifty form of compliment by which one sermon could be made to serve many patrons. Robert South compiled this list.

To the Reverend, Learned, and very worthy Dr. Rreind, headmaster of the Westminster School, together with the other subordinate masters of the same; as likewise to all such as heretofore in their several times have been, and those who at present actually are, members of that Royal Foundation. . . .[143]

Far more inclusive is a dedication by Thomas Brooks:

To all the Lords, Knights, Ladies, Gentry, Ministers and Commons of England, (and the Dominions thereunto belonging) that have but the least desire, the least mind, or the least will to escape hell, and to go to heaven, or to be happy in both worlds. . . .[144]

Thomas Reeve prefers specific mention:

To Charles II

To the Duke of Somerset, George Duke of Albermarle, Thomas Earle of Southampton, James Earle of Northampton, Lionel Earle of Midersex, George Earle of Nowich, and the rest of the Nobilities of the Kingdome of England, unstained honour, and undoubted Salvatione.

To the Right reverend Fathers in God, Gilbert Lord Bishop of London, Matthew Lord Bishop of Ely, George Lord Bishop of Rochester, and the rest of the reverend Bishops of the Kingdome.

To the Right honorable Sr. Robert Foster, Lord Chief Justice of the Kings bench, Sr Orlando Bridge-man Lord Chief Justice of the common pleas, Edward Atkins one of the Barons of the Exchequer and the rest of the honorable Judges.[145]

The dedications of those sermons which were preached on special occasions, as before the king, before parliament, at the universities, before the Lord Mayor, at funerals, and so on were virtually preëmpted. A man could hardly preach a sermon by request and then dedicate the sermon to someone entirely uninterested. There may be found, therefore, numbers of formal, colorless Epistles addressed to the group or the individual that had invited the preacher to deliver a sermon. Especially are the parliamentary ser-

[143] *Works*, III, 67.
[144] *The Crown and Glory of Christianity*, etc.
[145] *Sheba's Head Cast over the Wall*, etc.

mons introduced in this manner,[146] but a man of independence like Peter Sterry will refrain from flattery; and a disturbing spirit like Hugh Peters will neglect to deprecate his performance, though otherwise their dedications are according to rule.[147]

The dedications of university sermons are usually constructed in the preferred manner. Robert South takes nearly one thousand two hundred words to offer a group of sermons to the university of Oxford. There is nothing of a religious flavor about the opening lines: "These discourses . . . having by the favour of your patience had the honour of your audience, and being now published in another and more lasting way, do here humbly cast themselves at your feet, imploring the yet greater favour and honour of your patronage, or at least the benevolence of your pardon." [148]

These bachelors and doctors of divinity were much too clever not to see the absurdity of the exaggerated compliments showered on men of social or political importance. Edmund Calamy permits himself to be satirical when he dedicates his sermon, the *Noble-Man's Patterne,* to "the Right Honorable House of Lords," before whom he had spoken. "If all noble-men were as good and religious as they are presented to the world in the Epistles prefixed to the Books that are dedicated to them, we should not have so much cause to complaine of great mens Iniquities or of poor mens flatteries. . . . It is the custom to send sermons out into publicke view under the Patronage of some Nobleman or other. This sermon hath this preheminence, That it comes forth under the Patronage and by the command not

[146] See the dedication of the sermon preached by Stephen Marshall, Dec. 22, 1641; Henry Scudder, Oct. 30, 1644; John Greene, Feb. 24, 1646; W. Craddock, July 21, 1646; Thomas Manton, June 28, 1648; Joseph Caryl, Oct. 8, 1656. There are, too, many stereotyped dedications from the pens of men of reputation as speakers and writers, such as Owen, Calamy.
[147] Sterry: *The Spirit Convincing of Sinne,* preached Nov. 26, 1645; Peters: A Thanksgiving Sermon, preached Nov. 1, 1649.
[148] *Sermons,* Vol. I, 264 (Preached 1667).

only of one Lord, but of a House of Lords. The Lord
make it to obtaine that end for which it was preached."
The writer of that dedication has no idea of fooling himself
or anybody else, but while he is about it, he is willing to
turn his phrases neatly and offer a pretty play on the word
Lord.

The very prince of clerical dedicators is Thomas Fuller.
He riots in preliminary compliments; never does he miss
an opportunity. Where another man writes one or two
dedications for a book, Bishop Fuller writes them for each
section of a book. He dedicates everything: sermons, histories (church, college, personal), allegories, romantic tales.
Being Thomas Fuller he does not write his dedications by
formula. In his *Pisgah Sight of Palestine,* each book is
dedicated to the heir of some nobleman, the first, for
example, being inscribed to Esme Stuart, not yet a year old
but a most important infant, son and heir to James, duke of
Richmond and Lennox. In the *Church History* which
Fuller so faithfully "endeavoured," as he says on his title
page, he adjusts his compliment to the particular person
he is addressing. There is nothing transferable about
Fuller's dedications. His brief chapter on the third century, in his *Church History,* is offered as a compliment to
Mr. Simon Bonnell, Merchant, and the author says gracefully, "It is proportionable to present a century short in
story to one low in stature, though deservedly high in the
esteem of your friend. . . ." [149] The name of Thomas
Bide, Esq., of London, stands at the head of Section V
because of his love of mathematics, "there being much of
surveying in the chapter." Some of the dedications are in
Latin, as is that to Thomas Adams, Lord Mayor of London,
who is hailed as Maecenas and praised for his disinterested
generosity. [150] A few of the preliminary compliments are
addressed to women, as is the very charming one, "To the
Noble Lady Elenor Roe, Relict to the Honourable Sir

[149] Vol. I, Section 3. [150] Vol. I, Section 8.

Thomas Roe"; [151] and that to Mistresse Anne Davis, telling her not to be embarrassed, "seeing yourself left alone, surrounded on all sides with masculine dedications." [152]

Bishop Thomas Fuller never felt, evidently, that he should make any difference between his secular and his religious publications: both follow the literary fashion of the day. The *Church History of Britain*, which is theological in intention but agreeably worldly in execution, shows the same variety of flattering foreword that appears before the good-naturedly satirical *Ornithologie* (dedicated to Roger L'Estrange), or the allegorical *Antheologia* (dedicated to William Stafford, merchant of Bristol), or the stirring tale entitled *Triana; or, A Threefold Romanza, of Mariana, Paduana, Sabina* (dedicated to the Reader). Fuller's published sermons are a means of paying extravagant compliments to the Lady Elizabeth Newton,[153] and to Lady Frances Manners, Countess of Rutland; in these, the elaboration of *conceit* could not be surpassed by Cowley or Dryden.[154]

The nonconformist John Owen was as much a follower of the fashion in using dedications as was the established and more literary Thomas Fuller. There is none of Fuller's geniality about Owen's preliminary pages, though he can turn a graceful phrase and play with an original fancy. Rather does he take advantage of the opportunity custom gives him, to plant one more blow in the sinner's defenses. The Puritan preacher is quite ready to adopt the secular habit of naming a sponsor for his printed work and addressing a courteous Epistle to him, but Owen adapts the popular custom to his own personality, which is, after all, exactly what Fuller does. The difference is that Fuller had a most engaging personality. Many of Owen's published sermons had been previously delivered before parliament: at openings, at Fast Days, and Days of Solemn

---

[151] Vol. I, Section 9.
[152] Vol. I, Section 3.

[153] *Comfort in Calamitie, etc.*
[154] *Cause and Cure, etc.*

Humiliation. Usually, these sermons are dedicated to the assembly which had heard them,[155] but one of the parliamentary sermons is dedicated to "his highness the Lord Protector." Lord Fairfax is complimented by an ascription at the head of two sermons, and here Owen is as modish as any charming courtier poet of the day: "What thoughts concerning your person, my heart is possessed withal, as in their storehouse they yield me delightful refreshment, so they shall not be drawn out, to the disturbance of their self denial." (But for conscience' sake, he adds that he will pray for Fairfax.[156])

Nathaniel Hardy is plainly enjoying himself when he writes the dedication of his sermon, *Wisdomes Character: or, The Queen of Graces,* to the High Sheriff of the county of Buckingham. "Sir, At your command this small Barke was first launched into the River, and is now put forth to Sea; I know the season is perillous, and perhaps she may meet with a contrary winde, but her Anchor of Truth will preserve her. . . . The Commodities which she bringeth are the incomparable Jewell of Wisdome, the Amber of Purity, the Gold of Peace, the Silkes of Gentlenesse, the Oyl of Mercy, all sorts of pretious Fruits, the Diamonds of Impartiality, Sincerity, and these fetched out from the uttermost Indies, or any places of the earth, but the uttermost Heaven of Heavens."

Barten Holyday, who was a poet and playwright as well as a preacher, knew how to turn a compliment in fashionable phrasing. He dedicated his sermon, *On the Serpent and the Dove,* to Sir William Bulton, assuring him: "To be a Favourer of Knowledge is from a Bounty of Goodness; yet the Honour of many: to be a Favorite of Knowledge is from a Bounty of Nature; yet the Honour of few: Each in

---

[155] E.g., Jan. 31, 1649. The subject of this sermon is Tolerance. It is a mild discourse and contains no reference to Charles's death; only determined interpretation can find an allusion.

[156] *Ebenezer.* Other parl. sers., Feb. 28, April 19, 1649; Oct. 30, 1656, represent Owen's adherence to the popular manner in dedications.

itselfe is Happinesse; Both in your selfe a Double Happinesse."

The dedication that shows a genuine, personal sense of
obligation or affection may be illustrated by Hardy's Epistle
to the "Worshipfull Roger Price, Esq.," which stands at
the head of the funeral sermon for Mr. Richard Goddard,
"late minister of S. Gregories by Pauls." Mr. Price had
been the patron of the minister, who had been buried from
Mr. Price's house.

A grateful note of appreciation appears also in the dedication prefixed to Thomas Adams's two sermons: *God's
Anger; Man's Comfort.* Most of Adams's work belongs to
the early part of the seventeenth century. The sermons of
those years are good reading.[157] as they should be, for
Adams was called "the Shakespeare of divines"; but the two
sermons published in 1653 tell, through the dedication, a
tale of lean years. "To the most honorable and Charitable
Benefactors whom God honoured for his Almoners and
sanctified to be the dispensers of the fruits of his Charity
and Mercy to me in this my necessitous and discrepit old
age, I humbly present this testimony of my thankfulness. . . ."

A more unusual reason for selecting dedicatees is that
given by the publisher of Christopher Love's sermons some
months after the minister's execution. To "the Rt. Worshipful, my Worthy Friends, Mr. Edward Bradshaw . . . and
Mrs. Bradshaw his wife" are the compliment and the explanation offered. "It is not that the works of the worthy
Author need any Patrociny. . . . But indeed, the reason
of this dedication (besides the publicke expression of my
respects to you both) is the consideration of that special
interest you both have to anything of Master Loves. Your
interest, Sir, is undoubted to this Treatise, as having
married his widow, whereby God hath made the solitary to

---

[157] Sample titles: *The Devil's Banquet; Leucanthropy, or The Wolf
Worrying the Lambes.*

dwell and rest in the house of her husband, and hath caused a mournful widow to forget her sorrows. And your right (deare Mistresse Bradshaw) is several yeares to be the wife of this eminent servant and Ambassador of Jesus Christ." [158]

The Reader frequently has a complimentary preface of his own which usually follows modestly after the Epistles addressed to definite and important individuals. Occasionally, it happens that a sermon goes out into the world of printed matter unsponsored, save by the impersonal Reader. Such a dedication relieves the author or publisher from the necessity of devising something new in compliments applicable to a particular person. The vague Reader is, however, addressed in conventional dedication language, for a professional writer could hardly fail to construct his clauses and contrast his ideas according to accepted usage. Observe John Owen, when addressing the Reader: "Had I been my own, it had not been thine. My submission unto others judgments being the only cause of submitting this unto thy censure." [159] Nicholas Bernard, too, addressed the Reader gracefully: "In this following narration, expect no guilded stile, unfitting a Mourner; painted glass may be more costly, but plainer is more perspicuous, and 'tis truth and clearnesse I only pretend unto." [160] Christopher Love's friends, when publishing his sermons, were careful to forestall possible criticism of their serious quality by informing the Reader that: "It is the unhappiness of our age, that men desire rather to have their ears tickled, then their hearts affected; and it is the sin of many jingling Preachers, that they minde rather the humoring of their hearers fancies, then the saving of their soules. . . ." [161] There is stronger feeling in the opening pages of *The Naturall Mans Case Stated, or, An Exact Map of the Little World Man,* a posthumous publication of seventeen sermons

[158] *The Combat between Flesh and Spirit;* pub. posthumously.
[159] *A Country Essay, etc.*
[160] *Fun. Ser.* for Usher.
[161] *The True Doctrine of Mortification.*

of Christopher Love's. The address to The Reader begins: "The exuberant spawns of illiterate books proceeding from the polluted wombs of the overloaded and bejaded adulterate presses which are all painted with fair titles, I can compare to nothing so fitly as a cheating Lottery." [162]

Those clergymen who were known to be especially adept at wording an introductory page found their services in steady demand. Whether they received anything more than gratitude for the assistance they gave, it has not been possible to discover. So popular were Baxter's Prefaces that he wrote them faster than he read the books to which they were to be affixed. "I have not read over this Book, being desired suddenly to write this Preface," he tells the Reader of Clark's *Lives of Eminent Persons*. Another work of Clark's, *The Marrow of Ecclesiastical History*, has Prefaces by Calamy (To the Christian Reader), John Wall (likewise to the Christian Reader), Simeon Ash, and poems by Thomas Dugard (in Greek), an anagram by John Clark, and other poems by Fuller, William Jenkins, Samuel and John Clark.

The preachers wrote dedications, whether for sermons or other works, that are worth reading, though it is true that not many are worth remembering. Thomas Fuller knew that a dedication had other uses than those prompted by gratitude or greed. "The Genius of the author," he declared, "is commonly discovered in the dedicatory epistle. Many place the purest grain in the mouth of the sack for chapmen to handle or buy: and from the dedication one may probably guess at the work, saving some rare and peculiar exceptions." [163]

In spite of its mechanical and conventional qualities, the sermon dedication is an interesting composition. It sometimes gives an intimate glimpse into the personality of the

[162] Other examples of secularly flavored dedications to the Reader: Robert Sanderson (1657), *Works*, I, 68; Fuller (to introduce Spencer's *Things New and Old*); the Publisher of Zachary Crofton's sermon, *The Hard Way to Heaven* (1662).
[163] *Holy and Profane State*, 214.

man who pays and the one who receives a compliment; it reflects the manners, customs and language of the day when it was composed; if it is connected with a great event or a great man, it will show them through a medium which is unconcerned with the future rating of either.

CHAPTER IV

THE SECULAR INTERESTS OF THE CLERGY

MANY clergymen found it quite possible to combine secular and religious occupations. For some this was especially easy because a Bachelor of Divinity might be a fellow or lecturer in a university where, although he would preach when requested to do so and lecture at stated times, there would be at his disposal many hours which he could devote to any avocation that attracted him. Another man who had entered the ministry, might be bitterly poor or over-worked; still another might become an ecclesiastical personage with many formal duties attached to his office. Whatever his environment might be, the man who had opportunity and leisure and the man who was seemingly too low or too high to have either found a way to pursue almost any avocation, if he sincerely wished to do so. Along through the years between 1640 and 1670, bishops and other clergy did serious work in science, language, and history, in poetry, music, and drama.

For the preachers were as normally human as the congregations they preached to. An intelligent, well-educated clergyman, living in the age of Milton or of Dryden, could not fail to be interested in subjects outside of school divinity any more than a man of like ability and the training of our own day could ignore the discoveries and developments of the twentieth century. Secular studies and points of view are entirely legitimate on the part of gentlemen of the clergy. Godliness is in no way lessened, and usefulness is certainly increased, by an intimacy with sciences and arts.

137

These men of varying religious sects, living in a time when creeds and politics were so intermingled that it was not possible to touch one without arousing another, felt a responsibility toward the preservation and increase of learning, and the encouragement of creative art. Spiritual truth, they thought, was not unallied with knowledge, therefore they gave long hours of study to languages, mathematics, and philosophy. Fine Arts, they thought, were wholly compatible with, perhaps complementary to, religion, therefore some of them wrote plays and poetry, and loved music greatly. Yet among the very men whose secular pursuits were most conspicuous may be found those who obeyed in all simplicity the command recorded by the prophet: ". . . to do justly, and to love mercy, and to walk humbly with thy God."

I

Learned Avocations

Antiquities

The church antiquary was so established as a type by the middle of the seventeenth century that Thomas Fuller included him among the *Characters* that make up the *Holy and Profane State*. Dr. Fuller numbers his observations on what constitutes the true church antiquary, and any modern student will read Numbers 5, 6, and 7 with appreciation:

> He is not peremptory but conjectural in doubtful matters.
> He thankfully acknowledgeth those by whom he hath profited.
> He affects not fanciful singularity in his behaviour.[1]

A too conspicuous interest in ancient objects or subjects sometimes brought suspicion upon a minister, it being feared

[1] *Holy and Profane State,* p. 55.

"that the rust of his old Inscriptions cankered his Soul with as old Superstition." This was a charge brought against John Barkham, says Lloyd, but it was disproved by the very fact that Barkham was a profound scholar: "When it is in the study of Antiquity, as it is in that of Phylosophy a little skill in either of them inclines men to Atheism or Heresie, but a depth of either study brings them about to their Religion." [2]

Some of the antiquarian interests of the clergy were general, some were narrowed to one subject. Hugh Cressey (whose Roman Catholic faith gave Anthony à Wood no uneasiness) liked to discourse "of divers matters relating to antiquities"; [3] but Thomas Ellis had a specialty, his "natural geny" leading him to British history, particularly that of Wales. Ellis experienced one of those tragedies of scholarship that hang suspended over every investigator. He was aiding another enthusiast in bringing out a new edition of Dr. Powell's *History of Cambria,* "but a Percie Enderbie published a book on the same subject in 1661, and Ellis threw away his notes." [4] William Fulman probably was a "true church antiquary" of whom Bishop Fuller approved, for Fulman's information regarding English genealogies and etymologies was extensive, yet his manner was unaffected. So modest, indeed, was this scholar that "being totally averse from making himself known, and that choice worth treasured up in, his great learning did in a manner dye with him." [5] Samuel Fairclough found his own scholarship to be a snare: "He had undoubtedly consumed his whole Life and buried himself in History and Antiquity, and in the knowledge of all humane Arts and Sciences, if God had not touched his Conscience by that Text of Scripture, viz. *The World by Wisdom knew not God.*" [6] Peter Heylin compiled an impressive volume, entitled: *A Help to English History, containing a succession of all the Kings*

[2] Lloyd: 279.
[3] Wood: *Ath. Ox.,* III, lxv.
[4] *Ibid.,* III, 993-4.
[5] Wood: *Ath. Ox.,* IV, 240.
[6] Clark: *Em. Lives,* p. 159.

*of England, the English Saxons, and the Britons, the Kings
and Princes of Wales; the Kings and Lords of Man, the
isle of Wight.* As also *Dukes, Marqueses, Earls and
Bishops . . . Viscounts, Barons, Baronets. . . .* Henry
Jackson evinced an unusual taste, having made a collection
of manuscripts of Abelard, and revised and compared them.
But in 1642, the parliamentary soldiers who sacked the
house, scattered the collection.[7]

Dr. Philip King (brother of the more important Henry
King, Bishop of Chichester) is credited by Hearne and
Wood as the author of *The Surfeit,* published in 1656, which
contained "some curious particulars concerning old English
literature." [8]   Dr. Gerard Langbaine, the elder, was an
authority on English history and antiquities; [9] so was John
Langley (the great schoolmaster), of whom Edward Rey-
nolds said, in his funeral sermon for Langley, "he was a
great Antiquary in the most memorable things of this
Nation." [10]   Samuel Lee published in 1656 his *Chronicon
Cestrense: An exact Chronology of all the Rulers and
Governors of Cheshire and Chester, both in Church and
State, from the Time of the Foundation of the City of
Chester to this very day.*[11] Bishop Lloyd of St. Asaph's was
interested in English history and made a special investiga-
tion of Geoffrey of Monmouth's chronicle.[12]   Robert San-
derson "spent much time (particularly in his retirement be-
fore the Restoration) in perusing old Registers." [13]   Brian
Twine studied charters, bulls, etc., relating to Oxford.[14]
Usher's "study and diligent perusal of our ancient Manuscripts and Records of all sorts made him more eminently

[7] Wood: *Ath. Ox.,* III, 577.
[8] *Reliq. Hearnae,* III, 237 (Appendix IX).   John Fell purchased
a number of ancient mss. from the collection of Cornelius Bee, among
them some of the Cotton mss., and writings of William of Malms-
bury.   Somner: Life (prefixed to *A Treatise, etc.*), p. 65.
[9] *Ibid.,* p. 28.
[10] *Sermon touching the Use of Humane Learning.*
[11] Wood: *Ath. Ox.,* IV, 346.
[12] Gutch: *Coll. Curiosa,* II, 253ff.
[13] *Reliq. Hearnae,* III, 35.
[14] Wood: *Sur. of the Antiq. of Ox.,* pp. 17-18 (Editor's note points
out Wood's heavy indebtedness to Twine).

learned, able, famous at home and abroad, than any other of our Divines." [15] Thomas Widdowes wrote *A Short Survey of Woodstock*.[16] Matthew Wren was unremitting in his pursuit of knowledge, if one may believe the tradition both his descendants and Thomas Herne set down: "Bishop Wren was a true antiquary. He has left collections wherever he went, as Pembroke hall, where fellow, Peter house, where master, Windsor, where dean, and Ely, where bishop. . . ." [17] William Somner "was consulted as a Druid or a Bard," in "all the history of use and custom." [18]

Chronology

James Usher must lead the way into any mention of Chronology. Of all the things that the good man did and said and wrote, his *Chronologia sacra* is today the most outstanding. There are many persons who never heard of James Usher, archbishop and primate of all Ireland, by name or title, but they accept his conclusions as to the age of the world quite literally as gospel, with no questions as to the accuracy of his calculations. In various editions of the Old Testament, Usher's figures have stood at the top of the first page of Genesis, and for generations their authority was unquestioned. Even today they usually go unchallenged by the average reader because of the familiarity of their appearance and the respect engendered by their surroundings. The first part of the Chronology (*Annales Veteris et Novi Testamenti*), to 3828 B.C., appeared in 1650; the second part in 1654. When Usher died in 1656, the great work was not fully completed, and on his deathbed he asked that his close friend and fellow specialist, Gerard Langbaine, would go on with the work. This Langbaine willingly undertook to do, but "he dyed 1657 of an

[15] Prynne: *Demurrer*, p. 144.
[16] Wood: *Ath. Ox.*, III, 399.
[17] Wren, Chris.: *Parentalia*, p. 44; *Reliq. Hearnae*, III, 8.
[18] Life of Somner (prefixed to *A Treatise, etc.*), p. 11.

extream cold taken by sitting in the University Library whole Winter days, and then after his return home, continuing in his study whole Winter nights, without any food or fire; being intent upon Bishop Usher's Chronicle, and Brian Twines Antiquities of the University of Oxford, with other exquisite Pieces of much Learning and Importance. . . ." [19]

Christopher Fowler had "a singular gift in Chronology" which he directed toward religious Prophecies; [20] William Fulman was "admirably well vers'd in Chronology." [21] Adam Littleton published a work: *Tabula Chronologica Personarum Illustrium et Rerum Memorabilium, praesertim quae Latinam Historiam spectant.* The entries begin:

A.M.
1   Orbitus conditus
    Adam formatus
130 Seth nascitur
930 Moritur Adam

Burnet testifies that William Lloyd was "the most punctual in chronology of all our divines." [22] Henry Newcome was interested in the subject, but there is an unhappy entry in the Diary, which reads: "Studdyed about something in Chronology. Wee were at a barrell of oisters at Mr. Meare's. I was troubled at something, I know not well what I studdyed all the forenoone." [23]

Mathias Prideaux prepared, for "the Towardly Young Sonnes" of Sir Thomas and Lady Katherine Reynell, *An Easy and Compendious History, etc.* It has seven parts, five of which have to do with the Bible or the Church. The Dynasty of the Britains begins with Samothes, the sixth son of Japhet. The Saxon Heptarchi is given. John Swan's book, *Calamus Mensurans: The Measuring Reed. Or, The Standard of Time,* came out in 1653. It places

[19] Lloyd: 517; Wood: *Ath. Ox.,* III, 447.
[20] Calamy: *Abridg.,* II, 98.
[21] Wood: *Ath. Ox.,* IV, 249.
[22] Vol. I, p. 186ff.
[23] *Diary,* Dec. 3, 1662.

Adam's death at 931 (the 22nd of April), compares the
Hebrew and Julian Calendars, and presents "an exact
Compulation of the Yeares of the World, from the Creation
thereof, to the time of the destruction of Jerusalem. . . ."
Two poems are included in the introductory material, one
of which, by John Booker, plays inevitably on the author's
name. The tribute concludes:

> Then thank our Author, a most learned Man.
> Sure when he dyes, He will sing like the Swan.

Francis Tallents worked on chronological tables for many
years, finally publishing the result in 1684, as *A View of
Universal History*. In mentioning the work, Calamy judges
it to be "one of the greatest Performances of the Age, and
will make his Name famous to Posterity." [24] Ezrael
Tongue was reputed to understand chronology well.[25]

Coins

To be a numismatist requires both capital and opportunity. A collector of books has relatively an easy time
because books are everywhere. But ancient coins and
medals are not stacked on stalls and in shops, and having
an intrinsic value, they are not parted with easily. An
ignorant man might not know the full value of a piece of
money that had come into his possession; but he would
know that it was money. Clergymen, therefore, who in the
seventeenth century collected coins and medals, are not
numerous; that is, there are few references to that particular avocation. There may have been scores of ministers
who cherished examples of money dating from the early
settlements of Britain, and from ancient peoples in other
lands; but unless the collection was sufficiently large to be
known by a learned public, it would not be likely to reach
the knowledge of contemporary writers.

[24] Calamy: *Abridg.*, II, 550.   [25] Wood: *Ath. Ox.*, III, 1263.

Archbishop Laud had a famous collection of coins, which he presented to the Bodleian Library. Even when he was a prisoner in the Tower, his coins were in his thought, and he wrote to Dr. Barkham (who had given many of them to him) regarding their arrangement.[26] Usher's library included "a choice (but not numerous) collection of ancient coins";[27] and John Langley, schoolmaster and "most judicious divine," had a good many coins which with his histories and antiquities "were sold by his brother merely for money's sake."[28] Another collection, Timothy Nourse's, went intact to the Bodleian: "his coins and medals, whether of gold, silver or copper . . . the coins amounted in all to 532 . . . chiefly Greek and Roman."[29] Two letters from John Rastick to Ralph Thoresby of Leeds, give an account of Roman coins found at Flete in Lincolnshire, and other antiquities found at Spalding.[30]

Heraldry

Heraldry would inevitably demand the attention of any student of genealogy and history; moreover, a certain amount of general information regarding coats of arms of nobles and gentry would still be a matter of course in the seventeenth century. That heraldry was a diversion more than ordinarily secular, may be inferred from Calamy's rather defiant statement regarding Mr. Matthias Candler's avocation: "He had one peculiar Study and Diversion that made him acceptable to Gentlemen, which was Heraldry and Pedigrees. He had really been a fit Man to have wrote the Antiquities of his Country. Let none condemn him for this, least they condemn their own great Bishop Sanderson who was much more swallow'd up in the same Studies."[31] Robert Sanderson undoubtedly took this diver-

---

[26] Letter quoted in Th. Hearne's *Collection of Curious Discourses,* II, 40; also Wood: *Ath. Ox.,* III, 36.
[27] *Reliq. Hearnae.,* I, 100.
[28] Wood: *op. cit.,* III, 435-6.
[29] *Ibid.,* IV, 449.
[30] Palmer: II, 164.
[31] Calamy: *Abridg.,* II, 652-3.

sion seriously, collecting wherever he went, not only coats of arms, but pedigrees, monumental inscriptions, and arms in churches and windows.[32]

John Barkham (Barcham) found Heraldry as interesting as he did coins. When a young man, he had published a book on Heraldry, but evidently feeling a certain lack of dignity in his performance, he permitted the book to come out in the name of John Guillim, an acquaintance of his who had made some study of the subject. The work proved popular and was reprinted a number of times. Pepys bought a copy in 1667, but he makes no comment on it. It was probably a book no gentleman's library could be without.[33]

William Oughtred found time to be "a great lover of Heraldry."[34] David Whitford does not seem to have made any original investigations in inscriptions or blazonry, but he rendered a service to those who did by translating into Latin the notes of his patron, Edward Bysshe, on old authors that have written of arms and armory.[35] Edward Waterhouse wrote two books on Heraldry;[36] Matthew Wren left some records of his study of the ancient arms of the French Kings, and of the Order of the Garter.[37] Peter Heylin made a study of Heraldry. He was sufficiently well known as an authority to be included in a satire on "An Oxford Incindiary" (published 1643). "I suppose him lineally descended from St. George's fiery dragon, and, if you please to inquire of Dr. Heylin, he may chance to make good the heraldry."[38]

Naturally enough, theological antiquaries were anxious to trace the origin of heraldry to the Bible. Bishop Hall says, in his *Impresse of God:* "If the testament of the

[32] Wood: *Ath. Ox.*, III, 623; Walker: Pt. II, 105.
[33] *Ibid.*, 36. (In *Rob Roy*, Ch. XI, Squire Osbaldistone takes up "Gwillym" as Sunday reading.)
[34] Aubrey: II, 110.
[35] Wood: *Ath. Ox.*, III, 1017.
[36] Wood: *Fasti*, II, 163.
[37] Wren: *Parentalia*, 144.
[38] Quoted in Aldington, R.: *Book of Characters*, p. 368.

patriarchs had as much credit as Antiquity, all the patriarchs had their armes assigned them by Jacob: Judah a
lyon, Dan a serpent, Nepthali an hinde, Benjamin a wolfe,
Joseph a bough, and so the rest." [39] Fuller had the same
idea: "They [arms] may seem in some sort to be *jure
divino* to the Jews, having a precept for the practice
thereof: 'Every man of the children of Israel shall pitch
by his own standard, with the ensign of their father's
house.' " [40]

Astrology

There has always been a certain charm about Astrology,
and the seventeenth-century divine was not indifferent to
its attraction. In that day, natural astrology (the study
of the stars which predicts the motions of heavenly bodies
and eclipses of the sun and moon) and judicial astrology
(the study of the stars which predicts the influence of con-
stellations on men and events) were still an active interest,
though astrology no longer enjoyed prestige. Natural astrology began to grow nearer to astronomy and pure mathematics, and judicial astrology leaned toward personal and
political flattery and invective.

A pleasant flavor of magic hung about the astrologer's
performances; and this fact made a conscientious preacher
doubt the propriety of associating himself in the public mind
with those who claimed to have the power to divine the
future, and to bring strange things to pass in the present.
True, there was the precedent of Saul's appeal to the witch
of Endor; but there was also the Apostle Paul's disapproval
of exorcists and their practices, a disapproval so forcefully
expressed that "many of them also which used curious arts,
brought their books together, and burned them before all
men: and they counted the price of them, and found it

[39] Browne, Sir Th.: *Works,* II, 35 (The Scutcheons of the Jews).
[40] Fuller: *Worthies,* I, 65 (*Numbers* II, 2).

50,000 pieces of silver." [41]   Perhaps a knowledge of that incident is the reason that Charles Hotham who "in his Younger Years . . . had study'd judicial Astrology . . . gave express Orders in his Will that all his Papers and Books relating to that Art should be burnt." [42]   Samuel Lee knew the same qualms: "He had studied the astrological art, and when he became acquainted with it, durst not approve it, and burnt near an hundred books, the design of which was to give an insight into it. . . ." [43]

Thomas Gataker recklessly engaged in a quarrel with the leading astrologer in England, William Lilly. The contention lasted three years, 1652-1653-1654. It began with a sermon of Gataker's on the text: "Learn not the way of the heathen, and be not dismayed at the signs of heaven; for the heathen are dismayed at them (*Jeremy* x, 2)." "Dr. Gataker," says Lilly, in his *Life,* "made a scandalous exposition, and, in express terms, hints at me, repeating verbatim from one of my former *Anglicus.* The substance of my epistle was that I did conceive the good angels of God did reveal astrology to mankind, etc. but he in his annotations called me blind buzzard, etc." The quarrel continued until "I was persuaded by Dr. Gauden, late Bishop of Exeter, to let him alone; but in my next year's *Anglicus* in August observations, I wrote '*Hac in tumba presbyter et nubulo,*' in which very month he died." [44]   Lilly had no objection, however, to acknowledging his professional debt to the clergy. When he was but a beginner in astrology, he looked up to William Breden, "a profound divine, but absolutely the most polite person for nativities in that age." [45]   In 1632 he learned astrology of "one Evan, a minister in Staffordshire." [46]   Later he was much indebted to a collection of works on astrology, made by a Mr. A. Bedwell, minister of Tottenham high-cross. After his death, his library was sold, and from it Lilly acquired

[41] Acts xix, 19.
[42] Calamy : *Abridg.,* II, 413.
[43] Wood : *Ath. Ox.,* IV, 348.
[44] Lilly : *Hist., etc.,* p. 80ff.
[45] *Ibid.,* p. 35.
[46] Wood : *Ath. Ox.,* I, 36.

what he referred to as "my choicest books of astrology." [47]
The most conspicuous inclusion among Lilly's *Collection of
ancient and modern Prophecies Concerning these present
Times, with Modest Observations thereon,* is his "Scheam"
for Archbishop Laud. His Inclination, Preferments, and
fatal Period are shown, with the position of the stars on
twenty occasions in his life, from the time when he went
as a poor scholar to Oxford to his death on the scaffold.
The book was published the year after Laud's death. [48]

John Butler, who was chaplain to that important person,
the Duke of Ormond, was a specialist in astrology. He, like
Gataker, entered into a controversy regarding fine points
of interpretation, his opponent being a brother clergyman,
Dr. Henry More, the Platonist. [49] William Oughtred included astrology among his many avocations. His son Ben
was confident his father understood magic, a belief shared
by Aubrey who says that Oughtred was "very lucky in
giving his judgments on nativities; he would say that he did
not understand the reason why it should be so, but so it
would happen; he did beleeve that some genius or spirit
did help." [50] Robert Burton was a calculator of nativities,
and the story goes that he foretold his own death (by calculations) "and was suspected of making the prediction
come true." [51]

Of course the gentlemen of the cloth wrote books on
astrology and allied subjects. Joshua Childrey published
in 1652, his *Indago Astroloica; or, a brief and modest Inquiry into some principal Points of Astrology.* [52] On hear-
say evidence we learn "that Bishop Fell intended to have
printed all fryar Bacon's pieces in two volumes in folio." [53]
John Geree wrote a book, in 1646, against astrology,
Astrologo-mastix; [54] and Seth Ward denounced astrology,
calling it "that gullery." [55] Ward was answering John

[47] Lilly : *op. cit.,* pp. 28-9.
[48] *Op. cit.,* p. 52ff.
[49] Wood : *Ath. Ox.,* III, 373.
[50] *Ibid.,* II, 653.
[55] *Vindiciae Academiarum,* pp. 30-1.

[51] *Ibid.,* III, 903.
[52] Wood : *Ath. Ox.,* III, 902.
[53] *Reliq. Hearnae,* II, 153.
[54] Wood : *op cit.,* III, 245.

Webster, who in his *Academiarum Examen* had dared to reproach the universities with slighting, neglecting, and scoffing at astrology, though it is "so noble and beneficial a science." [56] Thomas Hall also answers Webster, and also scorns his belief in astrology, especially condemning his admiration for "that lying, rayling, ignorant Wizard, Ly-ly, who hath not only reviled the most learned and Reverend Mr. Gataker, with the Orthodox Ministry of the land . . ." but both Church and State.[57] Fuller, too, is opposed to it. When he is listing the qualities that should be possessed by "the General Artist," he says sweepingly: "as for judicial astrology which hath the least judgment in it, this vagrant hath been whipped out of all learned corporations." [58]

This quotation is taken from Fuller's Holy and Profane *Characters,* published in 1642. It is impossible that he should not at that time have known some astrologers who were respected as dignified, learned men. The Society of Astrologers was a recognized body of scholars; as such they invited ministers to preach before them, and these men, judging by the forewords of the printed sermons, were much complimented by the invitation. Certainly Robert Gell had no misgivings regarding the propriety of his act when he preached "before the learned Society of Astrologers," August 1, 1649. His dedicatory epistle expresses his appreciation of the honor done him not only in the request for a sermon, but in the insistence that he print it. The quarto bears the title: *Stella Nova, a New Starre, Leading wisemen unto Christ.* . . . It was sold "at the Signe of the Sun on Garlick-Hill." The sermon itself is appropriate but not interesting. Mr. Gell says that God governs the world "by the influence of the Starrs and Angells, which, I believe makes much for the glory of God, because thereby

---

[56] *Op. cit.,* p. 51.
[57] *Histrio-Mastix,* p. 207.
[58] *Holy and Profane State,* p. 58. (Sidrophel, in *Hudibras,* embodies all the undesirable traits of the seventeenth-century astrologer.)

his mighty power is made known. . . ." And he quotes the
wise men of the East led by a Star; the stars in their
courses that fought against Sisera; the heavens that de-
clare the glory of God—all the apposite texts. That sermon
is an honest, intelligent piece of work. It has been spoken
of at some length because it shows a dignified attitude
toward the better class of astrologers; except for that fact
it has no secular interest. Yet another sermon of far less
promising appearance turns out to be delightful and worldly
reading. It is by Dr. Nathanael Ingelo, and it was
preached "before the University of Cambridge, at the
Commencement, July 4, 1658." When printed, it bore the
title, *The Perfection, Authority, and Credibility of the Holy
Scriptures*. A wayfaring reader might be excused for putting that sermon aside as deserving to be read by title only.
But even the opening line is worth while: "Parables are
vocall Hieroglyphicks, lively images of usefull Truths;
fitted for instruction."

Dr. Ingelo denounces Porphyry (whose antichristian activities had ceased in the fourth century), and in a work-
manlike manner answers his arguments, especially one
touching Apollonius Tyanaeus whom the very long dead
Porphyry had extolled. All of that is conventional enough.
But under cover of exposing ancient iniquities, the preacher
tells this sort of thing: "Among his Magical devices I
reckon his seven rings, which he called after the names of
the seven Planets, which he wore each day differently
according to the name of the Planet which the day bore.
These he received of the Indians, whom Philostratus con-
fesses Magicians, and tells many pretty stories of them,
as of their Tables, which moved of themselves, and brought
in dinner of bread, fruits, and herbs, which put themselves
in order, better than any Cook could do. As also of their
Cisterns, two of wine, and two of water; one hot, one cold,
which came into the Dining-room of themselves, and of little
pages of black brass, which mingled the wine with water,

also of two Hogs-heads, one filled with water, another with wind. . . ." [59]

John Selden had been dead four years when this sermon was preached; had he heard it, he would have been even more convinced of the truth of his assertion: "There never was a merry World since the Fairies left Dancing, and the Parson left conjuring." [60] Selden, we remember, had no spiritual responsibilities. Anthony Burgess did, and he devoted one of his one hundred and forty-five sermons on the seventeenth chapter of John to this matter of conjuring: Sermon LXXV: *That the Scripture might be fulfilled (Joh. 17. 12) Against Judicial Astrology and Witchcraft.*

It was the belief that Scripture authorized the study of the stars, that led Richard Carpenter to preach a sermon which he published under the title: *Astrology Proved Harmless, Useful, Pious.* This sermon was delivered before the Honorable Society of Astrologers, from the text, "And let them be for Signs . . ." (Gen. i, 14); and the dedicatory epistle was addressed to the noted astrologer and scholar, Elias Ashmole (*Doctissimo Domino et Amico meo, etc.*). The quarto has thirty-six pages, the margins of which bristle with references to the Bible (of course), and to authorities of unimpeachable respectability such as Plato, Josephus, Seneca, Jerome, and Aquinas. The reader is assured that since the children of Seth made "diligent and ferverous enquiry into the stars," it is "probable, if not evident, That Adam had authorized the Work, and plained their path before them." Carpenter went on to say: "We may lawfully, and without impeachment of our Duty, enquire into the Nature, Motions, and Actions of the Angels: therefore we may lawfully and without infringement of our obligations, enquire into the Nature, Motions and Actions of the Heavenly Bodies. . . ." ". . . Scripture cannot be rightly understood without enquiry into Astrology," as those texts which treat of lunatick persons.[61] John Swan, most

[59] Pp. 96-9.   [60] *Table Talk*, p. 119.   [61] Pp. 4, 19.

respected preacher of sermons and student of chronology, also defended Astrology: "For pure Astrology and unde-filed," he says in his *Signa Coeli*, "will observe no such times as may bring any dishonor unto God, and yet it may observe times too." It is ignorance and superstition, he feels, that have brought astrology into ill repute.[62]

Chemistry

Chemistry was a declared avocation of only a few eccle-siastics. That the number was not larger is accounted for by the fact that a tincture of black art still clung to the study, and by the more practical explanation that "elabo-ratories" were rare. Charles Hotham was a "searcher into the Secrets of Nature, and much addicted to Chymistry." [63] William Oughtred worked ambitiously over chemical ex-periments and "told John Evelyn . . . not above a year before he dyed, that if he were but five yeares (or three yeares) younger, he doubted not to find the philosopher's stone. He used to talk much of the mayden earth for the philosopher's stone. It was made of the harshest cleare water that he could gett, which he lett stand to putrify, and evaporated by simmering. Ben (his son) tended the fur-naces." [64] Evelyn testifies directly: "Came that renowned mathematician, Mr. Oughtred to see me. . . . Amongst other discourse, he told me he thought water to be the philosopher's first matter, and that he was well persuaded of the possibility of their elixir; he believed the sun to be a natural fire, the moon a continent, as appears by the late Selenographers. . . ." [65]

Thomas Vaughan (twin brother of Henry Vaughan), after being "disturbed in his rectory," retired to Oxford

[62] P. 24.
[63] Calamy: *Abridg.*, II, 413. Also, Samuel Ogden: "He could readily tell you what had been said by the several parties among Philosophers to solve the several Phenomena about Fire, Gravity, etc.," *ibid.*, 193.
[64] Aubrey: II, 109-10.
[65] *Diary*, August 28, 1655.

"where he became a very Eminent Chymist. . . . He was a zealous brother of the Rosie Crusian Fraternity." [66] Vaughan (who always wrote as Eugenius Philalethes) published in 1650, *Magia Adamica; or the Antiquity of Magic and the Descent thereof from Adam downward proved*. He did not feel that there was any contradiction between his religious and scientific activities; indeed, he found it quite possible to regard them as one. "Magic," he explained, "is impiety with many but religion with me. . . . Magic is nothing but the wisdom of the Creator revealed and planted in the creature. . . . Magicians were the first attendants our Saviour met withal in this world." [67] A tradition says that Vaughan died by an explosion in the course of chemical experiments.

Stephen Marshall, in his sermon, *Reformation and Desolation*, took a practical view of such studies. He considered them harmless, even praiseworthy, because of "what learned men say of them who have studied for the Philosophers stone, though they could never find out the Elixar; yet in their search after it they found out many excellent thinges, admirably usefull for mankinde. . . ." [68] The Duke of Newcastle had a sympathetic assistant in "Dr. Payne, a divine and my chaplain, who hath a very witty, searching brain of his own, being at my house at Bolsover, locked up with me in a chamber to make Lapis Prunellae, which is saltpetre and brimstone inflamed. . . ." [69] Ezrael Tongue "spent much time and money in the art of alchemy"; [70] and the preacher of his funeral sermon "sayes that he haz left two tomes in folio of alchymie. His excellency lay there." [71] John Thornborough "was much commended for his skill in Chymistry,

---

[66] Walker: Pt. II, 389.
[67] *Works* (ed. A. E. Waite), pp. 121, 132.
[68] P. 28.
[69] Newcastle, Margaret: *Life of the Duke of Newcastle*, p. 200. See Robert Boyle (*Works*, I, 93ff.): "the noblest of Metals may be Mechanically transmuted."
[70] Wood: *op. cit.*, III, 1262.   [71] Aubrey: II, 261.

a study but seldom followed in his time; and 'tis thought by some helps from it it was that he attained to so great an age." [72]   Wallis experimented with gunpowder, and compared it with lightning; he "considered their effects so similar, that they might, without hesitation, be ascribed to the same cause"—a view that was also held by Sir Thomas Browne.[73]

In 1649, "J. H." complained (in his *Humble Motion to Parliament*) that at the University there was "no chimestry which hath snatcht the keys of nature from the other sects of philosophy. . . ." [74]   In 1663, Wood says there was a "Chimical Club" which flourished at Oxford "under the noted chimist and rosicrucian, Peter Sthael of Strasburgh." [75]   In the group, besides Anthony à Wood, were Francis Turner (later, Bishop of Ely) and Benjamin Woodroffe (later, canon of Christ Church).   An earlier class had included Dr. Ralph Bathurst (a physician and, afterward, Dean of Wells), Nathaniel Crew (afterward, Bishop of Durham), and John Wallis who achieved distinction in mathematics, not chemistry.

Law

An ecclesiastic of any real importance, living in the uncertain times of the Commonwealth and the Restoration, would have found it essential to know something of the civil as well as of the church law.   His own rights and those of his party were constantly subject to criticism or attack. To be certain of just how far he or his opponent might go, legally, was useful information.   Even more surely did the parson of no importance, who had no influential friends and no money, who lived and served in some isolated parish,

---

[72] Wood: *Ath. Ox.*, III, 4.
[73] *Works of Sir Thomas Browne,* I, 178 (Note).
[74] P. 27.
[75] Wood: *Ath. Ox.*, I, lii-liii.   (Robert Boyle brought Sthael to Oxford in 1659.)   Wood says, "This P. Sthael who was a Lutheran and a great hater of women, was a very useful man . . ." (I, lii).

have need of a knowledge of many simple points of law
if he were to protect himself and advise his ignorant people. "The Countrey Parson," George Herbert had written,
"desires to be all to his parish, and not only a pastour, but
a lawyer also and a phisitian." [76]

Among the clergymen who gave attention to matters of
law were some who held degrees in law, some who gave advice informally (as many did in medicine), and others who
were well read in legal works, finding the subject one of
abstract interest.

Dr. Thomas Barlow was "so profoundly Learned, both
in Divinity, and the Civil, and Canon Law; that he was
often applied to as a casuist, to resolve Cases of Conscience
about Marriage. . . ." [77] Mr. Benlows became (after the
1662 ejectments) a counselor at Law, and a Justice of the
Peace.[78] Christopher Elderfield (private chaplain to Sir
William Goring) was "well read in the civil, canon and common law. . . ." He wrote: *The Civil Rights of Tithes*
(1650).[79] William Fuller held a degree of Doctor of Laws;
afterwards he became Bishop of Limerick, and, later, of
Lincoln.[80] Bishop Juxton, in his youth, took first a bachelor's and then a doctor's degree in law.[81] William Parsons
(ejected by the Puritans, but after the Restoration, Vicar
of Great Dumnow in Essex) was a bachelor of law.[82] Dr.
William Paul was "a shrewd man in business, whether of
Trade, Husbandry, Buying and Improving Land, Disposing
of Money; carrying a great command over the factions about
him by his money (which he could lend to advantages, to
the most considerable men of that party) in those sad times,
when others of his Order submitted to them; exceedingly
well versed in the Laws of the Church and land. . . ." [83]
Dr. John Richardson, Bishop of Ardagh, was "as good and

[76] *A Priest to the Temple*, p. 258 ("The Parson's Completenesse").
[77] *Dr. Barlow's Genuine Remains*, p. 351.
[78] Calamy: *Abridg.*, II, 513.   [80] *Ibid.*, *Fasti*, II, 231.
[79] Wood: *Ath. Ox.*, III, 336-7.   [81] Lloyd: *State Worthies*, p. 1038.
[82] Wood: *Fasti*, II, 231.
[83] Lloyd: p. 611.

dexterous a Lawyer as Clerk, he compounded Differences, discharged Annuities and Pensions." [84] Matthew Robinson "understood the common and statute law . . . was a judge of good estates." [85] Robert Sharrock became "at length archdeacon of Winchester . . . being then accounted learned in divinity, in the civil and common law, and very knowing in vegetables, and all pertaining thereto." [86] Edward Stillingfleet "applied himself much to the study of the law and records, and the original of our constitution. . . ." [87] Richard Stuart was a doctor of laws "and afterwards a noted divine, and Eloquent Preacher. . . ." [88] Joseph Trueman "had a good share of skill, not only in the Statute and Common Law, but also in the Civil." [89] Richard Whitlock was a bachelor of the civil law, and did not take orders until after the Restoration.[90] Henry Willes was "of great skill in the Law." [91]

Languages

To the seventeenth-century preacher, Latin was a necessity, Greek a convenience, Hebrew and Arabic a desirable acquisition, and other languages a means to scholarly ends. Even in boyhood, Latin became a familiar medium of speech; it constituted the first step toward entrance into the learned professions; and it was a useful means of communication when traveling abroad or when receiving distinguished foreigners in England. Latin, moreover, was still the conventional vehicle for a university address or

[84] Lloyd: p. 607.
[85] *Autobiography*, pp. 52-3; see, too, Thomas Hill (Palmer: II, 489) and Edward Moore (Palmer: I, 217).
[86] Wood: *Ath. Ox.*, IV, 147.
[87] Burnet: *Hist. of his own Times*, p. 129.
[88] Walker: Pt. II, 48.
[89] Nelson: *Life of Bull*, p. 205; Calamy: *Life, etc.*, II, 528.
[90] Wood: *op. cit.*, III, 984.
[91] Calamy: *Abridg.*, II, 496.
Sir Simon Degge published in 1676, *The Parson's Counsellor, with the Law of Tithing.* Book I shows what makes a man legally a Parson, Vicar, etc. Book II concerns Tithes, Mortuaries . . . (The tithes include bees, pigeons, fish, etc.).
See Coate: *Social Life in Stuart England, passim.*

sermon, and the disputations were commonly conducted in
Latin. A grammar-school boy was also drilled in writing
Latin until he could compose not only readily but according
to classical standards, because many works were printed in
Latin, and also because a correspondence with learned
men abroad would be carried on in that language.[92]
Richard Carpenter added an irritable postscript to a work
of his, placidly entitled *The Perfect Law of God,* which
reads: "If any Man be griev'd at aught I have here written, and cannot subdue his grief from festering into a
Quarrel: I desire that his Answer may be returned in
Latin. First, Because I will not enter the Lists with any
Adversary, but a Scholar, and Secondly, Because I will not
be Sea-bounded, and judg'd concerning my future Discourse, by an Iland. . . ." Francis Cheynell has by no
means the same feeling that a man ignorant of Latin is
unworthy his attention. *Sions Memento and Gods Alarum*
is preceded by a deprecatory epistle to the Courteous
Reader: ". . . in the book you will meet with much Latine
which is not translated, yet if you turn over but the first
foure or five leaves, you may without the help of Latine, if
you read attentively, pick out the scope of the book; some
questions were scholasticall and would not beare English,
some are full of blasphemies, others there are that will seem
superfluous to any but a scholar, who delights to know
every circumstance." [93] Baxter, unashamed, says that he
had no great skill in languages. He excuses himself for not
writing *The Reformed Pastor* in Latin: "If the ministers
of England had sinned only in Latin, I would have made
shift to admonish them in Latin, or else have said nothing to
them; but if they will sin in English, they must hear of
it in English." [94]

[92] See "John Warren" in Palmer: *Nonconf. Mem.,* I, 507, on colloquial use of Latin. "The ministers in his neighborhood [Hatfield]
held monthly meetings for Latin sermons and disputations, and de-
terminations . . . which might have entertained an academical
auditory."
[93] *Autobiog.,* p. 9.   [94] Pp. iii-iv.

A foundation in Greek was usually laid in the grammar school, with the result that some boys could speak Greek as easily as they did Latin.[95] This ability, however, was rare; a knowledge of Greek was common, but there was little practical use of it as a spoken language. Wood tells a story of a London merchant, "with a long beard and haire over-grown," who came to Oxford, "faigning himself a Patriarch," and John Harmar, the Greek professor of the university, "appeared very formally and made a greek harangue before him. Whereupon some of the company who knew the design to be waggish, fell a laughing and betrayed the matter. . . . Mr. Will Lloyd, then living in Wadham college in the quality of tutor, was the author of the trick." [96] Calamy relates much the same story, substituting "the pretended Archbishop of Samos" for the Patriarch, and making him visit Samuel Ogden "who entertained him in the Greek Tongue." [97] Either tale serves as evidence that there were English divines who could talk Greek as well as read and write it.

Hebrew might also be a part of a curriculum at a school such as Westminster or St. Paul's.[98] An intending clergyman sometimes reached the university well equipped in the three languages that led the way to a degree in divinity. John Pell, for instance, "at thirteen yeares and a quarter old . . . went as good a scholar to Cambridge, to Trinity College, as most Masters of Arts in the University. (He understood Latin, Greek, and Hebrew.)" [99]

But a man of really scholarly inclinations considered those three tongues but the beginning of an acquaintance

[95] Watson, Foster: *The English Grammar Schools to 1660*, pp. 5-6. John Rowe "had such a knowledge of Greek that he began very young to keep a Diary in that language," Palmer: I, 142. Mr. Richard Blackerby kept three diaries: one in Greek, one in Latin, one in English (Clark: *Geographicall Des.*, p. 63).

[96] Wood: *Ath. Ox.*, I, xxxviii.

[97] Calamy: *Account, etc.*, II, 192.

[98] Watson, Foster: *The English Grammar Schools to 1660*, p. 528; *Autobiography of Matthew Robinson*, pp. 87, 96, 97; Hoole: *New Discovery, etc.*, Ch. III, 214ff.

[99] Aubrey: II, 122.

with ancient languages. Mr. John Gregory knew, in addition to the ordinary trio, "Syriac, Chaldee, Arabick, Aethiopick, etc." [100] He owed, he declared, his introduction to oriental learning to "John Dod, the decaloguist, whose society and directions for the Hebrew tongue, he enjoy'd one vacation at his benefice in Northamptonshire." [101] Dr. Thomas Comber was "dexterous in Hebrew, Arabick, Coptick, Samaritane, Syriac, Chaldee, Persian, Greek, Latine . . . great abilities very much sweetened by his great Modesty and Humility." [102] Mr. George Bindon "improv'd his Knowledge in the Latin, Greek, Hebrew, Chaldee, and Syriack Tongues, to an exacter degree than is common." [103] The learned Henry Jessey had a more than ordinary acquaintanceship with Syriac and Chaldee when he left the university, besides being (one may say, of course) well versed in Greek, Latin, and Hebrew; he continued his studies when he was private chaplain to a gentleman in Suffolk, and did not lay aside his scholarly investigations when he became a Baptist minister, with all the persecution and controversy pertaining thereto.[104] Manasseh ben Israel, the great Jewish divine, knew Hebrew, Latin, Dutch, Spanish, and English; [105] Dr. John Conant "knew most of the Oriental languages and was particularly well versed in Syriac." [106] Robert Baillie knew thirteen languages; Ephraim Pagit knew fifteen or sixteen. And of Dr. William Fuller, Lloyd says magniloquently, ". . . those Languages which parted at Babel in a confusion, met in his soul in a method." [107]

Other well-known orientalists were: Robert Baillie,[108] Thomas Cawton,[109] Samuel Clarke,[110] Thomas Gataker

[100] Lloyd : p. 86. (John Johnson had "much studied the Egyptian hieroglyphics," Palmer : I, 197.)
[101] Wood : *Ath. Ox.*, III, 205.
[102] Lloyd : pp. 447-8.
[103] Calamy : *Abridg.*, II, 602.
[104] Neal : *Hist. of the Puritans*, II, 253.
[105] *Jewish Encyclopedia; Dict. Nat'l Biog.*
[106] *Biog. Brit.*, I, 436.
[107] Lloyd : p. 509.　　　　[109] Palmer : *Nonconf. Mem.*, I, 196.
[108] *Dict. Nat'l Biog.*　　　[110] Wood : *Ath. Ox.*, III, 1108.

("the ablest man of the whole synod of divines in the oriental tongues," says William Lilly),[111] Dr. Thomas Hyde,[112] John Lightfoot,[113] Narcissus Marsh,[114] Samuel Ogden,[115] Wm. Outram,[116] John Owen,[117] William Pell,[118] Christian Ravis (who was invited by Usher from Berlin, and who taught Orientals in Gresham College, London, in 1642),[119] Lazarus Seaman,[120] and Thomas Vaughan.[121]

An Arabic lectureship was founded at Oxford by Archbishop Laud in 1636, Edward Pocock being the first reader of the Arabic lecture. The next year, Laud sent Pocock to Constantinople "to seek for books of the Eastern tongues, and to improve his knowledge of them." [122] During his absence, Dr. Pocock deputed Thomas Greaves to read the Arabic lecture, this clergyman, also, being an authority on Oriental languages.[123] Richard Heath was, on the authority of Calamy, "one of the Greatest Masters of the Age" in the Oriental tongues, especially in Syriac and Arabic.[124] James Lamb wrote a *Grammatica Arabica* and other studies of Arabic words and constructions.[125]

John Reynier, a brilliant young divine who died in early manhood, thought Arabic valuable as an aid to the understanding of the Scriptures; [126] naturally that consideration does explain in part the interest that was taken in Eastern

[111] Lilly: *Hist. of His Life, etc.*, p. 80.
[112] Wood: *op. cit.*, III, 523.
[113] Masson: *Milton*, VI, 295.   [115] Calamy: *Abridg.*, II, 192.
[114] *Dict. Nat'l Biog.*   [116] *Dict. Nat'l Biog.*
[117] Calamy: II, 53. "Mr. Wood, the Oxonian, after some Reflections that are as Black as the Vapours of the Infernal Cell, where they were forg'd, thinks fit to own, That the Doctor was a Person well skill'd in the Tongues, Rabbinical Learning, and Jewish Rites and Custons. . . ."
[118] *Ibid.*, p. 289.   [120] Calamy: *op. cit.*, p. 16.
[119] Wood: *op. cit.*, IV, 591.   [121] Wood: *op. cit.*, III, 723.
[122] Wood: *op. cit.*, IV, 318ff. (Edmund Castle was professor of Arabic at Cambridge in 1661.)
[123] Walker: Pt. II, 112. (On the death of Pocock, in 1691, Thomas Hyde became Arabic lecturer, having long been recognized as an authority on that language. Wood: *op. cit.*, IV, 523.)
[124] Calamy: *op. cit.*, II, 548.   [125] Wood: *op. cit.*, III, 668.
[126] Calamy: *Abridg.*, II, 84. See *Ichabod*, p. 22: "How do you think poor souls can clear divine truths, lying hid in the depths, darkness and ambiguity of Original words, without skill in Languages?"

languages by clergymen who were sincerely anxious to understand completely the Word of God which they preached so conscientiously and so continuously. But not all those who could speak with authority thought the study of Arabic necessary or even advisable. Abraham Wheelock, who held the Arabic lectureship established in Cambridge by Sir Thomas Adams,[127] was definitely discouraging when Isaac Barrow and Samuel Sprint went "to discourse with him about the Arabick Language, which they were desirous to learn: But upon hearing how great Difficulties they were to encounter, and how few Books there were in that Language, and the little Advantage that could be got by it, they laid aside their Design." [128] Usher told Evelyn that it was a great loss of time to give much study to Eastern languages; "that, except Hebrew, there was little fruit to be gathered of exceeding labour; that, besides some mathematical books, the Arabic itself had little considerable. . . ." [129]

Hebrew

The Arabic specialist, Edward Pocock, was also extraordinarily learned in Hebrew, and he became professor of Hebrew at Oxford in 1648. So great was his reputation, that he was left undisturbed at the time of the university ejectments in 1654, John Owen and other Puritans testify-

---

[127] ". . . he hath served the University of Cambridge by erecting an Arabick Lecture. . . ." N. Hardy: *The Royal Common-Wealths Man*, Lond., 1668, p. 37. Also, Fuller: *Hist. of the Univ. of Camb.*, etc., p. 231: "Thomas Adams (thou citizen, since lord mayor) of London . . . founded an Arabian Scholarship, on condition it were frequented with competency of auditors. And, notwithstanding the general jealousy that this new Arabia (happy, as all novelties at the first) would soon become desert; yet it seems, it thrived so well, that the salary was settled on Abraham Wheelock. . . ."
Wheelock's successor, Edmund Castell, aroused less enthusiasm. It is said that in the third year of his occupation of the chair, he found his lectures much neglected. Finally, he posted up on the Schools' gate: *Arabicae linguae professor cras ibit in desertum* (Wordsworth: *Scholae Acad.*, p. 163).
[128] Calamy: *op. cit.*, II, 340.
[129] *Diary*, Aug. 21, 1655.

ing to Pocock's great value to learning.[130] It was before a group of nonconformists of less education that Christopher Hindle was summoned for examination, and "being an excellent Scholar and particularly well vers'd in the Hebrew Tongue, he most shamefully exposed them." [131] Joseph Cooper's "chief Excellency lay in the Hebrew Tongue"; he used this knowledge primarily to interpret the Hebrew text of the Scriptures; "he read the Masorah, and other Jewish and Rabinical Commentaries as if they had been in Latin." [132] Dr. Nathanael Ball willingly gave instruction "in the Hebrew and Oriental Languages, in which there were few that equall'd, and scarce any that exceeded him. With the greatest Ease in the World would he offhand, render any Part of the Hebrew Bible into proper English." [133] Robert Burhill (or Burghill) was "right learned and well grounded in the Hebrew tongue," and so firm was his reputation even in his youth for an exact knowledge of ancient languages, that Walter Raleigh sought aid from him whenever *The History of the World* needed an explanation of Hebrew or Greek quotations.[134] Jacob Houblon (the clergyman son of the conspicuously successful merchant family of that name) knew Hebrew as well as Greek and Latin.[135] The gifted and cultured anabaptist, John Tombes, was a Hebrew scholar, although his greatest proficiency lay in the Greek.[136] Richard Crashaw knew Hebrew, Greek, and Latin.[137] Richard Blackerby was reckoned one of the

---

[130] See Owen's letter to Thurloe (March 20, 1654/5); *Coll. of State Papers*, III, 281.
   Wood: *Ath. Ox.*, IV, 318. (Dr. James Duport, though not a presbyterian, remained professor of Greek at Cambridge during the Civil War. He was, however, asked to resign in 1654. Mullinger: *Camb. in the 17th Cent.*, pp. 181-2.)
[131] Walker: Pt. II, 268.
[132] Calamy: *Life, etc.*, II, 767. See, too, Thomas Cawton, Palmer: *Nonconf. Mem.*, I, 196.
   Zachary Bogan published in 1658 a comparison of Homer with the Hebrew text of the Scriptures. He wrote in Latin but gave all his illustrations in Hebrew and Greek.
[133] *Ibid.*, p. 363. (Milton in his tract *On Education*, advises that Hebrew be gained so far as to read the Scriptures in the original.)
[134] Wood: *Ath. Ox.*, III, 18.   [136] Aubrey: II, 258.
[135] *The Houblon Family*, p. 191.   [137] Wood: *Fasti*, II, 15.

best Hebricians in Cambridge; [138] Timothy Roberts was famous for his skill in that tongue; [139] and Ralph Cudworth made profound studies in Hebrew writings, the results of which he gave to the world in a Latin treatise "of a polemicall nature." [140] Francis Potter had merely "a competent knowledge of Hebrew, but not a critique." [141] Dr. Humphrey Prideaux, too, did not meet the highest standards of scholarship, being, in the opinion of Dr. Henry Aldrich, "an unaccurate muddy-headed man." Prideaux's chief skill was supposed to be in "Orientals, and yet even there he was far from perfect . . . unless in Hebrew, which he was well versed in." [142] Probably a number of these preachers agreed with Fuller: "Hebrew is a language which Hierome himself got with great difficulty, and kept with constant use (skill in Hebrew will quickly go out, and burn no longer than it is blown). . . ." [143] When Francis Osborne wrote his *Advice to a Son,* he said, under Religion, that: "a Prosecution of the Oriental Tongues (beyond an ability to understand them) is like Musick or Fencing, unable to requite the time they consume: Hebrew being observed to grow for the most part in Soils apter to produce Roots than Flowers. . . ." [144]

One explanation of the wide interest in Eastern languages lies in the plan and execution of the Polyglot Bible. [145] The scheme of the arrangement belongs largely to Brian Walton, but other scholarly ecclesiastics gave him advice. Evelyn writes, under the date of November 22, 1653, "I went to Londin, where was proposed to me the promoting that great work (since accomplished by Dr. Walton, Bishop of Chester) *Biblia Polyglotta,* by Mr. Pierson, that most learned divine." Usher advised Walton, so did his father-in-law, William Fuller, Dr. Bruno Ryves, and Dr. Juxton. Nine

[138] Clark : *Em. Lives,* p. 57.
[139] Palmer : *Nonconf. Mem.,* II, 495.
[140] Thurloe : *State Papers,* VII, 593.
[141] Aubrey : II, 164.   [143] *Holy and Profane State,* p. 26.
[142] *Reliq. Hearnae,* III, 157.   [144] P. 83.
[145] Burnet : *Hist. of his own Times,* p. 131.

languages were used, but every part did not appear in Latin, Hebrew, Syriac, Chaldee, Samaritan, Arabic, Aethiopic, Persic, and Greek. Each language, whenever employed, had its own Latin translation joined to it. A number of preacher-specialists corrected the text of those languages in which they were particularly well informed, as: Edmund Castle, Samuel Clark, Henry Ferne, Thomas Greaves, Richard Heath, Thomas Hyde, Edward Pocock, David Stokes, Herbert Thorndyke, Abraham Wheelock, and Thomas Winniffe.[146]

The *Prefatio* gives due credit to those scholars who revised the texts, or wrote learned explanations. In the *Prolegomena* is an essay, *De linguarum natura, origine, divisione, numero, mutationibus, et usu*, which explains the origin of language as being divine, not in any way natural to man. *De lingua Hebraica* discusses man's first speech, which was presumably Hebrew.[147] The stupendous undertaking was encouraged by Cromwell to whom, very properly, it was planned to dedicate the work. Cromwell died before the publication of the six folio volumes was completed, and Walton cannily canceled two leaves of grateful and admiring acknowledgment to Cromwell, substituting others which extolled the virtues of Charles II.

Anglo-Saxon

The love of knowledge for its own sake, and the habit of searching and researching for scripture sources, led some of these men, naturally enough, to the Fathers in Anglo Saxon, and to the early history of the British isles. Archbishop Usher's name at once suggests the famous "Chronology," but he was connected as participant or patron with most of the scholarly enterprises of his day, and with many

[146] Walker: Pt. II, 22ff.
[147] Vol. VI.
See also: Heylin's argument with Fuller, regarding Adam's probable use of Hebrew (*Appeal of Injured Innocence*, p. 398ff.) ; Wilkins on the origin of language (*Real Character*, Pt. I, p. 2).

of the political ones as well.[148] He was a generous friend
to scholars and encouraged learning wherever he found it,
whether at home or abroad. His most interesting foreigner,
from the point of view of English scholarship, was Franciscus Junius. Junius had come to England in 1620, and
became librarian to the Earl of Arundel. Later, he went
to Oxford for the sake of the libraries, but especially for
contact with Dr. Thomas Marshall who was "a great critic
in the Gothic and Saxon languages." [149] By this time,
Junius had attracted the attention of Usher who thereafter
gave him much assistance. Before making his special study
of Anglo-Saxon, Junius had acquired "Gothic, Francic,
Cimbric or Runic, and Frisic," and he could, therefore,
appreciate the importance of his discovery in the Bodleian
and Cotton libraries, of "divers Saxon books of great antiquity." [150] With Usher's approval and assistance, Junius
published in Amsterdam (in 1655) the *Caedmonis Para-
phrases Poetica Geneseos.*[151] Dr. Abraham Wheelock was
another student who "discovered" the language of long-ago
England. In 1643 he published Bede's *Ecclesiastical History,* with the Anglo-Saxon version of King Alfred. Lloyd
says that the translation and learned Notes in this edition
"excelled in Greek." [152] In 1644, Sir Henry Spelman settled thirty pounds a year on Dr. Wheelock "to explain the
Saxon tongue publick in the University." [153]

Dr. John Fell's gift to Oxford of a type foundry, included "Saxons" as well as black-letter, Orientals, Roman
and Italic fonts.[154] Meric Casaubon planned an elaborate
study: *De quatuor Linguis Commentationis Pars prior;*

[148] Usher's "model," designed to make it possible for the presbyterian ministers to conform, and his other conciliatory propositions,
belong to the sectarian history of the time.
[149] Wood: *Ath. Ox.,* III, 1141.
[150] *Ibid.,* 1140.
[151] For other works, including the transcriptions of the Silver Codex
of Ulfilas (which he found in Holland), see Wood: *op. cit.,* 1138-
1143. For Marshall's work in Saxon and Gothic, his notes and glossa-
ries, see Wood: *op. cit.,* II, 121; IV, 171.
[152] Lloyd, p. 517; Petheran, p. 58.
[153] Lloyd, p. 517.
[154] Plomer: *Eng. Printing,* p. 214.

quae, de Lingua Hebraica: de Lingua Saxonica, etc.; but
he did not finish the other two languages, Greek and
Latin.[155] It was "by the advice and persuasion of Dr.
Meric Casaubon," that William Somner began to study
Anglo-Saxon. He found it extremely difficult,[156] although
he knew "Gothic, German, Danish and other Northern
languages." In 1659, appeared his *Dictionarium Saxonico-
Latino-Anglicum*. The Saxon words are defined first in
English, then in Latin. Aelfric's Saxon Grammar is included, followed by a Latin glossary. The volume was well
equipped with introductory poems, praising Somner as "the
great Restorer of the Saxon Tongue." His name offered
the chance for a conceit; for instance:

> Te somno, Somnere, premi cui dicere fas est?
> Testatur doctus te vigilare liber.

Another of the poems, signed Johannes de Bosco, says
frankly that the Dictionary will not find many readers:

> Hadd'st thou some Bible Dictionary made;
> A Concordance, or dealt in such like trade:
> Hadd'st thou some Gospel-truths, some common place
> Presented to this fighting-preaching race;
> Or to our sword-Divines assistance lent
> By Paraphrase, Expounding, or Comment:
> Thou mightest have (haply) found more Readers: now
> The many won't thy learned pains allow.

Somner quotes George Hicks as an authority in Anglo-
Saxon; Edward Stillingfleet refers to the "Gothic Eddas"
as source material in his *Origines Sacrae;* Charles Butler
published in 1633 an English Grammar containing a collection of Saxon and English words, with a comparison between the two languages.[157] John Wilkins made a study of

---

[155] Wood: *Ath. Ox.*, III, 937.
[156] *Life of Somner*, p. 22 (prefixed to his *Treatise of the Roman
Ports, etc.*).
[157] Petheram : p. 68.

language groups in his *Real Character;* he asserts that the Saxon is responsible for "the several Languages of the English, the Scots, the Frisians, and those on the North of Elve." [158]

John Wallis is much more definite. He knows something of the history of Anglo-Saxon in Britain,[159] and in his *Praxis Grammatica* analyzes the words of the Lord's Prayer, showing the derivation of each native English word from the Saxon, and its equivalent in other languages. The following is an example of Wallis's method.

> Pro *which* antiquatus dicebant *Whilk,* atque Scoti etiamnum, aut etiam *Quilk;* Anglo-saxones *Hwilk,* Dani *Hvilk,* Germani *Welch, Welche,* Belgae *Welk, Welke,* Galli *Quel, Quelle;* omnia a Latino *Quali;* sicut, a Quo, *who;* a Quando, *whan, when;* et forte a Quare, *where* and *where-fore.* Nam pro Latinorum Qu, posuerunt non raro Cambro-britanni Chw, Anglo-saxones *Hw,* et nos *Wh.*[160]

Welsh

Mr. Stephen Hughes was so much devoted to the study of Welsh that he printed Welsh books at his own charge, among them "the excellent Welsh poems of Mr. Rees Pritchard, Vicar of Llanymddfrid, which contain the Summary of Christian Duties in British Verse." So accurate was Mr. Hughes's knowledge of Welsh, that he was asked to assist in the correction of the Welsh Bible.[161] Stephen Marshall encourage Welsh by allotting £50 to Anthony Thomas for preaching in that language;[162] and Thomas Gouge engaged teachers at a penny, or two-pence a week to teach Welsh children English. John Davies gave

[158] P. 3.   [159] *Grammatica Lingua Anglicanae* (Ad Lectorem).
[160] Pp. 138-9. See also Petheram: *Hist. Sketch of . . . Anglo-Saxon Lit. in Eng.,* p. 49ff; Wordsworth: *Scholae Acad., etc.,* p. 159ff.
[161] Calamy : *Abridg.,* II, 718.
[162] Wood : *op. cit.,* II, 588. Thomas Gouge, at his own expense, had Welsh translations made from the Bible and other books (*Dict. Nat'l Biog.*) ; also, Clark: *Em. Persons,* pp. 204-5; Baxter: *Autob.,* pp. 249-50.

much time to ancient authors of Wales. He published his *Antiquae Linguae Britannicae nunc communiter dictae Cambro-Britannicae a suis Cymraecae vel Cambricae, ab aliis Wallicae Rudimenta,* etc., as early as 1621, a *Dictionarium Britannico-Latinum* in 1632, and at the time of his death in 1644 had the reputation of being "an indefatigable searcher into ancient scripts, and well acquainted with curious and rare authors." [163] Thomas Powell left an unpublished manuscript entitled *Fragmenta de Rebus Britannicis. A Short Account of the Lives, Manners, and Religion of the British Druids and the Bards, etc.*[164] Samuel Tapper "perfectly understood the Welsh language." [165] Heylin quarreled with Fuller about the Welsh language, though Fuller insisted that he intended only to honor Welsh when he said it was "no daughter or niece," but a mother and original language.[166] Heylin prided himself on his Welsh descent, and spoke of Welsh speech and history with the emphasis of one having authority.[167] Samuel Clark, in his *Geographicall Description,* with no suggestion of close acquaintance, comments cautiously on the language and people of Wales: "The Welsh Language is least mixed with foreign words of any used in Europe, but having many Consonants in it, is lesse pleasing. The People are cholerick and hasty, but very loving to each other." [168]

A knowledge of Welsh was not common, if one may judge from the hilarity that a Welsh inventory caused when the pious and scholarly Henry Newcome tried to read it to a group of friends.[169]

Irish

The Irish language attracted Archbishop Usher, not only because he found genuine enjoyment in struggling with any

[163] Wood: *op. cit.,* III, 508.
[164] *Dict. Nat'l Biog.*
[165] Palmer: *Nonconf. Mem.,* I, 284.
[166] *Appeal of . . . Innocence,* p. 396.
[167] *Cosmography,* p. 326.
[168] P. 106.
[169] *Diary,* May 1, 1662.

ancient language, but because he was a native of Ireland and knew something of the modern form of Irish. The man who did serious and definite work in the field of Irish history and language was Geoffrey Keating (Scathrun Ceitinn). Keating was a Roman Catholic priest, poet, and historian. He was also a forceful preacher, and there is a pleasant story that a lady became so angry because of what she considered to be a personal attack in one of his sermons, that she persuaded the President of Munster to enforce the Conformity Act, and drive Keating from the pulpit. The means she took to avenge a petty vanity worked altogether for good, because Keating, forbidden to preach and in hiding, devoted himself to his History of Ireland. The English authorities were, it appears, in sympathy with his project, because he wandered where he would in search of materials. This history includes a list of records and annals from which he drew his facts, and offers many delightful old and romantic tales that are woven with the history.[170] Narcissus Marsh, when Provost of Trinity College, Dublin, insisted that the Irish-born students should learn the Celtic language grammatically. Furthermore, he coöperated with Robert Boyle in preparing a translation of the Old Testament into Irish.[171] William Bedell, Bishop of Kilmore, learned Irish sufficiently to compose a grammar in that language. The New Testament and Prayer Book were already translated into Irish, which fact encouraged the Bishop to attempt the translation of the Old Testament. He made considerable progress in this scheme, being aided by a native Irishman named Murtagh King.[172]

Modern Languages

Modern languages, except for the convenience they afforded when a man traveled on the continent, were not

[170] Keating: *Hist. of Ireland* (ed. John O'Mahony), p. xiii. Eleanor Hull: *A Text Book of Irish Literature*, Pt. II. 133-42. [171] *Dict. Nat'l Biog.* [172] Burnet, J.: *Life of Bedell*, pp. 117, 118-9.

a prized intellectual possession among the seventeenth-century preachers. Nathanael Ball "spoke French so wel, that he has often been taken for a native Frenchman"; [173] and the same compliment was paid Herbert Palmer.[174] Archbishop John Williams also knew French well.[175] Isaac Barrow spoke "severall languages." [176] Thomas Comber was "dexterous" in French, Spanish, and Italian.[177] Richard Crashaw knew Italian and Spanish, ". . . whereof he had little use, yet he had the knowledge of them." [178] John Gregory had "a useful command of French, Italian, Spanish, and Dutch." [179] Jacob Houblon "was acquainted with Italian, and was a lover of Petrarch"; [180] Dr. Bargrave knew Italian so well, that Sir Henry Wotton left the bulk of his Italian library to him.[181] John Pell could speak and write Italian, French, Spanish, High-Dutch and Low-Dutch.[182]

Translations

The general knowledge of languages naturally brought about some work in translating. Quite as naturally, the majority of the translations were religious in subject matter; but a few examples of secular material will help to show the wide interests of divines who, tireless in the service of the church, yet found time to do other things. Edmund Chilmead turned into English Campanella's Latin *Discourse touching the Spanish Monarchy*. The book did not sell, and the resourceful publisher wrote "an epistle and caused this title to be printed and put before the remaining copies: *Thomas Campanella a Spanish Frier his*

173 Calamy: *Abridg., etc.*, II, 363.
174 Clark: *General Mar.*, p. 476.
175 Hacket: *Life of Williams*, p. 209.
176 Aubrey: I, 88; Wood: *Fasti*, **II, 178.**
177 Calamy: *op. cit.*, p. 363.
178 Wood: *Fasti*, II, 5.
179 Lloyd: p. 86.
180 *The Houblon Family*, 191.
181 Walton: *Lives* (Wotton).
182 Aubrey: II, 122.

Advice to the King of Spain, for the obtaining of the Universal Monarchy of the World." [183]

Thomas Hall published an English translation of the second book of Ovid's *Metamorphoses,* calling it, *Phaeton's Folly: or the Downfall of Pride.* Hall, who was a nonconformist schoolmaster and bachelor of Divinity, had a nice taste in titles; and when he put together, for professional purposes, an "Explanation and Grammatical Translation of the 13th Book of Ovid's Metamorphoses," he printed it as *Wisdom's Folly.*[184]

John Harmar reversed the usual process by changing from English into Latin James Howell's *A Treatise or Discourse concerning Ambassadors* [185] "and one or more of the plays of Margaret dutchess of Newcastle, for which he was well rewarded." [186] Jasper Mayne translated Donne's Latin epigrams into English for the 1652 edition of his poems. A letter from Thomas Hyde to Dr. Barwick, dated May 4, 1659, says: "I shall only tell you (that you may not believe that we have laid aside the thoughts of Books, and all good learning) that Dr. Creighton hath been these many Months in preparing the History of the Council of Florence in Greek, which he translates into Latin from a Copy which will be judged very authentick, and sure will be a Work very welcome to the World. . . ." [187]

From French into English, Chilmead translated, *A treatise of the Essence, Causes, Symptoms, Prognosticks, and Cure of Love, or Erotique Melancholy* (written by Jam. Ferrand, doctor of Physick).[188] Gilbert Wats translated Davila's *History of the Civil Wars of France* from Italian into English, but did not print it because "Charles Cotterell and William Aylesbury having had the start of him in that work," he felt it unnecessary to continue.[189]

[183] Wood : *Ath. Ox.,* III, 350-1.
[184] *Ibid., Fasti,* II, 219.
[185] *Ibid., Ath. Ox.,* III, 680.
[186] *Ibid.,* 920.
[187] Kennett, White, p. 14.
[188] Wood : *Ath. Ox.,* III, 350.
[189] *Ibid.,* 433.

Philology

Archbishop Usher, who may appropriately introduce a paragraph on almost any seventeenth-century topic, lay or clerical, recommended to Evelyn the study of philology above all human studies.[190] The word had a broader application than it has today. Fuller explains the term: "Indeed Philology properly is terse and Polite Learning, *melior literatura,* (married long since by Martianus Capella to Mercury) being that Florid shell, containing onely the Roses of learning, without the prickles thereof, in which narrow sense thorny Philosophy is discharged as no part of Philology. But we take it in the larger notion, as inclusive of all human liberal Studies, and preposed to Divinity, as the Porch to the Palace."[191] As a philologist, Robert Burton was declared to be "thro' pac'd,"[192] John Harmar to be "most excellent,"[193] Dr. Adam Littleton, "most exquisite."[194] Sometimes the word was applied to the compiler of a dictionary. Many of the schoolmasters prepared lexicons for the use of their pupils; other scholars were interested in definitions and English equivalents for foreign languages, preferably ancient languages. An unusual volume of the sort was *An English Greek Lexicon, containing the Derivations and various Significations of all the Words in the New Testament.* This work was published in 1661, all the contributors being nonconformists. John Wilkins wrote: *An Essay toward a real Character and a Philosophical Language,*[195] in which he proposes Hebrew as the groundwork for a universal language. He discusses Phonetics and gives a phonetic representation of the Creed and the Lord's Prayer. The author talks on many subjects connected with language. For example, language was

---

[190] *Diary,* August 21, 1655.
[191] *Worthies,* I, 26.
[194] Walker: Pt. II, 109.
[192] Wood: *Ath. Ox.,* II, 652.
[193] Calamy: *Account, etc.,* II, 339.
[195] An Oxford student, in 1668, paid 15s. for this book (*The Flemings at Oxford,* p. 440).

preserved by Noah and his family. A picture of the Ark is included, with a cross section showing a reasonable, if extremely compact, arrangement of the animals. Wilkins also wrote: *An Alphabetical Dictionary: wherein all English Words according to their various Significations are either referred to their places in the Philosophical Tables, or explained, etc.* Adam Littleton's *Linguae Latinae Liber Dictionarius Quadripartitus* follows this plan:

1. An English-Latin
2. A Latin-Classical
3. A Latin-Proper (Names)
4. (1) Latin-Barbarous
   (2) The Law Latin

Learning

Knowledge was necessary, many thought—those in the pew as well as those in the pulpit—to a profitable preaching of the Word of God. Anyone could read plainly written in Ecclesiastes: "And further, because the preacher was wise, he taught the people knowledge." Yet Chillingworth offers a warning in one of his sermons: ". . . knowledge be so dangerous a ware, (it is something like gunpowder; a man when he has it must take heed how he uses it) . . ." [196] An emphatic publication entitled *Ichabod: or, Five Groans of the Church* demands a learned clergy. The anonymous author says the preacher must know languages, history, for, "How is it possible for those poor creatures to understand sundry passages of Scripture depending upon propriety of words and idioms, or upon the Customs, Rites, Proverbs, Formes, Usages, Laws, Offices and Antiquities of the Assyrian, Persian, Greek and Roman Governments, without a competent portion of humane Learning?" [197] This outburst was published in 1663 and was directed against the divines of the established church. Almost twenty years

[196] Works, II, 563. [197] P. 22.

before, in 1645, Parliament had passed an Ordinance for
the Ordination of Ministers, that asserted: "Every Candidate must be 24 years of age, at least, and must be tried not
only in respect of piety, character, preaching ability, and
knowledge of divinity, but also in respect of skill in the
tongues and in Logic and Philosophy." [198]

Probably, candidates were accepted who did not meet all
these requirements; probably, too, there was, when *Ichabod*
was published, a large majority of preachers well informed
as to Semitic idioms and Assyrian peculiarities; but what
the two quotations show is that in the early days of the
Puritan régime and in the early years of the Restoration,
there was a like demand that only a thoroughly educated
man should serve the church as a preacher. So general was
the feeling that biographers of divines recognize the necessity of mentioning that a man is widely informed, saying
"he was a learned man" almost automatically. When the
writer adds something to his conventional statement, when
he shows in what way or to what degree a particular
preacher was learned, then one may be sure that man knew
more than most. Dr. John Gregory, in addition to his
ability in languages (he knew Latin, Greek, Hebrew,
Syriac, Chaldee, Arabick, Aethiopick, etc., Saxon, French,
Italian, Spanish and Dutch), had "a deep insight into
Philosophy, a curious faculty in Astronomy, Geometry and
Arithmetick, a familiar acquaintance with the Jewish
Rabbins, the Ancient Fathers, the Modern Cricks and
Commentators, a general History and Chronology, and indeed a Universal Learning." [199] Sometimes, the biographer
offers corroboration of his assertion, as, "Mr. John Lomax
was a man of great learning even in the Opinion of Bishop
Cosins. . . ."[200] When speaking of John Tombes—Tombes
was a conscientious, disputing Baptist—Aubrey includes as

[198] Nov. 8, 1645. See Masson: *Milton*, III, 398-9; Henry Thurman's *Defence of Humane Learning in the Ministry;* Reynolds's *A
Sermon Touching the Use of Humane Learning;* Thomas Hall's *Vindiciae Literarius.*
[199] Lloyd: p. 86ff.   [200] Calamy: *Abridg.*, II, 510.

evidence of the same fact, "Bishop Ward respected him for his learning." Furthermore, Robert Sanderson and Thomas Barlow were his friends.[201] Even a seventeenth-century anabaptist could not be ignored intellectually or socially with such support.

At other times the mention of a minister's possession of more than the common supply of learning, is combined with the notice of some trait of personality—Mr. Henry Newcome, for example (he of the delightful *Diary*): "His Parts and Learning were admirably set off by a singular Fitness for Friendship and Conversation, in which he was amiable above many. . . . A most sincere and inartificial Humility at once hid, and adorn'd his other Excellencies." [202] Although Mr. John Wood was "reckon'd as great a Critick in the Greek and Latin Tongues, as any in the University," he was "one of the most shiftless Men in the World . . . a Learned Man, but wanted the Faculty of Communicating." [203] Nicholas Bernard, in his funeral sermon for Usher, speaks especially of "the communicativeness of his studies." [204] Thomas Gilbert offers yet another combination of excellence: "He had all the School-men at his Fingers-ends; and which is a little unusual, took a great Delight in Poetry. . . ." [205]

Mr. William Smith, of Packington, "enjoy'd a greater measure of health than most Students, and laborious Preachers do." [206] That comment leads naturally to the semi-invalid, hard student, and untiring preacher, Richard Baxter. He was not a university man, but he was a learned one; he had been duly ordained by the Bishop of Worcester.[207] Baxter possessed extraordinary energy, and did

---

[201] Aubrey : II, 259. Tombes was at one time tutor to John Wilkins.
[202] Calamy : *op. cit.*, p. 392.
[203] Calamy : *Abridg.*, II, 85.
[204] The House of Commons, in 1647, ordered that £100 quarterly be paid to Usher "for his present support, subsistence, and incouragement in his studies." In 1649, the allowance was renewed (Thurloe : I, 112).
[205] Calamy : *op. cit.*, 109.
[206] *Ibid.*, 423.
[207] *Ibid.*, I, 11-12.

not waste a moment; he preached; he catechized; he made pastoral visits; he wrote nearly two hundred books. This achievement is the more remarkable because his health was never good. It seems incredible that a man, seldom free from bodily discomfort even if not in actual pain, could have accomplished so much in so many ways; especially is it surprising that he should have accumulated a vast store of book knowledge. Even Bishop Burnet, who is not particularly fond of Baxter, says that "if he had not meddled in too many things, he would have been esteemed one of the learned men of the age." [208] Baxter himself condemned the action of Parliament in imprisoning Dr. Daniel Featley, "because whatever the facts were, he was so learned a man, as was sufficient to dishonour those he suffered by." [209] It was honor shown to learning that left Dr. James Duport and Dr. Edward Pocock undisturbed in their professorships during the civil war, though neither man was a presbyterian.

This learning, which so many of the preachers possessed in generous measure, was achieved by means of systematic, unceasing study. Dr. John Bryan was so fearful of wasting time, that "to prevent vain Thoughts in the Night Season when he could not sleep, he would run over a Greek Catechism, Herberts Poems, or some other useful thing he was Master of." [210] John Gregory studied sixteen hours a day for many years; [211] Dr. Henry Hammond rarely went to bed "till after midnight, sometimes not till three in the morning, and yet certainly rising to prayers at five"; [212] Matthew Robinson "fixed upon a settled resolve, to study seven hours per day at least; four of these hours he spent in philosophy, his morning study; the afternoon hours he devoted *litteris amoemoribus,* viz., to Greek and Latin poets until he had left none of moment unread, to history, geog-

---

[208] *Hist. of his own Times,* p. 128.
[209] Calamy: *Abridg.,* I, 75.
[210] *Ibid.,* II, 736.   [211] Lloyd: p. 86.
[212] Fell: *Life of Hammond,* p. 48.

raphy, etc." [213]   Dr. Wallis would sit at his studies twelve or fourteen hours together; [214] Dr. Matthew Wren worked, "never seeing Fire in the coldest time . . . seldome a bed till eleven at night, and always up at five in the morning." [215] William Gouge "was at his study by five a clock in the morning and alwayes by four in the summer"; [216] Mr. Herring "was often willing to miss a meal, that he might the more satisfy himself in conversing with his books." [217]

Some of these gentlemen who read and wrote so assid-uously were subject to constant interruption from other scholars and from parishioners, and also from curious visitors; one wonders that a man, active preacher in a large parish, or equally active executive in a university, could produce in scholarship as well as in religious disputations. Henry Jessey finally grew so resentful of the stream of friends, controversalists, and beggars that came to his study, that he put a sign over it:

> Amicis, quisquis huc ades;
> Aut agita paucis, aut abi;
> Aut me, laborantem, adjuva.[218]

William Oughtred, who knew so much and wished to know so much more, might have discovered the philosopher's stone and other useful objects if he had been permitted to study as much as he wished to; but "his wife was a penurious woman, and would not allow him to burne candle

[213] *Autobiography*, p. 19.
[214] *Reliq. Hearnae*, II, 222-3.
[215] Lloyd : p. 612.
[216] Jenkins : *A Shock of Corn*, pp. 40-1.
[217] Clark : *General Mar.*, p. 467.
[218] Crosby : *Hist. of the Baptists*, I, 307ff. This anecdote reminds one of a somewhat similar story told of Lancelot Andrewes. He al-ways studied all the forenoon and disliked interruption : "he doubted they were no true scholars that came to him before noon" (*Biog. Brit.*, I, 144). Francis Junius, when studying under Dr. Thomas Marshall at Oxford, "being troubled by often visits, he removed his quarters to an obscure house in Beef-hall-lane" (Wood : *Fasti*, II, 357). Baxter tells that "one said openly that I had killed a man with my own hand in cold blood ; that it was a tinker at my door ; that because he beat his kettle and disturbed me in my studies I went down and pistolled him" (*Autob.*, pp. 241-2).

after supper, by which meanes many a good notion is lost,
and many a probleme unsolved; so that Mr. Henshawe,
when he was there, bought candle, which was a great comfort to the old man." [219] No one checked Thomas Fuller,
who gave himself without stint to people and books and
politics and the pulpit. When the dean of Worcester
preached Fuller's funeral sermon, a dramatic result of these
labors was anounced: "a while after his death, an effusion
of blood burst forth at his temples, which was thought to
have been settled there by his sedate and intense application to his studies." [220]

The inception and development of the Royal Society is
the most notable proof of the learned avocations of the mid-
seventeenth-century clergy. As early as 1645, there were
weekly meetings of a group that included Wilkins, Wallis,
the physician, Jonathan Goddard, and others who were
interested in mathematics and physical science. After the
civil war, when Wilkins was made Warden of Wadham
College, the meetings were held at his lodgings, and among
those who were in constant attendance were Seth Ward,
Robert Boyle, Sir William Petty, Matthew Wren, Goddard,
Christopher Wren (Doctor, not Sir), Laurence Rooke,
Ralph Bathurst, besides Wilkins and Wallis. Bishop
Thomas Sprat, in his *History of the Royal Society*,[221] tells
of the experiments made and the subjects investigated, the
letters sent abroad requesting information on learned topics,
the projects suggested; but to his thinking, the greatest
service done by the Society is that it brings together men
of all kinds. "There the Soldier, the Tradesman, the
Scholar, the Gentleman, the Courtier, the Divine, the Pres-

---

[219] Aubrey, II, 110. Evelyn included Oughtred among the extraordinarily learned of ancient and modern times (*Diary*, Dec. 20, 1668).
[220] *Biog. Brit.*, III, 2018.
[221] P. 53ff. See Masson: *Milton*, VI, 391.
Among the original Fellows of the Royal Society were: Isaac
Barrow, B.D., Edward Cotton, D.D., William Holder, D.D., John Pell,
D.D., Thomas Sprat, D.D., John Wallis, D.D., Matthew Wren, Esq.
(entered the church, subsequently). *The Record of the Royal Society*,
Lond., 1912, p. 16ff.

byterian, the Papist, the Independent, and those of Orthodox Judgment, have laid aside their names of distinction,
and calmly conspir'd in a mutual agreement of labors and
desires: A blessing which seems even to have exceeded that
Evangelical Promise, That the Lion and the Lamb shall
lie down together." [222] Sprat published his History in 1667,
by which time the "Invisible College," as the informal
gatherings were first called, had become an important institution whose members enjoyed social as well as intellectual
advantages; but its beginnings were among a small group
of learned men in which Puritan divines largely pre-
dominated.

It was not only in England that a learned Englishman
might win recognition. Meric Casaubon was invited into
Sweden by the famous Cristina to inspect her universities,
but he refused.[223] John Hales was often consulted "by
learned men beyond, and within, the seas"; [224] William
Oughtred was invited to Italy by the Duke of Florence
during the civil wars, "and offered him 500 *li*. per annum;
but he would not accept it because of his religion." [225]
Archbishop Usher was invited to France, and also to
Holland, the Hollanders "offering him the place of being
Honorius Professor at Leiden, which had an ample stipend,
but he refused both." [226] Patrick Young was consulted by
most of the "Great and Learned Men then in Europe." [227]
Students came from beyond the seas to learn from John
Conant.[228] When Gataker traveled, foreigners "came and
lodged in his house for instruction." Clark (in *Ten
Eminent Divines*) names ten of the many who "were as
ambitious of being entertained by him as if they had been
admitted into a University." [229] German, Danish, and

---

[222] *History, etc.*, p. 403.
[223] Walker: Pt. II. 8 (Casaubon was born in Geneva, but lived in
Eng. from 1611 to his death in 1671, at Oxford).
[224] Wood: *Ath. Ox.*, III, 411.   [226] *Eighteen Sermons* (Preface).
[225] Aubrey: II. 110.   [227] Walker: Pt. II, 50.
[228] Watson: *Religious Refugees, etc.*, p. 96.
[229] *Ibid.*, p. 97; Clark: p. 146.

French students came to England to be taught by John Prideaux.[230]

Yet in spite of the achievements of scholarship, the dignities to which these learned divines attained, the reputation which was theirs, the term "scholar" often carried with it a connotation far from complimentary. When Isaac Barrow went about with "his hatt up, his cloake halfe off and halfe on, a gent. [sic] came behind him and clapt him on the shoulder and sayd, Well, goe thy wayes for the variest scholar that ever I met with." [231] John Harmar was "a meer scholar, and therefore mostly in a poor and shabbed condition. . . ." [232] Joshua Hoyle is called "a careless person and no better than a meer scholar." [233]

Libraries

They were bookish men, these "painful" studious divines. Books, it is true, were their tools, but besides an appreciation of the practical usefulness of ancient tomes and manuscripts in interpreting texts and in answering opponents, there may often be seen that love of books which in some persons passes the love of any other thing in life.

Patrick Young, "the most Celebrated Grecian of his Age," was Library-Keeper at St. James's until he was turned out in 1649.[234] Another official book-man was Dr. Thomas Barlow, Provost of Queen's College and Proto-bibliothecus of the Bodleian Library. Evelyn mentions a visit to him, and tells of the curiosities he showed his guests.[235] This Dr. Barlow was, in his simpler environment, as ready to help a scholar as was Laud or Usher. There was at Oxford, keeping a modest "coffey house," a

---

[230] Watson : op. cit., p. 95.
[231] Aubrey : I, 90-1.
[232] Wood : Ath. Ox., III, 919.
[233] Ibid., p. 383.
[234] Walker : Pt. II, 50 (The keys were given to Hugh Peters, who was consequently charged with plundering the medals and mss., and selling some of them to Sir Simonds D'Ewes).
[235] Diary, July 11, 1654.

young man, Cirques Jobson, a Jew and a Jacobite. "He read whenever he could in the university library and by conversing with books not used by the vulgar students, especially MSS., he was taken notice of by Mr. Tho. Barlow, the head keeper of the said library, who began thereupon to express some kindness towards him, with the offering his assisting hand." [236] John Dury, out of his own practical experience, wrote a book which he called, *The Reformed Librarie-Keeper*. Dury, a modest, studious clergyman, served as deputy to Bulstrode Whitelock who in 1649 was appointed keeper of the King's medals and library. The little book is practical throughout: a Catalogue should be made "so that it may alwaies bee augmented"; the Library-Keeper should trade books at home and abroad; Librarians should be paid better salaries. This material is in the form of two letters to Samuel Hartlib, with whom Dury was associated in educational projects.[237]

To some scholarly clergymen, books came without effort, as to Edward Martin, Dean of Ely ". . . who had six Ancestors in a direct line, learned before him, and six Libraries bequeathed to him. . . ." [238] Edward Davenant, equally fortunate, "had a noble library, which was the aggregate of his father's, the bishop's, and his owne." [239] Other men built up their collections, volume by volume, manuscript by manuscript, gladly expending a fortune, if they possessed one, on old books and new books, illuminated parchments and badly printed pamphlets.

It must have been particularly hard to see such an accumulation disappear. The ever-memorable John Hales had gathered a library at a cost of £2500, but after his sequestration he was obliged to part with it in order to feed and clothe himself, receiving, it is said, about £700 for it from Cornelius Bee, a London bookseller.[240] Most of this

[236] Wood: *Ath. Ox.*, I, xxiii.
[237] See Dirchs: *A Biog. Memoir of Samuel Hartlib*, p. 18.
[238] Lloyd: p. 461.
[239] Aubrey: I, 201.   [240] Wood: *Ath. Ox.*, III, 411.

money, Hales gave to other sequestered ministers, and if they tried to repay him, he would refuse to accept a penny.[241] John Prideaux was another scholar whose books proved to be his only possession of money value, after he had been "plundered." He took his misfortunes cheerfully, according to accounts. When someone said to him: "How doth your lordship do? Never better in my life, said he, only I have too great a stomack; for I have eaten that little plate which the sequestrators left me, I have eaten a great library of excellent books, I have eaten a great deal of linnen, much of my brass, some of my pewter, and now I have come to eat iron, and what will come next I know not." [242]

Archbishop Usher's library was notable even in a day of great private libraries. It contained about ten thousand books and manuscripts, and its value made him feel that he ought to leave it to his daughter though he had intended, in more prosperous times, to bequeath it to Dublin College. The soldiery stationed in Ireland bought it for Dublin College (Trinity College, in Dublin) paying £2200 for it, but as it was stored for many years, much of it was lost or damaged.[243]

Archbishop Laud's library was famous and deserved its fame, for he had had unusual opportunities of gratifying a collector's ambitions. He was notably generous to scholars; when he sent such men as Edward Pocock and John

[241] Walker: Pt. II, 94.
One who with his whole family was for a time supported by John Hales, was Anthony Farrington, Vicar of Bray, and Preacher at Windsor. He was a particularly honest and sincere man, and consequently more than one chronicler tells with gusto the old anecdote of the sixteenth-century Vicar of Bray who kept strictly to his principles, that he would live and die Vicar of Bray. In the keeping of this resolve, he submitted himself to the religious exigencies of Henry VIII, of Edward VI, of Mary, and of Elizabeth, ending his life complacently in the Vicarage of Bray (Lloyd: p. 542).
Lazarus Seaman, "the learned nonconformist," had a library which, it is said, was the first disposed of by auction, in England. The books brought in £7000 (Calamy: *Abridg.*, II, 16).
[242] Wood: *Ath. Ox.*, III, 273; Walker: Pt. II, 78. Timothy Woodroffe was unfortunate in suffering from both armies; he was "plundered of a very good library" (Wood: *Ath. Ox.*, III, 1113).
[243] Burton: I, 384 (Note); *Reliq. Hearnae*, I, 49.

Greaves to the East to buy medals, coins, and manuscripts for him, he was not only gratifying his own desire to possess such things, but he was giving an experience to his agents that would be of great service to them professionally. Pocock, for example, became professor of Hebrew at Oxford (he was already Arabic lecturer), and Greaves was professor of Astronomy at Oxford, and, later, of Geometry at Gresham College in London.[244] In June, 1639, Laud sent 576 manuscripts to the public library at Oxford, to be added to the 700 he had sent previously; in 1640 he sent still more, feeling, no doubt, that they were safer at a distance from himself.[245]

Isaac Vossius, most secular of clergymen, had a library for which Oxford offered £3000. This sum was refused and the books were carried to Leyden where the university of that city purchased them for, it is said, £3000.[246] Bishop Stillingfleet's collection of books was sold to Narcissus Marsh (Archbishop of Armagh) for £2500, but eventually it, too, went out of England.[247] Evelyn mentions that he tried to buy Dean Cosin's library "which was one of the choicest collections of any private person in England," but he does not say whether he was successful.[248]

Great men in the church had, naturally enough, the money and the opportunity to gather together rare and valuable works; but there were men of what one may call the middle class of the clergy who loved books of many kinds, who bought, borrowed, and read books; there were men who denied themselves bread that they might have the books that they craved more than food. Dr. William Bates, however, was never in such straits. He was typical of the well-educated, successful, nonconformist minister who read and studied as indefatigably as he preached. He was considered one of the great preachers of the late 50's and early 60's, and Pepys (that barometer of a man's fame) made a

[244] Wood : *op. cit.*, 325.
[245] *Ibid.*, 330.
[248] *Diary*, April 15, 1652.
[246] *Reliq. Hearnae*, I, 206-7.
[247] *Ibid.*, 49.

point of going to St. Dunstan's on the twenty-seventh of
August, 1662, to hear Dr. Bates's farewell sermon. One
explanation of his popularity is found in his habit of illustrating his points by simple, secular references to matters
of common knowledge in books and in life. When Dr.
Bates died, the preacher of the funeral sermon said, "He
had lived a long studious life; an earnest gatherer of
books. . . ." And then, "Whatsoever belonged to the more
polite sort of literature, was most grateful to him when it
fell into a conjunction with what was also most useful.
Nothing mean was welcome onto his library, or detained
there, much less thought fit to be entertained and laid up in
the more private repository of his mind." [249] In another
funeral sermon, that of Simon Patrick for Samuel Jacomb,
there is, again, a mention of what books may mean to a
man; but Dr. Patrick had evidently known instances where
a love of books degenerates into selfish absorption, for he
issues a warning: ". . . this is not to be forgotten, that
though he was of excellent learning . . . yet he lived not
alway among his Books, which is to die among the living,
and to live among the dead. . . . But he was exceeding free
to all good converse, and let his Friends enjoy so much of
him, that sometimes he could scarce enjoy himself, but only
in them." [250]

Henry Newcome was a genuine lover of books. The mere
looking at them and handling of them gave him pleasure;
cataloguing was a joy so great that he more than suspected
it to be a sin. The arrangement of the English library, the
books of which were to be chained in the Byrom chapel in
the Collegiate Church,[251] gave him deep concern. He is
ashamed because he wishes to be "the chief doer in setynge
up the bookes," and resents sharing the placing of them in
their permanent location.[252] Finally, he records: "I did
after dinner take order about the chaininge of the rest of

[249] Bates: *Spiritual Perfection*, p. xix.   [251] *Diary*, p. 30 (Note).
[250] *Divine Arithmetic*, p. 59ff.   [252] *Ibid.*, Dec. 11, 1661.

the bookes for the English library. . . ." [253] But another pleasure awaits him, because, only two weeks later, he writes: "I put prices to my cozen Dunster's books." [254] Early in the next month, "Mrs. Hiet desired mee to direct her in the choice of bookes, for by will the library is to goe to Mr. Edmonson and his son, save only his wife may take what she pleaseth for her owne use. I desired to deale uprightly in busynes and so noted out several bookes that were most practical, as the Book of Martyrs, and English Annotations, Burgess' *Spiritual reviveinge,* and Perkin's, Beeston's, Sibs, Hooker, Bolton, Love, Watson's Workes, so many of them as were there. No bookes tho English that are above her capacity that I medled with." [255]

When Newcome's sister (a person with a disposition much like that of Pepys's sister) writes for five pounds to retrieve a cow, Henry Newcome lists four reasons against, and eight reasons for, giving her the money. No. 7 of the latter group is: "If I had some bargaine of bookes I should goe nigh to straine myself to doe it." [256] He knows very well that his own library is a snare: "Then I writ in my own Catalogue havinge a little perused my sermon for to-morrow." On another occasion he records, "I saw a vanity in lookinge on my bookes which the mice had hurt before I went to Church which was by accident, and this kept my minds company sometime in the very publicke service this day." [257]

Though Newcome might select the *Book of Martyrs* and other devotional literature for a bereft widow, he himself enjoyed books of many sorts. He read the *Compleat Ambassador* and Davila's *History of the Civil Wars in France,* the Duke of Holstein's ambassador's travels (which he read in a stationer's shop), Peter Heylin's *Geography* and Sandys's *Travels.* He read *Hudibras* and was as puzzled as Pepys to account for its popularity: "He would

[253] March 11, 1661–2.
[254] March 26, 1661–2.
[255] April 8, 1622.
[256] Dec. 15, 1661.
[257] Jan. 23, 1662–3.

be wicked but is without wit." [258] Of course he read Du
Bartas, borrowing the book from his friend Mr. Buxton.

It was not only a pleasant and convenient thing for a
minister to possess books, but it was hardly respectable not
to possess them. As Lloyd observes: "Many mens excellent parts are kept low for Want of a well contrived, and by
reason of a scant ill chosen Library. The knowledge of
Books, as it is a specious, so he would say (Lloyd now
quotes "Mr. Launce of St. Michael in the Quern") it was
an useful part of Learning, as whereby upon any emergent
doubt or difficulty, a man may have recourse unto the advice
of grave and learned men. . ." [259] Francis Potter's lack
of a good library gives Aubrey an opportunity to speak
slightingly of Potter's knowledge of languages; after which
follows the comment: "He had but few bookes, which
when he dyed were sold for fifty-six shillings, and surely
no great bargaine." [260]

To Henry Jessey, books were an absolute necessity.
After his father's death "he had not above three pence a
day for his maintenance, yet he so economically managed
the small pittance as to spare some of it for hiring
books." [261] Chillingworth did not hire, but he plainly borrowed with the finality of action which attends borrowing.
Witness John Hales (in a Letter to a Person Unknown):
"You require of me the use of Crellius against Grotius; I
am sorry, in mine own behalf, that I cannot pleasure you.
My good friend, Mr. Chillingworth (a gentleman that
borrows books in haste, but restores them with advice)
hath got it into his hands, and I fear me I shall hardly see
it again; for he had borrowed it twice: by this symptom
I judge what the issue will be; for no man yet borrowed
the same book twice of me, that ever restored it again." [262]

[258] *Diary*, Jan. 31, 1662–3. [259] P. 522. [260] II, 164.
[261] Neal: II, 253. Cf. Josselin: *Diary*, Jan. 30, 1645.
[262] *Works*, I, 199. Baxter, in his *Autobiography*, p. 235, laments:
"I was so long wearied with keeping my doors shut against them
that came to distrain on my goods for preaching, that I was fain
. . . to hide my library first and afterwards to sell it."

Edmund Calamy must have been more fortunate, or perhaps, on the other hand, he intended a reproof when, in a
funeral sermon for Simeon Ashe, he said: ". . . let us
therefore do with them [ministers] as we do with Books
that are borrowed; if a man borrows a Book, he knows he
must keep it but for a day or two, and therefore he will be
sure to read it over; whereas if the Book be a mans own, he
laies it aside, because he knows he can read it at any time.
Remember your ministers are but lent you, they are not
your own. . . ." [263]

Thomas Lydiatt represents the extreme type of student:
". . . he laid out what money he got upon books, so that
he was, in a manner starved to death; which made Dr.
Potter, when he sent him a benevolence of five pounds, give
him strict charge to spend none of it in books, but to take
care to get what might recruit his macerated body." [264]
Lydiatt was the sort of man who would read understand-
ingly St. Paul's request of Timothy: "The cloke which I
left at Troas with Carpus, when thou comest, bring with
thee, and the books, but especially the parchments." [265]

Mathematics

Mathematics was a major interest with a number of
clergymen, and a necessary branch of knowledge with others
who felt that the proof of religion rested in part on
chronological tables, a knowledge of "Eclyps," the date of
Easter, and so on. Henry Thurman wrote a *Defence of
Humane Learning in the Ministry,* in the course of which
he demanded: "How can a Divine without Geometry answer
an Atheisticall Julian or a scoffing Lucian, that laugh at the
arke for a Mosaicall figment, to be reported to contain
Noah . . . ?" Yet, says Mr. Thurman, an excellent mathematician has shown that there was place for all and twelve-

[263] *Farewell Sermons* (bound in the 1662 edition), p. 402.
[264] *Reliq. Hearnae,* I, 101-2.   [265] II Tim. iv. 13.

months victuals for them besides.[266] This author would
not have a clergyman go too far: "in a minister is required
not singular excellency in the Sciences, but a convenient
mediocrity." [267]

Henry Hammond's attitude toward mathematics was distinctly patronizing. In the second part of the seventh
sermon of his collection of nineteen sermons, he says
(having already quoted Aristotle on the subject):
". . . History and Geometry, and the like, go down
pleasantliest with those which have no design upon Books,
but only to rid them of some hours, which would otherwise
lie on their hands.[268] Thomas Fuller shows his General
Artist as only moderately given to mathematics, not suffering it "to be so unmannerly as to jostle out other arts." [269]
Baxter says frankly: "And for the mathematics, I was an
utter stranger to them, and never·could find in my heart to
divert any studies that way." [270] Pepys would have made
the same criticism of that speech as he did of a sentence
in a sermon preached by the Duke of Albemarle's chaplain.
"All our arithmetique is not able to number the days of a
man," he had said; and Pepys, quoting it, added, "which,
God knows, is not the fault of arithmetique, but that our
understandings reach not the thing." [271]

William Oughtred was only twenty-three when at Cambridge he wrote his *Horologiographia Geometrica*. Histories of mathematics give him the credit of systematizing
elementary arithmetic, algebra, and trigonometry; [272] besides this, he introduced the symbol x ·for multiplication,
and :: as that of proportion.[273] His *Clavis Mathematica*,
first published in 1631,.was reissued in 1648, and again in
1652.[274] By way of climax, he was extraordinarily suc-

[266] P. 29.
[267] P. 34.
[268] P. 102.
[269] *Holy and Profane State*, p. 56.
[270] *Autobiography*, p. 9.
[271] *Diary*, Nov. 5, 1665.
[272] Rouse Ball: *Hist. of the Study of Math. at Cambr.*, p. 30.
[273] Cajori: *A Hist. of Math.*, p. 167.
[274] William Harvey is said to have been reading this book, and working the problems, not long before he died (1657) ; Wyatt: *William
Harvey*, p. 163.

cessful as a teacher of mathematics.[275] John Wallis, at one time a pupil of Oughtred's, intended first to be a doctor, then took orders, and in 1649 went to Oxford as professor of Geometry.[276] He attracted attention by his application of the methods of Descartes and Cavalieri, especially in Conic Sections.[277] Wallis and Lord Brounker together solved a problem proposed by the French mathematician, Pierre de Fermat, and published the result in 1658. The solution was printed again in an algebraic work brought out by John Pell in 1668, and thereafter was known as "Pell's problem." [278] Wallis had a controversy with Hobbes that lasted twenty years. Hobbes asserted that he had discovered the quadrature of the circle; Wallis told him he was mistaken, whereupon Hobbes published *Six Lessons to the Professors of Mathematics in Oxford;* Wallis replied with *Due Correction for Mr. Hobbes for not Saying his Lessons Right.*[279] With other men, Wallis had innumerable personal disputes, most of them based on the charge that Wallis borrowed ideas too freely, without any acknowledgement of indebtedness.[280]

Isaac Barrow, after a brief experience as Greek professor at Cambridge, became in 1662 professor of geometry at Gresham College; the next year he received the first appointment to the professorship of mathematics which had just been founded by Sir Henry Lucas. Between 1655 and 1669, when he resigned his chair to Isaac Newton, Barrow published a number of studies in mathematics. Aubrey con-

---

[275] See under "Schoolmasters," p. 209.

[276] Aubrey says that his "old cozen, Parson Whitney," told him "that in the visitation of Oxen in Edward VI's time, they burned mathematical bookes for conjuring bookes, and, if the Greeke professor had not accidentally come along, the Greeke Testament had been thrown into the fire for a conjuring booke too" (Aubrey: II, 297). See also Hobbes: *Leviathan,* p. 370, on mathematicians and "diabolical arts."

[277] Cajori: *op. cit.,* p. 192ff.

[278] Cajori: p. 181.

[279] Chambers: *Book of Days,* II, 656.

[280] " . . . he lies at watch, at Sir Christopher Wren's discourse, Mr. Robert Hooke's. Dr. William Holder, etc. ; putts downe their notions in his note booke, and then prints it, without owneing the authors. This frequently, of which they complaine" (Aubrey, II, 281).

cludes the list by assuring the reader that there was then printing "22 initiating lectures about mathematics, to which will be subjoined some lectures that he read about Archimedes, proving that he was an algebraist, and giving his thoughts by what method Archimedes came to fall on his theorems." [281] Barrow also wrote volumes and volumes of sermons. He died at the age of forty-seven.

Mathematics filled most of John Pell's life. He did not take orders until the Restoration, and continued to study mathematics and philosophy in spite of his new responsibilities. "He was not adroit for preaching," Aubrey testifies; from Wood one learns that tenants and relatives "cozened him out of the profits of his parsonages and kept him so indigent that he wanted necessaries, even paper and ink, to his dying day." [282] His whole career was concerned with mathematics; divinity was his avocation. He did not even make excursions into medicine or poetry, as was the habit of many of his contemporaries. In 1643, Pell filled the chair of mathematics at the university of Amsterdam, and in 1646 at Breda. He "produced" steadily: from 1630 to 1635, he had printed studies *On the quadrant, On logarithms, Astronomical history*, etc.; in 1644 he wrote on *Easter;* in 1650, *On an Idea of Mathematics;* in 1668 he used in a translation from the Dutch, the symbol ÷ for division—this being its first use; [283] in 1672, he wrote a book with the title: *A Table of the Square Numbers, namely of all the Square Numbers, between 0, and an hundred millions, and of their Sides or Roots, which are all the Whole Numbers between 0 and ten thousand. With an Appendix concerning the Endings, or last Figures of all square Numbers.*[284] Anyone buying that book would have a pretty clear idea of what it contained.

Seth Ward was another of Oughtred's famous pupils. He was appointed to the Savilian chair of astronomy in

[281] Aubrey: I, 91.
[282] Wood: *Fasti,* I, 462.
[283] Rouse Ball: p. 41.
[284] Wood: *Fasti,* I, 463.

1649, in the place of John Greaves who was ejected; and next became professor of mathematics at Oxford. He published a work on comets, and one on the planetary orbits,[285] besides a number of others on Trigonometry, etc.[286] He was famous, as a teacher, for his method of drawing "his geometricall schemes with black, red, yellow and green, and blew ink to avoid the perplexity of A. B. C. etc." [287] Ward was much interested in philosophy and was one of the group of thinkers and disputants that developed eventually into the Royal Society. With all his absorption in mathematics, he did not ignore his religious duties. He took his degree in divinity in 1654, after which he advanced steadily in the church, becoming Bishop of Sarum, and finally Bishop of Salisbury. When Pepys is in Salisbury (June 11, 1668), he goes to the minster, "and I looked in and saw the Bishop, my friend Dr. Ward." Before he died, Ward "fell under a loss of memory and understanding," a pitiful conclusion to the life of a man "who was both in mathematics and philosophy and in the strength of judgment and understanding, one of the first men of his time." [288]

Many other parsons found an *extra*-interest in mathematics. Among them are men whose names are easily recognizable; a number, however, are names only, the label "mathematician" being attached to them by contemporary writers, without comment.

> Thomas Baker published *The Gate of Equations Unlock'd,* etc. (Wood: *Ath. Ax.,* IV, 286).
> George Burdon (Calamy: *Abridg.,* II, 603).
> Robert Burton was "an exact mathematician . . . and one that understood the laying of lands well" (Wood: *op. cit.,* II, 652-8).
> John Bushnell (Calamy: *op. cit.,* II, 693).
> William Chillingworth was so practical a mathematician that he laid out fortifications around Gloucester and other places, being called "the Kings little Engineer, and Black-art man" (Lloyd: p. 542).

[285] Rouse Ball: pp. 36-8.
[286] Wood: *Ath. Ox.,* IV, 249-50.
[287] Aubrey: II, 284.
[288] Burnet: *History, etc.,* p. 442.

Edmund Chilmeade (Wood: *op. cit.,* III, 350).

Gilbert Clerke wrote a book on Oughtred's *Clavis* (Nelson: *Life of Bull,* p. 512).

Richard Cumberland made a study of Jewish Measures and Weights, comparing them with the standard in England. He dedicated the work to Samuel Pepys (Wood: *Fasti,* II, 205).[289]

Edward Davenant was, in Sir Christopher Wren's opinion—as quoted by Aubrey—"the best mathematician in the world about 30 or 35 yeares ago. But being a divine he was unwilling to print, because the world should not know how he had spent the greatest part of his time" (Aubrey: I, 200).

Thomas Gataker, "the most famous mathematician of all Europe," declared William Lilly though he was the sworn enemy of Dr. Gataker (Lilly: *History of his Life, etc.,* p. 60).

Dr. John Gregory had "a curious faculty in Astronomy, Geometry and Arithmetic" (Lloyd, p. 86).

John Goad worked over his book, *Astro Meteorologica,* from about 1650 to 1686; "the whole discourse is founded on sacred authority and reason" (Wood: *Ath. Ox.,* IV, 26).

Thomas Greaves (Walker: Pt. II, 112).

Thomas Grundy (Calamy: *op. cit.,* II, 690).

Joseph Hall knew enough of mathematics to have that study classed as one of his recreations (Lloyd, p. 419).

Thomas Hyde translated a Persian study of the longitude and latitude of fixed stars (Wood: *op. cit.,* IV, 525-6).

John Janeway, while still at Eton, made an almanack and calculated eclipses (Clark: *Em. Lives,* p. 61).

Jonathan Jephet was "Eminent . . . in . . . some parts of the Mathematics: And us'd often to practice Dialling and Surveying for his Recreation" (Calamy: *op. cit.,* II, 117).

Archbishop Laud gave a store of mathematical instruments to St. John's at Oxford (Evelyn: *Diary,* July 12, 1654).

---

[289] Cumberland gave careful attention to his profession, and ended as Bishop of Peterborough. But when Pepys saw him in the spring of 1667, he was far from prosperous looking "in a plain country-parson's dress." He was a St. Paul's and Cambridge man, like Pepys himself, who knew Cumberland well and liked him—"a most excellent person . . . and one that I am sorry should be lost and buried in a little country town, and would be glad to remove him thence; and the truth is, if he would accept of my sister's fortune, I should give £100 more with him than to a man able to settle her four times as much as, I fear, he is able to do; and I will think of it, and a way how to move it, he having in discourse said he was not against marrying, nor yet engaged" (March 18, 1666/7).

Franciscus Linus (Father Hall) printed a discourse of dialling (Aubrey: II, 34).

Adam Martendale (Calamy: *op. cit.*, II, 35).

Launcelot Morehouse was one of the argumentative preacher-mathematicians and wrote violently "against Mr. Francis Potter's book of 666, and falls upon him, for that 25 is not the true roote, but the propinque root; to which Mr. Potter replied with some sharpnes, and that it ought not to be the true roote, for this agrees better with his purpose" (Aubrey: II, 86).

Charles Moreton's "Eminency lay in the Mathematics" (Calamy: *op. cit.*, II, 144).

John Newton published studies in geometry and trigonometry, as: *Exhibiting the Doctrine of the Sphere, and Theory of Planets decimally by Trigonometry and by Tables* (London, 1656); and also such practical works as: *Description of the Use of the Carpenter's Rule, and the Art of practical Gauging of Casks and Brewer's Tuns* (Wood: *op. cit.*, III, 1190).

John Oldfield was "a great Master in the Tongues and Mathematics" (Calamy: *op. cit.*, II, 72).

Samuel Ogden "was a good Mathematician, and took delight in Algebra, Trigonometry, and the several parts of the Mathematicks. He was acquainted with some of the greatest Men of the Age in that Science, and Taught his Scholars that were Studious and Ingenious the Elements of the Mathematicks, on purpose to charm them into a love of those Studies, that they might there find Manly Pleasure, and not be drawn to Debauchery under a Pretense of Pleasure, and he was us'd to observe that very few good Mathematicians were Lewd and Scandalous" (Calamy: *op. cit.*, II, 193).

George Stratford (Walker: Pt. II, 112).

Herbert Thorndyke—"as I am informed by Seth Ward, Lord Bishop of Sarum, and other learned men, one of the best . . . mathematicians of this age" (Aubrey: II, 257).

John Thornton "(Household Chaplain to the late first Duke of Bedford) . . . a great mathematician" (Calamy: *op. cit.*, I, 95).

John Wilkins was inclined toward the astronomy side of mathematics. His *Discovery of a New World: or a Discourse tending to prove that 'tis probable there may be Another habitable World in the Moon,* was published in 1638, and went through four editions by 1684. He also, in

1640, published a Discourse "tending to prove that 'tis probable our Earth is one of the Planets."

Henry Willes—"a considerable mathematician" (Calamy: *op. cit.*, II, 496).

John Winchurst—"of a subtil head, a good mathematician" (Wood: *op. cit.*, I, xcvi).

Dr. Christopher Wren (the Dean of Windsor) "was well skill'd in all Branches of the Mathematicks" (*Parentalia*, p. 142).

Medicine

The same investigating turn of mind that led one man to search for sources in language and history and religious dogma, would lead another man to inquire into the structure of the human body, the flow of the blood,[290] and the cause and cure of disease. Since spirit and flesh have many interests in common, it was inevitable that the man of God who was so often in the presence of physical and mental suffering, should attempt to give ease to the body as well as strength to the soul. There was no lack of biblical precedent for the combining of preaching and healing, and there were certain practical advantages in possessing a knowledge of medicine that a clergyman could hardly be blind to. Milton put this last point of view plainly before anyone who would read his unamiable: *The Likeliest means to remove Hirelings out of the Church.* "Those preachers among the poor Waldenses . . . bred up themselves in trades and especially in physic and surgery as well as in the study of scripture . . . that they might be no burden to the church. . . ."[291]

When Richard Baxter was working among the poor in Kidderminster, he found it so necessary to give medical advice that this service interfered seriously with his religious duties. Finally, he established "a Diligent Skilful

---

[290] Harvey's *Exercitatio de motu cordis et sanguinis* appeared in 1628. It was, of course, well known to preacher-physicians.
[291] *Prose Works*, p. 167.

Physician" among his parishioners, promising not to practice himself.[292] George Fox tells of consulting "one Macham, a priest in high account. He would needs give me some physic, and I was to have been let blood. . . ."[293] Fox had at one time some idea of combining physic with his vocation of preaching, but the Lord opened to him reasons why he should not do so.[294]

With the readjustment that followed upon the Parliamentary or Restoration ejectments, many a minister found "Physick" to be a resource that would provide subsistence for his family. Men who were genuinely interested in medicine, and who possessed some means, studied seriously before attempting to practice, securing a degree either in England, in Holland (at Leyden), or in France, or in Italy (at Padua).

Ralph Bathurst was made a Doctor of Physick at Oxford in 1654, but returned to divinity after the Restoration.[295] Robert Bruistry took his degree in medicine at Leyden, following his ejectment from Emmanuel College, and practiced at Yarmouth.[296] Mr. Abraham Clifford (another nonconformist), Bachelor of Divinity, was a "Licensed Practitioner" in London, but he had previously taken his degree at Leyden.[297] Edward Hulse also secured his degree from Leyden, after being ejected from Emmanuel, and practiced in London.[298] Thomas Holyoake obtained a license from Oxford to practice and did practice until the Restoration, when he returned to the church.[299] Martin Llewellyn was a Master of Arts, and had been a chaplain in the Service. He retired to London after his ejectment by parliament, studied medicine, and was admitted Doctor of his Faculty. He did not return to the

---

[292] Calamy: *Life of Baxter*, I, 30; Baxter: *Autobiography*, p. 78. See also Timothy Woodroffe (Wood: *Ath. Ox.*, III, 1113).
[293] Fox: *Journal*, p. 5.
[294] *Ibid.*, p. 17.
[295] Wood: *Fasti*, II, 183. Also, "George Bathurst" in Wood: *Ath. Ox.*, II, 544; III, 430.
[296] Calamy: *Abridg.*, II, 84.
[297] *Ibid.*, p. 90.
[298] *Ibid.*, p. 84.
[299] Wood: *Ath. Ox.*, III, 1041.

church after the Restoration, but continued to practice. **(In 1664, while still practicing medicine, he was made Justice of the Peace for the County; and as "he was esteemed a good poet" also, Mr. Llewellyn appears a man of considerable intellectual experience.**[300]**)** The learned Manasseh ben Israel, who presented the plea of the Jewish people to parliament in 1655, was both a divine and a physieian.[301]

Matthew Robinson was fairly forced to practice medicine. He had taken his degree in divinity in 1648, but having little hope of prosperity for his church party, he devoted himself to the study of "physic, drugs, apothecary shops, chymical experiments, anatomy, vividesection of dogs, being much aided by Dr. Brown [Thomas] of Norwich." As it was the study rather than the practice that attracted him, he was much embarrassed if not annoyed by the constant interruption of his studies by people who insisted on his treating them. His reluctance being ascribed to modesty and a proper hesitation to practice without authority, some official person "sent to him under the seal of the office a license to practice physic."[302]   William Rowland's claim to be included among English clergymen who held a degree or license in medicine, is slight, but Wood says that he did "take the degrees in arts, holy orders, and was made either a reader or a curate of St. Margaret's church in the city of Westminster." He went over to Rome "early in the troubles," but did not try to enter the priesthood, his secular side having full sway in a cheerful, irresponsible career, a part of which included the acquiring of a degree in medicine, "as I have heard," Wood adds cautiously.[303]   Gilbert Rule left his Northumberland charge in 1662 and went to Holland, where he took his degree in medicine.[304]   Dr. Thomas Wren (a son of the Bishop of Ely) was created Doctor of Physick at Cambridge by the Chancellor's Letters, in 1660.   Later, he became archdeacon of Ely.[305]

[300] Walker: Pt. II, 108.
[301] Masson : *Milton*, V, 71.
[302] *Autobiography*, pp. 38-9.
[303] Wood : *Ath. Ox.*, III, 486.
[304] Calamy : *Abridg.*, II, 515.
[305] Wren : *Parentalia,* pp. 55, 180.

Since it was not at all uncommon for a preacher to pre-
scribe acceptably without a degree, only two of these
amateur physicians thought it worth while to pretend to
hold credentials which did not exist. One was a Thomas
Frankland, sometime of Brasenose, "who forged the university seal and set it to a writing whereby it tested that the
said Frankland had taken his degree of Doctor of physick
in this university. . . . He did take his degree of Bachelor
of Divinity and renouncing his orders practised physick."
The historian of Oxford observes, "He hath forged a will
also," but offers no details or evidence.[306] Another man
who, duly entered into the church, practiced medicine under
a pretense that he was a licensed physician of Oxford, was
Aaron Streater. He flourished before the times of sequestrations and ejectments, therefore his change of profession
was not the result of political or religious oppression, but
he "being a fantastical person" followed what was probably a natural bent. As early as 1641 he published a study,
*Of an Ague and the curing thereof, whether Quotidian,
Tertian, or Quartan.*[307] He did not, apparently, settle the
matter, for twenty-four years later Pepys quotes the chaplain of the Duke of Albemarle as saying in a sermon: "All
our physicians cannot tell what an ague is. . . ."[308]

The enforcement of the Act of Uniformity in 1662
brought about numerous transfers of activity from the
pulpit to "Physick." Frequently the nonconformist
preachers retained a hold upon their vocations, slipping in
a sermon here and there, sometimes in a church, sometimes
in a private house, sometimes at the bedside of a patient.
They were very human gentlemen, composed of many in-
gredients besides the *Westminster Confession,* the *Shorter
Catechism,* "or equivalent," and they must have derived
considerable sinful satisfaction from doing two things at
once: obeying the law, and outwitting it. Calamy tells of

---

[306] Wood : *op. cit.,* I, lxxviiiff.
[307] Wood : *Ath. Ox.,* III, 55.   [308] *Diary,* Nov. 5, 1665.

a number who were successful in this respect: Mr. John Bulkley seldom visited his patients "without reading a Lecture of Divinity to them, and praying with them." [309] Mr. Giles Firmin "practis'd Physick for many Years, and was still a Constant and Laborious Preacher." [310] Mr. John Lomax "practis'd Physick: And preach'd when he had an Opportunity." [311] Mr. Robert Parrot "had two Strings to his Bow; but neither of them was very strong. He practis'd Physick and profess'd Divinity." [312] Mr. John Pringle followed two professions (and was "not unpleasing in Conversation").[313] Mr. Richard Resbury "preach'd afterwards at his own hir'd House at Oundle, and practis'd Physick with good Success." [314] Mr. John Reynolds practiced and preached.[315] Mr. Thomas Titus did likewise, and furthermore "he married a gentlewoman of very good Circumstances, that enabled him to be more useful." [316]

Other nonconformist ministers, less resourceful, or with a different variety of conscience, practiced medicine exclusively, after St. Bartholomew's Day; among them were:

Mr. Andrew Barnett	(Cal.: II, 567)
Mr. Stephen Baxter	(" " 770)
Mr. Richard Birch	(" " 414)
Mr. John Brett	(" " 697)
Mr. Patrick Bromfield	(" " 511)
Mr. Sam. Burnet	(" " 542)
Mr. Daniel Capel	(" " 317)
Mr. Richard Capel	(Clark: *General Mar.*, 523-4.)
Mr. Stephen Charnock	(Pal.: II, 160)
Mr. Ichabod Chauncey	(Cal.: II, 610)
Mr. John Clark	(" " 529 [317])
Mr. Richard Core	(" " 813)
Mr. Luke Cranwell	(" " 165)
Mr. William Flood	(Pal.: II, 238)

[309] Calamy: *Abridg.*, II. 311.
[310] *Ibid.*, 296.
[311] *Ibid.*, 510.
[312] *Ibid.*, 92.
[313] *Ibid.*, 504.
[314] *Ibid.*, 493.
[315] *Ibid.*, 624.
[316] *Ibid.*, 565.
[317] "Tho he never undertook the Practise of Physick for Gain: What he did that Way was Gratis."

Mr. Richard Gilpin	(Cal.: II, 154)
Mr. Josiah Holdsworth	(" " 810)
Mr. Richard Inglet	(Pal.: I, 180)
Mr. Henry Jessey	(Neal: II, 253)
Mr. Samuel Lee	(Wood: *Ath. Ox.*, IV, 347)
Mr. John Manship	(Pal.: II, 448)
Dr. William Marshall	(Cal.: II, 414)
Mr. Edmund Matthews	(" " 491)
Mr. Richard Moreton	(" " 625)
Mr. Samuel Oldershaw	(" " 423)
Mr. John Panton	(" " 697)
Mr. William Pell	(" " 289)
Mr. Richard Perrott	(" " 784)
Mr. Richard Reyner	(" " 884)
Mr. Gilbert Rule	(Pal.: II, 241)
Mr. Henry Sampson	(" " 212)
Mr. Richard Smith	(Cal.: II, 613 ³¹⁸)
Mr. Anthony Stevenson	(Pal.: II, 594)
Mr. James Stevenson	(" " 369)
Mr. Samuel Stodden	(" " 352)
Mr. Andrew Tristram	(Cal.: II, 565)
Mr. Edmund Warren	(" " 293)
Mr. Bartholomew Westley	(Pal.: I, 442)
Mr. John Wilson	(Cal.: II, 109)

All these men left the church (perforce, it is true) for medicine; but occasionally it happened that men, of their own volition, left medicine for the church. Pepys speaks quite respectfully of hearing "the Doctor that is lately turned Divine, Dr. Waterhouse. He preaches in a devout manner, not elegant nor very persuasive, but seems to mean well, and that he would preach holily; and was mighty passionate against people that make a scoff of religion. And the truth is I did observe Mrs. Holworthy smile often, and many others of the parish, who, I perceive, have known him, and were in mighty expectation of hearing him preach, but could not forbear smiling, and she particularly on me, and I on her." [319] Henry Brunsell also had been formally

---

[318] "A Man of great Repute, as a Gentleman, a Physician, and a Divine."
[319] *Diary,* Jan. 31, 1668/9.

admitted to practice medicine and had been successful; but after the Restoration, "laying aside that faculty, he betook himself to divinity." [320]

There were preacher-physicians who became specialists in their new—or, at least, their concentrated—field. Nicholas Cary cured "ill affected Eyes and Ears." [321] John Cortman's difficult specialty was "in paralytic Distempers and distracted People." [322] Valentine Greatrakes (Greatrick, Gratrix) was not an ordained minister, but on the testimony of Wood, had "spent some years in studying humanity and divinity" under John Daniel Getsius, minister of Stoke Gabriel in Devonshire.[323] About 1662, Greatrakes was strongly convinced that the gift of healing was his, especially in the King's Evil; and because of his method of treatment for that disease, he became known as "the stroaker." He aroused much enmity among the regular clergy, but also some admiration in the same group. "Mr. Grattrix the stroaker, grows in that esteem among us that I heard the Bishop of Hereford [Herbert Crofts] yesterday say he had done thinges, to his owne certain knowledge, beyond all the power of nature. . . ." [324]

William Holder (mathematician, musician, philologist, and member of the Royal Society) worked out a method of teaching the deaf and dumb to speak. "He was," says Aubrey, "beholding to no author: did only consult with nature." [325] Unfortunately, Dr. John Wallis later gave a few lessons to young Mr. Popham (Holder's most conspicuous patient) and claimed the credit of teaching him to speak. A professional quarrel ensued, with charges and counter charges.[326]

---

[320] Wood: *Fasti*, II, 233.
[321] Kennett: *Register*, 473.
[322] *Ibid.*, 492.
[323] Wood: *Fasti*, II, 233.
[324] *Hatton Correspondence*, I, 49. See *The Great Abnormals*, by T. B. Hyslop, pp. 108-9.
[325] John Bulwer had suggested an academy for the mute, in 1644 (Watson, Foster, p. 451).
[326] Aubrey: I, 404. A Note, p. 599, in Dr. Burney's *Hist. of Music* says that Dr. Holder was so disagreeable as sub dean of the Chapel Royal, that he was called "snub dean."

It was "Botanism" that most attracted the nonconformist Samuel Ogden, though "he had a considerable insight into Anatomy, and several parts of Physick. . . . 'Twas a rare thing to him to meet with a Herb that he could not readily Name in Latin and English: And as to most, he would tell you the Nature and Effects." [327]   Matthew Robinson was especially successful "in consumptions." [328]   Thomas Vaughan, who, like Robinson, was of the established church, retired to Oxford "and in a sedate repose prosecuted his medicinal geny," which in his case was the "chymical" part. Later, he went to London and made wider and deeper studies "under the protection and patronage of that noted chymist sir Rob. Murrey or Moray knight." [329]

A number of the outstanding clergymen were interested in one or another phase of "Physick," although they did not consider themselves physicians, even of an informal variety. Isaac Barrow studied medicine for some years; [330] Robert Burton died at the very beginning of the period to which this discussion of clergy-interests is roughly limited, but his influence continued because of his *Anatomy of Melancholy,* which, originally published in 1621, went through eight editions in the next fifty years.[331]   Richard Cumberland "had a good judgment in Physick and he knew everything that was curious in Anatomy." [332]   Though Nicholas Ferrar never went beyond deacon's orders in the church, he was more spiritual than most of the divines named in this chapter. With his strongly religious qualities, he combined a love of beauty and of knowledge. One of his intellectual interests was medicine, which he had studied at Padua.[333]

[327] Calamy : *Account, etc.,* II, 194.
[328] *Autobiography,* p. 40.
[329] Wood : *Ath. Ox.,* III, 722.
[330] *Works,* I, xi.
[331] Osler : *The Library of Robert Burton (Trans. of the Bibl. Soc.,* Vol. X, Lond., 1912). Also, Saintsbury : *Hist. of Elizabethan Literature,* p. 429.
[332] *Biog. Brit.,* III, 1594.
[333] *Autobiography of M. Robinson,* p. 27 (Note).

Dr. John Wallis gave his first interest, when a student at the university, to medicine, and when he took his B.A. in 1637, he maintained the circulation of the blood in a disputation ("the first time the theory was publicly maintained in a disputation").[334] Dr. John Wilkins was enthusiastic on the subject of transfusion of blood. Pepys (of course) chanced "to go to a tavern, where Dean Wilkins and others: and good discourse; among the rest, of a man that is a little frantic, that hath been a kind of minister, Dr. Wilkins saying that he hath read for him in his church, that is poor and a debauched man, that the College [The Royal Society] meeting at Greenwich College have hired for 20s to have some of the blood of a sheep let into his body; and it is to be done on Saturday next. They purpose to let in about twelve ounces; which they compute, is what will be let in a minute's time by a watch."[335] This secular interest of Dr. Wilkins's was not unique among the scientifically inclined preachers. Eighteen years earlier, Francis Potter had told John Aubrey of "his notion of curing diseases, etc. by transfusion of blood out of one man into another, and that the hint came into his head reflecting on Ovid's story of Medea and Jason, and that this was a matter of ten years before that time. About a year after, he and I went to trye the experiment, but it was on a hen, and the creature to little and our tooles not good. . . ."[336]

Teaching

Teaching is not, strictly speaking, an avocation of the seventeenth-century divine. It is, rather, an associated or

[334] Ball Rouse: *Hist. of Math. at Camb.*, p. 41. (Wallis took orders after receiving his M.A. in 1640.)

[335] *Diary*, Nov. 21, 1667. For Pepys's account of a public anatomy, see his entry of Feb. 27, 1662. (The opportunities to attend public anatomies were limited; even surgeons had to get permission from the Barber Surgeons Company or from the College of Physicians, to dissect dead bodies in private. Wyatt: *William Harvey*, p. 67.)

[336] Aubrey: II, 166. (See, same page, Potter's letter describing with a diagram his experiment in transfusion.) Also, Wood: *Ath. Ox.*, III, 1156.

allied vocation. The Fellows in the university lectured
to undergraduates; many a country clergyman added to his
scant income by receiving into his home young men whom
he would instruct as well as lodge and board; and the
private chaplain was always expected to teach the children
of his patron. The headmastership of a private school was
one of the recognized openings for university-trained men
who had won their degrees but no preferment in the
church; and after the sequestrations and ejectments that
always emphasized Puritan or Anglican authority, deprived
ministers often found a refuge behind the schoolmaster's
desk. When Fuller is enumerating the Fellows who were
ejected from Cambridge in 1643, he remarks that the situation reminds him of the Greek saying, "He is either dead
or teacheth school," which was applied to the soldiers of
Nicias who had fought unsuccessfully against the Sicilians.
"No calling," observes Bishop Fuller broadmindedly,
"which is honest being disgraceful, especially to such who,
for their conscience' sake, have deserted a better condition." [337] The ejectments of 1662 also sent many of the
clergy (nonconformists, this time) to school-keeping.[338]

There was always, then, a reason why a parson taught
school. He did not select the work because he enjoyed
young people, or because he liked the excitement of making
two ideas grow where one or none had been before, or because he wished to share his knowledge; he taught school
because he saw no other way to get a living. Having unwillingly become an usher or a private tutor, the young man
who had planned to be an archbishop, or the old man (of
the 1662 group) whose prosperity was behind him, would
not be likely to feel any enthusiasm about teaching. There
were, however, mitigating circumstances in some teaching
positions, for the young usher might be associated with

[337] *Hist. of the University of Cambridge*, p. 237.
[338] See *Original Records of Early Nonconformity*, 2 vols. The ejected
ministers are reported "as Heads and Teachers, at most as Preachers,
never as Ministers," p. xii.

such great teachers as Thomas Farnaby or Richard Busby (the latter being himself a Doctor of Divinity); [339] or he might make it his ambition to prepare others for the career that had been denied to him and do his teaching so well that, years afterwards, he could take credit to himself for the success of certain pupils who became famous clergymen. Dr. Richard Busby, for example, "educated more youths that were afterwards eminent in Church and State, than any master of his time." [340] Richard Reeve (a Roman Catholic, by the way) was "so sedulous in his profession of pedagogy, that he hath educated 60 ministers of the Church of England and about 40 Roman priests." William Fuller "bred as many (Preachers) under him in the Church, as he did Scholars in the University." [341]

The social position of the teacher is made plain by contemporaneous comment. "I know not how it comes to pass," says Robert South in a sermon,[342] "that this honorable employment should find so little respect (as experience shews it does) from too many in the world. For there is no profession which has, or can have, a greater influence upon the public. . . . Nay, I take schoolmasters to have a more powerful influence upon the spirits of men than preachers themselves." And Francis Cheynell insists that the schoolmaster's office is as honorable as it is useful, adding practically: "let their maintenance be as honourable as their office." [343]

When Thomas Jacombe preached the funeral sermon of the Reverend Richard Vines, and mentioned that after leaving the university, Mr. Vines was for some time a schoolmaster, Dr. Jacombe hastened to say, "And let this be

[339] Two great clergymen-teachers died just before the beginning of our period: Alexander Gill (1635) and Joseph Meade (1638).
[340] Wood: *Ath. Ox.*, IV, 418.
[341] Lloyd: p. 509.
[342] *Sermons*, III, 83-4.
[343] *A Plot for the Good of Posterity*, p. 43; also, Reynolds's funeral sermon for Langley, p. 26: "And I scarce know a greater defect in this Nation, than the want of such encouragement and maintenance as might render the Calling of a Schoolmaster so honorable, as men of great Learning might be invited into that service."

no disparagement; I could instance in rare instruments of God's glory in the church of Christ, who began with that employment." [344] Fuller's *Character* of the Good School-master explains the unsatisfactory qualities of the typical master in this way: 1. Young men teach before they finish the university: 2. they teach because they are waiting for preferment; 3. because they are disheartened; 4. they grow rich and delegate the work to ushers. [345]

A list of preacher-teachers in the times of Cromwell and the Restoration would be long. So very many divines taught at some time in their lives that, as has been said, the schoolmaster occupation can hardly be considered an avocation. Only those men will be named, therefore, who have some special interest attaching to them, as of personality, or pedagogical method, or extraordinary success as a teacher.

Dr. John Bois was able to attract students to his Greek lectures at four o'clock in the morning. They gathered around his bed, so Thomas Gataker says, while he discoursed to them. [346]

Dr. Richard Busby, the chief master of Westminster School for fifty-five years, was an active influence in the life of many a notable man of the seventeenth century. He was a particularly awe-inspiring disciplinarian, with a propensity, like that of Alexander Gill, for whipping everybody who came within reach of his cane. A *Spectator* paper (No. 229) shows Sir Roger standing before Busby's monument in Westminster Abbey, exclaiming: "Dr. Busby, a great man! he whipp'd my grandfather; a very great man! I should have gone to him myself if I had not been a Blockhead; a very great man!" Burton, in his Diary, uses the schoolmaster's name as a general reference (March 23, 1658/9): "The House rose at two. The Chair behaves

---

[344] *Enochs Walk and Change.* Cf. Clark: *Em. Lives,* p. 127, on "Richard Mather."
[345] *Holy and Profane State,* p. 85.
[346] Funeral Sermon by Simeon Ashe (*Narrative of the Life of Mr. Gataker*).

like a Busby amongst so many school-boys; and takes a little too much on him, but grandly." [347] Dr. Busby was held in such public esteem, that he was invited to walk in the funeral procession of Cromwell. Somewhere in the list of persons (filling nearly eleven octavo pages) one finds:

> Clerks of the household kitchen, His Highness's kitchen
> Master of Westminster School, Mr. Busby
> Usher of the Exchequer, Mr. Beyer [348]

Anthony à Wood credits Busby with having "educated more youths that were afterwards eminent in the church and state than any master of his time." [349] This statement does not necessarily convey a compliment to the pupil. Wood cites Robert South as a pupil at Westminster where he "obtained a considerable stock of grammar and philological learning, but more of impudence and sauciness." [350]

William Chappell (who wrote *The Preacher, Or, the Art and Method of Preaching*) was "famous for his many and eminent Pupils." [351] Thomas Cheesman is mentioned as a successful teacher. This is an interesting statement because he had been blind from the age of four. He took both his first and second degrees at Cambridge and later became "a useful Preacher." [352]

Dr. Thomas Comber, master of Trinity, Cambridge, deserves special mention because of his efforts to preserve a standard of scholarship, "commonly making this return when he was solicited by Powerful Friends in favour of an unqualified Lad, Persuade your Gardner to Plant a Withered Tree in your Garden." [353] Dr. John Conant,

---

[347] *Memoirs,* IV, 243.   [348] *Ibid.,* II, 518.
[349] *Ath. Ox.,* IV, 418. In Nichols, IV, 395, is a letter, dated Dec. 13, 1640, which accompanied a gift of ten dozen bottles of "Cyder" to Busby. It is a gay, friendly letter that gives an unusual view of the austere master. See G. F. R. Russell's *Memoir of Richard Busby,* for a study of the man, and of Westminster School in the seventeenth century.
[350] *Ibid.,* p. 631.
[351] Lloyd: p. 607. Milton is, of course, the most famous; but their association was brief. He also taught Henry More, Lightfoot, and Robert Gouge.
[352] Calamy: *Abridg.,* II, 103.   [353] Walker: Pt. II, 9.

Rector of Exeter College, was also a conscientious executive: he "instructed the tutors in the need of conscientious instructing, watched over the students, punishing them by exercises instead of fines." [354]   When Ralph Cudworth was a tutor at Emmanuel College, Cambridge, he had at one time twenty-eight pupils.[355]   Dr. James Duport was equally popular as a tutor.

Bishop Duppa was the carefully selected instructor of the Prince of Wales, afterwards Charles II.   The Duke of Newcastle recommended Duppa in a letter that must have given him pride and pleasure, if he ever saw it, though the praise is not concerned with his ability as a churchman.   The prince is congratulated on "your tutor, sir, wherein you are most happy, since he hath no pedantry in him; his learning he makes right use of neither to trouble himself with it or his friends; reads men as well as books . . . has travelled, which you shall perceive by his wisdom and fashion more than by his relations; and in a word strives as much discreetly to hide the scholar in him, as other men's follies to show it; and is a right gentleman, such a one as man should be." [356]

Alexander Gill, the younger, was both a clergyman and teacher but his reputation is so overshadowed by that of his father (who died in 1635) that he has little personal consequence.   Thomas Godwin was one of those disappointed university men who waited long for recognition by the church: "Broken and wearied out by the drudgery of a school," he at length had a rectory conferred upon him.[357] Of quite another type is the "pretie little man" John Hales, who became a private tutor because a kindly person sought

[354] *Biog. Brit.*, III, 1435.
[355] Mullinger: *Cambridge Characteristics in the 17th Century*, p. 155.
[356] Newcastle, Marg.:   *Life of the Duke of Newcastle*, pp. 326-7. For Charles I's letters to the prince, regarding Duppa, see Clarendon: IV, 78-9.
[357] Wood: *Ath. Ox.*, III, 51-2.   See A. K. Cook, *About Winchester College*, p. 57ff, "A Head-Master has been known to go directly to a bishopric."

an excuse to provide for him after he was ejected. "My lady Salter . . . had him to her house, indeed, but 'twas to teach her sonne, who was such a block head he could not read well." [358] "Meek Dr. Heyward" was "forced to keep School" after his ejectment, but he was more fortunate than most of the impromptu schoolmasters, "there being no Art or Quality, as Musick, Arithmetick, Writing, etc., but he was able to teach, as if he had been professor of it." [359] Dr. William Holder is an outstanding figure among the school-teachers and tutors, because he made a special study of the deaf and dumb.[360]

Dr. Ralph Kettle would furnish copy for a book. He was the sort of schoolmaster to whom anecdotes attach themselves. He had "ways," he had prejudices. He was always saying or doing something that could be laughed at. This is Fuller's testimony: "I have heard Dr. Whistler say that he wrote good Latin, and Dr. Ralph Bathurst . . . that he scolded the best in Latin of any one that ever he knew. He was of an admirably healthy constitution. . . . He was a very tall, well grown man. His gown and surplice and hood being on, he had a terrible gigantique aspect, with his sharp gray eies. . . . One of his maxomes of governing was to keepe down the *juvenilis impetus*. . . . One of the fellowes was wont to say that Dr. Kettle's braine was like a hasty pudding, where there was memorie, judgement, and phancy all stirred together. . . . He hated long haire and he would bring a paire of cizers in his muffe. . . . I remember he cut Mr. Radford's haire with the knife that chipps the bread on the buttery hatch, and then he sang (this is in the old play—Henry Viii's time—of Grammar [sic] Gurtons Needle)

"And was not Grim the Collier finely trimm'd?
Tonedi, Tonedi." [361]

[358] Aubrey: I, 283. [359] Lloyd : pp. 512-13.
[360] Wood : *Fasti*, II, 245 (For the controversy on the subject see under "Medicine," p. 200).
[361] *Church History of Britain*, II, 17.

John Langley was accounted a great schoolmaster in a day that knew many men of more than ordinary ability who were at the head of famous schools. He too had a personality though not as eccentric a one as Kettle's. He was an antiquary, linguist, and grammarian, and so earnest a master, that in a sickness he desired "if he should then have died, to have been buried at the school door." [362] There is the best sort of proof that Dr. Samuel Marsh was particularly successful as a teacher, because "among his Scholars and Pupils were: three Bishops, four Privy-Counsellors, two Judges, three Doctors of Physick." [363] Equally able was Dr. Lambert Osbaldeston who ". . . 'tis said, Had above 80 Doctors in the Three Great Faculties, in the Two Universities, that did gratefully acknowledge their Education under him. . . ." [364] Lloyd's comment on him gives an idea of what was unusual in the manner and practice of a teacher: "he being not pedantick in his carriage and discourse, was by some not thought rich in Learning, because he did not jingle with it in his discourse. . . . He never dulled a quick head by mawling it, nor awed a fluent tongue into stuttering by affrightments, nor commuted correction into money, nor debased his authority by contesting with the obstinate, turning such out when he could do them no good, and they might do others much hurt, studying the Children's dispositions, as they did their books: the invincibly dull he pityed, consigning them over to other Professions, Shipwrights, and Boat-makers, will chuse those crooked pieces of Timber, which other Carpenters refuse." [365]

Dr. William Oughtred was an exceptional teacher of mathematics, as may be shown by a mention of some of his students: "Seth Ward, M. A. (now Bishop of Sarum) came to him and lived with him halfe a yeare (and he would not take a farthing for his diet), and learned all his mathe-

[362] Reynolds's funeral sermon for Langley, p. 31.
[363] Lloyd : p. 504.
[364] Walker : Pt. II, 91.
[365] Lloyd : p. 616.

matiques of him. Sir Jonas More was with him. . . . Sir
Charles Scarborough was his scholar; so was Dr. John
Wallis. . . . so was Christopher Wren; so was Mr. Smith-
wyck, *Regius Societatis Socius*. One Mr. Austin . . . was
his scholar, and studyed so much that he became mad, fell
a laughing, and so dyed, to the great grief of the old gentleman. Mr. Stokes, another scholar, fell mad, and dream't
that the good old gentleman came to him, and gave him
good advice, and so he recovered, and is still well. . . . He
taught all free." One learns, too, that "he could not endure
to see a scholar write an ill hand; he taught them all presently to mend their hands." But even Oughtred was not
always successful: "He had nine sonnes (most lived to be
men). . . . None of his sonnes he could make scholars." [366]
(He probably made no attempt to teach his four daughters.
Edward Davenant did instruct his daughters; they were
Algebraists.) [367]

Still another example of ability to inspire pupils is Thomas
Pashe, doctor of divinity and teacher. "And it will perchance be thought no contemptible Evidence of his great
Worth, that three Bishops, Four Privy-Counsellors, Two
Judges, and Three Doctors of Physick, all of which had
been his Pupils in the University, came in one Day to pay
him a Visit." [368]

"Sometimes ordinary scholars make extraordinary good
masters," says Fuller, when picturing the qualities of The
Good Master of a College. "Yes, a little alloy makes gold
to work the better, so, perchance, some dullness in a man
makes him fitter to manage secular affairs. . . ." [369]
Hannibal Potter and Ralph Kettle were of this sort;
". . . if they were not so ready Scholars, yet could they
build and govern Colledges . . . the Whetstone is dull its

[366] Aubrey: II, 105ff.
[367] *Ibid.*, I, 201.
[368] Walker: Pt. II, 141. (This is exactly the same statement Lloyd
makes regarding Samuel Marsh. Lloyd's is the earlier book. The
array of notables could be duplicated for many teachers.)
[369] *The Holy and Profane State*, p. 79.

self that whets the things." [370]   Dr. John Pottinger must
have had executive ability: "The very discipline and method
of his excellent School, was able to instill learning (like a
watch once well set that goeth always) even without him
to the dullest capacity, and his fancy, parts and incouraging
temper, put life into that Learning. . . ." [371]   But Ellis
Rowland had no gift either for teaching or managing, consequently his wife "kept school and he was forced to make
Flourishes and Patterns for the girls to sew by." [372]

Edward Sylvester sounds like an amiable, long suffering,
competent college professor of any time or place. "He was
the common drudge of the university, either to make, or correct or review the Latin sermons of certain dull theologists
thereof before they were to be delivered at St. Mary's, as
also the Greek or Latin verses of others (as dull as the
former) that were to be put in, or before, books that occasionally were published. He lived to see several of his
scholars to be heads of houses in this university: John
Owen, dean of Christ-Church, John Wilkins, warden of
Wadham College, Henry Wilkinson, principal of Magdalen
hall, etc. who with other scholars of his that were doctors,
batchelors of divinity, law and physick and masters of arts,
had an annual feast together; to which their master was
always invited, and being set at the upper end of the table,
he would feed their minds with learned discourses, and
criticisms in grammar." [373]

Ezrael Tongue who was "governour, or one of the professors of an academy at Durham, followed precisely the
Jesuites method of teaching; and boyes did profit wonderfully." At one time, Dr. Tongue gave up teaching and lived
as an active clergyman in Kent, "but being much vex'd with
factions, parishioners and quakers, left his benefice, and
returned to teaching." He seems to have been a resourceful teacher. "Ezerel Tong, D. D. invented . . . the way

[370] Lloyd: p. 542.
[371] Lloyd: p. 616.
[372] Calamy: *Account, etc.*, p. 787.
[373] Wood: *Fasti*, II, 34.

of teaching children to write a good hand in twenty dayes time, by writing over, with blacke inke: viz. the children (scilicet, about 8 or 9 aetatis) were to do it four howers in the day; i.e. 2 howers or 2 halfe-howers in the morning at a time (as the boyes temper could endure it without trying him),—and then to play as long; and then to it again, to keep up the idea in the child fresh." [374]

Thomas Triplet lives, if he lives at all, through his ballad on Alexander Gill, the elder.[375] Benjamin Whichcote was much praised by Tillotson; [376] and Theophilus Wodenote deserves remembrance because of advice he gave John Aubrey: "when I was a school-boy . . . he did me much good in opening of my understanding; advised me to read lord Bacon's Essayes and an olde booke of proverbs (English). . . ." [377] There may have been other clergymen-teachers who recommended to their pupils the reading of English literature, but their pupils do not mention the fact.

Many of the teachers wrote textbooks for their classes, the majority, naturally enough, being Latin Grammars, derived more or less from Lily's immortal work.[378] Richard Busby published eight textbooks in Latin and Greek,[379] and is said to have taught from a Hebrew Grammar of his own composition that was not printed.[380] There were also lexicons compiled by these men, phrase-books, and studies in composition; but they were as a general thing useful aids to knowledge, not excursions into new methods of pedagogy. Textbooks for very young children offer more interest. Francis Cheynell suggests an unusual way to learn an alphabet. "The Holy Spirit," he says, "hath composed

[374] Aubrey: II, 262. (This is the Tongue who was connected with Titus Oates and the Popish Plot. See Burnet: *History, etc.,* I, 424, 510.)
[375] Aubrey: II, 264. See under *Poetry,* p. 234.
[376] Neal: I, 483.
[377] Aubrey: II, 307. Brinsley, in *A Consolation, etc.,* recommends "Maister Chapman's translation in English meeter; whom we may rightly call the English Homer," p. 73-4.
[378] For Lat. Gr. more or less independent of Lily, see Foster Watson, *Eng. Grammar Schools,* p. 273ff.
[379] Wood: *Ath. Ox.,* IV, 418.
[380] Watson, Foster, p. 529.

some abcedarian Psalms in Akrosticall verses, according to the Hebrew Alphabet, that Children might learn an alphabet of godlinesse . . . the first letters of the verses of certain Psalmes, the 25. 34. 37. 119. are set down according to the order of the Alphabet, etc." [381] A livelier work is a plain and Easy Primer for children (probably by Charles Hoole), "wherein the Pictures of Beasts and Birds for each Letter in the Alphabet are set down." [382] Thomas Lye brought out *The Child's Delight,* a spelling book "wherein all the Words of our English Bible are set down in an Alphabetical Order and divided into their distinct syllables." [383] John Newton printed: *School Pastime for Young Children: or an easy and delightful Method for the Teaching of Children to read English directly.*[384] Ezrael Tongue goes further and puts his English Grammar into verse:

> Noun substantives the names of things declare,
> And adjectives, what kind of things those are.[385]

II

The Clergy and the Fine Arts

Drama

The Drama had fallen on evil days at the beginning of the period of Puritan control,[386] and the clergy, even though play-minded, would not be likely to devote time to a subject that offered no return either in money or in public consideration. The dry-as-dust explorations into

---

[381] *A Plot for the Good of Posterity,* p. 26.
[382] Wood: *op. cit.,* III, 759.
[383] Wood: *Ath. Ox.,* IV, 136.
[384] *Ibid.,* III, 1191.
[385] *Ibid.,* p. 1266.
[386] For successive ordinances against Stage Plays, see Rushworth: Oct. 18, 1687; Jan. 22, 1647/8; Jan. 31, 1647/8; Feb. 9, 1647/8; Jan. 1, 1648/9.

"the fathers" and commentators had no money results, it is true, yet such work was a means of bringing a man to the notice of his fellow scholars who might give him aid in securing preferment in the church, or who could recommend him to the notice of a generous patron. Furthermore, the learned avocations often led to lively controversies which gave pleasure to all the participants. If a man had a peculiar genius for the pursuit and identification of sources and parallels and influences, if he had a logical faculty that urged him to analyze, subdivide, and support his propositions and theories, then such a man would be sure of stirring up interest among those who agreed or disagreed with the point of view presented.

It is easy to see why few men of the church gave serious attention to the composition of plays during the forties and fifties of the seventeenth century. A man who writes a play wants to see it acted, he wants to compare it with other performances, he wants to talk about it to people who are interested in plays and actors. No one of those desires could be easily satisfied in the Commonwealth times, but, on the other hand, no one of them was utterly impossible. Plays and parts of plays were acted, even if disguised in various ways,[387] plays were published, and there were a number of clergymen living at the beginning of the civil war, who had written plays earlier in the century and who would hardly have lost all interest in dramatic art merely because it was under suspicion.

Among those who had written plays before 1640, William Cartwright is easily the most important from a literary standpoint. He was only thirty-two when he died in 1643, but he had already made a reputation as a dramatist, poet,

[387] See, Rollin, H. E.: A Contribution to the History of English Drama (*Studies in Phil.*, Vol. 18).
Nettleton: *Eng. Drama of the Restoration and 18th Cent.*, Ch. II (The Dramatic Interregnum, 1642-1660). The Thomason Catalogue includes the titles of many plays published when the Puritans were in power.
See Evelyn (Feb. 5, 1648/9) for comment on a tragi-comedy at the Cockpit.

lecturer in metaphysics, and preacher of well-planned sermons. He wrote tragi-comedies: *The Lady Errant, The
Royal Slave, Siege: or, Love's Convert,* and a comedy, *The
Ordinary.*[388] The serious-minded Dr. Daniel Featley,
though he never composed a play himself, yet gave his
approval to the practice by writing one of the dedication-
prefaces to Phineas Fletcher's *Purple Island.* Dr. Featley
concludes with a sweeping invitation: "I invite all Sorts
to be readers; all Readers to understand; and all who understand to be happy." [389] Richard Flecknoe's pastoral, *Love's
Dominion,* was printed in 1654; and his critical study of
drama, *A Short Discourse of the English Stage,* appeared
in 1664.[390] In a preface to his *Erminia* (1661), he had
written that he could "say without vanity that none knows
more of the English Stage than he, nor any seen more of
the Latin, French, Spanish and Italian." [391] Thomas Hall
was the author of a tract entitled *Funebria Florae, The
Downfall of May-Games.* The arguments against May
Games are presented in what is virtually a one-act play,
embedded in the sterner and much duller paragraphs of re-
proofs and exhortation, objections and answers. Court
procedure is followed, and the indictment of Flora is according to prescribed form; a Jury is made up, and testimony given. The choice of witnesses for the prosecution
shows considerable imagination: Holy Scriptures, Pliny,
Lactantius, Synodus Francica, Charles the Second, Order
of Parliament, Solemn League and Covenant, Order of the
Council of State, Bishop Babbington, Bishop Andrewes,
and Ovid. As each person testifies, a reference in the
margin shows the source of the opinion given.[392]

The prolific Peter Heylin wrote a tragedy (*Spurious*)
and a comedy (*Theomachia*) in his youth but neither was

[388] Wood: *Ath. Ox.,* III, 67-70.
[389] "To the Reader," p. ix.
[390] Spingarn: *Crit. Essays of the 17th Cent.,* II, 91.
[391] Graves, T. S.: Notes on Puritanism and the Stage (*Studies in
Phil.,* Vol. 18).
[392] Pp. 19-30.

ever printed.[393] Barten Holyday's unamusing comedy, *Technogamia, Or, The Marriage of the Arts,* was both acted and printed but its reception was not encouraging, and the author found a more satisfactory avocation in poetry and translations of Persius, Juvenal, and Horace.[394] Dr. Henry Killigrew's tragedy, *The Conspiracy,* was written when he was a mere boy, but the play was sufficiently good to tempt someone to print it in 1638 without the author's consent; consequently he published, in 1652, a new edition under a new title, *Pallantus and Eudora.*[395] Jasper Mayne published a comedy, *The City Match,* in 1639, which had another edition in 1659.[396] Pepys saw it played in 1668— "not acted these thirty years, and but a silly play." Mayne also published a tragi-comedy, *The Amorous War,* in 1648.

Henry Newcome did not print anything of a secular nature, but he was much interested in his brother minister's play, *The Benefice.* Robert Wilde, its author, had written it in youth, just as the other preacher-playwrights referred to had written plays when drama was the popular form of composition; but, unlike them, he worked his play over when play writing again became profitable, and Newcome apparently did much of the rewriting.[397] Bishop Thomas Sprat was another assistant playwright, tradition says, and Buckingham's *Rehearsal* had the benefit of his suggestions.[398] Samuel Sheppard wrote a few short farces. Wood is authority for the assertion that James Shirley "entered into Holy Orders" and "became a minister of God's word."[399] But this statement has been denied, and it does not seem possible to offer Shirley as a divine with drama as his avocation.[400] William Strode, however, did combine sermon and play constructing. He, like Cartwright, died in the early years of the civil war, but his play

[393] Wood : *op. cit.,* 557.
[394] Wood : *Ath. Ox.,* III, 522-3.
[395] *Ibid.,* IV, 621.
[396] *Ibid.,* III, 972.
[397] *Diary,* Jan. 31, 1662/3 ; July 21, 1663.
[398] Wood : *op. cit.,* IV, 209 ; *The Rehearsal* (Introduction), p. 17.
[399] *Ibid.,* III, 151.
[400] Nason : *James Shirley, Dramatist,* pp. 31-2.

with the delightful title, *Passions Calmed, Or, the Settling of the Floating Island,* had been acted before the King and Queen in 1636. It was published in 1655, with its title abbreviated to *The Floating Island.* Below the name of the author is printed: "The Aires and Songs set by Mr. Henry Lawes, servant to his late Majesty in his publick and private Musick." Strode had been dead ten years when his play was published, and the writer of the Epistle to the Reader feels that he must prevent any misconception as to the character of the author. "He wrote it at the instance of those who might command him; else he had scarce condescended to a *Play,* his serious thoughts being fill'd with notions of deeper consideration." George Wilde had two unprinted plays in his past.[401] Robert Wilde's play has already been spoken of.

The only ordained preacher whom tradition puts literally on the stage is the always dramatic Hugh Peters. The often repeated story tells that he was expelled from college, and for some time thereafter was an actor, in this way acquiring his extravagance of language and gesture.[402] The explanation of the gossip that makes Peters an actor, probably lies in the man's personality. He was a vigorous, colloquial preacher who used timely, often unseemly illustrations that his audience could enjoy and retail. He was prominent in politics; he was tremendously admired and fiercely hated. Current anecdotes gained in popularity if they could be connected in some way with Hugh Peters, and brief stories, old and new, were published as *Hugh Peter Jest Books.* He was the sort of person of whom any spectacular report is easily believed, to whom any wild action is credited. His death was a climax of many public appearances, and the spectators found great satisfaction in the hanging, drawing, and quartering of the man who, rumor said, had stood on a scaffold eleven years before and

[401] Wood: *Ath. Ox.,* III, 720.
[402] Burnet: *History of his own Times,* p. 106.

struck the king's head from his body. It is no wonder, then, that he was believed to be an actor as well as many other things.[403]

Drawing

Religion and Art have always been willing associates, but none of these preachers turned painters, and none of the painters or engravers of the day selected preaching as an avocation. Many of the clergy allowed themselves music and poetry as a serious diversion, but no parson gave the same attention to Art.[404] There is nothing mysterious about this fact; in the first place, there was no general interest in painting or sculpture, and in the second, both painting and sculpture were connected in the English protestant mind, with the church of Rome. Consequently, only a few divines are mentioned as experimenting with pencils and brushes or as caring for beauty as some man has fixed it on canvas. There must have been the usual proportion of people, among the clerical group, who had skill in drawing; but it was not an ability that would win admiration or seem worth comment from a biographer.

Thomas Comber, whose special and conspicuous gift was in languages, cared for painting also, but not to the extent of creating anything;[405] Richard Crashaw had some practice in "Drawing, Limning and Engraving";[406] William Holder, that many-sided preacher, had "good judgement in painting and drawing";[407] Francis Potter, even more generously endowed with assorted talents, "was from a

[403] In the *Memoir of Richard Busby*, by G. F. R. Barker, we are told that at Christ Church, Busby once acted in Cartwright's *Royal Slave* before the king and queen with such brilliant success "that he seriously thought at one time of adopting the stage as a profession," p. 34.

[404] Evelyn, in *Sculptura; or The History of Calcography*, p. 98, speaks of English engravers, but names no divines of his own time. Peacham's *Compleat Gentleman* (1622), Ch. XII, says the author was beaten by his schoolmasters because he drew persons, or maps.

[405] *Dict. Nat'l Biog.*

[406] Lloyd: p. 619.

[407] Aubrey: I, 404.

boy given to drawing and painting. On the buttery-dore in his parlour he drew his father's picture at length, with his booke (fore-shortened), and on the spectacles in his hand is the reflection of the Gothique south windowe"; [408] Peter Sterry could refer to Vandyke and Titian as if the names meant a real acquaintance with the work of both artists; [409] and Samuel Ward was an emblematist after the manner of Francis Quarles.[410] Wilkins's books on mechanical devices contain elaborate designs, diagrams, and use of perspective. It does not follow, of course, that he drew the figures himself.

Music

Although organs and musical instruments were not permitted in the churches while the Puritans were in authority, music did not disappear entirely from knowledge or practice. "Right glad am I," says Thomas Fuller, "that when music was lately shut out of our churches, on what default of hers I dare not to inquire, it hath since been harboured and welcomed in the halls, parlours, and chambers, of the primest persons of this nation." [411] Dr. Burney is responsible, in his *History of Music,* for the statement that, while officially frowned upon, "yet it [Music] seems to have been more zealously cultivated, in private, during the usurpation, if we may judge by the number of publications, than in the same number of years, at any former period." [412]

The turmoil of the civil war, and the subsequent readjustments, social and financial, would not offer much opportunity for creative work in musical composition. Sing-song measures sufficed to carry the stall ballads, but music as an expression of high and beautiful thought was

[408] *Ibid.,* II, 162.
[409] *Freedom of the Will,* pp. 22-3.
[410] *Dict. Nat'l Biog.*
[411] *Worthies,* I, 41. See Webster (*Acad. Examen* (1654), p. 42) on the neglect of the highest form of music.
[412] Vol. III, 408.

crowded out—crowded out, rather than stamped out. Cromwell was himself extremely fond of music, as is well known, and it was with his approval that Davenant, in 1656, opened "a kind of theatre," at Rutland house, in Charterhouse-square for "an Entertainment in Declamation and Music, after the Manner of the Ancients."[413] In the same year Davenant produced the *Siege of Rhodes;* and, too, a petition was presented for the foundation of a College of Music.[414] In 1658, Sir William Davenant provided daily, at the Cockpit in Drury Lane, a lively "opera" called *The Cruelty of the Spaniards in Peru,* in which both vocal and instrumental music were made use of.[415] In 1659, *The History of Sir Francis Drake* was "Exprest by Instrumentall and Vocall Musick, and by Art of Perspective in Scenes."

After the Restoration, music returned with no apparent effort to its former dignified position. It has been said that this fact proves that there had been no general cessation of interest in music;[416] but even if it had been literally silenced during nearly twenty years, that would be too short a time to obliterate, or even seriously to blur, a great art. Music would still have remained a part of the mind and spirit of any person who knew and loved good music. Nor would men who had been reared in the Established church before the Commonwealth era be likely to forget the harmonies, the chants, the tremendous swelling chords that were woven through the liturgy. No sensitive person, however spiritually and intellectually Puritan, could, even if he would, divest himself of an emotional experience of years.[417]

A knowledge of music, as a matter of fact, could be of practical service even in Puritan times. Edmund Chilmead,

---

[413] *Worthies,* III, 420.
[414] Watson, Foster: *Hist. of Eng. Grammar Schools,* p. 219.
[415] Burney: *op. cit.,* III, 420.
[416] Watson, Foster: *op. cit.,* p. 219.
[417] Pepys's first mention of music in the church is on June 17, 1660: "This day the organs did begin to play at White Hall before the King"; but he makes no comment.

after his ejectment from a chaplaincy in Christ Church, Oxford, "was forced . . . to obtain a living by that which before was only a diversion to him, I mean by a weekly music meeting which he set up at the Black Horse in Aldersgate in London." [418] Dr. Robert Creighton (Evelyn spells it Greighton; Pepys, Crayton, Creeton and Critton; Burney, Creyghton) was almost a professional musician. He studied abroad while in attendance on Charles II. He composed two complete services, one in E flat and one in C natural. "He was not gifted with great original genius for musical composition," says Dr. Burney carefully, "yet he has left such pleasing and elegant proofs of his progress in the art, as manifest judgment, taste, and knowledge." [419] William Holder is praised by Dr. Burney as one who had "studied and practiced counterpoint . . . with the application of a diligent professor." [420] Aubrey also testifies as to the quality of Dr. Holder's avocation: "he is very musicall, both theoretically and practically, and he has a sweet voyce. He hath writt an excellent treatise of musique in English, which is writt both doctis et indoctis, and readie for the presse." [421] Henry More "play'd sometimes on the Theorbo"; but found his pleasure was "so overcomingly great, that he hath been forc'd to desist. [422]

A musically inclined preacher did not always have a real gift for musical composition. He might merely like to sing, as Dr. Ralph Kettle did. He had a shrill high treble, and the story goes—Dr. Kettle was the sort of person who inevitably attracts ridiculous anecdotes—that a certain disrespectful J. Hoskyns, who had a higher voice, "would play the wag with the Doctor and make him strain his voice up to his." [423] Bishop Barnabas Potter loved music and could and did sing, which fact, Fuller says, contradicts the assertion that the bishop was so puritanically inclined "that

[418] Wood : III, 350.
[419] Burney : *op. cit.*, III, 599-600.
[420] *Ibid.*, p. 598.
[421] Aubrey : I, 404.
[422] *Life*, p. 54-5.
[423] Aubrey : II, 24.

organs would blow him out of the church." [424]   John Prideaux, when Bishop of Worcester, liked to tell the story of how his failure in a voice contest was really the beginning of his success.   As a young man he applied for the position of parish clerk, relying upon his "pretty good tuneable voice" to secure the office for him.   But a competitor appeared and after a trial (one candidate tuning the psalm in the forenoon and the other in the afternoon) the place was given to Prideaux's opponent.   "Upon which, after he was advanced to one of the first dignities in the church, he would frequently make this reflection, saying, If I could have been clerk of Ugborough, I had never been bishop of Worcester." [425]

Thomas Salmon, whose vocation made him rector of Mapsal in Bedfordshire, took a keen and scientific interest in music, producing, among other studies, a work that was "approved by both the mathematical professors of the university of Oxford with large remarks upon the said treatise, by the learned Dr. John Wallis." [426]   This work was: *A Proposal to perform Music in perfect and mathematical Proportions, containing 1. The State of Music in general. 2. The Principles of present Practice, according to that Art. 3. The Tables of Proportions calculated for the Viol, and capable of being accommodated to all sorts of Music* (London, 1689). [427]

A real lover of "musique" among the preachers was Dr. Robert Sanderson.   He not only played on the base viol, but also sang to it. [428]   In one of his sermons (delivered at Whitehall, 1641), Dr. Sanderson uses music for an explanatory comparison.   He is speaking of the need of sustaining one another: "The whole concert will be out of tune if one string is."   And then, "Anything that is toler-

[424] *Worthies*, III, 306 ; Clark : *General Martyrology*, p. 464.
[425] Wood :   III, 271-2.
[426] *Ibid.*, IV, 184.   See, also, Dr. Burney's *History*, III, 600.
[427] Salmon's book was not published until late in the century, but he had, of course, been at work on it for years.
[428] Aubrey :   II, 212.

able will pass among country people; but the least discord in the world will offend a choice and delicate ear." Even if all be in tune, yet if "one would have a grave pavin, another a nimbler galliard, a third some frisking toy or jig," what a hideous confusion must result.[429] Peter Sterry finds musical terms equally convenient in making clear his idea of the unity of the will of God: "The Flats and Sharpes, the Bases and Trebles, the Concords and Discords of Musick are all comprehended by the spirit of the Musicians in one Act of Harmony. . . . This single Act of Harmony, by its proper force, first invented and formed all Musical Instruments, prepared them for it self through all diversions of touches and Motions. . . . In like manner, the far greater perfection, the Will of God . . . containeth originally eminently within it self, complacency and aversion, love and hatred, with their several objects, in their several forms and degrees, in their several risings and fallings, most properly and harmoniously suited to each other." [430]

Strode tried, in a translation from Strada, to reproduce the musical notes of the nightingale, which is represented as imitating a lutinist.[431] Early in the century (1609) Charles Butler wrote a song—music and words—to imitate the humming of bees.[432]

Dr. John Wallis found an interest in music—not many possibilities of interest escaped him. He published a work entitled: *Claudius Ptolemy's Musica*. Thomas Hearne quoted Henry Aldrich as saying that this was Wallis's masterpiece; but Hearne adds, "Dr. Wallis understood nothing of the practice of musick." [433] Dr. John Wilkins gave open encouragement to music even in Puritan

[429] *Sermons* (Twelfth Sermon), p. 309.
[430] *Freedom of the Will*, pp. 22-3.
[431] *Works*, pp. 16-18.
[432] *The Feminine Monarchie*, Ch. V. (In 1634 the book was printed in phonetic spelling.) See p. 77: "In the Melissomelos, or Bees Madrigall, musicians may see the grounds of their Art."
[433] *Reliq. Hearnae*, II, 79.

times. When he was Warden of Wadham College, the violinist Thomas Balsar (Baltzar) came to Oxford, and Wilkins invited him "and some of the musitians to his lodgings in that college purposely to have a consort, and to see and heare him play." [434]

Anthony à Wood tells of weekly gatherings of music lovers in Oxford in the year 1656. They met at the house of Will Ellis; and in this group were a number of men who later became eminent in the church. Henry Bridgeman became an archdeacon; Christopher Coward, a mere rector; but Nathan Crew ("a violinist and violist, but always played out of tune, as having no good eare") lived to be bishop of Durham; Christopher Harrison was "a maggot-headed person and humorous; he was afterwards parson of Burgh. . . ." Matthew Hutton ("an excellent violist") became a rector; Thomas Ken, afterward bishop of Bath and Wells; Narcissus Marsh (later archbishop of Armagh in Ireland) "would come sometimes among them but seldom played, because he had a weekly meeting in his chamber in the said college (Exeter) where masters of music would come . . ."; and Samuel Woodford, later prebendary of Winchester. [435]

Other divines who were interested in music were: Charles Butler; [436] Edward Gibbons; [437] Dr. Joseph Hall ("so innocent that Musick, Mathematick, and Fishing were all his Recreations"); [438] Nathaniel Ingelo, an active patron of musicians; [439] Samuel Ogden; [440] Thomas Pierce, referred to by Evelyn as a learned minister and excellent musician; [441] George Stradling who "kept his fellowship during the times of trouble and usurpation, being accounted a rare lutenist and much valued by Dr. Wilson the music professor"; [442] a "Mr. Wilson" who after his ejectment,

[434] Wood: *Ath. Ox.*, I, xxxii.
[435] Wood: *Ath. Ox.*, I, xxxivff.
[436] *Ibid.*, III, 209-10.
[437] Walker: Pt. II, 32.
[438] Lloyd: p. 419.
[439] Wood: *Fasti*, II, 306.
[440] Calamy: *Abridg.*, II, 193.
[441] *Diary:* Entry of Oct. 2, 1656.
[442] Wood: *Ath. Ox.*, IV, 237.

Calamy says, found in his music a "comfortable Subsistence, by instructing the Scholars there [in Cambridge] and Young Gentlemen all the country round, in that noble Art;[443] and Thomas Wren (second son of the Bishop of Ely), who was much addicted to music.[444]

Poetry

Poetry was a by-product of many a sermon writer. In some instances poetry was a clergyman's chief contribution to his generation, and such a man belongs primarily, by reason of his special gift, to literature rather than to religion. The connection with the church may be almost lost sight of, not only by readers of the twentieth century but by writers of the seventeenth century. Wood, for example, gives but scant space to "Robert Heyrick's" vocation, saying vaguely that he had a benefice conferred on him ("in Devonshire, I think"). But Wood does know about *Hesperides* and *Noble Numbers*. Herrick himself from what little is really known of him, did not, apparently, feel that he was indissolubly joined to the church. When he was ejected from Dean Prior in 1648, he lived in London as a layman, even publishing his poems as the work of "Robert Herrick, Esq.";[445] and after his return to Devonshire, tradition connects him with a highly secular publication, the almanac *Poor Robin*. Herrick is said to have used "Poor Robin" as a *nom de plume*, but there exists a stronger claimant in the person of Robert Winstanley of Saffron Walden.[446]

The poetry of Richard Crashaw does not furnish a great deal of proof of secular relaxation, the most of it being strongly religious; but the *Delights of the Muses* does include *Wishes, Love's Horoscope*, and sentimental *Songs*

---

[443] Calamy : *Abridg.*, II, 118.
[444] *Parentalia*, p. 55.
[445] Masson : *Milton*, VI, 292.
[446] *Notes and Queries*, 6th series, VII, 321-3.

"out of the Italian," Crashaw's style is of his time, and he
can on occasion out-*conceit* Cowley or Dryden or any contemporary poet.[447] Crashaw's vocation is usually mentioned by those who discuss him, probably because of his
change of religion. A transfer to or from (sometimes to
and from) the Roman Catholic church was always an item
worth putting into print. Crashaw's secular abilities are
not overlooked by professional biographers; Wood praises
his learning, especially his excellence in five languages
(adding that he was "a meer scholar and very shiftless");[448] Lloyd contributes the information that the
poet was interested in "Musick, Drawing, Limming and
Graving." [449]

William Cartwright was a poet as well as a playwright
(and preacher). When the Matchless Orinda wrote a
poem in memory of him, she apostrophized him as "Prince
of Fancy," making no allusion to his clerical side.[450] Isaac
Walton, when contributing a complimentary poem to the
1651 edition of Cartwright's comedies, said nothing about
his sermons;[451] nor does Aubrey except for one slight
reference.[452] Thomas Vaughan (who also contributed a
poem to the 1651 edition) does not speak of the plays, but
dwells at some length on Cartwright's service to Oxford.[453]
Herrick, Crashaw, and Cartwright are too well known and
too easily within reach of readers, to need explanatory
comment on secular tastes. Henry More, as a poet, is

[447] As the famous description of Mary Magdalen's tears: "Two
walking baths, two weeping motions. . . ."
[448] Wood: *Fasti*, II, 5.
[449] Lloyd: p. 619.
[450] Poems by the most deservedly Admired Mrs. Katherine Philips.
Sir John Pettus wrote of Cartwright:

> ". . one rich soul
> That filled the Stage, the Schools, the Pulpit, too;
> An universal wit,
> All things, and men, could fit;
> So shap'd for ev'ry one
> As born for that alone" (Lloyd: p. 423).

[451] *Waltoniana*.
[452] Vol. II, 148.
[453] *Works*, pp. 474-6.

always dignified, and often difficult. It is encouraging to know that a brother mystic found More's poems somewhat vague: "Dr. More," writes Peter Sterry in his *Freedom of the Will*, "whose Books full of excellent Wit, Learning and Piety I always read with much pleasure and profit, although I be not alwayes so happy, as to find my Understanding tuned to a comfort and harmony with his, seemeth to me like a Prophet as well as a Poet, to sing this mystery, drawn forth from the sacred retreats of the divinest Philosophy in his Poems." [454]

Another generally accepted poet is Henry King; but poetry was only one of the milestones that marked his aesthetic and spiritual progress: "When he was young he delighted much in the studies of music and poetry, which with his wit and fancy, made his conversation much accepted; when he was elder, he applied himself to oratory and philosophy, and in his reduced age fixed on divinity." [455] Henry King's most quoted lyric is "Tell me no more how fair she is"; perhaps as well known as his *Sic Vita*, a poem thoroughly characteristic of its school: the transitoriness of life pictured by a succession of comparisons and *conceits*. Richard Flecknoe's name is also a familiar one, not through his poetry, but because Dryden borrowed the name which, with a prefix, he made to serve as a transparent cover for an attack on Shadwell. There was small chance for Flecknoe to be remembered as a poet; his interest in drama has done more for his fame. Here is an example of his verse:

The Ant

Little think'st thou, poor ant, who there
With so much toil, and so much time
A grain or two to thy cell dost bear,
There's a greater work i' the world than thine.[456]

---

[454] P. 31 : More wrote an admiring tribute to the Duchess of Newcastle; *Letters and Poems in Honour of the Duchess of Newcastle.*
[455] Fuller : *Worthies*, I, 202 ; also, Wood : *Ath. Ox.*, III, 839.
[456] *Specimens of the Early English Poets*, III, 310.

William Chillingworth is hardly recognizable as a poet; it is as a polemical divine, as a mathematician and as a philosopher that he fills paragraphs and whole pages in seventeenth-century studies. His claim to be included among the poets rests upon a line in Sir John Suckling's *Session of the Poets:*

> There was Selden and he sat hard by the chair,
> Weriman not far off, which was very fair;
> Sands with Townsend, for they kept no order;
> Digby and Shillingsworth a little further.

And the same authority makes a poet of John Hales:

> Little Hales all the time did nothing but smile
> To see them, about nothing, keepe such a coile.

It should not be forgotten that writing Latin verses was part of a schoolboy's training, and in consequence the mechanics of verse construction were familiar to all educated men. This fact accounts for the frequent and casual mention of this man or that being "a good poet"; for even a man who lacked fancy or a sense of harmony might produce fair workaday verse which would serve various purposes, such as to celebrate some local or national event, or to embellish a funeral sermon.[457] A man who was connected with one of the universities would be likely to write in Latin, as Isaac Barrow did, his poems being dignified, occasional, and uninspired, even when he has as lively and secular a subject as a fight with Algerine pirates.[458] A

[457] Brinsley: "Though Poetry be rather for ornament than for any necessary use; and the maine matter to be regarded in it, is the purity of phrase and of stile: yet because there is very commendable use of it, sometimes in occasions of triumph and rejoycing, more ordinarily at the funerals of some worthy personages, and sometimes for some other purposes; it is not amisse to traine up schollers even in this kinde also . . ." (*Ludus Lit.*, p. 191ff.).
Hoole: *New Discovery, etc.*, p. 190.
D'Ewes kept his exercise-book, in which he wrote verse at Bury School. It contained "two thousand eight hundred and fifty verses, Latin and Greek" (*Journal*, I, 102).
[458] *Iter maritinum a portu Ligustico Constantinopolim.* Vol. VIII, 445. Barrow's biographer, Abraham Hill, says Barrow was always addicted to poetry, and at Cambridge would aid the juniors "though

man who was a part of London life would find a subject
for poetry always ready to his hand. Innumerable verses
were written to Cromwell, to Charles II, to lords and
ladies; there were rhymes on the Dutch War,[459] and on the
Fire and the Plague; there were rhymes on political and
religious issues. Probably many persons admired the
stilted couplets of *An Apology for Bishops, or, A Plea for
learning.* It rehearses the services of bishops to England:

> Witness grave Morton whose judicious head
> Found means to join the white rose with the red.[460]

Still another outlet for the parson who was not a poet
but who liked to compose verses, was in the eulogies attached to the printed funeral sermons that were so extraordinarily popular in the seventeenth century. It had long
been a custom to contribute admiring poems, as well as
dedicatory epistles, to printed plays or poems,[461] and the
publisher of funeral sermons found this an excellent
fashion to imitate. The persons who enjoyed seeing their
poems in print, welcomed the opportunity to do so, and if
they were scholarly divines, they expressed their regret
for the loss of a friend in Greek or Latin. Thomas
Jacombe's funeral sermon for the Reverend Richard Vines
is preceded by thirteen poems in Latin and English, most
of them playing skillfully on the name Vines. One of the

---

for all the exercises he made for them in verse and prose, he never
received any recompense but one pair of gloves" (I, xi). In poetry
he most valued description; "but the hyperboles of some modern poets
he as much slighted" (p. xii).

[459] Dryden: *An Essay on Dramatic Poesy:* "I have a mortal appre-
hension of two poets, whom this victory, with the help of both her
wings, will never be able to escape" (*Works,* I, p. 37). Both Robert
Wild and Richard Flecknoe wrote poems on the defeat of the Dutch.

[460] Anonymous, Lond., 1640. Becket is mentioned, and Bonner,
Gardiner, Cranmer, Ridley, Hooker, Farrar. Laud is the only living
contemporary cited. As the poem was (wisely) printed without the
name of its author, it cannot be claimed as a preacher-production, but
certainly the chances are in favor of such authorship.

[461] Herrick and Crashaw offer many examples of verse-compliments.
John Fell and Ralph Bathurst both wrote poems for the 1651 edition
of Cartwright's poems.

English poems is by a fellow minister, Robert Wild, who, in his day, had considerable repute as a poet. It begins:

> "Art thou gone too, (thou great and gallant minde)
> And must such sneaks as I be left behinde?"

The memorial verses often reflect the literary taste of a day that approved of tricks of phrasing, *conceits,* and strained comparisons. John Whitefoot was a fortunate man who could preach a funeral sermon and compose a funeral poem according to popular taste. When Dr. Whitefoot preached the funeral sermon of Bishop Joseph Hall, he included a poem in the dedication. The preacher-poet feels under no obligation to sing the piety of the late prelate; nor in poem or sermon does Dr. Whitefoot refer to Bishop Hall's writings. One stanza will illustrate the style of the verse:

> What rich Embroidery of Wit and Grace
> Like sparkling Diamonds set in Golden Case;
> Like the pure white and red, in beauties cheek,
> With sweet contention the Precedence seek,
> > Possest
> > That brest.[462]

Nicholas Bernard contributed a poem to Dr. Whitefoot's quarto, which shows a recollection of a controversy of which Joseph Hall was a great part:

> His holy life, a silent check to all
> The rout of Vices, was: his Pen the Maul
> > Of Sects
> > And Smects.

It happened that the author of the *Humble Remonstrance* and the *Satires* died a few months after Usher, thereby giving Bernard a metaphysical opportunity:

[462] *Deaths Alarum.*

> Learned Armagh to honour this his day,
> His Usher was, and Heaven-ward led the way.
> When aged Durham shall remove his station,
> How great, how glorious a Constellation
> In th' Orb Empyreal wil they make those three
> That will out-shine the radiant Cassiopee.

A poem, *The Mourners Blazonry,* by Samuel Fairclough, written as a tribute to the memory of Sir Nathaniel Barnardiston, accompanies a picture of a combined family tree and a coat of arms. It begins:

> Hark, how the doleful bittern sadly moans
> And tunes her withered reed to dying groans.
> The streaming Spots of Ermine, seem to weep
> That innocence itself (their Type) doth sleep.
> The Crosses once dyed Gules, with Saviours blood,
> Turn pale with grief, as if they understood.

> The Gospels loss is his: The Azure Field
> (Heav'ns Hieroglyphick) shews, Faith was his Shield.[463]

A poem *On the Death of Mrs. Elizabeth Wilkinson* is so constructed as to make every other line begin with a letter of the lady's first name, and every one of the intervening lines, with a letter of her last name.[464] Still another chance to get one's verses before men, was found in the custom of adorning the hearse of a literary man with poems. Dr. Barten Holyday, when archdeacon of Oxford, composed the following lines, "Upon the death of his vertuous and prudent friend Mr. Edw. Wood in the beginning of his proctorship of the universitie of Oxon.":

> Chosen he was a censor of the times
> He chose to dye, rather than view the crimes,
> The Cynique's lanterne he far wiser thought,
> That for an honest man at high-noon sought,

---

[463] Clark: *Eminent Lives,* p. 117.
[464] Clark: *General Martyrology,* p. 546.

Then bring a midnight sinner to the light,
Whose darker actions do outshade the night.
Friend, thou was wise, with honour thus to dye,
Fame is thy epitaph, thy tombe the sky.[465]

There were more cheerful though no more popular varieties of verse in which a preacher might indulge. Even before *Hudibras* made doggerel the fashion, James Smith had experimented with the form, and in 1658 he published, with other poems, a burlesque: *Penelope and Ulysses.*[466] In 1655, James Smith and Sir John Minnis published as joint authors and editors a small volume, entitled *Musarum Deliciae,* which was reissued the next year.

William Strode, doctor of divinity, playwright and poet, had some of his poems set to music by Henry Lawes. The following stanza begins a song *In Commendation of Music:*

When whispering straynes doe softly steale
With creeping passion through the hart,
And when at every touch wee feel
Our pulses beate, and beare a part;
When threds can make
A hartstring Shake
Philosophie
Can scarce deny,
The soul consists of harmony.[467]

There is nothing of pulpit ancestry about this selection:

To a Lady putting off her Veil

Keep on your maske and hide your eye,
For with beholding you I dye;

---

[465] Wood: *Ath. Ox.,* I. xxiv. (This brother of Anthony à Wood died May 22, 1655.) Calamy, in speaking of the death of Edward Bowles, says: Many Copies of Verses were made to adorn his Hearse, some of them are not contemptible" (*Abridg.,* II, 783). A Note following Wood's account of John Langley's funeral says, "Verses instead of escutcheons were hung about the corpse" (*Ath. Ox.,* III, 436).
[466] Courthope: *Hist. of Eng. Poetry,* III, 363-4.
[467] *Works,* p. 2.

> Your fatall beauty, Gorgon like,
> Dead with astonishment will strike;
> Your piercing eyes, if them I see,
> Are worse than basilisks to mee.[468]

Smallpox tempted him, as it had others, to a display of invention:

> "Love shott a thousand darts,
> And made those pitts for graves to bury hearts.[469]

Examples of Strode's work were included in many of the collections of the day, such as *Parnassus Biceps, Wit Restored, Musarum Deliciae.*

A book of poems—frivolous poems, at that—once did good service to a clergyman-poet of this time, serving as a veritable "neck-verse." When Thomas Weaver was on trial for his life, his book, entitled *Songs of Love and Drollery,* was produced in court as evidence against his character. The judge read a few pages, then: "Gentlemen, the person we have here before us is a scholar and a wit. Our forefathers had learning so much in honour, that they enacted that those that could but as much as read, should never be hanged, unless for some great crime, and shall we respect so little as to put to death a man of parts?" [470] The jury acquitted him.

John White "wrote three volumes full of fooleries and impertinences" after he was safely back in divinity, having practiced physic from the time of his ejectment until the Restoration. The first volume, Wood says, contained anagrams and epigrams on the kings and nobility of England; the second volume satirized bishops and lesser clergy, and the third was on "the gentry and other persons." [471] Abraham Wright (of *Five Sermons* fame) god-fathered a collection of poems published under the title, *Parnassus*

---

[468] *Works,* p. 3.
[469] *Works,* p. 49.

[470] Wood: *Ath. Ox.,* III, 622.
[471] Wood: *Ath. Ox.,* III, 943.

biceps. Or several choice Pieces of Poetry, composed by the best Wits that were in both the Universities before their Dissolution. In his Address to the Reader, Wright laments the Golden Age "when it was held no sin for the same man to be a Poet, and a Prophet."

Inevitably there were jocular lines on schoolmasters. Not even a devout, ordained minister could always forget the tyrant who had made learning a physically painful process; but such verses can hardly find a place even at the end of such uninspired examples as have been presented. The only one that has any measure of fame, is Thomas Triplet's on Alexander Gill the elder. Dr. Gill had a whipping-obsession and Triplet's ballad shows the schoolmaster impartially beating every pupil and tradesman who came within reach of his cane. The story is told with a good deal of humor of a Rabelaisian quality and it is easy to understand its popularity.[472]

There remains to be mentioned but one other sort of enjoyment of poetry among the preachers, and there is but one example to offer as an illustration of an unusual variety of poetic temperament. This is Isaac Vossius, a Dutch scholar who had been invited to England because of his learning. Charles II had made him Canon of Windsor, and afterwards, prebendary of Windsor, but Vossius did not permit these favors to hamper his expressed views or his actions. Certainly there was little of church quality about him; he would say if questioned that he did not believe in the divine origin of religion, and when he attended chapel at Windsor, he read Ovid's *Ars Amandi* during the service. His peculiar pleasure in poetry he derived not from the ideas or pictures suggested, but from the rhythm alone. He liked to have his hair combed by a measured stroke, and he preferred barbers who were skilled in prosody. In

---

[472] Aubrey: II, 263-6. Dr. Triplet was at one time tutor and chaplain to Lord Falkland at Great Tew (*Letters of Lady Falkland*, p. 45). When Triplet was himself a schoolmaster, he was quite as brutal as his old master.

a Latin treatise on rhythm, published at Oxford in 1673, he says: "Many people take delight in the rubbing of their limbs, and the combing of their hair; but these exercises would delight much more, if the servants at the baths, and the barbers, were so skillful in this art, that they could express any measure with their fingers. I remember more than once, I have fallen into the hands of men of this sort, who could imitate the measure of songs in combing the hair; so as sometimes to express very intelligently iambics, trochees, dactylls, etc., from whence there arose to me no small delight." [473]

Among the divines who are briefly mentioned below are men of widely varying importance and ability. Richard Baxter and Jeremy Taylor, for example, are great men, the one in theology, the other in literature. But neither was a great poet. There are men in the list who are not important in any way at all; but their rhymes pleased their friends and these men were labeled poets. Baxter, Ken, Taylor, and Sprat may be found in Encyclopedias and literary studies of various kinds; but many of the so-called poets must be sought in half-forgotten *Anthologies,* in *Collections* and *Selections* whose yellowed pages are seldom turned. The majority of these "painful" poets wrote on religious subjects, an outgrowth of their vocation; it is their indulgence in the composing of verse that makes the practice an avocation.

Clement Barksdale was the author of *Nympha Libethris,* or, the *Cotswold Muse* (Wood: *Ath. Ox.,* IV, 222).

Richard Baxter's poems show no originality of thought and certainly no play of fancy, but there is a dexterity of versification and an evenness of structure that make his poetry easy and pleasant reading; *The Vain Show,* for instance, and *The Valediction.* Baxter's own judgment of his poetry is, "they take not with those that expect more art, they profit two sorts, women and vulgar Christians and persons in passion by

[473] Chambers: *Book of Days,* I, 16.

afflictions; and some in devotional exercise of affection. . . ."
(*Autobiography*, p. 249).

Bunyan's simple, commonplace lines often have good rhythm,
and in the verses for boys and girls, something of invention.
There is no sign in any of his poems of an abiding influence
from the days of his unregeneracy when he loved "a ballad,
a news-book, George on horseback, or Bevis of Southampton"
("A Few Sighs from Hell," *Works,* III, 711).

Joseph Beaumont (Walker: Pt. II, 153).

Robert Burghill was "in his younger years, a noted Latin
poet" (Wood: *Ath. Ox.,* III, 19).

William Cooper was "a fine poet, especially in Latin"
(Palmer: I, 137).

John Fell is a poet by virtue of writing commendatory
verses in other people's books.

John Flavel was not regularly ordained, but he preached
energetically for many years, and grew rich "by marrying
wives," says Wood. Flavel's poetry is pretty bad but a
selection is sometimes included in anthologies of sacred poetry.
Happiness for All represents his style; it begins:

> Oh, what a dull, desponding heart is mine,
> That takes no more delight in things divine. . . . (*Speci-*
> *mens of Early Eng. Poetry,* III)

Henry Greisley had "some small things in the way of Poetry"
(Walker: Pt. II, 108).

John Harmar was particularly a Latin poet (Calamy:
Abridg. etc., II, 339; Wood: *Ath. Ox.,* II).

Peter Heylin was "an excellent poet, but very conceited
and pragmatical" (Wood: *Ath. Ox.,* III, 557). His *Memorial
of Bishop Waynflete* (160 stanzas) describes Magdalen College
and its surroundings.

Barten Holyday translated from Latin poets (Wood:
op. cit., 523).

Richard Jones "had a vein of Poetry, in Latin, English,
and Welsh" (Calamy: *Abridg.* II, 844).

Thomas Ken (Bishop of Bath and Wells) wrote religious
poetry, one of his hymns being the well-known *Morning Hymn,*
beginning:

> Awake my soul, and with the sun
> Thy daily stage of duty run;
> Shake off dull sloth, and early rise
> To pay thy morning sacrifice.

Philip King (Lloyd: p. 507).

John Kirby—"and sometimes he would divert himself in making Verses . . . as to which it must be own'd the Sense is far beyond the Poetry" (Calamy: *op. cit.*, II, 795).

Adam Littleton composed a Latin poem, *Tragi-comoedia Oxoniensis*, describing satirically the visit of the parliamentary visitors to Oxford. (The work is ascribed to Littleton, but the eight page quarto does not give author, place, or date.)

Martin Llewellyn was, Walker says without enthusiasm, "esteemed a good Poet, and hath several Things of the Kind Extant." Among the "Things" is

Celia in Love

> I felt my heart, and found a flame
> That for relief and shelter came;
> I entertain'd the treacherous guest
> And gave it welcome in my breast.
> Poor Celia! whither wilt thou go?
> To cool in streams, or freeze in snow? . . .

There are eight more lines, and it is all pretty bad poetry, and all undeniably secular (Walker: Pt. II, 108).

David Lloyd, *Songs, Sonnets, Elegies* (Wood: *Ath. Ox.*, III, 652-3).

Thomas Master (Wood: *op. cit.*, 84.)

George Maxon "could imitate Horace so exactly as not to be distinguished without Difficulty" (Calamy: *Abridg.*, II, 128).

Robert Mead was "a Stout and Learned Man, a good Poet" (Walker: Pt. II, 108).

Samuel Ogden: "often would he divert himself with making a Copy of Verses upon any Subject that offer'd; but most commonly his subjects were serious" (Calamy: *Abridg.*, II, 193).

Thomas Pierce was "esteemed a good poet" (Wood: *op. cit.*, IV, 299).

Matthew Robinson—"yet in his severest studies, he could bestow one hour daily upon poetry and poetical exercises" (*Autobiography*, 21).

William Rowland (who changed his name to Rolandus Palingenius) wrote *Varia Poemata* in Latin, English, and some French (Wood: *op. cit.*, III, 486).

John Sheffield "had a genius both for witty and divine poetry" (Palmer: I, 149).

Samuel Sheppard apologizes for a former work, "incompatible with his profession." But his poem *In Memory of our famous Shakespeare* needs another apology. One stanza will suffice:

> Plautus sigh'd, Sophocles wept
> Tears of anger, for to hear
> (After they so long had slept)
> So bright a genius should appear. . . .(*Specimens of Early Eng. Poetry,* III, 300)

Peter Smart wrote in Latin and English, and was said to be the author of "Old Smart's Verses" which Wood had seen mentioned "in auction catalogues" (Wood: *Ath. Ox.,* III, 41).

Thomas Sprat (Bishop of Rochester)—"Pindaric Sprat"—wrote a good deal of carefully composed poetry, as *The Plague of Athens,* a eulogy of Cromwell, and religious pieces.

Richard Stuart, was "a good Poet and Orator, and afterwards a noted Divine, and eloquent Preacher. . . ." (Walker: Pt. II, 48)

Jeremy Taylor wrote much better poetry when he was writing prose than he did when he broke up his lines into stanzas. Many of his uneven lines look and read like one variety of twentieth-century verse; for instance, *Immanuel,* or *Of Heaven.* Here are a few lines from the latter:

> Where the great King's transparent throne
> Is of an entire jasper-stone;
> There the eye
> Of th' chrysolite,
> And a sky
> Of diamonds, rubies, chrysoprase,
> And above all, thy holy face,
> Makes an eternal charity.

Herbert Thorndyke—"I have seen a poemation of his on the death of Gustavus Adolphus, King of Sweden, in Latin hexameter, about 100 verses or better" (Aubrey: II, 257).

Thomas Vaughan, twin brother of Henry Vaughan, wrote Latin poetry, on Cynthia, on Chloe, etc. (*Works,* pp. 453-73).

Robert Wilde: "In the evening comes Mr. Pulling . . . and very good company, he reciting to us many copies of good verses of Dr. Wilde's, who writ Iter Boreale" (Pepys: *Diary,* Dec. 25, 1667; also, Thoresby: *Diary,* I, 31).

Samuel Woodford (Wood: *Ath. Ox.,* I, xxxv; IV, 730).

The joint responsibilities of religion and poetry are presented by Davenant in his Preface to *Gondibert:* "For Poesy, which (like contracted Essences seems the utmost strength and activity of Nature) is as all good Arts, subservient to Religion; all marching under the same Banner, though of less discipline and esteem. . . . And when the Judges of Religion (which are the Chiefs of the Church) neglect the help of Moralists in reforming the People (and Poets are of all moralists the most useful) they give a sentence against the Law of Nature . . . as Poesy is adorn'd and sublim'd by Musick, which makes it more pleasant and acceptable; so morality is sweetened and made more amiable by Poesy. And the Austerity of some Divines may be the cause why Religion hath not more prevailed upon the manners of Men; for great doctors should rather comply with things that please . . . than lose a Proselyte. . . ." [474]

Other Literary Interests

The craft of fiction found few practitioners, for the seventeenth century was not a story-telling period. If a writer conceived plot situations he put them into plays; if he were convinced that a man or woman was a type, he offered such a person as a *Character;* if he were emotional or sentimental, he made verses. It is not surprising that Thomas Fuller tried his hand at a Romance. Its title is: *Triana; or, A Threefold Romanza, of Mariana, Paduana, Sabina,* and it is a lively tale in all its sections; but certainly it cannot boast of originality. Mariana has been placed in a convent by her father who wishes to make his peace with heaven, but she is loved by a poor and pleasant young man, Fidelio, who arranges her escape, being aided by a resourceful friend, Ardelio, and the discovery of an underground passageway leading to a vault beneath the convent. The two young people are apprehended and condemned to death,

[474] Pp. 64-5.

but both escape the penalty by time-honored means. Fuller himself recognized that his tale bore a family resemblance to other narratives, and in his foreword to the Reader he declares that he is not presenting a translation from the Spanish or Italian, although "this is the common Pander to men's fancy, hoping to vent them under that title, with the more applause. These my play-labours never appeared before, and is an essay of what hereafter may be a greater volume."

Nathaniel Ingelo published in 1660 a religious romance, *Bentivolio and Urania,* which was so successful that it was reprinted in 1669, 1673, and 1682. It is a complicated and most tiresome work of six hundred and sixty-seven folio pages. A Table explains the proper names: "Bentivolio here denotes good will; Urania, Heavenly Light; Pammelaena, All dark. By this name the state of Ignorance is represented," and so on. There is much criticism, thinly veiled under allegory, of catholics, dissenters, and quakers.[475] Prayers and hymns are introduced, invocations fill many paragraphs, and letters couched in grandiose language are inserted frequently. Moral as the work is, its author, being a doctor of divinity, was uneasy as to the effect it might have on one who should misunderstand its purpose. The writing and reading of romances, he tells the Reader, is one of the impertinences that clip the soul. "For my own part," the troubled author goes on, "I do not desire that all books should be as dull as many are, and none compos'd, as all are not, to delight; but I would have that delight true, and the quicknesse not evaporate into Lightnesse and Vanity."

Bishop Joseph Hall once wrote an uninspired Latin romance, *Mundus Alter et Idem,* which was characterized by Smectymnuus as, "that wretched pilgrimage over Minsheu's Dictionary." David Lloyd (the poet, not the biographical writer) did not trouble to dress his fiction in a

[475] Pp. 135, 141, 159.

serious garment. He wrote a burlesque of a Welsh poem, calling his work *The Legend of Captain Jones*. It appeared in 1669, in two parts: "The first part relateth his adventures at sea, his first landing, and strange combat with a mighty bear. The second begins with his miraculous deliverance from a wreck at sea by the support of a dolphin." [476] A curious conflict between religion and worldly tastes is seen in the attitude of Nicholas Ferrar toward the plays, heroical poems, love songs, and romances he had gathered together and keenly enjoyed before he consecrated himself to the life of service he developed at Little Gidding. He could not bear to destroy the volumes he still loved, but he packed them in great hampers and stored them out of sight. When he was near death, he gave orders about the place of his burial, and then directed that the books long hidden should be brought forth and burned at the spot where his grave would be.[477]

That there lurks a dangerous charm in romance was explained by Adam Littleton in a Good Friday sermon, preached in 1668: "If a Romantick Story, made up with poetical language and impertinent fictions can entertain us with that concerned affection, that we are impatient and unsatisfied, till we have discovered the whole Plot, and traced all the turnings and windings of it to the very Close and Issue of all the fabulous Adventures: what a shame were it for us Christians, not to be very well vers'd in all the passages of our Saviour's Sufferings."

They were not story-tellers, these brethren of the pulpit. The lengthy romances of La Calprenède, of Mademoiselle de Scudéry, were widely circulated in England, but no preacher tries to imitate them, or to repeat the stories —as Mrs. Pepys struggled to retell *The Grand Cyrus*.[478] Nor did any philologically inclined parson collect fables or fairytales as La Fontaine and Perrault were doing in France

[476] Wood: *Ath. Ox.*, III, 652.
[477] Carter: *Nicholas Ferrar, etc.*, pp. 82, 266.
[478] Pepys: *Diary*, May 12, 1666.

in the latter half of the century.[479]   The clergyman who
came nearest to writing story narratives was Thomas Fuller
with his *Triana,* and his allegories of birds and flowers.[480]
But the omission of tales of love and chivalry argues no lack
of imagination on the part of the seventeenth-century divine.
All the successful preachers dealt in high adventure and
failure and achievement.   "In preaching," John Selden
observed, "they do by Men as writers of Romance do by
their chief Knights, bring them into many Dangers, but
still fetch them off: So they put Men in fear of Hell,
but at last bring them to Heaven." [481]

Description could be used as successfully in the pulpit
as in a printed narrative, and the creeping horrors which,
a century later, were to give identity to the Gothic novel
were a familiar inclusion in a seventeenth-century sermon.
Gloom and gruesome detail are as effectively used in Jeremy
Taylor's *Apples of Sodom; or the Fruits of Sin* or in
Nathaniel Hardy's *Lamentation, Mourning and Woe, Sighed
forth in a Sermon* as when they are employed to give at-
mosphere to Otranto or Udolpho; and the author of *Vathek*
does not make the Hall of Eblis more vivid than a "Winter-
Preacher" whom James Howell quotes, made the place of
everlasting punishment, "dwelling so on the fires of Hell
that a Sythian or Greenlander would have thought it
Paradise." [482]

Travel-records

The members of the clergy who went to far-away places
as chaplains, or as collectors of manuscripts and ancient
coins and medals, sometimes allowed themselves the worldly
recreation of writing about what they had seen and heard.
Lancelot Addison (father of Joseph Addison) was one of

---

[479] La Fontaine's first group of Fables was published in 1668; Perrault printed his *Contes* in 1697.
[480] See pp. 253. 256.
[481] *Table Talk,* p. 140.   [482] *Letter XXVI,* p. 604.

these. He lived a number of years at Tangier where he gathered the material which he printed in 1671 under the title: *West Barbary: or, a short Narrative of the Revolution of Fez and Morocco, with an Account of the present Customs, sacred, civil, and domestic.*[483] John Bargrave "had an especial hand in *An Itinerary containing a Voyage made thro' Italy in 1646 and 1647* (London 1648).[484] Edmund Ludlow, in his *Memoirs,* speaks of a "Mr. Gage," a priest, who died on an expedition to Jamaica. He had written *The English American, his Travaill by Sea and Land,* published in 1648.[485] Peter Heylin, who wrote so many books, included a travel-book among his works: *Full Relation of two Journies. The one into the main Land of France: The other into some of the adjacent Islands, in 5 Books* (London, 1656).[486] But the most interesting recorded experience was that of Edward Terry, he having been chaplain to the great mogul in East India for more than two years. His book has the explicit title: *Voyage to East-India. Wherein some Things are taken Notice of in his Passage thither, but many more in his Abode there within that rich and most spacious Empire of the Great Mogul* (London, 1655).[487]

The personal essay, like the romance, did not attract the bachelors and doctors of divinity. Fuller imitated John Earle's *Characters,* but the studies of human nature were discreetly labeled *The Holy and Profane State* when they appeared in 1642. The preachers liked to write essays on everyday topics, usually publishing them in the guise of sermons, but occasionally they came out as frankly secular pamphlets. An entertaining illustration of this type of diversion is: *A Discourse of Artificial Beauty, In Point of*

[483] Wood: *Ath. Ox.,* IV, 518.
[484] Wood: *Fasti,* II, 267.
[485] *Memoirs,* I, 417. For references to Thomas Gage, see Burnet: *Hist. of his own Time,* I, 137; Thurloe: *Diary,* V, 59-61.
[486] Wood: *Ath. Ox.,* III, 563.
[487] *Ibid.,* p. 506. ("Afterwards it was added to the travels of Pet. de la Valle, and abridged in Sa. Purchas his second part of Pilgrims, book 9.")

Conscience between two Ladies.[488] It is a deadly serious work which could hardly fail to give keen joy to a twentieth-century reader. Thirteen Objections to Painting the Face are presented in orderly succession, and authorities are cited, particularly "the Fathers and Modern Divines" who are quoted as expressing disapproval of a practice that is "very scandalous, and so unlawful." Jezebel looms large as a warning. It was in 1662 that the little book was published. A decade earlier, in 1652, there had been re-issued in London John Donne's *Paradoxes, Problems, Essayes, Characters,* and in the first group is a brief paper, "That Women ought to Paint," in which the author, out of the other half of him that did not become the Dean of St. Paul's, lays down good and aesthetic reasons why the faces of women ought to be painted.

It is impossible to judge how much purely secular reading these preachers may have done, especially among English writers. Ministers of all denominations quoted prodigally from the classical poets and philosophers because it was the fashion to do so. It is possible that they were equally familiar with the earlier literature of their own country and refrained from making allusions to Chaucer or Spenser or Shakespeare because such a departure from established custom would not be approved by either listeners or readers.

The seventeenth-century section of Dr. Caroline Spurgeon's *Five Hundred Years of Chaucer Allusion and Criticism* includes examples from John Barkham, Fuller, Joseph Hall, Gerard Langbaine, Thomas Plume, Thomas Sprat, and John Wallis; but except for the quotations from Fuller and Hall, the references are slight; and not even those two show any intimacy with the man who could love a parson,

---

[488] John Gauden is reputed to be the author of the work; and so is Jeremy Taylor. The latter refers to painting the face in more than one sermon, as, " . . . sometimes we see a decayed beauty besmeared with a lying fucus, and the chinks filled with ceruse; besides that it makes no real beauty, it spoils the face, and betrays evil manners . . . " (*Works,* I, 739).

or laugh at him, and who displayed his keenest irony through an imitation of fourteenth-century sermon-mechanics. Fuller found Chaucer "a Refiner and Illuminer of our English tongue,—and if he left it so bad, how much worse did he finde it?" Fuller also gives biographical information, including a reference to the popular though unsubstantiated anecdote of Chaucer's fight with the Franciscan Friar in Fleet Street.[489] Bishop Hall quotes from the *Pardoner's Tale,* the *Parlement of Foules,* the *Book of the Duchess,* and from *Lydgate's Complaint of the Black Knight* (which he ascribes to Chaucer).[490] Another Chaucer-reading clergyman, not mentioned in the *Allusion* book, is John Hackett, who quoted a couplet from the *House of Fame,* as if he really knew the poem.[491] Dryden quotes John Hales as saying "that there was no subject of which any poet ever writ, but he would produce it much better done in Shakespeare." [492] Robert Sanderson, in a sermon at Whitehall, in speaking of pamphleteers who demand church reform, said they were "just as one of our own poets (of good note in his time) hath long since described error's children; a numerous brood, but never a one like other, saving only in this, that they were all ill-favoured alike." [493] John Hackett quotes a line from Ben Jonson.[494] Scant references such as these are to be found now and then in a sermon or other composition, but so infrequently that it is impossible to think that English authors were widely or carefully read; for even though literary usage required Latin and Greek allusions and quotations, a genuine knowledge of Chaucer or Shakespeare would have been impossible to hide. A man's reading will out.

There were literary groups in the seventeenth century that attracted men of like tastes, and in each of these com-

[489] *Op. cit.,* I, 230. [490] *Ibid.,* I, 222.
[491] *Life of Archbishop Williams,* p. 217.
[492] *Works,* I, 99.
[493] Sermons, II, 309 (Delivered July, 1641). The allusion is, of course, to the *Faerie Queene.*
[494] *Life of Archbishop Williams,* p. 217.

panies, some of the clergy are found. John Hales and possibly Chillingworth (Suckling's "Shillingworth") were familiar with the quite unclerical world in which Ben Jonson and his friends lived: [495] both men were also, at a later date, members of the philosophical and literary gatherings at Great Tew. Jeremy Taylor was one of the mutually admiring circle that acknowledged the Matchless Orinda as leader. He willingly answered, as a member of the *précieuse* group, to the name of Palaemon; he even wrote a *Discourse on the Nature, Offices and Measures of Friendship*, dedicating the work to Orinda. The very adaptable John Hales who had found the "Tribe of Ben" congenial, and had been one of the scholars whom Lord Falkland made welcome at Great Tew, also enjoyed the friendship of the peaceful household at Little Gidding which was not finally broken up until 1646, although the community dwindled after the death of Nicholas Ferrar in 1637. There, too, had gone in earlier days, Herrick, Sandys, Crashaw, Henry Vaughan, Wither, Giles Fletcher, Robert Burton—a mixture of clergy and laity who gave and received much from one another, and learned much more from the extraordinary family to whom beauty was a part of religion, the acquirement of knowledge a service to God, and the stitching and binding of books an expression of fine and high personality.[496]

Miscellaneous Avocations

All of the avocations mentioned in the preceding pages have been of an intellectual character. Plainly, the seventeenth-century divine, established or nonconformist, considered that mental alarums and excursions were the only forms of relaxation creditable to a person dignified by the

[495] See Suckling's *Invitation to Town* (*Works*, p. 28).
[496] Carter, T. T.: *Nicholas Ferrar. His Household and His Friends*.
Hutton, W. H.: *History of the English Church* (1625-1714).
Walton: *Life of Herbert*, p. 312.

priestly office. In speaking of recreation in connection with Dr. George Bull, his biographer says: "I cannot find that after he entered into Holy Orders, he was ever addicted to any innocent Pleasure. . . . If there was anything that looked like a Diversion, it was the Enjoyment of agreeable Conversation. . . ." [497] But John Williams, archbishop of York, thought diversion a necessity. "The greater the performance was (whether a Speech, or a Sermon, or a Debate) he was to undertake, the more liberty and recreation he took, to quicken and open his spirits, and to clear his thoughts. . . ." [498]

Isaac Barrow was an engrossed, almost an obsessed student, but he allowed himself two indulgences: "If he was guilty of any intemperance, it seemed to be in the love of fruit"; and the second weakness was tobacco, "which he used to call his Panpharmacon or Universal Medicine, and imagined it helped to compose and regulate his thoughts." [499] Henry Newcome permitted himself a good many cheerful moments, one learns from his diary. Chief among his active diversions was bowles. He is a little uncertain about the propriety of this indulgence and he writes: ". . . went to bowles at 5. I hope I shall not be much taken with it only merely for refreshment and preservinge health, if the Lord blesse it to me for that purpose." [500] On another occasion, he records: "After dinner I went to bowles at the broad holme, where wee spent the afternoone. I desired to thinke of several things which might be spiritually applyed in bowling, whereby one might remember and hint some good from what may be good for the body." [501] A friend and his wife drop in to

[497] Nelson: *Life of Bull*, p. 84. Also, Thomas Wilson: "He was never given to any Recreations (tho never so innocent) but he was exceeding sparing in his Expence of Time" (Clark, *Em. Lives*, p. 34). Dr. Robert Harris's "only play time was Saturdays in the afternoon: then he used to unbend and disburden himself by some innocent recreations, but only *ad ruborem.*" (Clark: *Gen. Martyr.*, p. 531).
[498] Lloyd: p. 379. [499] *Works*, I, 509.
[500] May 19, 1663. Fuller says Bowling teaches Mathematics and Proportion (*The Holy State*, p. 183ff.).
[501] Sept. 23, 1663,

spend the evening, and "after dutys" they draw valentines; another night, "wee were very merry about turneinge our pancakes. Was sad afterward." He goes to the fair, to the gardens with his wife, and to see the mountebank. This last recreation he feels is a dangerous one. Once, "Wee foolishly fell into heat this night about the mountebanke. What a folly it is in us to be angry if wee be not all in one thought." [502] Again, he and his wife "fooleinge . . . spent too much time in seeinge the mountebanke. It is not so grave as becomes a minister, and also time might be better bestowed, and besides wee see sin acted. The foole that makes himselfe a foole is not to be encouraged, and then I heard him to swear too, and therefore I intend to see them no more if the Lord will." [503] But Newcome's real recreation is tobacco. It is very bad for him, but he likes it. One may watch his struggles from page to page:

> My base heart is but too much concerned with this tobacco.
> I prayed in secret and I was sensible . . . how tobacco doth too much fill my thoughts, and selfe denial about such a stinkeinge thing might doe well.
> I resolve to let this tobacco alone and to studdy to forget it, for it doth me no good.
> I felt myself lorded over by tobacco and surely I must not give way to it, when it is thus minded by mee as it is.
> I doe see my slavery with this tobacco. When it can hasten a duty to be at it, and when I know it doth not benefit mee, but allmost allways makes mee sicke, it is high time to dismisse it. But sometimes to deny it when it is so desired were but a small degree of selfe denial.[504]

When the brief diary ends, Newcome is still enslaved, but he never deceives himself as Barrow does about the effect tobacco has upon him.

[502] June 22, 1663.
[503] March 22, 1662. (He did see them again as the date of the preceding quotation shows.)
[504] *Passim*, Nov., 1661 to Sept., 1663. Lilly tells (*Life*, p. 35) of William Breden, a parson, who "was so given over to tobacco . . . that when he had no tobacco, he would cut the bell-ropes and smoke them."

John Owen relaxed with flute playing and athletics;[505] John Prideaux indulged in shooting and bowles;[506] Robert Sanderson was fond of shooting and of bowles;[507] Usher liked cards but he gave them up, as he did poetry, "least it should have taken him off from more serious studies";[508] and Seth Ward was "perhaps somewhat too fond of athletics, at which he was very proficient."[509] Josselin reproached himself for "unseasonable playing at chesse."[510]

Mechanics

A number of divines found an interest in devising mechanical contrivances of a useful or ornamental nature. John Aubrey believed that "Francis Potter's genius lay most of all to the mechanicks; he had an admirable mechanicall invention, but in that darke time wanted encouragement. . . . He had excellent notions for the raysing of water, using a wheel with steps to walk on as if you were going up staires, and an ordinary bodye's weight drawes up a great bucket. . . ."[511] Aubrey set down a memorandum "to send to Mr. Francis Potter for his notions of flying and of being safely delivered upon the ground from great heights with a sheet."[512] This resourceful gentleman also "invented a paire of beame compasses, which will divide an inch into a hundred or a thousand parts."[513]

Dr. John Wilkins had a warm admirer and sympathizer in Evelyn: "He . . . showed me the transparent apiaries, which he had built like castles and palaces, and ordered them one upon another, as to take the honey without destroying the bees. . . . He had also contrived a hollow

[505] *Dict. Nat'l Biog.*
[506] Lloyd: p. 536. See, too, Wm. Somner: *Life* (prefixed to his *Treatise*) p. 10.
[507] Lloyd: p. 537.
[508] Bernard: *Funeral Sermon for Usher (Eighteen Sermons)*, pp. 24, 25.
[509] Aubrey: II, 283.　　　　　　[511] Aubrey: II, 162.
[510] *Diary*, Feb. 23, 1647.　　　　[512] *Ibid.*, p. 128.
[513] *Ibid.*, p. 166. See also, Burnet: *Hist. of his own Times*, I, 186-7.

statue, which gave a voice and uttered words by a long concealed pipe that went to its mouth, whilst one speaks
through it at a good distance. He had . . . variety of
shadows, dials, perspectives, and many artificial, mathematical, and magical curiosities, a way-wiser, a thermometer,
a monstrous magnet, conic, and other cestions, a balance on
a demi-circle; most of them his own, and that prodigious
young scholar Mr. Christopher Wrene. . . ." [514] On another occasion, Evelyn "called at Durdans, where I found
Dr. Wilkins, Sir William Petty, and Mr. Hoole, contriving
chariots, new rigging for ships, a wheel for one to run
races in, and other mechanical inventions." [515] Aubrey has
another memorandum below the one in regard to Potter's
flying machine, reminding himself to inquire about "Dr.
Wilkins his notion of an umbrella-like invention for retard-
ing a ship when she drives in a storm." [516] Aubrey also says
that Wilkins's head "ran much upon the perpetuall
motion." Evelyn made Wilkins a present of "my rare
burning-glass"; [517] and a month later went to see him at
Whitehall where he was found with Sir P. Neal, famous
for his optic glasses.

Wilkins tells the Reader that Mathematical and Philosophical Enquiries have been a recreation in leisure hours.
Dr. Wilkins must have been extraordinarily active during
those times if one may judge by *Mathematical Magic; or the
Wonders that may be perform'd by Mechanical Geometry.*[518]
The first part of the book is truly mechanical, but the
second is a glory of imagination. Here are a few chapter
headings:

> Ch. II. Of a Sailing Chariot, that may without Horses
> be driven on the Land by the Wind, as Ships are on the Sea.
> Ch. IV. Of the Moveable and Gradient Automata, repre-
> senting the Motions of Living Creatures, various Sounds of
> Birds, or Beasts, and some of them articulate.

[514] *Diary*, Aug. 27, 1655.　　[516] Aubrey : II, 328 ; 300.
[515] *Ibid.*, Aug. 4, 1665.　　[517] *Diary*, April 12, 1656.
[518] One of the Flemings bought this book twice, once for 5s. 8d.,
again for 4s. 6d. *The Flemings at Oxford,* I (App. C), pp. 388, 442.

Ch. V. Concerning the Possibility of framing an Ark for Submarine Navigations. The Difficulties and Conveniences of such a Contrivance.

Ch. VII. Concerning the Art of flying. The several ways by which this has been or may be attempted.

Ch. IX. Of a perpetual Motion. . . . The several Ways whereby it hath been attempted; particularly by Chymistry.

Ch. X. Of subterranean Lamps.[519]

A man who had great skill "in the optiques" was Father Franciscus Lines (i.e. Hall). He wrote a discourse *de coloribus,* and "a pretty little booke in 8vo (or lesse) of natural philosophy," the name of which Aubrey unfortunately forgot.[520]

Evelyn's visits to scientific friends seem frequently to have been so fortunately timed as to coincide with those of other interesting men, and consequently it is not surprising that when he is calling upon John Wallis and finds him in the tower of the schools (at Oxford), there, also, are Robert Boyle and Dr. Christopher Wren "with an inverted tube, or telescope, observing the discus of the sun for the passing of Mercury that day before it; but the latitude was so great that nothing appeared. . . ."[521] Dr. Wallis, in collaboration with Mr. Huygens, published a study on the laws of motion at the same time that Sir Christopher Wren completed a tract on the same subject, "and these three great men, without knowing anything of one another's thoughts, agreed exactly in the same proportions."[522]

Edward Barlow, a Catholic priest, worked for many years on clocks, and perfected his invention of repeating-

---

[519] Wilkins did not let his many scientific interests creep into his sermons. They are thoroughly conventional; he was not led astray even when he selected such a text as the following: "For God shall bring every work into judgment, with every secret thing, whether it be good, or whether it be evil" (Eccles. xii. 14). Preached before the King, Feb. 27, 1669/70.

[520] Aubrey: II, 34.

See Joseph Glanvill: *Scepsis Scientifica, or, Confest Ignorance, the Way to Science.*

[521] *Diary,* Sept. 24, 1664.

[522] *Reliq. Hearnae,* II, 63. Dr. Christopher Wren, afterwards Dean of Windsor, is not to be confused with Sir Christopher Wren.

clocks, about 1676. Later, he introduced a similar device into watches.[523]

Mr. John Oldfield "had a Mechanical Head and Hand, capable of any thing, he had Opportunity to get insight into." [524] Thomas Powell published in 1661: *Humane Industry: or a History of most manual Arts, deducing the Original, Progress, and Improvement of them.*[525]

Outdoors

If many of the seventeenth-century clergy were out-of-doors men, the people who wrote about them found no interest in that fact. One man may like to walk, and one may like a ride,[526] but such tastes are rarely mentioned. A poet—as Herrick, of course—may talk of nature in his poetry, and a preacher may introduce an elaborate tree or flower comparison into his sermons, but no Gilbert White is to be found among the clergy of the time. There is a certain relief in coming upon Dr. John Dod as he sits holding a flower in his hand, firmly refusing to inspect a beautiful house built by Sir Christopher Hatton. "In this flower," said Dr. Dod, speaking entirely out of order—seventeenth-century order—"I can see more of God than in all the beautiful buildings in the world." [527] It is, curiously enough, George Fox who leads us into one of the few gardens that appear in the accounts written by and about preachers. Fox, on this occasion, was troubled as to the ground of despair and temptations, and he went to an ancient priest in Warwickshire and reasoned with him about

---

[523] *Dict. Nat'l Biog.*
[524] Calamy: *Account, etc.*, II, 172.
[525] *Dict. Nat'l Biog.*
[526] Juxton enjoyed long walks (Lloyd: p. 504); so did Richard Blackerby (Clark: *Em. Lives*, p. 58); and Matthew Robinson (*Auto.*, p. 48), who also liked to hunt, and furthermore he bred horses and sold them. Seth Ward, also, was fond of hunting (Aubrey: II, 283). Fuller says that "Running, Leaping, and Dancing, the descants on the plain song of walking, are all excellent exercises" (*The Holy State*, p. 184). Many of Henry More's *Dialogues* show his delight in summer evenings, out of doors.
[527] Fuller: *Church History*, I, 307.

it, but the priest (Fox terms all salaried ministers "priests") could only suggest that he take tobacco and sing psalms. "Tobacco was a thing I did not love, and psalms I was not in a state to sing; I could not sing." He applied to a second priest without gaining any relief; a third he found in a garden, and this man seemed willing to talk in the way Fox wished. Unfortunately "now, as we were walking together in his garden, the alley being narrow, I chanced, in turning, to set my foot on the side of a bed, at which the man was in such a rage as if his house had been on fire. Thus all our discourse was lost. . . ." [528]

Francis Potter devised an interesting garden, as he devised many other things. Aubrey saw it: "He had a pretty contrived garden there, where are the finest box hedges of his planting that ever I saw. The garden is a good large square; in the middle is a good high mount, all fortified (as you may say) and adorned with these hedges, which at the interstices of . . . [sic] foot have a high pillar (square cutt) of box, that shewes very stately and lovely both summer and winter." [529] Probably Fuller is only conventional in his *Antheologia: or, The Speech of Flowers* but he sounds rather affectionately disposed toward his imaginary garden. The flowers talk about themselves, the Rose being the leader. The author explains the situation in his dedication. The Rose scorns the Tulip, "a well-complexioned stink, an ill savour wrapped up in pleasant colours;" ". . . and yet this is that which filleth all gardens, hundreds of pounds being given for the root thereof, whilst the Rose is neglected and contemned . . . fit only to grow in the gardens of yeomen." [530]

The Physic-garden at Oxford gave an impulse to the scientific study of plants. William Browne, with the collaboration of Philip Stevens (who was not a divine), com-

---

[528] *Journal*, pp. 4-5.   [529] Aubrey: II, 164.
[530] Bound with *Joseph's Party-Coloured Coat*, pp. 279-80. The "tulipomania" had raged about 1634. See Josselin on Roses: *Diary*, Apr. 19, 20, 1646; May, 23, 1647.

posed a catalogue of the Botanical Garden at Oxford.[531] Francis Drope was a horticulturist who studied and wrote on the care of fruit trees.[532] Ezrael Tongue also made a study of trees, particularly the Sap in trees, and the Bleeding of Walnuts.[533] Robert Sharrock (who later reached the dignity of archdeacon of Winchester) was "very knowing in vegetables and all pertaining thereto." [534] John Wray (Ray) wrote a *Catalogus Plantarum Angliae* (1670).[535] Wilkins, in his *Real Character,* used Wray's list of trees, herbs, flowers, etc., and Willoughby's tables of fish and animals.

A use of nature similes is no sign of a knowledge of or affection for growing things; every man who had been educated in the Grammar School and the University must have had at hand, ready for use, scores of Greek and Latin comparisons to birds and trees and flowers. A few examples, however, may be interesting. Chillingworth, who spent much of his time at Oxford in walking in the groves seeking whom he might dispute with, perhaps looked about him as he did so and saw this himself, "for as the shadows are longest when the sun is lowest, and as vines, and other fruit trees, bear the less fruit, when they are suffered to luxuriate and spend their sap upon superfluous suckers, and abundance of leaves; so commonly, we may observe. . . ." [536] John Owen in a Thanksgiving Sermon preaching before Parliament after the destruction of the Scots army at Worcester, takes Ezekiel xvii. 24 as his text ("And all the trees of the field shall know. . . .") and for seven folio pages, he carries out a tree-simile.[537] Jeremy Taylor uses flowers for decorative purposes in his sermons. A famous example is the following: ". . . if you thrust a

[531] Wood: *Fasti*, II, 282. John Greaves described one side of the "greatest Egyptian pyramid" as being "693 feet. So that it is twice as much as our Physick Garden at Oxford." (*Reliq. Hearnae*, I, 215-6.) The Physic Garden was opened in 1632.
[532] Wood: *Ath. Ox.*, III, 941.
[533] Wood: *Ath. Ox.*, III, 1263.
[534] *Ibid.*, IV, 147.
[535] Calamy: *Abridg.*, II, 87.
[536] *Works*, p. 530.
[537] *Sermons*, p. 399.

jessamine there where she [nature] would have a daisy
grow, or bring the tall fir from dwelling in his own country,
and transport the orange or the almond-tree near the fringes
of the north-star, nature is displeased, and becomes unnatural, and starves her sucklings, and renders you a return
less than your charge and expectation: so it is in all our
appetites. . . ." [538]

The list of clergymen who found recreation in the study
of birds is brief. John Ray (Wray) is the only parson,
apparently, who actually worked at ornithology. He
"viewed, corrected, and digested into order, the Ornithology
of Mr. Francis Willoughby." [539] The two men made their
investigations together, using Willoughby's original manuscript as a foundation. Sir Thomas Browne aided them,
placing at their disposal his own notes, "including a number of coloured drawings." [540] He refers to their book
as if it were a volume easily procurable, "There is a handsome figure of an ostrich in Mr. Willoughby's and Ray's
Ornithologia." [541] In his *Vulgar Errors,* Sir Thomas quotes
Dean Christopher Wren as an authority on the size and
manner of growth of frogs.[542]

Rhetorically, birds have a much better chance of catch-
ing the interest of the preachers. Thomas Fuller may have
had a natural liking for birds, or a cultivated one derived
from the richness of allusion in the Bible. His most complete collection of birds is in a sermon which had been
preached in St. Clement's Church, London, and which was
published under the title, *Comfort in Calamitie.* "We may
observe," says Dr. Fuller, "that David is much pleased
with the Metaphor in frequent comparing himselfe to a
Bird, and that of severall sorts: first to an Eagle, Psal.
103.5. Thy Youth is renewed like the Eagles: Sometimes
to an Owle, Psal. 102.6. I am like an Owle in the Desart:
Sometimes to a Pelican, in the same verse, Like a Pelican in

[538] *Works,* I, 695.
[539] Wood: *Fasti,* II, 246.
[540] *Works,* I, lvii.
[541] *Ibid.,* III (Tracts).
[542] *Ibid.,* II, 290.

the Wildernesse: Sometimes to a Sparrow, Psal. 102.7. I watch, and am as a Sparrow: Sometimes to a Partridge, as when one doth hunt a Partridge. I cannot say that he doth compare himselfe to a Dove, but he would compare himselfe, Psal. 55.6. Oh, that I had the wings of a Dove, for then I would fly away and be at rest.

"Some will say, Howe is it possible, that Birds of so different a feather, should also so flue together as to meet in the Character of David." (He then explains that David in prosperity is the eagle; in adversity, the owl, etc.)

In a short allegory, Fuller made use of birds, as many satirists before and after him have done, to embody ideas of leadership. In *Ornithologie; or, The Speech of Birds,* the whole species is commanded to appear at a specified time, and choose a leader; "it was also proclaimed that all antipathy should cease between all Birds during their meeting." There is a good deal of social and local satire in the discussions, and Fuller's vocation is not noticeable. The book was printed in 1655, and was dedicated to Roger L'Estrange who may have already evinced an interest in animal fables, but he did not publish his own book of Aesop's fables until 1692.

Jeremy Taylor is as much addicted to bird comparisons as he is to flower similes and metaphors. The sentence that is oftenest quoted when the Bishop's literary mannerisms are being discussed, is that which begins, "For so I have seen a lark rising from his bed of grass, and soaring upward. . . ." and which ends some thirty-two lines down the page, the comparison being that of the lark's flight and the prayer of a good man.[543] Virtually all the preachers employ birds in their figurative expressions and one such phrase is hardly to be distinguished from another, so conventional is the wording. It is a pleasure to find Mr. Ralph Josselin to be a man who knows birds in trees, not merely on a printed page; for example, (Oct. 23, 1644) "I saw

[543] *Works,* I, 638.

a young rooke yt fell out of the nest in the priory yard
y^s day; I have not knowne ye like in all my dayes y^t they
should build and breed at this time of the yeare." [544]

Farming

Just as, after sequestration or ejectment some preachers
became schoolmasters as the quickest way to gain a living,
so other preachers became farmers. To those who had
known only the small positions in the church, the work
could not have been new. The curate and the ill-paid
rector had been accustomed to making their own hay, and
digging their own gardens. The sequestrations in Puritan
times, were usually directed against men who held fairly
good, if not very good, livings, and these ousted men were
likely to have some social or financial resources which
would aid them in securing usherships or chaplaincies.
This was not always the case, of course. There was Will
Davis, a loyalist parson, "being forced out of meer Necessity for a Subsistence as I nave ᵇ   from a
Reverend Person who had it fr   marry
an Ordinary Woman with a very small Estate, and to turn
Farmer, or rather Day-Labourer upon it; the Value of it
being so little, that he was forced to Thrash in the Barn
for his Lively-hood, and to go to Market to sell
Cheese. . . ." [545]

The St. Bartholomew ejectments were sweeping. After
August 24, 1662, the average nonconforming minister was
looking for some way of supporting himself and his family.
Some men found it possible to conform, as did Edward
Reynolds (who was made Bishop of Norwich), and Wallis,
and Wilkins (who lived to be Bishop of Chester); some
were cared for by generous patrons; some wrote books.
But a great number of the lesser preachers turned farmer.
Calamy, who names many, often states the fact with the

[544] *Diary*, p. 21.   [545] Walker: Pt. II, 73.

barest comment; as, "Mr. Humphrey Bell was content to turn Farmer for a Livelihood"; [546] or, "Mr. Burnand retir'd to the Desert Places in Austin-More and there took a Farm." [547] But if he has any excuse he gives an individuality to his farmer. Mr. William Benton "took a Farm, and apply'd himself to Husbandry for the necessary Maintenance of his Family: and afterwards he followed the Mault Trade. He was a Man of Parts, Presence, and Assurance." [548] "Mr. Ralph Wickleff took a Farm which he liv'd upon; and yet preach'd in his own Home, and taught Youth in the Latin Tongue." [549] Mr. Thomas Joseph "spoilt an ingenious Husbandman to become an Ignorant Preacher." [550]

The unnamed author of the forty-eighth sermon in the collection entitled *The House of Mourning* knew something about farming and what to expect of the weather. Listen to him: "Man might have Fallowed, and Stirred, and Plowed, and Sown, and Harrowed, and Rouled, and Weeded and Mown, and yet not have brought home to the Barn. . . . How may a Snowy January, Frosty February, Dusty March, Showry Aprill, Windy May, Warm June, Hott July (all very kindly in their kinds) be married with a constant and continued raign in August . . . ?" [551] Ralph Josselin was an unusually successful farmer. [552] In his Diary, sermons and wheat, prayers and cattle, are closely associated.

Fishing

Among the by-occupations of the Cromwell and Stuart clergymen, fishing is scarcely mentioned; perhaps the biographers and preachers of funeral sermons thought angling undignified, or perhaps, on the other hand, it was

[546] Calamy: *Abridg.*, II, 513.
[547] *Ibid.*, II, 158.
[548] *Ibid.*, p. 791.
[549] *Ibid.*, p. 305.
[550] *Ibid.*, p. 732.
[551] *Ibid.*, p. 539.
[552] E.g., see the goodly portions he was able to give his daughters when they married, *Diary*, p. viii.

a matter of course and did not need a specific statement. No occupation could be more correctly god-fathered
from an ecclesiastical point of view. Isaac Walton makes
this fact quite clear: ". . . it is observable that it was our
Saviour's will that these, our poor fishermen, should have
a priority of nomination in the catalogue of his twelve
Apostles, as namely, first St. Peter, St. Andrew, St. James,
and St. John. . . ." He proves conclusively that Moses
and Amos were anglers; and then offers, as evidence of a
desirable combination of preacher and fisherman, a certain
long-ago Dean of St. Paul's who spent a tenth part of his
time in angling. He lived to ninety-five, his mind and
senses unimpaired: " 'Tis said that Angling and Temperance were great causes of these blessings." [553]   John Donne
is highly praised for his verses mainly because, Walton says
frankly, he alludes to rivers and fish and fishing; [554] Phineas
Fletcher is "an excellent Divine, and an excellent Angler;
and the author of excellent piscatory Eclogues, in which
you shall see the picture of this good man's mind: and
I wish mine to be like it." [555]   None of Walton's examples
belong to the period under discussion, but he himself is
writing in that time—the *Angler* was published in 1653—
and he took his fishermen where he found them. [556]

[553] *The Compleat Angler*, p. 53.
[554] *Ibid.*, p. 178.
[555] *Ibid.*, p. 200.
[556] Walton would have enjoyed a sermon preached to the fishes by a
contemporary, Antonio Vieryra, in Portugal. On St. Anthony's day,
he addressed himself directly to the fishes, saying it was better on the
Festival of the Saints, to preach like them rather than to them. The
fish are reminded that they were created before beasts, fowls, or men;
that Moses mentions the whale by name but never a beast; that Aristotle says fish alone cannot be tamed or domesticated; that at the
flood all fish escaped; that though beasts were sacrificed to God, fishes
never were . . . (Neal: *Mediaeval Preachers* . . . p. 321ff).

CHAPTER V

THE PREACHER AND THE SOCIAL ORDER

THE social position of the English clergyman varied, naturally enough, with the inheritance of social consequence to which he had been born and with the official rank which he attained in the church. In the Established Church he might become a bishop or archbishop with a revenue of impressive proportions, though some bishoprics were notably obscure, lacking both dignity and income.[1] In nonconformist sects, there were few men from the great families of England, though many could claim the title of "gentleman," and some had influential connections through marriage or friendship. The lesser clergy, of any sectarian group, ranked "below the small freeholders, slightly above the farmers, and not very much above the tradescraftmen." [2] The unordained, irregular, uneducated preacher, or the spontaneous quaker, had no social existence.

But not even bishops were safe from charges of low birth and insufficient breeding. In 1641, "came forth the Lord Brook his book against bishops, accusing them in respect of their parentage to be . . . of the dregs of the people, and in respect of their studies no way fit for government, or to

[1] Dr. Richard Holdsworth refused the bishopric of Bristol, "not out of covetousness . . . because so small the revenues thereof . . . but for some secret reason." Fuller: *Hist. of Camb.*, p. 207.
A letter from Daniel Fleming to Bishop Guy Carleton of Bristol (Feb., 1671) expresses the hope that Carleton may be translated to an old bishopric, a new one such as Bristol—a creation of Henry VIII's time—being small in revenue. *The Flemings at Oxford*, I, 190.
[2] Sydney, W. C.: *Social Life in England, 1660-1690*, p. 165.

be barons in parliament." It was the first of these accusa-
tions that stirred the active resentment of the bishops.
They held a meeting, "and in their own necessary defence
thought fit to vindicate their extractions, some publicly,
some in private discourse." Fuller tells of the evidence of
gentility offered by this or that lord bishop: "Dr. Williams
(archbishop of York) had purchased the two ancientest
houses and inheritances in North Wales, in regard he was
descended from them. . . . Dr. Juxton, bishop of London,
did or might plead that his parents lived in good fashion,
and gave him a large allowance, first in the university, then
in Grey's Inn, where he lived as fashionably as other gentlemen, so that the Lord Brook might question the parentage
of any inns-of-court-gentlemen as well as his. . . . Bishop
Morton of Durham averred that his father had been lord
mayor of York. . . . Bishop Cook of Herford, his father's
family had continued in Derbyshire, in the same house and
in the same means, 400 years at least. . . . Bishop Owen
of Asaph, that there was not a gentleman in the two counties
of Carnavon and Anglysea of 300 pounds a year but was his
kinsman, or allieman, in the fourth degree, which he thinks
will sufficiently justify his parentage." [3]

All these persons were church personages, and only
political feeling could have inspired so general a charge of
social inferiority. The term "gentleman" still had a definite
meaning in the seventeenth century. A bishop might courteously be considered *ex officio,* a gentleman, but when the
word is applied to an unimportant man of religion it is because the writer wishes to emphasize good breeding.
Samuel Palmer, who revised and added to the Calamy biog-
raphies, always uses the word deliberately. Of Nathaniel
Durant, we read, "His father was a gentleman;" [4] Joseph

---

[3] *Church History, etc.,* VI, 211ff. The dispute was "whether bishops
should sit still in the house."
   On Archbishop William's claims to long descent, see Lloyd: *State
Worthies,* p. 903. Joseph Hall's good birth is proved in the first pages
of his Life (bound with his *Contemplations*).
[4] Palmer: *Nonconf. Mem.,* I, 341.

Halsey "was much of a gentleman, and was generally honoured and loved by those who knew him;"[5] John Hodder "was so much of a gentleman, and of such singular ingenuity, that his very enemies admired him, and were proud of his conversation."[6] Thomas Holland was "a gentleman born";[7] Richard Wavel, when the title of gentleman was given to him in an indictment and "one that sat on the bench" objected to the use of the term, found himself promptly defended by the lord mayor who showed that the title of gentleman was legitimately Mr. Wavel's.[8]

Baxter quotes Judge Jeffreys as saying : "There is Bates, I saw him just now—I will say that for him, he is a gentleman and a scholar, and the best of the whole pack of them. . . ."[9] William Gouge was so fearful of pride in his good birth that he charged his executor "that he should not affix any Escutcheons to his Herse, though he were a Gentleman anciently descended; as if he had thought that the poverty of Christ was his patrimony . . . and Coat of Arms."[10] Samuel Clark is careful to give due respect to well-born clergymen. When he mentions Mr. Thomas Tregoss, he adds: "The Family whereof he was a Branch was not without Noble Blood in its veines. Some are of the opinion that it is more Ancient than the Norman Conquest, a Stem of the old Britans driven into and Planted in those parts."[11] Mr. Samuel Fairclough was "well descended by both Father and Mother, and to be born so, is reckoned an honour even by divine testimony . . . the children of illustrious Parents, having a preference given them in sacred Writ, Eccl. 10, 17."[12]

---

[5] Palmer : *Nonconf. Mem.*, I, 285.
[6] *Ibid.*, I, 452.
[7] *Ibid.*, II, 83 ; also, S. Hildersham, *ibid.* : II, 327 ; Geo. Newton, *ibid.* : II, 377 ; H. Lever, *ibid.* : II, 267.
[8] *Ibid.*, I. 164.
[9] *Autobiography* : Appendix, I, p. 260.
[10] Jenkins : *A Shock of Corn*, p. 36.
[11] *Em. Lives*, p. 109.
[12] *Ibid.*, p. 153. Th. Hall, in *Vind. Lit.*, speaks of Isaiah being "of the blood Royall," p. 12.

The most elaborate and best known of the contemporary judgments of the everyday—which means the average—clergyman is that of John Eachard, who was himself a minister of the church of England, and was also, in 1679 and 1695, vice-chancellor of the university of Cambridge. His book, *The Grounds and Occasions of the Contempt of the Clergy and Religion,* was published anonymously in 1670. The Preface to the Reader reveals a good deal of the author's personality. He explains that he is not a seeker after tithes; nor is he disgruntled because of disappointed ambitions; nor is he one "of those occasional Writers, that missing preferment in the University, can presently write you their new Ways on Education; or being a little tormented with an ill chosen wife, set forth the Doctrine of Divorce to be truly Evangelical." [13] Nor is he "one of those people who insist that no one can be a profitable Instructor of the People, unless born when the sun is in Aries, etc., nor go through the work of the Ministry unless, for three hundred years backward it can be proved that none of his family ever had a Cough, Ague, or grey Hair." [14]

The author asserts that the dignity of the church is lowered by the custom of putting into the ministry the weakest, least promising member of a family. This same charge is also made by Robert South in one of his sermons, and he is more definite than Eachard: ". . . matters have been brought to pass, that if a man amongst his sons had

[13] Milton's pamphlet on Education had been written in 1664; that on Divorce, in 1643.

[14] Eachard's open reproof and satirical comment are directed at clergymen as a class, and not at any one group. Sectarian vituperations were matters of course and are not to be considered as evidence of the attitude of the general public to the ordained minister. After the Restoration, it was the fashion to ridicule the nonconforming preachers but they did not lack defenders among scholars, or even among members of the established church. In the Preface to his *Account* of ejected ministers and others, Edmund Calamy says plaintively: "They [the Dissenters] have born all the Obloquy that the Stage, the Tavern, the Press, or the Pulpit could well vent against them. . . . And yet, they have some Footing, and some Credit still left."

any blind, or disfigured, he laid him aside for the ministry; and such a one was presently approved, as having a morti- fied countenance. In short it was a fiery furnace which approved dross, and rejected gold . . . when God refused the defective and the maimed for sacrifice, we cannot think that he requires them for the priesthood." [15]   Matthew Robinson once drew up a model "for the Maintaining of Students of Choice Abilities at the University, and Princi- pally in order to the Ministry." He wished to deflect from the ministry the "raw and unfurnished" young men who enter it through necessity, "to their own perpetual dis- couragement, and to the great mischief of the Church." [16] There are so many of that quality that they bring the church into contempt, and yet those very persons, Robinson feels, might be successful in some occupation outside of the church. This view is also held by the author of *The Pulpit Guarded,* who complains of the habit of "thrusting into Ecclesiastical or Literary offices at the university a many of persons who had they been suffered to obey their owne inclinations, and followed some Trade or Handcraft, might have ranked themselves amongst the ablest of their Pro- fessions." [17]   Baxter, too, advised against a hasty or care- less choice of the ministry as a convenient way of providing for a son.[18]

Many men thought of attendance at the university as pro- viding a claim to social recognition, and as a preparation for a church appointment. The university itself did not rate the clergyman high in the social scale. At Oxford, dur- ing the Commonwealth, the entrance fees marked the fol- lowing descending order:

---

[15] *Sermons,* I, 86ff.
[16] *Autobiography* (Appendix), pp. 162 ; 174-5. The author of *The Gentleman's Calling* laments that gentlemen, who have more time than other men, will not put this time to advantage by studying Divinity ; "but Divinity is beyond all others under prejudice with them, decried not only as a crabbed, but ungentile study."
[17] T.[homas] H.[all], p. 16ff. Cf. Ascham : *The Schoolmaster,* pp. 22-3.
[18] *The Reformed Pastor,* p. 79.

	£	s	d
The son of a Peer............................	2	0	0
The son of a Baronet.........................	1	6	8
The son (eldest) of a Knight (Miles)..........	1	0	0
The son (not eldest) of a Knight, of an Armiger, and a Doctor......................	0	10	0
The son of a Generosus (or gentleman).......	0	5	0
The son of a Clergyman, or of a Plebeius.....	0	2	0
A Serviens, or a Chorister[19]..................	0	0	0

Both the nobleman and the country parson, having sent a son to the university, felt that the institution was under obligations to provide a livelihood for that son if he took his degree in divinity, however unfitted he might be for his profession, mentally or spiritually. Edmund Ludlow gives an account of a talk with Dr. Earle who told him "that by abolishing episcopacy we took away all encouragement to it [learning]; for that men would not send their sons to the university had they not some hopes that they might attain to that preferment. To this I replied that it would be much more honest for such men to train their children at the plow, whereby they might be certainly provided with a livelihood, than to spend their time and money to advance them to an office, pretended to be spiritual, and instituted for spiritual ends, on such a sordid principle and consideration." [20] Pepys had the same idea as John Earle about the responsibility of the university to provide for young divines and, troubled as to the future of his unpromising brother John, decides "that I will either send him to Cambridge for a year, till I get him some church promotion, or send him to sea as a chaplain where he may study, and earn his living." [21]

When James Harrington created the Commonwealth of Oceana, he did not neglect to settle this troublesome question as to how the university should provide for the clergy-

[19] Burrows: *The Register of Visitors at . . . Oxford, 1647-1658*, p. 468.
[20] *Memoirs*, I, 81-2.
[21] *Diary*, Oct. 10, 1667.

men it produced. This is the reasonable arrangement Harrington suggests: When a minister dies or removes from the parish, the congregation assembles and deputes one or two elders, by ballot, to repair to one of the universities with a certificate to the Vice-Chancellor, giving the facts of death or removal. The Vice-Chancellor calls a convocation, "and having made choice of a fit person, shall return him in due time to the Parish." He serves as probationer for a year, after which he is voted on by the congregation as a permanency.[22]

No position in all the range of church appointments was as much ridiculed and scorned as that of the private chaplain. Eachard draws his picture as a timid, servile creature, receiving perhaps ten pounds a year, taking care of the garden, looking after the horses, and humbly leaving the table after a course or two, "picking his teeth, and sighing with his hat under his arm; whilst the Knight and my Lady eat up the tarts and chickens." [23] John Taylor, the Water-Poet, puts the self-effacing chaplain into rhyme:

> His Worship's Chaplaine, twice (with double grace)
> In feare and trembling, takes and leaves his place,
> And (having read his Chapter) still must say,
> Thus ends your Worship's Lesson for the day.[24]

When Cowley set forth his *Proposition for the Advancement of Learning,* he devoted one paragraph of his presentation of an ideal college to the duties of the chaplain (after giving four pages to the duties of the professors); and he states that the chaplain is to eat at the masters' table. He also states that the chaplain "shall not trouble himself or his

[22] Pp. 83-8.
[23] *Grounds and Occasions, etc.,* p. 19ff. In a later work, *Observations on an Answer to the Enquiry* . . . Eachard says in his Preface: "if any of you hear of a Second Answer coming out against my Former Letter, concerning my putting the Tarts before the Chickens (for I am given to understand that such an Objection is urged) . . . by all means presently stop the Press; for most certainly Chickens ought to have the Precedence of Tarts, both by an indispensable right of Nature, and by the justest and oldest Traditions of Cookery."
[24] *Works,* VII (Differing Worships).

Auditors with the controversies of Divinity." [25]   Anthony
à Wood, wishing to show his superiority to a chaplain relates that when Sir Leolin Jenkyns introduced him to the
archbishop of Canterbury, who was at dinner, he, "A.W.,"
saw "John Eachard, the author of the *Contempt of the
Clergy,* who sate at the lower end of the table between the
archbishop's two chaplayns . . . being the first time that
the said Eachard was introduced into the archbishop's company.   After dinner the archbishop went into his withdrawing roome, and Eachard with the chaplaynes . . . to
drink and smoak.   Sir L. Jenkyns took then A.W. by the
hand, and conducted him into the withdrawing roome to the
archbishop. . . ." [26]

One of the most important sermons delivered by the
Reverend Mr. Vines, was at the funeral of the Earl of
Essex, on which occasion, having many gentlemen of position among his auditors, he seized the opportunity to slip in
a word for the private chaplain.   First, commands Mr.
Vines, "submit your cheeke to reproofes;" then, "frowne not
your Chaplains into a meale-mouth'd basenesse, so that they
dare no more make a darke or oblique reflexion upon your
darling sinnes, then take a Beare by the tooth." [27]

The private chaplain was supposed to accommodate himself to any plans of his patron.   He might even be requested
to marry my lady's maid or a relative of the family with a
damaged reputation.   Eachard says this satirically, but
that there was truth in his statement is shown by the testimony of writers contemporaneous with Eachard who are
not holding a brief, as he is, for reform but who speak out
of a familiar knowledge of conditions.   Edward Chamberlayne declares in a chapter on "The Social Position of the
English Established Clergy," "as it now is in England . . .
they are accounted by many as the dross and refuse of the

[25] *Essays and Other Prose Writings,* p. 38.
[26] Wood: *Ath. Ox.,* I, lxxff.
[27] *The Hearse of the Renowned,* p. 21.   Also, Cheynell: *A Man of
Honour,* p. 65.

Nation. Men think it a stain to their blood, to place their Sons in that Function, and Women are ashamed to marry with any of them." [28] No doubt ambitious and personable house chaplains were sometimes able to marry into the immediate family of the patron even when the lady was young, attractive, and untouched by slander. Pepys repeats the gossip that Jeremiah White, "formerly chaplain to the Lady Protectress," tried to marry Cromwell's daughter, Frances.[29] The story is that the Protector one day found White on his knees before Frances Cromwell, and the chaplain excused himself by saying that he had been begging that the Lady Frances would use her influence with her waiting-woman with whom he declared himself to be in love. Oliver, being suspicious of the chaplain's sincerity, forced him to marry the waiting-woman soon after. Among Flecknoe's *Sixtynine Enigmatical Characters* is one of a nobleman's chaplain. The picture is much like that drawn by Eachard, emphasizing the chaplain's servility, and his patron's scorn. We see the nobleman silencing the man who is regarded as an upper servant, refusing him a place even at the lower end of the table; and we watch the chaplain claiming the higher end of the steward's table, and seizing an opportunity to make love "in godly manner to the Chambermaid or Waiting-gentlewoman." [30]

All chaplains, of course, were not of the type that lent itself so easily to satirical treatment; nor were all patrons overbearing and selfish. There were men who gave their chaplains not only a home but the opportunity for study and for acquaintance with scholars. A library such as that of the Earl of Arundel would alone be sufficient attraction for

---

[28] *Angliae Notitiae*, p. 383ff. Donald Lupton shows the country chaplain, in 1632, as companion of the butler and other servants (*London and the Country Carbonaded*, p. 37ff.).

Bunyan speaks of "Your trencher chaplains, that thrust themselves into great men's families, pretending the worship of God, when in truth the great business is their own bellies . . ." (*Works*, "On Praying in the Spirit, p. 637).

[29] *Diary*, April 18, 1660.

[30] P. 44.

a man of studious tastes to content himself with the position of private chaplain.

Many householders take the chaplain as a matter of course, mentioning him in diaries without enthusiasm or animus. Mistress Alice Thornton refers to "a godly and orthodox divine . . . who had married my father's steward's widdow;" [31] but she makes no comment on the man or his wife. She expresses herself as much pleased with Mr. Thornton's plan to ask a divine, Mr. Comber, "to have his table at Newton, which my husband would give him, with a horsse to be kept winter and summer, if he would please to come and live with him." Mistress Thornton considers that the minister's "learning, parts, and ingenuity would make him a very good companion to divert him [her husband] in his retiredness, and to seariousness a temper."[32] As an afterthought she adds that Mr. Comber could "performe family dutyes of prayers, and catechising the children."

Lady Mary Warwick always writes courteously if a trifle patronizingly of the household chaplains with whom she comes in contact in her father-in-law's house. The first one she mentions is the well-known John Gauden, but she makes no comment except that he was afterwards Lord Bishop of Worcester.[33] Somewhat later the Earl of Warwick had, as household chaplain, "one Mr. Walker, who being a very good natured, civil and ingenious person, I took much delight in conversing with." [34] This Anthony Walker preached the family funeral sermons: one on Lord Rich (the son of the earl) in 1664, on Lord Warwick in 1673, and finally Lady Mary's own in 1678. All were printed, the popularity of the last requiring a second edition in 1687.[35]

---

[31] *Diary*, p. 208.
[32] *Diary*, p. 217.
[33] *Autobiography*, p. 15.
[34] *Ibid.*, p. 20.
[35] Mr. Walker had a decorative style; for example, in his sermon for Lady Mary, he exclaims: "Oh, for a Chrysostom's mouth, for an angel's tongue to describe this terrestrial seraphine; or a ray of light condensed into a pencil, and made tactile, to give you this glorious child of light in *viva effigie*," p. vii.

Lady Anne Clifford plainly feels her own noble condescension as she records in her Diary that the minister has
had dinner with her. One entry gives an account of the
evening when her guests were "the Sheriff and his wife,
Mr. Geastly, our parson, my two Farmers here, William
Spedding and his wife, Jeffrey Bleamire and his son, so
after dinner I had them into my Room, and kissed the
Women, and took the men by the hand, and a little after,
Mr. Geastly, the parson, said Common Prayer and read a
chapter, and sang a Psalm . . . and when Prayers were
done they went away." [36]

Anne, Lady Halkett, draws in her Memoirs, an elaborate
character of the private chaplain of Sir Charles Howard
at whose home she paid an extremely long visit in her girl-
hood. At first she entirely approves of Mr. Nichols: "Hee
was a man of good life, good conversation, and had in such
veneration by all as if hee had beene their tutelar angel."
Even when Anne finds him guilty of double dealing and
convinces Sir Charles of the fact, the chaplain is not dismissed, "because Sir Charles had a respect for him, and
desired that all should respect him. . . ." Anne also has
this feeling regarding the dignity of Mr. Nichol's office;
during a stormy interview with the chaplain (who has made
every effort to misrepresent her to her hosts), she says:
"the respect I have to your calling, and the benefitt I have
had by your preaching and prayer, shall keepe mee from
divulging your faults." Later she records, probably with
some satisfaction, that Mr. Nichols "had not followed my
advice as to reforming butt traducing a person who came
there presently after I went away, who could nott suffer itt
as I had done, butt tooke a revenge suitable enough to the
fault, though unsuitable to one of his function." [37]

Lady Fanshawe, the wife of Sir Richard Fanshawe, says
that her father and mother were both great lovers and

[36] *Life, Letters and Work,* p. 266.
[37] *Journal,* pp. 31-69.

honorers of clergymen, and taught her to admire them. Sir Richard died in Madrid (where he was serving as ambassador); and Lady Fanshawe states in her Memoirs: "July the 4th, *stilo novo,* 1666, my husband was buried by his own Chaplain, Henry Bagshaw with the ceremony of the Church of England, and a sermon preached by him." [38]

Lettice, Lady Falkland, received chaplains and neighboring divines affably at Great Tew. The particular interest they had for her, was their need of guidance: "she was accustomed to hint unto them what virtues it would be proper to commend in their sermons." [39]

The court chaplains were selected from the most noted divines: "for the most part, Deans of Prebendaries, and all Principal Predicators," Chamberlayne says. He names among the forty-eight appointed for the year 1669: Pierce, Maine, Stillingfleet, Tillotson, Fell, Cartwright, Smith, Maggot, Barrow, Pearson, Creighton, Allestree, and Hardy. [40] These men are all of one group; but at the beginning of Charles II's reign, he had been careful to include presbyterians among the court chaplains. Calamy mentions the elder Calamy, Reynolds (who had not yet conformed), Ash, Spurstow, Wallis, Bates, Manton, Case, Baxter, who were made "the King's chaplains in Ordinary," but only five preached, once each. [41]

Mr. Samuel Pepys offers much evidence as to the attitude of the average man to the clergy as a class. The pulpit carries with it, in Mr. Pepys's opinion, no obligation to respect its occupant. He likes to hear bishops preach because they are well-advertised men, but he criticizes them exactly as he does nonconformists, or laymen. He is nearly always condescending toward his own minister, Daniel Mills.

---

[38] P. 241. For other chaplains sent abroad, see Cary: *Memorials,* I, 93-3, Thurloe: *Collection, etc.,* V, 522-3, as examples. The number was very large.

[39] Duncon, J.: *Lady Lettice, Viscountess Falkland,* p. 91.

[40] *Angliae Notitiae,* Pt. I, p. 180-1.

[41] *Abridg.,* I, 139; Baxter: *Autobiography,* p. 146; Ludlow: *Memoirs,* II, 283.

Many of his sermons are labeled dull, or lazy; he is invited to dinner reluctantly, and when he comes without invitation, "he is a cunning fellow, and knows where the good victuals is. . . . However, I used him civilly, though I love him as I do the rest of his coat." Once Pepys writes airily: "Mr. Mills preached, who, I suspect, should take it in snuffe that my wife did not come to his child's christening the other day." [42]

Mr. Mills's cloth does not protect him from Pepys's scorn: "My wife and I the first time together to church since the plague, and now only because of Mr. Mills his coming home to preach his first sermon; expecting a great excuse for his leaving the parish before anybody went, and now staying until all are at home; but he made but a very poor and short excuse, and a bad sermon." [43] Not that a plague-frightened clergyman was uncommon; his type was sufficiently familiar to serve as the subject of a Broadside: *A Pulpit to be let. Woe to the idle shepherd that leaveth his Flock. With a just applause of those worthy Divines that stay with us.* One stanza reads:

> Beloved: and he sweetly thus goes on,
> Now, where's Beloved? Why, Beloved's gon;
> No morning Mattens now, nor Evening Song.
> Alas! the Parson cannot stay so long. [44]

Pepys's old schoolmates who have become parsons always interest him. It is rather an amused interest, to which is added a puzzled surprise at a creditable performance in the pulpit; and there is no trace of extra respect because of his friend's vocation. A few entries will illustrate this attitude:

(May 29, 1661) . . . went to Walthamstowe . . . heard Mr. Radcliffe, my former school-fellow at St. Paul's (who is yet a merry boy) preach. He read all, and his sermon very simple.

[42] *Diary,* July 9, 16, 1662; May 29, June 3, 1667; Oct. 6, 1661.
[43] Feb. 4, 1666.
[44] Lemon: *Cat. of a Coll. of Printed Broadsides.*

(Dec. 25, 1664) To Mr. Rawlinson's church where I heard a good sermon of one that I remember at Paul's with me—his name Meggott: and very great store of fine women that is in this church, more than I know anywhere else about us.

(Aug. 5, 1666) To the church . . . and there I find in the pulpit Elborough my old schoolfellow, and in as right a parson-like manner, and in as good a manner as I have heard anybody.

(April 5, 1667) In the street met Mr. Sanchy, my old acquaintance at Cambridge, reckoned a great minister here in the City . . . which I wonder at; for methinks in his talk, he is but a mean man.

Edward Stillingfleet was also a former Cambridge associate, and Pepys made a special effort to hear him preach.[45] The Clerk of the Acts counted many clergymen among his friends, though he was inclined to consider most of them what the author of *Gangraena* called Poluppragmaticall;[46] and, as has been said, he did not feel that their position in society was superior to his own. When Mr. Mills quoted someone as saying "that if a minister of the word and an angell should meet together, he would salute the minister first;" Pepys commented mildly, "which I thought a little too high."[47]

As a government official, Mr. Pepys thinks the clergy should not overstep their bounds: "To White Hall chapel. . . . The Bishop of Chichester [Henry King] preached a great flattering sermon, which I did not like that clergy should meddle with matters of State."[48] Milton had expressed this same feeling in *The Tenure of Kings and Magistrates*: "I have something also to the divines . . . Not to be disturbers of the civil affairs, being in hands better able and more belonging to manage them. . . ."[49] D'Avenant in the Preface to *Gondibert* announced: "Chief

<hr>

[45] *Diary*, April 23, 1665. See Jan. 16, 1667: "He tells me, too, how the famous Stillingfleete was a Bluecoat boy."
[46] Thomas Edwards: P. 61.
[47] *Diary*, Aug. 9, 1663.
[48] *Ibid.*, July 8, 1660.
[49] *Prose Works*, p. 366.

Ministers of Law, think Divines in government should, like the Penal Statutes, be choicely, and but seldom us'd." [50] A little more than a decade earlier, Sir Simonds D'Ewes had reported, *in re* Commissioners for the town of Cambridge, that "the names of Doctors of Divinity were discussed and finally withdrawn. For it had been the olde grievance of England that clergie men did intermeddle with secular affaires. It was a great grievance now to be remedied." [51]

Although Pepys has his private opinion of individual preachers, and thinks that ministers as a class should not presume too far, he also believes that a degree of dignity attaches to their office. He disapproves of the way one of Bishop Morley's sermons is received, even if he does not forbear a fling at the man himself: ". . . down to the chapel again, where Bishop Morley preached on the song of the Angels. . . . Methought he made but a poor sermon, but long, and, reprehending the common jollity of the Court, for the true joy that shall and ought to be on these days, he particularised concerning their excess in plays and gaming. . . . Upon which it was worth observing how far they are come from taking the reprehensions of a bishop seriously, that they all laugh in the chapel when he reflected on their ill actions and courses . . . one that stood by whispered in my eare that the Bishop do not spend one groate to the poor himself." [52] Pepys laughs with the rest, on another occasion, when his old schoolfellow, Mr. Christmas, made "good sport in imitating Mr. Case, Ash, and Nye, the ministers"; but adds, to salve his own conscience, "a deadly drinker he is, and grown very fat." [53]

[50] P. 51.
[51] *Journal*, p. 223 (Jan. 1, 1640).
[52] *Diary*, Dec. 25, 1662. (See Evelyn's *Character of England*, p. 144, where he speaks of his satire having been taken seriously: "I am informed by a person of quality, and much integrity, that heard a learned and sober preacher quote the Character in his sermon, and reproach the people for their irreverent behaviour in the church in the very language of that book . . . ").
[53] *Ibid.*, Nov. 1, 1660.

Payment

The lesser clergy, conforming or otherwise, had extraordinarily little to live on. "You are wary of trusting them with more than you conceive due . . . you give them enough, if you give them meate and worke," accused Gaspar Hickes; "and so much I thinke you will give your horses." [54] Chamberlayne, in his *Angliae Notitiae* (1669) says that "the Revenues of the English Clergy are generally very small and insufficient," which reduces the dignity of the clergy, and this "is the last trick of the Devil . . . he invented the Project to bring the Clergy into contempt and low esteem, as it is now in England. . . ." [55] One of the many subjects, earthly and heavenly, to which Thomas Fuller gave attention was the matter "Of Ministers Maintenance." For eight pages does he give reasons why a parson should have a decent income, answering all possible objections. One argument sounds especially familiar: "Besides, the prices of all commodities daily rise higher; all persons and professions are raised in their manner of living. Scholars, therefore, even against their wills, must otherwhiles be involved in the general expensiveness of the times. . . ." [56]

But there was another point of view regarding ministers' salaries. Samuel Butler's *Remaines* includes a number of satirical references to those who get their living by Religion; as in the Character of the Modern Politician, "he thinks that no man ought to be much concerned in it [religion] but Hypocrites, and such as make it their Calling and their Profession; who, though they do not live by their Faith, like the Righteous, do that which is nearest to it, get their living by it"; [57] In another place, Butler declares: "Clergy-

[54] *The Life and Death of David*, p. 13. Funeral ser. for Wm. Strode, Esq. [55] Pp. 255, 258.
[56] *Holy and Profane State*, p. 240; also, in *Worthies*, I, 96 (the inferior clergy).
[57] P. 26 (These *Characters* were written from 1667-1669, Pref., p. iv).

men expose the Kingdom of Heaven to sale, that with the Money they may purchase as much as they can in this World; and therefore they extol and magnify the one as all Chapmen do a Commodity they desire to part with, and cry down the other, as all Buyers are wont to do that which they have the greatest longing to purchase, only to bring down the price. . . ." [58] Milton's entire essay on *The Likeliest means to remove Hirelings out of the Church* is a denunciation of the grasping minister. The author settles all financial questions such as tithes, fees for marriages, christenings, burials; he even disposes of the argument that the education of a parson is costly, and that he should be recompensed for his expenditure, by begging his readers to remember that most divinity students are in the university on scholarships, exhibitions, fellowships, "and seven years expense may be met by one year of a good benefice." [59]

With the quakers it was a matter of principle not to preach for money. One of the many occasions when George Fox was "moved of the Lord" to interrupt a sermon, was during the exposition of the text, "Ho, everyone that thirsteth. . . ." Fox promptly took his cue from the words, and shouted: "Come down, thou deceiver; dost thou bidst people come freely, and take the water of life freely, and yet thou takest 300 pounds a year of them, for preaching the Scriptures to them." [60] Fox did not object to contributions to the support of preachers; it was tithes and forced maintenance of the clergy that he condemned.[61] "When I heard the bell toll to call people together to the steeple-house, it struck at my life; for it was just like a market-bell to gather people together that the priest might set forth his ware to sale. Oh, the vast sums of money that are gotten by the trade they make of selling the Scriptures, and

---

[58] *Remaines,* p. 500. See, also, John Cooke's *Unum Necessarium, or, The Poor Man's Case* (Reprinted in *The Retrospective Rev.*, II, 26).
[59] P. 174ff.
[60] *Journal,* p. 43; also, pp. 23, 51, 100.
[61] Barclay: *The Inner Life of the Religious Soc. of the Commonwealth,* p. 270ff.

by their preaching, from the highest bishop to the lowest priest! What one trade else in the world is comparable to it." [62]

Robert South thought (and preached) that irregular exhorters, who delivered sermons in barns and from tubs, chose such a place and pulpit in order to set the people against men carefully brought up to the ministry, who must be maintained "at the charge of a public allowance." [63] John Gauden says succinctly, in a funeral sermon: "Preachers, like soldiers, must be paid." [64]

Mistress Alice Thornton mentions that Mr. Thomas Comber, whom her husband invited to live at Newton, received as curate, £40 a year. He was evidently not thought passing rich on that amount, as his patron bestirred himself to increase the stipend.[65] The very learned Thomas Gataker, when he was preaching at Lincoln's Inn, received at first £40 and never more than £60 a year.[66] Joseph Alleine, at the most, was paid £80 a year, and for a long time, only £40.[67] Launcelot Morehouse as minister of Pertwood, had £40 a year.[68] Lady Anne Clifford allowed £40 per annum to Dr. Fairfax when he was at Queen's; and an allowance of the same amount to her first husband's chaplains, Dr. King and Dr. Duppa. Bishop Morley received the same sum from her, and was remembered in her will.[69] Baxter, the year before he was silenced, preached in Milk Street, for £40.[70] Another £40-a-year man was Simon Lynch who had a living bestowed on him by a kinsman, Bishop Aylesmere, who said cheerfully, "Play, cousin, with this awhile, till a better comes." And, remarks Fuller, who intro-

[62] *Journal*, p. 23.
[63] Sermons, II, 363. See Glanvill's recommendations, *An Essay Concerning Preaching*, pp. 94ff.
[64] Funeral Ser. for Dr. Brownrig, p. 112.
[65] *Autobiography*, p. 220.
[66] Simon Ash's Funeral Ser. for Gataker (*Narrative of his life*, annexed).
[67] *Life*, p. 91.
[68] Aubrey : II, 86.
[69] *Life, Letters and Work*, p. 306.
[70] *Autobiography*, p. 160.

duces the anecdote in his *Worthies*, "Mr. Lynch continued therein . . . sixty-four years." [71]

John Shaw tells in his *Diary*, that when he was appointed to preach every Friday in Manchester, in 1643, he was promised £50 a year, but never got one penny. In the next year, he sets down the agreement (as registered in the town's books) to pay him £150 a year "and a good house," in return for his very active services; "of which they owe mee at this day about £1000 which I know not wel how to get." [72] A letter to Sir Henry Slingsby, written in 1642, mentions a desirable Vicarage, "if it bee as I heare worth about £100 a yeare, then many a Bachelour in Divinity in either Vniversity will readily accept of it who will discharge the place to your good likinge and mine." [73] Lawrence Addison, the father of Joseph Addison, thankfully enjoyed a rectory worth £120 a year,[74] but Richard Sherlock, "as curate for Dr. Joseph Mayne, in an obscure village . . . in Oxfordshire, had £16 per annum for his pains . . . and he gave a good part thereof away to the poor of that place." [75] An even smaller amount is all that is hoped for by an imaginary parson in a song which John Rous inserts in his Diary, among the Acts and Ordinances, and war news that make up the most of the little book.

The Schollers Complaint
(*to the tune of Alloo, Alloo, follow my fancy*)

In several verses the unhappy scholar laments that he can find no preferment

> After seaven yeares reading
> And costly breeding. . . .

and that he will have to go into some country village where no one will pay tithes.

[71] I, 523.
[72] *Life of Master John Shaw*, pp. 137, 141.
[73] *Diary of Henry Slingsby*, p. 330.
[74] Wood: *Ath. Ox.*, II, 970.
[75] *Ibid.*, IV, 260.

> But if I preach and Pray too on the suddaine,
> And confute the Pope too, extempore without studying,
> I've ten pounds a yeere, besides my Sunday pudding.
>> Alas, pore scholler!
>> Whither wilt thou goe? [76]

Sometimes a generous man endowed a professorship by which a clergyman might benefit, as Abraham Wheelock did when Thomas Adams (afterwards Lord Mayor of London) founded an Arabic lectureship at Cambridge "on condition that it were frequented by a competency of auditors." Fortunately, Arabic proved a popular elective, and the professor found himself in receipt of the usual £40 a year. [77] He was further enriched by £30 a year when Sir Henry Spelman settled that amount on him "to explain the Saxon tongue publick in the university." [78]

The regulation £40 appears in a different connection when we find Adam Eyre and fellow parishioners holding a meeting "about displacing the vicar, Mr. Dickinson; where wee promised him £40 on Thursday fornight, 18 Martii, and we are to go about and gather it in the interim." [79] Incidentally, Mr. Christopher Dickinson refused to leave even for £40, and it was some time before the parish could legally oust him.

Calamy does not always give the income of his ejected nonconformists; he includes it when the amount will emphasize the self-denial or suffering of some man who was forced to leave his parish after August 24, 1662. Mr. Simon Barret enjoyed "at least Eight Score Pounds per annum"; [80] Mr. Nathaniel Bradshaw "left many good People, and a living of between 3 and 400 Pound per annum for the ease and safety of his conscience." [81] Mr. Thomas Elford had a living worth £200 per annum. [82]

---

[76] *Diary*, p. 115ff. The verses have been credited to Robert Wilde, but Thomas Herbert has a better claim. See H. A. Rollins, *Cav. and Pur.*, p. 19.
[77] Fuller: *Hist. of the Univ. of Camb.*, p. 231.
[78] Lloyd, p. 517.
[79] *Diurnall*, pp. 14, 20. [81] *Ibid.*, p. 111.
[80] Calamy: *Account, etc.*, II, 103. [82] *Ibid.*, p. 467.

Mr. William Gough had a benefice worth £180 a year; and Calamy remarks parenthetically: "His father a Royalist was undisturbed in the Parliament times, and under Oliver's Protectorship, though the living (of Chivrel Magne in the Co. of Wilts) was of considerable value." [83] Mr. Philip Lamb "was offered 600 Pounds a year if he would have conformed. But it did not tempt him." [84] Mr. Anthony Sleigh (by way of contrast) "for Twenty Years together . . . had not above Twenty Shillings a Year from his People"; [85] and the popular, hard-working Richard Baxter did not receive more than £90 per annum at Kidderminster. [86]

A special payment was sometimes made for a special sermon. "William Tipping gave twenty shillings yearly to All-saints parish in Oxon for a sermon to be preached there every good Friday." [87] Mr. Peter Nicholls died, left £200 to the college (Merton) and £100 to St. Giles parish, that with the revenues thereof a sermon yearly be preached on St. Peter's day by the parson of St. Giles, who is to have 40s. and the rest to the poor of the parish." [88] John Vaux (once Lord Mayor of York) left the reversion of his property to the city of York, stipulating that from the income there should be given "to St. Martin's parish £3 for sermons; and also £3 to the poor hearing the sermons." [89] Mr. Pepys one day met with Dr. Ball, the Parson of the Temple, "who did tell me a great many pretty stories about the manner of the Parsons being paid for their preaching at Paul's heretofore, and now, and the ground of the Lecture, and for the names of the founders thereof, which were many, at some 5s., some 6s. per annum toward it: and had their names read in the pulpit every sermon among those holy persons that the Church do order a collect for,

[83] Calamy: *Account*, II, p. 100.
[84] *Ibid.*, p. 280.
[85] *Ibid.*, p. 161.
[86] Calamy: *Abridg.*, I, 30.
[87] Wood: *Ath. Ox.*, III, 244.
[88] *Ibid.*, I, lxxx.
[89] *Life of Master John Shaw*, p. 129 (Note).

giving God thanks for." [90]   Nehemiah Wellington tells of a
minister who refused to preach a November-fifth sermon
"unless he might have a share of 13s. 4d. out of the collection for the poor. . . ." [91]

[90] *Diary,* April 1, 1669.
[91] *Hist. Notices,* I, 203.   (Dr. Michael Roberts, "sometime principal
of Jesus College, died with a girdle loyned with broad gold about him,
100 l, they say," 1649).   Wood : *Ath. Ox.,* I, lxxxv.

CHAPTER VI

THE *CHARACTER* OF A PREACHER

THE vogue of the Character in the seventeenth century is easily understood. It utilized mannerisms of thought and language that were popular; it gave an opportunity for striking flatteries at a time when praise could never be too fulsome, and likewise for cutting irony in a day when men were quite literally at daggers' points on many questions. The *Character* was brief, it could be polished again and again, it could be readily appreciated, remembered, and quoted. The very term was useful, for everyone knew just what it implied. A preacher found it especially convenient: Chillingworth offered the story of the unjust steward as a *Character*;[1] Henry Bagshaw, in preaching the funeral sermon for Sir Richard Fanshaw, said, "God knows I have not studied to devise him a *Character*";[2] the publisher of a collection of sermons, *Sarah and Hagar,* by Josias Shute, explained: ". . . my design was but to hint a *Character* of him and not to write his Life.[3]

The best *Characters* of the seventeenth century were written when James I was on the throne—those of Hall, Overbury, and Earle. So successful were the brief sketches that they were reissued from time to time, particularly

[1] *Sermons,* IV, 614.
[2] *Fun. Sers. by Eminent Divines,* p. 28.
[3] See Samuel Butler's use of the term: *Remains,* p. 37.
There are many studies of the *Character* as a literary *genre.* The *Camb. Hist. of Eng. Lit.* gives a list in Vol. IV, 591-2. See, too, *A Book of Characters,* by Richard Aldington (Lond., 1924); Jusserand's discussion in his *Lit. Hist. of the Eng. People,* III, 485ff.; *Characters from the Hist. and Memoirs of the 17th Cent.* by David Nichol Smith (Oxford, 1918; *Retrospective Review,* III, 50.

Earle's *Microcosmographie* which, first published in 1628, had new editions in 1629, 1633, 1638, 1650, 1669. George Herbert's pictures of the Country Parson were not brought out until 1652, nearly twenty years after the author's death. The *Character* was a fashion equally admired in France, where La Bruyère was an especially successful producer of the sharply drawn pen-picture,[4] both countries, of course, deriving their treatment, even many of their ideas, ultimately from Theophrastus, and immediately from the vague but cogent something called the spirit of the age.

In England, there were two popular ways of presenting a *Character:* one was a general type-picture, imitated from the Theophrastus model (by way of Hall or Earle); the other was a criticism of a definite person, mentioned by name. In this variety of *Character,* the writer may try to give an impression of the whole man, or may merely emphasize a detail of mind, or manner, or appearance. The pithy, clever, or would-be clever, habit of presenting a personality in a few paragraphs or a few words is frequently evident in the comments made on the clergy, as types or individuals, who were active in many differing ways in England during the fourth, fifth, and sixth decades of the seventeenth century. There are quite simple reasons for this fact. The subjects of characterization—the clergymen themselves— were conspicuous; furthermore, the feeling for and against them was likely to be a strong emotion in the heart of the writer, an emotion not always of personal affection or enmity for the man of religion, but of loyalty to a cause. The religious side of these preachers is not omitted when personal criticism is made, nor is it consistently slighted. The point is that there is almost invariably an inclusion of secular matter in the presentation of a divine; not only are his achievements displayed in other than religious fields, but his personality and appearance are also commented on

---

[4] See David Nichol Smith : *Characters from the Hist., etc.,* introductory essay, p. xxviff., for the source and development of the French *Character.*

with a freedom which confirms the impression that a minister was regarded as one whose concerns and temperament were closely connected with this present world. They were very human, these long ago preachers. As Roger L'Estrange says wisely: "It is with Churchmen as with other mortals; there are of all Sorts, Good, Bad, and Indifferent." [5] Like any mortal, too, they were full of contradictions: they had friends and enemies; they possessed courage and weakness; they were self seeking and self denying; they were charming and repellant.

The outstanding chroniclers and biographers who write in *Character*-fashion, as Aubrey, Burnet, Baxter, Calamy, Clarendon, Fuller, Lloyd, and Wood, were men of sincere religious convictions and prejudices, who undoubtedly appreciated the high purposes of the divines about whom they wrote; but the reader often feels that the recorders are disposed to take the spiritual vocation for granted. They turn their best phrases and polish their most carefully selected epithets in the cause of personality and secular pursuits. These chroniclers and biographers do not lack personalities of their own. Baxter and Calamy are strongly and naturally biased in favor of nonconformists; Burnet and Clarendon are equally consistent in support of members of the established church; Fuller cannot deny himself a clever turn of phrase irrespective of its appropriateness to the subject; Lloyd is not considered reliable; Anthony à Wood is likely to be prejudiced against a man because of some personal contact with him. But veracity and impartial judgment are not the first considerations in making the quotations that follow: it is the secular point of view, the nonreligious angle that is most often presented. Gossip, for once, is as valuable as truth.

The conventional *Character* which presents a type through the assembling of a number of details that are easily recognized as embodied in oneself or one's neighbor,

[5] *A Memento*, p. 86.

is more literary and less interesting than the directly personal portrait. The traditional *Character* is so nearly fixed in form and manner that it may be dismissed with little comment. *The Holy and Profane State* follows established lines, so do the *Sixtynine Enigmatical Characters,* the *Confused Characters of Conceited Coxcombs,* and Samuel Butler's *Characters.* In each of these collections of types, there are pictures of preachers who, for the most part, are unworthy of their office. Eachard's satirical portrait of the private chaplain falls into the same class, as do the clergy-generalizations quoted in the preceding chapter, from Thomas Hall, Robinson, and South. Andrew Marvell's *The Divine in Mode* also belongs in this group, though, like Butler's *Characters,* the picture of Mr. Smirk was not printed until after 1670.

The second group of characterizations is composed of observations on certain ministers who in all cases are mentioned by name. Only those criticisms are included which show some influence of the conceits, the contrasts, and the artificial phrasing that mark the genuine *Character.* Broadly, the examples offered fall under good disposition, bad disposition, singularity, and appearance.

It is pleasant to see how often someone speaks of the cheerfulness and joy of life that was conspicuous in this minister or that. Joseph Alleine's joy was mild but his cheerfulness was invariable. His *Life* as written by his wife and Richard Baxter, and others near to him, draws the picture of a rarely beautiful nature. It was also a very firm nature, for preach Mr. Alleine would, though authorities and physicians forbade; and study and write he would, though he had neither the time nor strength for the work. Throughout the biography, Alleine is shown to be hard-working, gentle, considerate of others, ill much of the time. This portrait fills an entire book, and many of the minister's experiences in the pulpit, in his home and in jail are included; but there remains a single clear impression of his cheerful, persistent struggle with most untoward circumstances.[6] Wood, it must be owned, received a different impression from the book. His *Character* of Alleine and his wife reads: "His life spent in actions, busy, forward (if not pragmatical) and meddling without intermission. The said Theodosia [Alleine's wife] a prating gossip and a meer Xantippe, finding Jos. Alleine to be meer scholar and totally ignorant of Women's tricks, did flatter, sooth him and woo, and soon after married, and brought him to her lure." [7]

Mr. Robert Atkins's "innocent Mirth and Facetiousness render'd his Company very Acceptable." [8] Dr. Bates was not "wont to banish out of his conversation the pleasantness that fitly belonged to it; for which his large acquaintance with a variety of story, both ancient and modern, gave him advantage beyond most; his judicious memory being a copious promptuary of what was profitable and facetious. . . . To place religion in a morose sourness, was remote from his practice, his judgment, and his temper." [9] Dr. John Barneston was "an hospitable House-keeper, a chearful Companion, and a peaceable Man." [10]

Isaac Barrow, after a noticeably unregenerate boyhood,[11] became a learned professor, a preacher capable of delivering a sermon three hours and a half in length, and a court chaplain. He still retained a degree of lightheartedness which made it possible for him to exchange repartee with the Earl of Rochester. One day they met at court, and, each bowing low:

---

[6] Alleine was the author of that extraordinarily popular book, the *Alarm to the Unconverted*. 20,000 copies of which sold in 1672, and 50,000 when it was republished three years later under a new title, *The Sure Guide to Heaven*.

[7] Wood: *Ath. Ox.*, III, 822.

[8] Calamy: *Account, etc.*, II, 314.

[9] Fun. Ser. for Bates by Dr. Howe (*Spiritual Perfection*, p. xx).

[10] Lloyd: p. 613.

[11] "There was so little appearance of that comfort which his father after received from him, that he often solemnly wished, that if it pleased God to take away any of his children, it might be his son Isaac." *Works*, I, ix.

Doctor, I am yours to the shoetie
My lord, I am yours to the ground.
Doctor, I am yours to the centre.
My lord, I am yours to the antipodes.
Doctor, I am yours to the lowest pit of hell.
There, my lord, I leave you.[12]

Mr. William Blagrave was "a well accomplished Scholar and Divine, and Mighty in the Word and Prayer both. He was seldom seen without a smiling countenance." [13]   Mr. Edward Bright was "a very good man, and was endowed with a great deal of patience, which indeed he much needed, having the affliction of a very froward and clamorous wife. On this account many thought it an happiness to him to be dull of hearing." [14]

Clarendon shows Chillingworth's good temper as being particularly irritating to an opponent: "a man of so grea[te] a subtlety of understandinge, and so rare a temper in debate, that as it was impossible to provoke him into any passyon, so it was very difficulte to keepe a mans selfe from beinge a little discomposed by his sharpnesse and quicknesse of argument and instances, in which he had a rare facility, and a greate advantage over all the men I ever knew." [15] Mr. Thomas Clark's good temper was humourously inclined —that is, in the modern sense of the word. At Westminster Hall, he heard a man say that "the Presbyterian Parsons were such silly Fellows that none of them could say Boh to a goose; Mr. Clark immediately holding out his Hand towards him, said Boh. . . . And Mr. Clark told him with the greatest Calmness and Composure imaginable, that it was to let him see that a Presbyterian could say Boh to a Goose." [16]

[12] *Dict. Nat'l Biog.*
[13] Calamy : *Abridg., Etc.,* I, 93.
[14] Palmer : *Nonconf. Mem.,* II, 62.
[15] *Characters and Episodes of the Great Rebellion,* p. 307.
[16] Calamy : *Account, etc.,* II, 346-7.
Isaac Walton quotes Herbert as saying: "Religion . . . does not banish mirth, but only moderates and sets rules to it." *Life of Herbert,* p. 306.

Nearly everyone who mentions John Earle says something about his kindliness and good nature; "of the sweetest and most obliging nature," Serenus de Cressy testifies. Thomas Fuller was also a thoroughly pleasant person to know, and talk to, and laugh with. It is easy to believe that he inspired this *Character* of himself and his book:

> Upon Mr. Fuller's Booke, called Pisgah-sight,
> Fuller of wish, than hope, methinks it is,
> For me to expect a fuller work than this,
> Fuller of matter, fuller of rich sense,
> Fuller of Art, fuller of Eloquence;
> Yet dare I not be bold, to intitle this
> The fullest work; the Author fuller is,
> Who, though he himself not himself, can fill
> Another fuller, yet continue still
> Fuller himself, and so the Reader be
> Always in hope a fuller work to see.[17]

Dr. William Fuller was "a grave man whose looks were a Sermon and affable withal." [18] John Hales had a "sweetness of nature and complaisance, which seldom accompany hard students and critics." [19] "Mr. Anthony Hodges, rector of Wytham in Berkshire, was a very good scholar, and fit, in many respects, to oblige posterity by his pen; but delighting himself in mirth, and in that which was afterwards called buffooning and bantering, could never be brought to set pen to paper for that purpose. He was the mirth of the company, and they esteem'd him their *terrae filius*." [20] Another gay parson was Henry Jeanes, "a scholastical man, a contemner of the world, generous, freehearted, Jolly, witty, facetious, and in many things represented the humour of Rob. Wild the poet. All which qualities do very rarely meet in men of the presbyterian persuasion, who generally are morose, clownish, and of sullen and reserved naures." [21]

[17] *Choyce Drollery*, p. 62.
[18] Lloyd : p. 509.
[19] Wood : *Ath. Ox.*, III, 410.
[20] *Ibid.*, I, xvii.
[21] *Ibid.*, III, 590.

Dr. William Juxton's cheerfulness was of another sort. He was ill a long time, "his disease the Stone, which he endured as chearfully as he did his pleasures; having patience to bear those pains, which others had not patience to hear of. . . ." [22]

Robert Leighton's cheerfulness seems to have been genuine, but of a negative quality. He "brought himself into so composed a gravity, that I never saw him laugh, and but seldom smile," says Gilbert Burnet; "and, tho' the whole course of his life was strict and ascetical, yet he had nothing of the sourness of temper that generally possesses men of that sort." [23] "That sort" may mean Leighton's character, or his presbyterian origin. He became Bishop of Dunblane after the Restoration. Dr. Potter, bishop of Carlisle, had such a good disposition that his presence automatically increased the value of property near his residence; "hundreds left their distant Habitations to be near him, though all accommodations about him were so much the dearer, as his neighborhood was so much the more precious." [24] John Prideaux "had a becoming festivity, which was Aristotle's not Paul's"; [25] William Rowlands (who called himself Rolandus Palingenius) was "a born droll, a jolly companion." [26]

Mr. Samuel Shaw had "quick Repartees, and would droll innocently with the mixture of Poetry, History, and other Polite Learning." [27] Mr. Benjamin Snowden displayed "Constant Serenity, sweet Affability, and an unclouded Alacrity shown in his Countenance. . . . His whole Conversation spake Quietness and Peace." [28] Alexander Strange was "no less prosperous than painful in compounding all differences among his neighbours, being a man of peace." [29] Dr. Weeks was "a cheerful man, that was good

---

[22] Lloyd : p. 597.
[23] *Hist. of his own Times*, p. 132.
[24] Lloyd : p. 154 ; cf. Fuller on Alexander Strange, *Worthies*, II, 386.
[25] Fuller : *Worthies*, I, 408.
[26] Wood : *Ath. Ox.*, III, 486.   [28] *Ibid.*, II, 476.
[27] Calamy : *Account, etc.*, II, 435.   [29] Fuller : *Worthies*, II, 386.

at making a Jest, but made not a trade of Jesting." [30]
William Wickens was as conscientious as he was pleasant:
"He was very cheerful in conversation; but commonly
would take care before he left any company, to drop something serious and savoury, which made his company profitable as well as pleasant." [31]   Robert Wild, the poet, was
"a fat, jolly and boon presbyterian," says Wood though
he had denied the sect any redeeming levity when he
sketched the character of Henry Jeanes. [32]

All the foregoing quotations have shown some degree of
geniality in the preachers mentioned, but there were men
who lacked friendliness and good nature, who gave much
of their energy to quarreling with parishioners or fellow
ecclesiastics, especially of other sects.   Robert South
preached four sermons on that wistful verse in Romans:
"If it be possible, as much as lieth in you, live peaceably
with all men."   "There are some persons," declares Dr.
South, "that, like so many salamanders, cannot live but in
the fire; cannot enjoy themselves but in the heats and
sharpness of contention; the very breath they draw does not
so much enliven, as kindle and inflame them; they have so
much bitterness in their nature, that they must be now and
then discharging it upon somebody." [33]

The majority of the controversies are political or religious, but some persons were "acquarrelled," as the author
of *Ahab's Fall* terms it, [34] on secular subjects.   Fell
quarreled with Anthony à Wood regarding the former's
right to expunge and insert whatever he wished while super-
vising the translating into Latin of Wood's records of
Oxford; Fuller exchanged animadversions with Heylin
who had pointed out Fuller's inaccuracies and laughed at
his multitude of dedications; Wallis and Hobbes wrote
against one another, on mathematical subjects, throughout
twenty years.   The Authorship of the *Eikon Basilike,* of

[30] Lloyd: p. 502.   [32] Wood: *Fasti,* II, 35.
[31] Palmer: *Nonconf. Mem.,* I, 84.   [33] *Sermons,* V, 169.
[34] Charles Herle.

the last three books of Hooker's *Ecclesiastical Polity,* of *The Whole Duty of Man,* furnished a starting point for debates and informal scolding scenes. These disagreements are useful in emphasizing secular angles of character but they do not provide the clean-cut statements about disagreeable preachers that may be found in other writings.

George Bull, like Barrow, gave little promise in youth of spirituality, or ambition. His biographer says this tactfully: "Yet notwithstanding that he was under the Direction of so zealous and orthodox a Divine [Baldwin Ackland], it must not be concealed that Mr. Bull lost much of the time he spent at the university." [35] Dr. Busby's disposition was so well known through so many years that people living near him would naturally expect something out of the common to happen at his death. In the *Hatton Correspondence,* we read "that ye people in ye streets, when he was expiring, saw flashes and sparks of fire come out of his window, wch made them run into ye house to put it out, but when they were there saw none, nor did they of ye house." [36]

"I saluted the old Bishop of Durham, Dr. Cosin," writes Evelyn, "to whom I had been kind, and assisted in his exile; but which he little remembered in his greatness." [37] Thomas Creesh had "the character of having been a man of excellent parts and sound judgment . . . but naturally of a morose temper, and too apt to despise the understanding and performances of others." [38] William Bartlet and his son John were a contrast to each other: "the father was called Boanerges and the son Barnabas, *this* healed where *that* had wounded, and both were rendered remarkably useful in their distinct characters." [39] Fuller tells of two brothers whose difference in opinion brought about an interesting exchange: "This John Reynolds at the first was a zealous papist, whilst William his brother was as earnest

[35] Nelson: *Life of Bull,* p. 12.   [38] Wood: *Ath. Ox.,* II, 523.
[36] Vol. II, 216.   [39] *Ibid.,* III, 265.
[37] *Diary,* April 17, 1663.

a protestant; and afterwards Providence so ordered it, that by their mutual disputation John Reynolds turned an eminent protestant, and William a inveterate papist, in which persuasion he died." [40] Charles Gataker "appeareth to have been a Person of great Violence in his Temper, but one well intentioned . . . and had he had but more Coolness of Thought, and had he withall read more of the Antients, and fewer of the Moderns, he would, I believe, have made no inconsiderable Writer." [41]

The quatrain beginning "I do not love thee, Dr. Fell," [42] has fastened a disagreeable personality on John Fell, Vice-Chancellor of Oxford. He disliked the amiable and popular Dr. Tillotson, he scorned the Royal Society, he treated Hobbes badly and Wood worse; also, he was a conscientious executive, a builder, a faithful preacher of many and readable sermons, a writer of a good biography, and a generous donor of a complete type-foundry that is in service today. [43] "Of an unsettled and inconstant temper," was Alexander Gill, like his father of the same name. "At length . . . he did quietly, yet not without some regret, lay down his head and dye." [44] Jasper Mayne, the preacher-playwright, had a resentful disposition. He left money to St. Paul's and to two of his Vicarages, but he bequeathed "nothing to the place of his education, because he (as Dr. Jo. Wall had done) had taken some distaste for affronts received from the dean of the college, and certain students, encouraged by him, in their grinning and sauciness toward him." [45]

Richard Sterne, archbishop of York, "was a sour, ill tempered man, and minded chiefly the enriching of his family." [46] A parson who realized his own weakness was

[40] Fuller: *Church Hist.*, V, 378.
[41] Nelson: *Life of Bull*, p. 145.
[42] For a discussion of the origin of the lines, see *Notes and Queries*, (5th series) Vol. VII, 166. For some of Fell's controversies, see D'Israeli: *Quarrels of Authors*, pp. 47-51; Wood: *Ath. Ox.*, I, lxviii, lxxi.
[43] Plomer: *Hist. of English Printing, Etc.*, p. 214.
[44] Wood: *Ath. Ox.*, III, 42-3.   [45] *Ibid.*, p. 973.
[46] Burnet: *Hist. of his own Times*, p. 382.

Ambrose Moston who "had some inclination to heat in his temper, and yet would be the first to censure himself for it".[47]   A thoroughly unpleasant person was Samuel Young: he possessed "a good share of classical learning; but had a wildness and irregularity in his temper litle short of madness, and was vehement and impetuous in everything he said or did. . . . His element was contention, and he could not live out of a tempest. . . . He died before he was quite mad." [48]

Clarendon has no sympathy for Archbishop John Williams: "a man of very imperious and fiery temper . . . being a man of great pride and vanity, he did not always confine himself to a strict veracity." [49]   Fuller, however, shows another side of the archbishop, quoting "a grave minister" to whom Williams had said: "I have passed through many places of honour and trust, both in church and state, more than any of my order in England this 70 years before; but were I but assured that by my preaching I had converted but one soul unto God, I should take therein more spiritual joy and comfort than in all the honours and offices which have been bestowed upon me." [50]

Richard Baxter was a prominent member of the Savoy Conference in which Anglicans and Presbyterians tried to agree upon sufficient points to keep them within the same religious fold.   In 1661, such an agreement seemed possible, and Baxter went to the meeting hopeful of a mutual spirit of compromise.   He was bitterly disappointed at the failure of those in power to concede anything, and he sets down in his *Autobigraphy* his frank opinion of the bishops who had irritated him most.   "Bishop Cosins was there constantly, and had a great deal of talk with so little logic, natural or artificial, that I perceived no one much moved by anything he said." [51]   Of Bishop Sanderson, Baxter

---

[47] Palmer: *Nonconf. Mem.,* II, 603.   [48] *Ibid.,* I, 426.
[49] *Hist. of the Rebellion,* II, 97.
[50] *Church Hist.,* VI, 326ff.
[51] *Autobiography,* p. 168.

writes: "his great learning and worth are known by his labours, and his aged peevishness not unknown." [52] Baxter criticizes, also, Gauden, Gunning, Pearson, Morley, Reynolds, Sterne and Thorndike. Of Pearson, he approved, and Gauden he mentions as "our most constant helper." The *Autobiography* was written long after 1661, but Baxter is still resentful against those who opposed him successfully at the Conference. Gunning was reported to have said that the nonconformists had lost nothing by refusing to conform, which statement drew from Baxter the angry exclamation: ". . . when he knew himself that I was offered a bishopric in 1660 and he got not his bishopric (for all his extraordinary way of merit) till about 1671 or 1672. . . ." [53]

To derive pleasure from the punishment of the wicked may not be evidence of an evil disposition, but it cannot possibly be a sign of a good one. The examples that follow show that retributive justice was regarded with the same satisfaction by sincerely religious persons of different sects. John Walker, the author of the *Sufferings of the Clergy of the Church of England,* records in connection with one Christopher Baitson: ". . . of Those who Articled against him, Three of the most forward Died in a very unhappy manner; One by a Fall from his Horse, Another was drowned, and the Third expired in a Raving and Distracted Condition." [54] Four persons, says Walker, were concerned in the prosecution and imprisonment of Richard Long: "The First of which died soon after; the Second was a little after taken Speechless, and never Spake more; the Third was somewhat Distracted in his Head before, and after grew downright Mad; and the last died in a Barn: and Two who were going to London to Swear against Mr. Long, died on the Road thither of the Small-Pox." [55] The non-

---

[52] *Ibid.,* p. 168. Sanderson disapproved equally of Baxter (Walton: *Lives,* p. 393).
[53] *Autobiography,* p. 223.
[54] Pt. II, 192.   [55] *Ibid.,* p. 298.

conformist Lucy Hutchinson tells of a mayor, "one Top-lady," who beat and kicked imprisoned nonconformists, and "he was one night taken with a vomiting of blood, and being very ill, called his man and his maid, who also at the same time fell a bleeding, and were all ready to be choked in their own blood, which at last stopping, they came to assist him; but after that he never lifted up his head, but languished for a few months and died." [56]   George Fox was no gentle, unresentful spirit; he frequently notes that misfortune falls on those that mistreat him.   One man who ridiculed him met with a dramatic punishment which Fox describes briefly.   "One man came in a bear's skin, and lolled his tongue out of his mouth.   On the way home he stopped at a bull-baiting.   The bull struck his horn under the man's chin into his throat, and struck his tongue out of his mouth so that it hung lolling out, as he had used it in that meeting.   And the bull's horn running up into the man's head, he swung him about on his horn." [57]

A number of preachers, while not actively ill tempered, or passively complacent when retribution fell upon their enemies, were possessed of traits that must have made them disagreeable to deal with.   William Cook "was very free in reproving his relations and all his acquaintance, as occasion required.   He was mightily concerned when he heard of the prosperity of any of them, that they might be provided against the temptations of their condition." [58]   John Torner, too, was one of those who feel it a duty to reprove the erring.   He seems to have been singularly courageous in doing so, if one may judge by an incident related by Calamy.   "Several ministers once agreeing to visit a certain lady, who was their hearer, but in some respects walked not

[56] *Life of Col. Hutchinson,* p. 430.
[57] *Journal,* p. 179.
See Buckle, *Hist. of Civilization,* II, 274ff., for examples of punishment visited on those who scoffed at, or refused to assist a minister. A *Note* adds a brief bibliography on the subject.
[58] Palmer; *Nonconf. Mem.,* I, 260; also, John Billingsby, *ibid.,* I, 314.

becomingly, in order to reprove; when it came to the point, all but Mr. Torner were for waiving what had been intended, for fear she should not endure them afterwards. . . . The lady did indeed resent his freedom, and for the present was angry; but doubly honoured him ever after." [59] Bartholomew Westley's attitude to his fellows was not unlike Mr. Cook's and Mr. Torner's. "He used a peculiar plainness of speech, which hindered his being an .acceptable popular minister." [60] Francis Turner's tiresome mannerisms were borrowed by Andrew Marvell for his satirical presentation of *Mr. Smirk: or, the Divine in mode,* "because in his conception he was a neat, starch'd and formal divine." [61] A more disturbing acquaintance was John Sadler: "it must be owned he was not always right in his head." [62] William Sedgwick also was "somewhat disordered in his head, and acquired the nickname of Doomsday Sedgwick from an unfortunate habit of interrupting conversations with the announcement that doomsday would occur the following week." [63]

Sir Simonds D'Ewes once phrased a *Character* of a certain Dr. Chaffin who had preached an indiscreet sermon in 1634, and six years later was called to account for it. The motion was made that he should be summoned to the House and "at the barre receive a sharpe admonition, and bee dismissed." Sir .Simonds volunteered his support for the preacher: "I stood upp and . . . said: That I had long known this man at the Temple and never tooke him to bee deepe scholar but to say noe worse of him a sociable man." [64] Other brief identifications that show more of the *Character* influence on the wording, are: "John Gregory was of honest though mean parents, yet rich enough to derive unto him the heriditary infirmity of the gout"; [65]

[59] Palmer: *Nonconf. Mem.,* II, 358.
[60] *Ibid.,* I, 442.
[61] Wood: *Ath. Ox.,* IV, 545.
[62] Palmer: *Nonconf. Mem.,* I, 210.
[63] Wood: *Ath. Ox.,* IV, 545.
[64] *Journal,* p. 419.   [65] Fuller: *Worthies,* I, 208.

Dr. John Hewitt "was born a gentleman and bred a scholar, and was a divine before the beginning of the troubles"; [66] Dr. Thomas Howell (brother of the better-known James Howell) appears as "a man not only flourishing with the Verdure and Spring of Wit, and the Summer of much Learning, and Reading; but happy in the Harvest of a mature Understanding, and a mellow Judgment in matters Politick and Prudential, both Ecclesiastical and Civil. . . ." [67] Stephen Marshall "was so supple a soul, that he brake not a joint, yea, sprained not a sinew, in all the alterations of the time"; [68] Dr. John Towers was "rich only in Children . . . and Patience"; [69] Dr. John Wall "spent his time in celibacy and books"; [70] John White "absolutely commanded his own passions and the purses of his parishioners, whom he could wind up to what height he pleased on important occasions." [71] Bishop Juxton held his purse strings firmly but without giving offense: "Such was the mildness of his temper, that Petitioners for money (when it was not to be had) departed well pleased with his Denials, they were so civilly languaged." [72]

Some preachers are marked by a singularity of temperament. Mr. Isaac Ambrose was one of these: " 'Twas his usual Custom once in a Year, for the space of a Month to retire into a little Hut in a Wood, and avoiding all Humane Converse, devote himself to Contemplation." [73] Peter Austin, on the contrary, found his happiness in active social service. His rakes had only five teeth so that there might be more wheat for the gleaners; and he sold his grain to the poor at less than the market price. "He employed a great many poor people in planting the common hedges

[66] Clarendon: *Hist., etc.,* IV, 65.
[67] Lloyd: p. 522.
[68] Fuller: *Worthies,* II, 105.
[69] Lloyd: p. 601.
[70] Wood: *Ath. Ox.,* III, 734. Walton (*Life of Sanderson,* p. 8) implies a good deal when he says: "Dr. Wall I knew, and will speak nothing of him, for he is dead."
[71] Fuller: *Worthies,* III, 24-5.
[72] Lloyd: *State Worthies,* p. 1038.
[73] Calamy: *Account,* etc., II, 409.

with plumbs, cherries, and other fruit trees, for the supply of the poor, and of travellers." [74] Samuel Fairclough's peculiarities had to do with things of the mind. When he was at the University, he duly performed all his Acts and Disputations, "and he sate in the Schools to be posed by all or any Master of Arts that would examine him"; but he went into the country the day he was actually to receive the degree, "his ensigns of honour," "and being asked the reason thereof, his answer was, that he came to Cambridge to study and gain Learning and Knowledge, and not to Commence or take Degrees." "We must look upon this person, "adds Samuel Clark, who is celebrating the eminent life of Mr. Fairclough, "as an Heteroclite, being a pure Moneptote, and invariably engaged in a way by himself. . . ." [75] Dr. Henry Hammond must have been something of a Moneptote, judging by Dr. Fell's statement regarding Dr. Hammond's projected marriage. He had been urged to marry, says his biographer, and "he gave some care to their advices: which he did the more readily for that there was a person represented to him, of whose Virtue as well as other more usually-desired accomplishments he had been long before well satisfied. But being hindered several times by little unexpected accidents," he retired in favor of a person "of a fairer fortune and higher quality. . . ." [76]

The clergy were much addicted to writing *Characters* in verse. Examples have been given under *Poetry* of stanzas celebrating the virtues or achivements of some man or woman, the lines usually being written as additions to funeral sermons. Many of Herrick's best-known poems are epitaphs; Crashaw wrote a number; William Strode and Fuller must have supplied anyone who asked for an elegy. Samuel Clark, in speaking of "Mr. Wilson," includes a poem of eleven stanzas, signed G. S., which is admirably

[74] Palmer: *Nonconf. Mem.*, II, 214.
[75] Clark: *Em. Lives*, p. 158.   [76] P. 102.

comprehensive as a tribute to departed clergy. One stanza reads:

> The Great Assembly, once renown'd,
> (Whose Fame in foreign parts did **found** [sic])
> Displeas'd on Earth, in haste remove
> Their Sessions to their House above.
> Seraphic Twiss went first, 'tis true,
> As Prolocutor, 'twas his due:
> Then Burroughs, Marshall, Whitake, Hill,
> Goug, Gataker, Ash, Vines, White, still
> Sharp Swords soon'st cut their Sheaths, **Pern, Strong,**
> Spurstow, Tuckney, Calamy, they throng
> The Gate of Bliss, as if their [sic] fear
> That Heaven would fill e'er they got there.[77]

In the Preface to Part II of Samuel Clark's *Marrow of Ecclesiastical History* are a number of *Character* verses written by clergymen in honor of Clark, who is still alive to enjoy them. The most striking of the compositions is an Anagram, signed F. P., in which the ingenious poet combines a compliment to Clark, an address to the Reader, and an advertisement of the book.

Samuel Clark
Anagram
Su(c)k All Cream
An Acrostick to the Reader of the Labour of
his Reverend Friend

Mr.

> Ah Reader, look, theSe chosen Vessels here
>   Most Richly filled Are with Milk sincere
> The Author scims theM and most sweetly strives
>   To make thee sUck the Cream of all their lives.
> From other Books (dEar friend) such Milk thou maist
> But in this precious Book aLl cream thou hast.
>   Then sweetly suck all Cream, and take thy fill;
>   Blessing the Lord of Life for the Authors skill
> This Book of Lives to reAd I need not woe thee;
>   The choicest food is heRe presented to thee:
>   All Cream then su(c)K: and much good may it do thee.

---

[77] *Em. Lives,* p. 41. Cf. a similar assembling of ministers in a funeral-sermon poem for Joseph Hall, p. 231.

In the pen sketch of a parson, the physical appearance
is often included, and as in the character hints, there is
shown no extra respect to the subject because of the pulpit
background. Richard Allestree, for example, was a noted
preacher, a popular author, a much-respected man who had
fought at Edgehill, and had served during the siege of Oxford; but these are not the reasons offered for his appointment to the provostship of Eton. The preferred explanation is that Charles II once defied a group to produce an
uglier man than the Earl of Lauderdale, whereupon Rochester went out on the street and chanced on a shabbily dressed,
ugly clergyman—Allestree. Charles admitted at once that
he had lost his wager, explained the situation, and apolo-
gized to Allestree, who promptly asked for preferment.
This he received, after some time, when he was made
provost of Eton.[78]

Mr. Robert Atkins "was a very comely little Man." [79]
Isaac Barrow was "strong and stout, and feared not any
man. . . . He was by no means a spruce man, but most
negligent in his dresse." [80] Mr. Birdsall of York "was very
temperate, and of a blameless Life; and any contrary Reflections, because of the flushing of his Face, which was
natural to him, were altogether groundless." [81] William
Cartwright was "ravishing by the comeliness of his presence
(for his body was as handsome as his soul). . . ." [82] William Chillingworth "was a little man, blackish haire, of a
saturnine complexion." [83] Edward Davenant's appearance
was even less impressive: "of middling statue, something
spare; and weake feeble leggs; he had sometimes the
goute." [84] The majority of the clergy of the time were
small men, if we may judge by the comments of their contemporaries. William Leo, in preaching the funeral sermon
for Daniel Featley, remarks that "it is an observation of

[78] Lyte: *Hist. of Eton*, p. 250.
[79] Calamy: *Account, etc.*, II, 217.
[80] Aubrey: I, 90.
[81] Calamy: *Account, etc.*, II, 793.
[82] Lloyd: p. 423.
[83] Aubrey: II, 172.
[84] *Ibid.*, I, 201.

the Physicians, that we are now of shorter stature, and of lesse livelihood then heretofore." Leo refers to Dr. Featley's small size which brought on him the ridicule of the Jesuits in Paris, though they admired the acuteness of his mind when he disputed with them. Leo adds: "The Jesuites in that contempt of theirs had forgot what that ancient Father Jerome said of Saint Paul, That although he was of a very little and low stature, yet for all that, that Homo tricubitalis ascendit in coelum." [85]

Thomas Hearne made an effort to have John Fell represented with some regard for the truth of his appearance. Hearne reproached the sculptor for making such a poor likeness of Fell: "All people that knew the bishop, agree that 'tis not like him, he being a thin, grave man, whereas the statue represents him plump and gay. I told the statuary that it was unlike, and that he was made too plump. Oh, says he, we must make a handsome man." [86]

Thomas Fuller was "of middle stature, strong sett; curled haire"; [87] Mr. Richard Gilpin's height "was of the middle sort, rather inclined to the lesser Size." [88] John Greene was "of a very pleasant aspect." [89] Aubrey describes John Hales as "a prettie little man, sanguine, of a cheerful countenance, very gentile, and courtious; I was received by him with much humanity: he was in a kind of violet colored gowne, with buttons and loopes (he wore not a black gowne) and was reading Thomas à Kempis." [90] Dr. Ralph Kettle was "a very tall well growne man. His gowne and surplice and hood being on, he had a terrible gigantique aspect, with his shap gray eies. The ordinary gowne he wore was a russet cloath gowne. He was, they say, white very soon. . . ." [91] Archbishop Laud is drawn by Fuller as "one of low stature, but high parts; piercing eyes, cheerful countenance, wherein gravity and pleasant-

[85] Funeral Sermon for Daniel Featley, pp. 12, 23.
[86] *Reliq. Hearnae*, II, 50-1.
[87] Aubrey : II, 257.
[88] Calamy : *Account, etc.*, II, 154.
[89] Palmer : *Nonconf. Mem.*, II, 205.
[90] Aubrey : I, 279.
[91] *Ibid.*, II, 17.

ness were well compounded." [92]   Thomas Manton, the noted presbyterian preacher, was "round, plump and jolly."   He was a commissioner at the Savoy Conference, and "Clarendon told Baxter that he should not have despaired of bringing that conference to a happy conclusion, if he had been as fat as Manton." [93]

Philip Nye made himself conspicuous by the singular cut of his beard.   No exact description of it is given, but the references show that it represented nonconformity. Samuel Butler wrote a long *Character*-poem, entitled *On Philip Nye's Thanksgiving Beard,* in which he shows the influential Mr. Nye, member of the Westminster Assembly, seeking to express his convictions by his beard.   He consulted the "ablest Virtuoso of the kind," says Butler, and requested that a design be drawn for him.   Then he sent for one

> that had the greatest Practice,
> To prune, and bleach the Beards of all Fantasticks. . . .

> To whom he showed his new-invented Draught,
> And told him, how 'twas to be copy'd out.

> Quoth he, 'tis but a false, and counterfeit,
> And scandalous Device of human Wit,
> That's absolutely forbidden in the Scripture,
> To make of any carnal thing the Picture.

Finally, the skilled and conscientious barber is convinced that he may, without sin, carry out Mr. Nye's design for his beard, and the minister goes forth to be regarded with astonishment by everyone he meets.   Just what the pattern of his beard is, no one can clearly state,

> And yet it was, and did abominate
> The least Compliance in the Church or State;
> And from it self did equally dissent,
> As from Religion, and the Government. [94]

[92] *Worthies,* I, 129.
[93] Burnet: *History of his own Times,* p. 206 (Note).
[94] *Remains,* p. 177-8.

William Oughtred was, like many of his cloth, a little man. He had "black haire, and black eies (with a great deal of spirit)." Once when Seth Ward and Charles Scarborough came to see him, "Mr. Oughtred had against their comeing prepared a good dinner, and also he had dressed himselfe, thus, an old red russet cloath-cassock that had been black in dayes of yore, girt with an old leather girdle, an old fashion russet hat, that had been a bever, *tempore reginae Elizabethae.*" [95] William Outram was "a tall spare leane pale consumptive man; wasted himself, I presume, by frequent preaching." [96] Of John Owen, the nonconformist, Wood, the firmly established, relates: "While he did undergo the said office of Vice-chancellor he, instead of being a grave example to the university, scorned all formality, undervalued his office by going to Quirpo like a young scholar, with powdered hair, snake-bone bandstrings (or bandstrings with very large tassels) lawn band, a large set of ribbonds pointed, at his knees, and Spanish leather boots, with large lawn tops, and his hat mostly cock'd." [97]

John Pell was "very handsome, and of a very strong and excellent habit of body, melancholic, sanguine, darke browne haire with an excellent moist curle." [98] Francis Potter is an exception to the usual lay-appearing preacher, because he "lookt the most like a monk, or one of the pastours of the old time, that I ever sawe one. He was pretty long visag'd and pale cleare skin and gray eie." [99] Samuel Shaw "was of a middle statue, and his countenance not very penetrating; like another Melancton, that could not fill a chair with a big look and portly presence; but his eye was sparkling, and his conversation witty, savoury, affable and pertinent." [100] Joseph Swafield "had a great

[95] Aubrey: II, 107.   [96] *Ibid.*, p. 114.
[97] Wood: *Ath. Ox.*, IV, 98. See, also, *ibid.*, 102. Josselin writes in his *Diary*, July 8, 1655: Heard how Dr. Owen endeavored to lay down all the badges of schollers distinction in the universities, hoods, caps, gowns, degrees. . . .
[98] Aubrey, I, 122.
[99] *Ibid.*, II, 122.
[100] Palmer: *Nonconf. Mem.*, II, 137.

and generous Soul in a little sickly Body; being one of a very low Statue, and tender Constitution"; [101] John Tombes was "but a little man, neat limbed, a little quick searching eie, sad, gray." [102] John Wilkins, on the contrary, "was a lustie, strong growne, well sett, broad shouldered person, cheerful, and hospitable"; [103] and from another authority we learn that he was "of a comely aspect and gentleman-like behaviour; he had been bred in the court, and was allso a piece of a traveller, having twice seen the Prince of Orange's court at the Hague." [104] Archbishop Williams was "of a proper person, comely countenance, and amiable complexion, having a stately garb and gait by nature." [105] Sir Philip Warwick penetrates beyond the archbishop's exterior: "if he had been look'd on in his inside, he was more a discontented Courtier, than an uncannonical Bishop." [106]

It is obvious that the quotations given in this chapter do not differ in type from the many already offered as illustrating various matters connected with divines. It has, however, seemed worth while, even at the risk of over-using examples, to bring together in these final pages a number of comments on a man's very self: his personality and appearance, not his ability, his interests, or his ecclesiastical quality.

Professionally, these men were ministers; many of them were theologians. Personally, they were like other educated persons in their day, or ours. To understand any one of them, his beliefs or his behavior, it is necessary to realize what a close resemblance that man bears to any one of us. Said the learned Dr. Daniel Featley in his preface to Phineas Fletcher's *Purple Island:* "He that would know Theologie must first study Autologie."

[101] Calamy : *Account, etc.,* II, 758.
[102] Aubrey : II, 260.
[103] *Ibid.,* p. 301.
[104] Wood : *Ath. Ox.,* III, 971.
[105] Fuller : *Church Hist.,* VI, 326.
[106] *Memoirs,* p. 92.

BIBLIOGRAPHY [1]

Adams, Thomas: Works (ed. Joseph Angus). Edin. 1862

Aldington, Richard: A Book of *Characters*. Lond. 1924

Alle, Thomas: A Breif Narration of the Truth of some particulars in Mr. Thomas Edwards his Book called Gangraena. Lond. 1646

Alleine, Theodosia, the Rev. Richard Baxter, and Others: Life and Death of the Rev. Joseph Alleine, A.B. Lond. 1838

Allestrey, Richard: Eighteen Sermons whereof fifteen Preached before the King. The rest upon Publick Occasions. Lond. 1669

[Allestrey, Richard]: The Gentleman's Calling. Lond. 1660

[Allestrey, Richard]: The Works of the Learned and Pious Author of The Whole Duty of Man. Oxford. 1704

Alsted, John Henry: Theologia Prophetica exhibens I. Rhetoricam Ecclesiasticam, in qua proponitur ars concionandi, et illustratur promptuario concionum locupletissimo. II. Politiam Ecclesiasticam. Hanoviae. 1622

[Amhurst, Nicholas]: Terrae-Filius: Or, The Secret History of the University of Oxford in Several Essays. Lond. 1726

Apology for Bishops, An, or, A Plea for Learning. . . . Anon. n. p. 1641

Ascham: The Schoolmaster (ed. James Upton). Lond. 1711

Aubrey, John: Brief Lives (ed. Andrew Clark). Oxford, 1898

[1] The known authors of works published anonymously are inclosed in brackets.

Bacchiler, John: The Virgin's Pattern: in the Exemplary Life, and lamented Death of Mrs. Susanna Perwick. . . . Lond. 1661

Baillie, Robert: Letters and Journals (1637-1662). Lond. 1841

Satan the Leader in Chief to all who resist the Reparaof Sion. Lond. 1643

Ball, W. W. Rouse: A Hist. of the Study of Math. at Camb. Camb. 1889

Barclay, John: Barclay his Argenis. Or, The Loves of Polyarchus and Argenis (Tr. by Kingsmill Long, Esq. 2nd. ed.). Lond. 1636

Barclay, Robert: The Inner Life of the Religious Societies of the Commonwealth. Lond. 1876

Barker, G. F. Russell: Memoir of Richard Busby, D.D. (1606-1695) with some account of Westminster School in the 17th cent. Lond. 1895

Barlow, John: The Genuine Remains of that Learned Prelate, Dr. Thomas Barlow, late Ld. Bish. of Lincoln. Lond. 1693

Barrow, Isaac: Theological Works (Life by Abraham Hill, prefixed) 8 vols. Oxford. 1830

Bates, William: Spiritual Perfection, unfolded and enforced: from 2 Cor. vii. (Intr. essay by the Rev. J. Pye Smith). Lond. 1840

Baxter, Richard: Autobiography (ed. J. M. Lloyd Thomas). Lond. 1926

A Call to the Unconverted (31st ed.). Lond. 1718

The Life of Faith, as it is the Evidence of things unseen. Lond. 1660

The Reformed Pastor. . . . An Appendix containing some hints of advice to students for the ministry, and its tutors (ed. Samuel Palmer). Wash. Penn. 1810

The Saints' Everlasting Rest. Boston. 1825

Beesley, Henry: The Soules Conflict with the Sins of Vain-glory, Coldnesse in professing Christ, Envie, Photinianism. . . . Lond. 1656

Benbrigge, John: Gods Fury, Englands Fire. Lond. 1646

Berkley, Sir John: Memoirs (in Maseres: Tracts. . .).
    Lond. 1815
Bernard, Nicholas: Funeral Sermon: The Pentitent Death
    of a Woeful Sinner, Or, The Penitent Death of John
    Atherton, Late Bishop of Waterford in Ireland
    . . . Executed at Dublin, Dec. 5, 1640. Lond. 1642
Fun. Ser. for Usher. Lond. 1656
Besant: Tudor London. Lond. 1904
Bogan, Zachary: Comparatio Homeri cum Scriptoribus
    Sacris quoad normam loquendi. Subnectitur Hesio-
    dus. Oxoniae. 1658
Bonhame, Joshua: A New Constellation. Lond. 1675
Bossuet: Oraisons Funèbres de Bossuet, précedés de l'es-
    sai sur l'oraison funèbre par M. Villemain. Paris.
    1855
Botsacco, Johanne: Promptuarium Allegoriarum et Simili-
    tudinum Theologicarum. Lubecae. 1626
Boyle, Robert: Works (ed. Richard Boulton). 4 vols.
    Lond. 1699
Braithwait, Richard: The English Gentleman; and the
    English Gentlewoman . . . and a Supplement lately
    annexed, and entitled The Turtle's Triumph. Lond.
    1641
Bramston, Sir John: Autobiography (ed. P. Braybrooke).
    Lond. 1845
[Brinsley, John]: A Consolation for our Grammar Schools,
    or, A faithfulle and most comfortable incourage-
    ment, for laying a sure foundation of all good Learn-
    ing in our Schools . . . More especially for . . .
    all ruder countries and places; namely for Ireland,
    Wales, Virginia, with the Sommer Ilands. . . .
    Lond. 1622
Brinsley, John: Ludus Literarius, Or, The Grammar
    School (ed. E. T. Campagnac. 1st ed., 1612).
    Lond. 1917
The Saints Solemne Covenant with their God. Lond.
    1644
Two Treatises. . . . The Doctrine of Christ's Media-
    torship; Of Mystical Implantation. Lond. 1651

Brooks, Thomas: An Arke for all Gods Noahs in a gloomy stormy day; Or, The best Wine reserved till last. Or, The transcendent Excellency of a believers portion above all earthly Portions whatsoever. Lond. 1662

The Crown and Glory of Christianity or Holiness, The only way to Happiness. Delivered in LVIII Sermons from Heb. 12. 14. Lond. 1662

Browne, Sir Thomas: Works (ed. Simon Wilkin). 3 vols. Lond. 1890

Brownrig, Ralph: Fourty Sermons. Lond. 1661

Buckle, H. T.: Hist. of Civilization in Eng. 2 vols. N. Y. 1892

Bunyan, John: Works. N. Y. 1833

Burgess, Anthony: CXLV Expository Sermons upon the whole 17th Chapter of the Gospel according to St. John: or, Christ's prayer before his passion Explicated, and both Practically and Polemically Improved. Lond. 1656

Burnet, Gilbert: Hist. of His Own Time. 2 vols. Lond. 1724

[Burnet, Gilbert]: The Life of William Bedell, D.D. Lond. 1685

Burney, Charles: A General Hist. of Music. 4 vols. Lond. 1789

Burrows, Montagu: Collectanea. Oxford. 1890

The Register of the visitors of The Univ. of Oxford, from A.D. 1647 to A.D. 1658. Lond. 1881

Burton, Robert: Anatomy of Melancholy (ed. the Rev. A. R. Shilleto). 3 vols. Lond. 1896

Burton, Thomas: Diary (1656 to 1657; ed. John Towill Rutt). 4 vols. Lond. 1828

Butler, Charles: The Feminin' Monarchi', or The Histori of Bee's. Oxford. 1634

Butler, Samuel: Genuine Remains (ed. R. Thyer). 2 vols. Lond. 1759

Hudibras and Other Works (ed. A. Ramsey). Lond. 1846

Cajori, Florian: A Hist. of Math. N. Y. 1895

Calamy, Edmund: Eli Trembling before the Ark. Oxford.
    1662
    Funeral Sermon for Simeon Ashe (included in the vol-
        ume of Farewell Sermons). Lond. 1662
    Funeral Sermon for Christopher Love. Lond. 1651
    Funeral Sermon for Lady Anne Waller: The Happinesse
        of those who Sleep in Jesus. . . . Lond. 1662
    God's Free Mercy to England a Pretious and Powerful
        Motive to Humiliation. Lond. 1642
    The Noble-man's Patterne of True and reall Thank-
        fulnesse. Lond. 1643
Calamy, Edmund (the younger): An Abridgment of Mr.
    Baxter's Life and Times (2nd ed.). 2 vols. Lond.
    1713
    An Account of the Ministers, Lecturers, Masters and
        Fellows of Colleges and Schoolmasters, who were
        Ejected or Silenced after the Restoration in 1660.
        (2nd. ed.). 2 vols. Lond. 1713
Cambridge University Transactions during the Puritan
    Controversities of the 16th and 17th centuries (eds.
    James Heywood and Thomas Wright).   Lond.
    1854
Carpenter, Richard: Astrology Proved Harmless, Useful,
    Pious. Lond. 1657
    The Perfect Law of God. Lond. 1652
Cartwright, Thomas: Diary (ed. the Rev. Joseph Hunter).
    Camden Soc. 1843
Cary, Henry: Memorials of the Great Civil War in Eng.
    from 1646-1652. 2 vols. Lond. 1842
Caryl, Joseph: Joy Out-Joyed, Or, Joy in overcoming evil
    spirits and evil men. Lond. 1645
Case, Thomas: The Root of Apostasy, and Fountain of
    true Fortitude. Lond. 1644
Castell, Edmund: Lexicon Heptaglotton. Lond. 1669
Caussinus, Nicholas: De Eloquentia sacra et humana (7th
    ed.). Lugduni. 1657
Cawdrey, Robert: A Treasury, or Storehouse of Similes
    (First pub. 1609). Bound with Spencer's Things
    New and Old. q. v.

Chamberlayne, Edward: Angliae Notitia; or, The Present
    State of Eng. (5th ed.). Lond. 1691

Chappell, William: The Preacher, or the Art and Method
    of Preaching. Lond. 1656

Cheynell, Francis: The Man of Honour. Lond. 1645
    A Plot for the Good of Posterity. Lond. 1646
    Sions Memento and Gods Alarum. Lond. 1643

Chillingworth, William: Works. Phil. 1841

Choyce Drollery (ed. J. Woodfall Elsworth).   Boston
    (Lincolnshire). 1876

Clarendon: The Hist. of the Rebellion and Civil Wars in
    Eng. (7 vols.). Oxford. 1839
    Characters and Episodes of the Great Rebellion. Oxford,
    1889

Clark (Clarke), Samuel: A General Martyrology. . . .
    Glasgow. 1770
    A Geographicall Description of all the Countries in the
    known World. Lond. 1657
    The Lives and Deaths of . . . the Great. Lond. 1675
    The Lives of Sundry Eminent Persons in this later age.
    In two parts. I Of Divines, II Of Nobility and
    Gentry of both Sexes. Lond. 1683
    The Marrow of Ecclesiastical History (3rd ed.). Lond.
    1675
    A Mirrour or Looking Glasse both for Saints and Sinners.
    Lond. 1654

Cleveland, John, The Poems of: (ed. John M. Berdan).
    N. Y. 1903

Clifford, Lady Anne: Life, Letters and Work (ed. George
    C. Williamson). Lond. 1922

Coate, Mary: Social Life in Stuart England. N. Y. 1924

Cobblers End, Or, His (last) Sermon, The. Lond. 1641

Collection of all the publicke orders, ordinances and
    Declarations of both Houses of Parliament from
    the Ninth of March 1642, Untill December 1646, A.
    Lond. 1646

Collins, John: The Spouses Hidden Glory, and Faithful
    Leaning on Her Welbeloved. Lond. 1647

Confused Characters of Conceited Coxcombs: or a Dish of

Trayterous Tyrants, dressed with Verjuice and pickled too [sic] posterity. By Verax Philobasileus (Lond. 1661); ed. James O. Halliwell. Lond. 1860

Cook, A. K.: About Winchester College. Lond. 1917

Cotton, John: God's Mercie mixed with his Justice. Lond. 1641

Courthope: A Hist. of Eng. Poetry. Lond. 1911

Cowley, Abraham: Essays and Other Prose Writings (ed. A. B. Gough). Oxford. 1915

Crawford, Bartholow V.: Questions and Objections. PMLA, XLI. No. 1.

Crofton, Zachary: The Hardway to Heaven. n. p. 1662

Crosby, Thomas: The Hist. of the Eng. Baptists. 4 vols. Lond. 1738

Dargan, Edwin C.: A Hist. of Preaching, A.D. 70-1572. N. Y. 1905

A Hist. of Preaching, 1572-1900. N. Y. 1912

D'Avenant, Sir William: Gondibert. Lond. 1651

The Siege of Rhodes. Dramatic Works. Lond. 1873

Degge, Sir Simon: The Parson's Counsellor, with the Law of Tithing. Lond. 1676

Dell, William: The Stumbling Stone . . . wherein the University is reproved by the Word of God. Lond. 1653

D'Ewes, Sir Simonds: Journal (ed. Wallace Notestein). New Haven. 1923

Digby: Letters between the Late Lord George Digby, and Sir Kenelm Digby, kt. concerning Religion. Lond. 1651

Dircks, H.: A Biographical Memoir of Samuel Hartlib. Lond. n. d.

D'Israeli, Isaac: Quarrels of Authors. 3 vols. Lond. 1814

Dolben, John: A Sermon preached before the King, Aug. 14, 1666, Being the Day of Thanksgiving for the late Victory at Sea. Lond. 1666

Donne, John: Paradoxes, Problems, Essayes, Characters. . . . To which is added a Book of Epigrams. Tr. from the Latin by Jasper Maine, D.D. as also Ignatius his Conclave, a Satyr. . . . Lond. 1652

Dowsing, William: of Stratford: Journal (ed. the Rev. C. H. Evelyn White). Ipswich. 1885

Dryden, John: Essays (ed. Edward Malone). 2 vols. Lond. 1800

Duncon, John: Lady Lettice, Viscountess Falkland (ed. M. F. Howard). Lond. 1908

Dury, John: The Reformed Librarie-Keeper. Chicago. 1906

Eachard, John: The Axe, against Sin and Error; and the Truth Conquering. Lond. 1646

Works (I) The Grounds and Occasion of the Contempt of the Clergy enquired into. . . . (II) Observations on an Answer to the Enquiry. . . . (III) Mr. Hobb's State of Nature considered; in a Dialogue between Philautus and Timothy. Lond. 1705

Edwards, Thomas: Gangraena: or, A Catalogue and Discovery of Errours, Heresies, Blasphemies and Pernicious Practices. . . . Lond. 1646

Erasmus, Desiderius: In Praise of Folly (ed. Horace Bridges). Chicago. 1925

Etherege, Sir George: The Comical Revenge, or, Love in a Tub. Lond. 1697.

Evelyn, John: A Character of England (Literary Remains; ed. William Upcott). Lond. 1834

Diary (ed. Austin Dobson). 3 vols. N. Y. 1908

Sculptura: or, The Hist. of Caleography (ed. C. F. Bell). Oxford. 1906

Exact Collection of Farewell Sermons, An. Lond. 1662

Eyre, Adam: Diurnall, 1646-47 (ed. H. J. Morehouse). Durham, 1877

Fairfax Correspondence, The (ed. Robert Bell). Lond. 1849

Fairfax, Thomas (Lord), Short Memorials of (in Maseres: Select Tracts. . .). Lond. 1815

Fanshawe, Lady: Memoirs. Lond. 1830

Farnaby, Thomas: Index rhetoricus et Oratoriae . . . cui adjiciuntur Formulae Oratoriae et Index Poeticus (5th ed.). Londini. 1654

Fell, John: The Character of the Last Daies. Oxford, 1675

The Life of the most Learned, Reverend and Pious Dr. Henry Hammond. Lond. 1661

A Sermon Preached Before the House of Peers. Oxford, 1680

Feltham, Owen: Resolves Divine, Moral and Political. Lond. 1640

Fénelon: Dialogues sur l'eloquence (Oeuvres choisies). Paris. n.d.

Ferrar, Nicholas: His Household and his Friends (ed. T. T. Carter). Lond. 1893

Ferriby, John: The Lawful Preacher. Lond. 1652

[Flecknoe, Richard]: Sixtynine Enigmatical Characters (2nd ed.). Lond. 1665

Flemings in Oxford, The, 1650-1700. 2 vols. (ed. John Richard Magrath). Oxford. 1904

Fletcher, Phineas: The Purple Island, or, The Isle of Man. Lond. 1783

Fox, George: Journal (ed. Norman Penney). Lond. 1924

Freeman, John: A Sermon preached without a Text. Lond. 1643

Fry, John: The Clergy in their Colours; or a brief Character of Them. Lond. 1650

Fuller, Thomas: Abel Redivivus, Or, The Dead yet Speaking (ed. William Nicholls). 2 vols. Lond. 1867

Antheologia; or, The Speech of Flowers (Bound with Joseph's Party-colored Coat). Lond. 1867

A Christening Sermon (Bound with Joseph).

Church Hist. of Britain, The (ed. the Rev. P. S. Brewer). 6 vols. Oxford. 1845

Hist. of the Univ. of Cambridge and of Waltham Abbey, The, With the Appeal of Injured Innocence (ed. James Nichols). Lond. 1840

Hist. of the Worthies of England (ed. P. A. Nuttall). Lond. 1840

Holy State, The. Camb. 1642

Holy State and the Profane State, The. Lond. 1840

Joseph's Party-colored Coat (ed. William Nicholls). Lond. 1867

Ornithologie, or, The Spirit of Birds (Bound with Joseph).

Triana; or, A Threefold Romanza, of Mariana, Paduana, Sabina (Bound with Joseph).

Truth Maintained, Or, Positions Delivered in a Sermon at the Savoy Since Traduced for Dangerous, now Asserted for Sound and Safe. Lond. 1643

A Sermon of Assurance. Fourteen Yeares agoe preached in Cambridge, since in other places. Lond. 1648

Two Sermons; the first, Comfort in Calamite teaching to Live well, The other, The Grand Assizes, minding to Dye well. Lond. 1654

Funeral Sermons by Eminent English Divines, 1650-1760 (ed. the Rev. John Page Wood). Lond. 1831

Gardiner, S. R.: Hist. of the Commonwealth and Protectorate. Lond. 1903

Gataker, Thomas: A Marriage Praier, Or, Succinct Meditations delivered in a Sermon. Lond. 1624

[Gauden, John]: A Discourse of Artificial Beauty. Lond. 1662

Gauden, John: Fun. Ser. for the Rt. Rev. Dr. Brownrig. Lond. 1660

Fun. Ser. for Robert Rich. Funerals Made Cordials. Lond. 1658

Gell, Robert: Stella Nova, a New Starre, Leading Wise Men unto Christ. Lond. 1649

Glanvill, Joseph. An Essay concerning Preaching, Written for the Direction of a Young Divine. Lond. 1678

Essays on Several Subjects on Philosophy and Religion. Lond. 1676

Scepsis Scientifica: or, Confest Ignorance, the Way to Science; in an Essay of the Vanity of Dogmatizing. . . . Lond. 1665

A Seasonable Recommendation and Defence in the Affairs of Religion. Lond. 1670

Some Discourses, Sermons and Remains (Collected by Anthony Horneck). Lond. 1681

Gouge, William: Fun. Ser. for Mrs. Margaret Ducke. Lond. 1646

Grammont, Count: Memoirs of the Court of Charles II (ed. Sir Walter Scott). Lond. 1891

Graves, T. S.: Notes on Puritanism and the Stage. St. in Phil., vol. 18

Gutch, John: Collectanea Curiosa . . . relating to the Hist. and Antiq. of Eng. and Ireland. 2 vols. Oxford. 1781

Hacket, John: A Memorial of John Williams, D. D. Lond. 1693

Hales, John: Works. 3 vols. Glasgow. 1765

Halkett, Anne, Lady: Journal (ed. John Gough Nichols). 1875

Hall, George: A Fast Sermon on the continuing Pestilence. Lond. 1666

H.[all], J.[ohn]: An Humble Motion to the Parliament concerning the Advancement of Learning and Reformation in the Universities. Lond. 1649

Hall, Joseph: Contemplations on the Hist. of the New Test. . . . Together with his Life and Hard Measure Written by Himself (ed. William Dodd). 2 vols. 1765

Hall, Thomas: Centuria Sacra, containing about one hundred Rules for the expounding and clearer understanding of the Holy Scriptures. Lond. 1654

    Examen Examinis (Histrio-Mastix. A Whip for Webster). Lond. 1654

    Funebria Florae, The Downfall of May-Games. 1661

    The Pulpit Guarded with XVII Arguments proving the Unlawfulness, Sinfulness, and Danger of Suffering Private persons to take upon them Publick Preaching. . . . Lond. 1651

    Rhetorica Sacra: or , A Synopsis. . . . Lond. 1654

    Vindiciae Literarum, The Schools Guarded: Or, The Excellency and Usefulness of Humane Learning in

Subordination to Divinity, and preparation to the Ministry; as also Rules for the expounding of the Holy Scriptures. . . . Lond. 1655

Halliwell, James O.: Books of Characters illustrating the Habits and Manners of Englishmen from the Reign of James I to the Restoration. Lond. 1857

Hammond, Henry: Several Sermons. Lond. 1664

Hardy, Nathaniel: Fun. Ser. for Sir Thomas Adams; The Royal Common-wealths Man, Or, King David's Picture. Lond. 1668

Fun. Ser. for Sir John Gayer. Lond. 1659

Fun. Ser. for Mr. Richard Goddard. Lond. 1653

Fun. Ser. for Mr. Adam Pemberton; The Epitaph of a Godly Man, especially a Man of God. Lond. 1655

Funeral Sermon for Mrs. Mary Smith; Death's Alarum, Or, Security's Warning Piece. Lond. 1654

Hope and Fear, The inseparable Twins of a Blest Matrimony. Lond. 1653

Justice Triumphing, Or, The Spoylers Spoyled. Lond. 1647

Lamentation, Mourning and Woe, Sighed forth in a Sermon. Lond. 1666

Mercy in her Beauty, or, The Height of a Deliverance from the depth of Danger. Lond. 1653

The Safest Convoy, Or, The Strongest Helper. Lond. 1649

Wisdomes Character; or, The Queen of Graces. Lond. 1656

Wisdomes Counterfeit: or, Herodian Policy Unmasked in a Sermon. Lond. 1656

Harley, Lady Brilliana: Letters (ed. Thomas Taylor Lewis). Lond. 1854

Harrington, James: The Commonwealth of Oceana (Intr. by Henry Morley). Lond. 1887

Harris, Robert: Funeral Sermon for Sir Thomas Lucy; Abners Funerall. Lond. 1641

Harrison, Dr.: Threni Hybernici; or, Ireland with England and Scotland, in a sad Lamentation for the loss of their Josiah. Lond. 1659

Manton, Thomas: England's Spiritual Languishing. Lond. 1648

Funeral Sermon for Christopher Love; The Saints Triumph over Death. Lond. 1651

Marshall, Stephen: Reformation and Desolation. Lond. 1643

A two-edged Sword out of the Mouth of Babes, to execute vengeance upon the Enemy and Avenger. Lond. 1646

Martin, L. C.: A Forgotten Poet of the 17th Cent. (Essays and St. by . . . the Eng. Ass'n.). Oxford, 1925

Marvell, Andrew: Works (ed. Edward Thompson). Lond. 1776

Maseres, Francis: Select Tracts Relating to the Civil War in Eng., in the reign of Charles I. 2 pts. Lond. 1815

Masson, David: The Life of Milton. 6 vols. Lond. 1877

Meggott, Richard: Funeral Sermon for Nathaniel Hardy. Lond. 1670.

Mercurius Rusticus: or, the Countries Complaint (Contains Querela Cantabrigiensis: or, the Universities Complaint, pp. 178-210). Lond. 1685

Milton, John: Prose Works (ed. George Burnett). 2 vols. Lond. 1809

Mollerus, Johan: Allegoriae profano-sacrae, das ist geistliche Deutungen, allerhand welticher auszerlesener Historien. Jena. 1655

Moore, John: The Crying Sin of England, Of not Caring for the Poor, wherein Inclosure, viz. such as doth unpeople Townes, and uncorn Fields, is Arraigned, Convicted, and Condemned by the Word of God. Lond. 1653

More, Henry: The Life of the Learned and Pious . . . to which are annex'd Divers of his Useful and Excellent Letters (ed. the Rev. Richard Ward). Lond. 1710

Morley, George, Ld. Bish. of Worcester: Sermon at the Coronation of Charles II. Lond. 1661

Mullinger, James Bass: Camb. Characteristics in the 17th Cent. Lond. 1867

A Hist. of the Univ. of Camb. N. Y. 1888

Neal, Daniel: The Hist. of the Puritans . . . from . . . 1517 to . . . 1688 (ed. John O. Choules). 2 vols. N. Y. 1843

Neale, J. M.: Mediaeval Preaching and Mediaeval Preachers. Lond. 1856

Nelson, Robert: Life of Dr. George Bull (2nd ed.). Lond. 1714

Newcastle: Letters and Poems in Honour of the Incomparable Princess, Margaret, Dutchess of Newcastle. Lond. 1676

Newcastle, Margaret: Life of the Duke of Newcastle (ed. C. H. Firth). Lond. 1886

Newcome, Henry: Diary (ed. Thomas Heyward). Lond. 1849

Newcomen, Matthew: Funeral Sermon for Mr. Samuel Collins. Lond. 1658

Nicholl's Literary Anecdotes of the 18th Century. 8 vols. Lond. 1848

Notes and Queries: 1st ser., vol. vi, 25; 5th ser., viii, 166; 7th ser., vii, 308

Original Records of Early Nonconformity under Persecution and Indulgence (Transcribed and edited by George Lyon Turner). 2 vols. Lond. 1911

Orinda to Poliarchus: Letters. Lond. 1729

Osborn, Francis: Works (Advice to a Son); (8th ed.). Lond. 1682

Osborne, Dorothy: Love Letters to Sir William Temple, 1652-1654 (ed. Edward Abbott Perry). N. Y. 1901

Owen, John: A Complete Collection of Sermons. Lond. 1721

The Shaking and Translating of Heaven and Earth. Lond. 1649

Palmer, Samuel: The Nonconformist's Memorial. . . . 2 vols. Lond. 1775

Parker, Irene: Dissenting Academies in England. Camb. 1914

Patrick, Simon: Funeral Sermon for Mr. Samuel Jacomb;

Divine Arithmetic, or, The Right Art of Numbe
our Dayes. Lond. 1657

Peacham, Henry: The Compleat Gentleman.
1906

Pepys, Samuel: Diary (ed. H. B. Wheatly). 9 vols
1895

Peters, Hugh: Gods Doings, and Mans Duty. L
The Tales and Jests of Mr. Hugh Peters. Lo

Petheran, John: An Hist. Sketch of the Pro
Present State of Anglo-Saxon Literature
land. Lond. 1840

Philips, Katherine: Poems by the most deserv
mired Mrs. Katherine Philips (The
Orinda). Lond. 1710

Pierce, Thomas: A Seasonable Caveat against the
of Credulity in our Trusting the Spirits b
Try them. Lond. 1678

Plomer, Henry: A Dictionary of the Booksel
Printers who were at work in Eng., Scot
Ireland from 1641-1667. Lond. 1907

A Short Hist. of Eng. Printing, 1476-1898. Lo

Powell, Vavasor: The Bird in the Cage Chirping f
tinct Notes to his Consorts abroad (2nd ed.)
1662

Price, Gulielmum: Ars concionandi. Amsteloda

Price, John: The Cloudie Clergie; or, A Mourn
ture for our Morning Lecturers. Lond. 16.

Prideaux, John: Conciliorum Synopsis. Oxoniae.
Fasciculus Controversiarum Theologicarum. O
1652
Scholasticae Theologiae Syntagma Mnemonicum.
oniae. 1651

Prideaux, Mathias: An Easy and Compendious Intro
tion For Reading all sorts of Histories. Oxf
1664

Prince, John: Danmonii orientales illustres: or, T
Worthies of Devon. Lond. 1810

Prynne, William: A Short Demurrer to the Jewes Long

discontinued barred Remitter into England (2nd
ed.). Lond. 1656

rio-Mastix. Lond. 1633

ncendiary, The: or, The Divinity and Devotion of
Ir. Calamy, Mr. Case, Mr. Cauton, Mr. Cranford,
d other Sion-Colledge Preachers in their Morning-
xercises. n. p. 1648

Edward Kelly: Magdalene College (College His-
ies). Lond. 1904

Francis: Emblems, Divine and Moral. N. Y.
54

homas: Sheba's Head Cast over the Wall. . . .
nd. 1661

ctive Review, I, II, III

, Edward: The Comfort and Crown of Great
ctions. Lond. 1657

l Sermon for John Langley; The Use of Humane
earning. Lond. 1658

Sermons on the 14th of Hosea (Pr. in 1645).
ond. 1827

infulnesse of Sin (5th ed.). Lond. 1651

ty Sermons. Lond. 1659

remiah: Charactery: or, a most Easie and Exact
Iethod of Short and Swift Writing whereby Ser-
ons and Speeches may be . . . taken. Lond. 1646

Josiah: A Nosegay of Rank-smelling Flowers.
. . Lond. 1646

gton, Francis: King Solomon's Directory. . . .
Lond. 1649

son, Matthew: Autobiography (ed. J. E. B. Mayor).
Camb. 1856

ns, Hyder E.: Cavalier and Puritan. N. Y. 1923

he Eng. Commonwealth Drama. St. in Phil., vol. 18.

s, John: Diary, 1625-1642 (ed. Mary Anne Everett
Green). Lond. 1856

ouse-Ball, W. W.: A Hist. of the Study of Math at Cambridge. Camb. 1889

Rushworth, John: Historical Collection, 1618-1648. 8
vols. Lond. 1721

Rust, George: Funeral Sermon for Jeremy Taylor (Taylor's Works, I, lxiv-lxxi). Lond. 1836

Saltmarsh, John: Perfume Against the Sulpherous . . . Lond. 1646

Sancroft, William: Lex Ignea: or, The School of Righteousness. Lond. 1666

Sanderson, Robert: Sermons (ed. the Rev. R. Montgomery). 2 vols. Lond. 1841

Sedgwick, Joseph: Sermon in reply to Dell's Stone. Lond. 1653

Selden, John: Table-Talk (2nd ed.). Lond. 16

Shaw, John: The Life of Master John Shaw (Diaries). Lond. 1877

S.[haw] S.[amuel]: The Voice of one Crying in ness. . . . Lond. 1666

Shute, Josias: Sarah and Hagar, Or, Gen. the 16t in XIX Sers. Lond. 1648

Simpson, John: The Herbal of Divinity. . . . Lon

Slingsby, Sir Henry: Diary (ed. the Rev. Dan sons). Lond. 1836

Smith, David: Characters from the Histories and of the 17th Century. Oxford. 1918

Smith, John, Gent.: The Mysterie of Rhetorique U . . . Lond. 1657

Somner, William: Dictionarium Saxonico-Latino-An Oxonii. 1659

A Treatise of the Roman Ports and Forts in Ke which is prefixt the Life of Mr. Somner. 1693

South, Robert: Sermons. 5 vols. Oxford. 1842

Spencer, John: Things New and Old (Pref. by Fuller; ed. the Rev. Richard B. Dickinson). L 1868

Spingarn, J. E.: Critical Essays of the 17th Centur 3 vols. Oxford. 1908

Sprat, Thomas: A Discourse . . . to the Clergy. . . Lond. 1696

The Hist. of the Royal Society of London (2nd ed.). Lond. 1702

Spurgeon, Caroline F. E.: Five Hundred Years of Chaucer Allusion. 3 vols. Camb. 1925

Spurstow, William: Funeral Sermon for Lady Honor Vyner; Death and the Grave no Bar to Believers Happinesse. Lond. 1656

Staunton, Edmund: Rupes Israelis. Lond. 1644

Steele, Richard: The Husbandmans Calling (12 sermons). Lond. 1668

Sterry, Peter: The Clouds in which Christ Comes. Lond. 1648

Sterry, Peter: A Discourse of the Freedom of the Will. Lond. 1675
Free Grace Exalted and thence Deduced. Lond. 1670
The Spirit Convincing of Sinne. Lond. 1645
The Way of God with his People in these nations. Lond. 1657

Stillingfleet, Edward: Originae Sacrae. 2 vols. Oxford. 1836
Six Sermons with a Discourse annexed. Lond. 1669

Strada, Famianus: Eloquentia Bipartita. Oxoniae. 1662

Strode, William: The Floating Island. Lond. 1655

Suckling, Sir John: Works. Lond. 1709

Swan, John: Calamus Mensurans. Lond. 1653
Signa Coeli. The Signs of Heaven. Lond. 1652

Sydney, W. C.: Social Life in Eng., 1660-1690. N. Y. 1892

Taylor, Jeremy: Works. 3 vols. Lond. 1836

Taylor, John: Works (Spencer Soc., Pub.). Manchester. 1870

T.[haddeus], J.[ohn](?): The Reconciler of the Bible: wherein Above 2000 seeming Contradictions . . . are . . . Reconciled. Lond. 1656

Thomason, George: A Coll. of the pamphlets, books, newspapers and mss. relating to the Civil War, the Commonwealth and Restoration, 1640-1661 (ed. G. K. Fortesque). 2 vols. Lond. 1908

Thoresby, Ralph: Diary, 1677-1724 (ed. the Rev. Joseph Hunter). 2 vols. Lond. 1830

Thorndike, Herbert: The due Way of Composing the dif-

ferences on foot preserving the Church. . . . Lond.
1660

Thornton, Mrs. Alice: Autobiography. Lond. 1873

Thurloe, John: A Coll. of the State Papers of, (ed. Th.
Birch). 7 vols. Lond. 1742

Th.[urman], H.[enry]: A Defence of Humane Learning
in the Ministry. Oxford, 1660

Till, Mr.: A Sermon of Consolation for all true Christians.
Lond. 1646

Tillotson, John: The Wisdom of being Religious. Lond.
1664

Tombes, John: Anthropolatria, Or, The Sinne Of Glorying
in Men, especially in Eminent Ministers of the
Gospel. Lond. 1645

Fermentum Pharisaeorum. Lond. 1643

Traherne, Thomas: Centuries of Meditations (ed. Bertram
Dobell). Lond. 1908

Trotter, Eleanor: Seventeenth Century Life in the Country Parish. Camb. 1919

Usher, James: Eighteen Sermons Preached in Oxford in
1640. Lond. 1659

Vaughan, Thomas: Works (ed. Arthur Edward Waite).
Lond. 1919

Verney Family, The: Memoirs (eds. Frances Parthenope
Verney and Margaret H. Verney). 2 vols. Lond.
1907

Vines, Richard: Funeral Sermon for the Earl of Essex;
The Hearse of the Renowned. Lond. 1646

Vossius, Gerard John: Elementa Rhetorica. Londini. 1724

W.[alker], G.[eorge]: The History of the Creation . . .
plainly opened and expounded in severall sermons.
Lond. 1641

Walker, John: The Sufferings of the Clergy of the Church
of Eng. Lond. 1714

Wallis, John: Grammatica Linguae Anglicanae (4th ed.).
Oxoniae. 1674

Walton, Brian: Biblia Sacra Polyglotta. Lond. 1657

Walton, Isaac: The Compleat Angler (ed. R. B. Marston).
Lond. 1905

Lives (ed. A. H. Bullen). Lond. 1884

Waltoniana (ed. R. H. Shepherd). Lond. 1878

Ward, Seth: A Sermon Against Resistance of Lawful Powers. Lond. 1661

Funeral Sermon for the Duke of Albemarle; The Christian's Victory over Death. Lond. 1670

Vindiciae Academiarum. Oxford, 1654

Warwick, Lady Mary (Boyle): Autobiography (ed. T. Crofton Croker). Lond. 1848

Warwick, Sir Philip: Memoirs. Lond. 1704

Waterhouse, Edward: An humble Apologie for Learning and Learned Men. Lond. 1653

Watson, Foster: The Curriculum and Text-Books of Eng. Schools in the first half of the 17th Century. Lond. 1903

The English Grammar Schools to 1660. Camb. 1908

Religious Refugees and English Education. Lond. 1911

Watson, Thomas: A Pastors Love Expressed to a Loving People. . . . Lond. 1662

The Righteous Mans Weal and the Wicked Mans Woe. Lond. 1662

Webster, John: Academiarum Examen, or, the Examination of Academies. Lond. 1654

Wellington, Nehemiah: Historical Notices. 2 vols. Lond. 1869

Westfield, Thomas: A Sermon preached at St. Paul's. Lond. 1641

Wheatley, H. B.: Samuel Pepys and the World he lived In. Lond. 1889

Whitaker, Jeremiah: The Danger of Greatness, or, Uzziah his Exaltation. Lond. 1646

White, John: The First Century of Scandalous Malignant Priests. Lond. 1643

Whitefoot, John: Funeral Sermon for Joseph Hall; Deaths Alarum. Lond. 1656

Whitlock, Bulstrode: Essays Ecclesiastical and Civil. Lond. 1706

Wilde, Robert: The Arraignment of a Sinner at the Bar of Divine Justice. Lond. 1656

Wilkins, John: The Discovery of a New World. Lond. 1640

Ecclesiastes: or, A Discourse Concerning the Gift of Preaching, as it falls under the Rules of Art. Lond. 1669

An Essay Towards a Real Character and a Philosophical Language. Lond. 1668

Mathematical Magick; or the Wonders That may be perform'd by Mechanical Geometry. In Two Books (5th ed.). Lond. 1707

Mercury: or the Secret and Swift Messenger (3rd. ed.). Lond. 1707

A Sermon preached before the King, Mar. 9, 1670. Lond. 1671

Sermons (Preface by John Tillotson). Lond. 1681

Wood, Anthony à: Athenae Oxoniensis (ed. Philip Bliss). 3 vols. Lond. 1817

Fasti Oxoniensis (ed. Philip Bliss). 2 vols. Lond. 1817

A Survey of the Antiquities of Oxford (ed. Andrew Clark). Oxford, 1889

Wordsworth, Christopher: Lives of Eminent Men connected with the History of Religion in Eng. from the Reformation to the Revolution (Selected and Ed.). Lond. 1810

Scholae Academicae. . . . Lond. 1877

Worthington, John: Diary (App. to Camb. Univ. Trans., Vol. II). Lond. 1854

Wren, Christopher: Parentalia, or Memoirs of the Family of the Wrens. Lond. 1750

Wright, Abraham: Five Sermons in five several styles; or Waies of Preaching. Lond. 1656

Wyatt, R. B. H.: William Harvey. Lond. 1924

INDEX [1]

Abridgement of the Life of Baxter, An, Calamy, *q. v.*

Abelard, Mss. of, 140

Abel Redivivus, Fuller, *q. v.*

Abner's Funeral, Harris, 62, 106

About Winchester College, Cook, 6, 245

Academiarum Examen, Webster, 16, 174, 260

Account of the Ministers, etc., An, Calamy, *q. v.*

Ackland, Baldwin, personality, 291

Active and Publick Spirit, The, Jacombe (Th.), 318

Adams, Elizabeth, 91

———, Thomas, cited, 48; sermon-titles, 133; dedication by, 133

———, Thomas (Lord Mayor), funeral sermon for, 96, 99; dedication to, 130; established Arabic lecture, 161, 281

Addison, Joseph, 242, 278

———, Lancelot, *terrae filius,* 14; travel, 243; payment, 278

Against Resistance, etc.: Ward (Seth), 93

Against Scoffing at Religion, Glanvill, 29

Ahab's Fall, Herle, 290

Alarm to the Unconverted, The, Alleine, 35, 286, 334

Albermarle, Duke of (see Monk)

Aldington, R.: *A Book of Characters,* 170, 330

Aldrich, H.: *Memoirs,* 192, 265

Alle, Th.: *A Breif Narration, etc.,* 305

Allegoria profano-sacra, Mollerus, 110

Alleine, Joseph, preaching, 35, 38; payment, 277; personality, 285, 286

———, Theodocia, 286

Allestry(-tree), James, 122

———, Richard, examiner, 6; cited, 24; supposed author of *The Gentleman's Calling,* 28; copyright of his sermons, 122; court chaplain, 271; appearance, 300

Alphabetical Dict., An, Wilkins, 173

Alsted, J.: *Theologia Prophetica,* 75, 107

Ambrose, I, personality, 297

Ambrosius, cited, 91

Amhurst, N.: *Terrae-Filius,* 13

Amorous War, The, Mayne, 216

Anatomy of Melancholy, The, Burton, 201

Ancient Rhetoric and Poetic, Baldwin, 6

Andrews, L., imitated, 19; cited, 48, 103, 215; hard student, 177

———, N., preaching, 41

Angliae Notitiae, Chamberlayne, 268, 271

Annales Vet. et Novi Test, Usher, 141, 275

Antheologia, Fuller, 131, 253

Anthropolatria, Tombes, 34

[1] Only the names of clergymen are followed by subheads.

Antiquae Linguae Britannicae, Davies, 168

Apleyard, Gam., preaching, 23

Apology for Bishops, An, Anon., 229

Apollonius of Tyre, 150

Appeal of Injured Innocence, Fuller, 164, 168

Apples of Sodom, Taylor, 242

Aquinas, cited, 151

Archimedes, 190

Areopagitica, Milton, 124

Aristotle, 4, 6, 19, 289

Arke for all Gods Noahs, An, Brooks, 120

Arraignment of a Sinner, The, Wild, 39

Ars conscionandi, Price, 46, 47, 110

Art of Preaching, The, Chappell, 43, 206

Art of Rhetoric, The, Hobbes, 7

Arundle, Earl of, 165, 268

Ascham: *The Schoolmaster,* 264

Ash(e), S., funeral ser. for him, 187; court chap., 271; imitated, 274; cited, 135, 277, 299

Ashmole, Elias, 151

Assize Sermon, An, Howe, 318

Assurance, A Sermon of: Fuller, 88

Astrologo-mastix, Geree, 148

Astrology Proved Harmless, Carpenter, 151

Athenae Oxoniensis, Wood, q. v.

Atherton, J., funeral ser. for him, 120

Atkins, R., preaching, 35; personality, 286; appearance, 300

Aubrey, J.: *Brief Lives,* 11, 31, 59, 66, 68, 76, 96, 145, 148, 152, 153, 158, 162, 163, 170, 174, 175, 178, 179, 181, 186, 189, 190, 191, 192, 193, 200, 202, 208, 210, 212, 218, 221, 226, 234, 238, 249, 250, 251, 253, 277, 284, 300, 301, 303, 304

Austin, Mr., student of Oughtred, 210

———, Peter, aided the poor, 29, 297

Axe against Sin and Error, The, Eachard, 123

Aylesbury, Wm., 171

Aylesmere, Bishop, payment, 277

Babbington, Bishop, cited, 215

Bacchiler, J., funeral ser. by him, 76

Bacon, Friar, 148

———, Lord, 5, 49, 212

Bagshaw, H., private chap., 271; use of the term *Character,* 282

———, Wm., prolific preaching, 37; funeral sermons, 98

Baillie, R., distributed his printed sers., 119; *Satan the Leader,* 124; orientals, 159

Baitson, Chr., retribution, 294

Baker, Th., mathematician, 191

Baldwin, Ch.: *Ancient Rhetoric and Poetic,* 6

Ball, N., orientals, 162; French, 170; payment, 280

———, Th., funeral ser. for him, 67

———, W. W. Rouse: *A Hist. of Math. at Cambridge,* 188, 190, 191, 202

Balsar (Baltzar), Th., music, 224

Barclay, R.: *The Inner Life,* 276

Bargrave, J., Italian, 170; travel, 243

Barker, G. F. R.: *Memoir of Busby,* 5, 218

Barkham, J., antiquary, 139; coins, 144; heraldry, 145; quoted Chaucer, 244

Barksdale, C., poetry, 235

Barlow, E., mechanics, 251

———, Th., law, 155; librarian,

180; aided students, 181; *Remaines,* 42; on Tombes, 175

Barnardiston, Sir Nathaniel, 231

Barnester (ton), J., personality, 286

Barnett, A., medicine, 198

Barret, S., payment, 279

Barrow, I., essay-sers., 87; preaching, 89, 114; Arabic, 161; linguist, 170; appearance, 180, 300; math., 189, 190; medicine, 201; poetry, 228; tobacco, 240; court chap., 271; fellow of the Royal Society, 178; boyhood, 286, 291

Bartlet, J., personality, 291
———, Wm., personality, 291

Basière(-ire), I., cited, 24

Batchcroft, Dr., cited, 16

Bates, Wm., memory, 66; funcral ser. 184; library, 183; considered a gentleman, 262; court chap., 271; personality, 286

Bath, R., delivery, 52

Bathurst, G., medicine, 195
———, R., chemistry, 154; Royal Society, 178; medicine, 195; on Kettle, 208, 229

Batten, W., 31

Baxter, R., at Blackfriars, 25; instructions on preaching, 46, 61, 69; delivery, 50; on Creighton, 57; sermon structure, 72; sermon content, 78; farewell sermon, 92; Prefaces, 135; Latin, 157; Welsh, 167; industry, 175, 177; library, 186; math., 188; medicine, 194; poetry, 229, 235; on candidates for the ministry, 264; court chap., 271; payment, 277, 280; *character*-writer, 284, 285; on members of the Savoy Conference, 293;

Beaumont, J., poetry, 236

Becket, Thomas à, 229

Bedell, Wm., Irish, 169

Bedwell, A., astrology, 147

Bee, Cornelius, 140, 181

Beesley, H.: *The Soules Conflict,* 34

Beheaded John Hewitt's Ghost, etc., 124

Behemoth, Hobbes, 16, 64

Bele (Bell), H., farming, 258

Benbrigge, J.: *God's Fury,* 306

Bendik, Sir Th., 93

Benefice, The, Wild, 216

Benlows, Mr., law, 155

Bentivolio and Urania, Ingelo, 240

Benton, Wm., farming, 258

Berkley, Sir John, *Memoirs,* 307

Bernard, N., funeral ser. for Usher, 68, 99, 105, 134, 175, 258; funeral ser. for Atherton, 120; poetry, 230

Besant, W.: *Tudor London,* 71

Bevis of Hampton, 236

Biblia Sacra Polyglotta, 163, 164

Bide, Th., 130

Billingsley, J., preaching, 295

Bindon, G., languages, 159

Biog. Brit., 29, 96, 122, 159, 178, 201, 207

Birch, R., medicine, 198

Bird in the Cage, The, Powell, 323

Birdsal, Mr., appearance, 300

Blackerby, R., ancient lang., 158, 162; walking for recreation, 252

Blagrave, Wm., personality, 287

Bluecoat Boy, 273

Bodley, Sir Th., 105

Bodleian Library, 144, 1

Bogan, Z.: *Comparat:* 162

Bois, J., Gree'

Bonha

Bossuet, funeral sers., 48, 95
Boswell: *Life of Johnson,* 79, 86
Botsacco: *Promptuarium Allegorium,* 109
Bourdaloue, 48, 59, 95
Bowles, E., poetry, 232
Boyle, R., 153, 154, 169, 178, 251
Bradshaw, E., 133
——, N., payment, 279
Braithwaite, R.: *The English Gentleman,* 28
Bray, the Vicar of, 182
Breden, Wm., astrology, 147; tobacco, 248
Breif Narration, A, Alle, 305
Brett, J., medicine, 198
Bridgman, H., music, 224
Brief Character of the Low Countries, A, Feltham, 38
Bright, E., personality, 287
Brinsley, J., disputations, 3; rhetoric, 6; sermon-notes, 60; sermon-divisions, 73; cited, 74; memorizing, 76; marginal notes, 122; on Chapman, 212; poetry, 228
Briscoe, M., delivery, 54
Broadley, Mr., preaching, 23
Bromfield, P., medicine, 198
Brook, Lord, 260, 261
Brooks, Th., sermon title, 120; sermon-dedication, 128
Broune, Mr., sermon-borrowing, 115
Brounker, Lord, 189
Browne, E.: *Journal,* 22
——, R., funeral sermon for Charles I, 100
——, Sir Th., 22, 146, 154, 196, 255
——, Wm., botany, 253
[B]rig, R., jocoserius, 14;
[preac]hing, 32; sermon struc[ture,] 112; funeral sermon [...], 85, 277; appear-

[...]cine, 195

Brydges: *Restituta,* 11
Buckhurst, Lord, 127
Buckingham, Duke of, 216
Buckle, H. T.: *Hist. of Civilization,* 295
Bulkeley, J., medicine, 198
Bull, Geo., delivery, 50; memory, 66; no recreation, 247; laziness in youth, 291
Bulton, Sir Wm., 132
Bulwer, J., 200
Bunyan, J., against vain-glory, 34; use of questions and answers, 73; sermon structure, 74; sermon-borrowing, 115; poetry, 236; on private chaps., 268
Burdon, G., math., 191
Burgess, A., serial preaching, 36; astrology, 151; *Spiritual Reviveing,* 185
——, C., examination of, 11
Burgess, D., jest of, 114
Burgoine, Sir Roger, 126
Burhill(-ghill), R., Hebrew, 162; Latin poetry, 236
Burnaud, Mr., farming, 258
Burnet, G., on Williams, 67; use of questions and answers, 73; on Gunning, 82; on Lloyd, 142; on Stillingfleet, 156; *Polyglot Bible,* 163; on Bedell, 169; Baxter, 176; S. Ward, 191; Tongue, 212; Peters, 217; Gage, 243; F. Potter, 249; Leighton, 289; Sterne, 292; Manton, 302; *Character* writing, 284
——, S., medicine, 198
Burney, Ch., 200, 219, 221, 222
Burning yet un-consumed Bush, The, Jenkyns, 92
Burroughs, Mr., 299
Burrows, M.: *The Register,* 14, 265
Burton, R., astrology, 148; philology, 172; math., 191; medicine, 201; at [...]

Burton, Th., on Manton, 33; Calamy, 40; Owen, 53; Reynolds, 113; Usher's library, 182; on Busby, 205

Busby, R., teacher, 204, 205, 206; text books, 212; actor, 218; death, 291

Bushnel, J., math., 191

Butler, Ch., rhetoric, 6; music, 223, 224

——, J., astrology, 148

——, S., *Hudibras*, 56, 73, 82, 149, 185, 232; *Remaines*, 275, 282, 285, 302

Bysshe, E., 145

Caedmonis Paraphrasis Poetica Geneseos, 165

Cajori, F.: *A Hist. of Math.*, 188, 189

Calamus Mensurans: Swan, 142

Calamy, E.: *Eli Trembling*, 123; funeral ser. for Anne Walker, 76; for Love, 103; for Ash, 187; *The Noble-man's Patterne*, 129; dedications, 129; prefaces, 135; bold preaching, 39, 40; court chap., 271; cited, 48, 49, 92, 113, 299

——, E. (the younger): *An Abridgement:* 35, 38, 50, 52, 65, 66, 67, 68, 72, 79, 98, 142, 143, 144, 147, 152, 156, 159, 160, 162, 167, 170, 172, 174, 175, 176, 182, 191, 192, 193, 194, 195, 196, 198, 199, 206, 224, 232, 236, 237, 254, 257, 271, 280, 287; *An Account,* 30, 33, 38, 40, 54, 56, 79, 81, 96, 158, 201, 211, 252, 263, 279, 280, 284, 286, 289, 300, 301, 304

Call to the Unconverted, A: Baxter, 62, 69

Calvert, P., payment, 97

Calvin, cited, 57

Cambridge, Univ. of, 3, 10, 14, 16, 18, 44, 150, 158, 160, 192,

Cambridge Characteristics in the 17th Century, Mullinger, 162

Cambridge Univ. Trans. during the 16th and 17th Cent., 309

Campanella, Th.: *Discourse concerning the Spanish Monarchy*, 170

Candler, M., heraldry, 144

Capel, D., medicine, 198

——, R., delivery, 52; medicine, 198

Carbury, Lady, funeral sermon for her, 103

Carleton, Bishop Guy, payment, 260

Carpenter, R., astrology, 151; Latin, 157

Carter, T. T.: *Nicholas Ferrar*, 241, 246

Cartwright, Th., shorthand, 77; court chaplain, 271

——, Wm., imitated, 19; plays, 214, 216; poetry, 226; elegiac verses for him, 229; appearance, 300; cited, 218, 229

Cary, H.: *Memorials*, 30, 58, 76, 271

——, N., medicine, 200

Caryl, J., indorsed Smith's *Rhetoric*, 7; delivery, 54; dedication, 129

Casaubon, M., Anglo-Saxon, 165; learning, 179

Case, Th., farewell sermon, 92; court chaplain, 271; imitated, 274

Castiglione, 10

Castle(-tell), E., Arabic, 161; *Polyglot Bible*, 164; *Lex. Heptaglotton*, 309

Catalogue of a Collection of Printed Broadsides, A, Lemon, 273

Catalogue of the Pamphlets, Books, etc., 1640 to 1661, Thomason, 214

Catalogus Plantarum Angliae, Ray, 254

Cause and C____ Wounded Con____ ____'uller, 131

Caussin, N.: *De Eloquentia Sacra*, 6, 109

Cavalier and Puritan, Rollins, 279

Cawdrey, R.: *Treasury of Similes, A*, 109

Cawton, Th., Hebrew, 162, 169

Centuria Sacra, Hall, Th., 110

Chadderton, L., preaching, 32; instruction preaching, 47

Chafin, Dr., personality, 296

Chamberlayne, E.: *Angliae Notitiae*, 267, 271, 274

Chambers: *Book of Days*, 114, 235

Chappell, Wm.: *The Art of Preaching*, 43, 44; teacher, 109, 206

Character of England, A, Evelyn, 59

Character of the Last Daies, The, Fell, 55

Characters, A Book of, Aldington, 145

Characters, Books of, Halliwell, 316

Characters, etc., Clarendon, 287

Characters from the Hist., etc., of the 17th Century, Smith, 282, 283

Charactery, Rich, J., 76

Charles I, 26, 32, 48, 100, 132, 207

Charles II, 48, 57, 89, 116, 123, 128, 164, 207, 215, 221, 229, 234, 271, 300

Charnock, S., medicine, 198

Chaucer, 99, 244

Chauncey, I., medicine, 198

Cheesman, Th., teacher, 206

Cheynell, F., Natural Hist., 4; preaching, 40; Latin, 157; on teaching, 204; on teaching the alphabet, 212; on private chaplains, 267

Childrey, J., astrology, 148

Child's Delight, The, Lye, 213

Chillingworth, Wm., controversy, ix; on preaching, 62; sermon structure ?? use of questions an?? 73: ser-

mon-length, 113; on knowledge, 173; a book borrower, 186; mathematician, 191; poetry, 228; of the Tribe of Ben, 246; nature similes, 254; personality, 287; appearance, 300

Chilmead, E., translations, 170, 171; math., 192; music, 220

Choyce Drollery, 288

Christening Sermon, A, Fuller, 313

Christian's Victory, The, Seth Ward, 102

Christmas, Wm., 91, 274

Chronicon Cestrense, Lee, 140

Chronologia sacra, Usher, 141

Chrysostom, cited, 91; on funeral sermons, 94; imitated, 269

Church Hist. of Britain, The, Fuller, *q. v.*

Cicero, 6, 8, 68

City Match, The, Mayne, 216

Clarendon: *The Hist. of the Rebellion*, 41, 127, 207, 284, 287, 293, 297, 302

Clark(e), J., popularity, 30; preaching, 23; medicine, 198; rhetoric, 7; poetry, 135

———, S.: Eminent Lives, 10, 12, 62, 67, 68, 75, 94, 135, 139, 159, 163, 164, 167, 179, 192, 205, 248, 252, 262, 298, 299; *General Martyrology*, 12, 47, 52, 68, 170, 177, 198, 222, 231, 248; *Geographical Description*, 158, 168; *Mirrour, etc.*, 109; *Marrow, etc.*, 299; poetry, 135

———, S. (not the divine), 164

———, Th., personality, 287

Clarkson, D., funeral sermon for Owen, 105

Clavis Mathematica, Oughtred, 188

Clergy in their Colours, The, Fry, 55, 59, 64

Clerke, G., math., 192

Cleveland, J.: *P*??

Clifford, A., medicine, 195
——, Lady Anne: *Life*, 114, 270, 277
——, S., memory, 66
Clouds in which Christ Comes, The: Sterry, 72
Coate, M.: *Social Life in Stuart England*, 156
Coates, S., delivery, 52
Cobblers End, The, Anon., 71
Collectanea Curiosa, Gutch, 140
Collection of Curious Discourses, A, Hearne, 144
Collection of . . . Prophecies . . . A, Lilly, 148
Collection of all the Publick Orders, A, 310
Collection of the State Papers of John Thurloe, A, 162
Collins, S., funeral sermon for him, 92
Comber, Th., delivery, 56; ancient languages, 159; modern languages, 170; teacher, 2⸱⸱ painting, 218
——, Th. (the youn⸱⸱ vate chaplain 277
Com⸱⸱ 203, 206, 279

⸱⸱ *The*,

⸱⸱ *cum Scrip-* ⸱⸱, 162
C⸱⸱ ⸱ *Rhetoricus*, Horne,

Compleat Ambassador, The, 185
Compleat Angler, The, Walton, 259
Compleat Collection of Farewell Sermons, A, 93
Compleat Gentleman, The, Peacham, 28, 218
Complete Collection of the Sermons of John Owen, A, 322

Conant, J., orientals, 159; learning, 179; executive, 206
Conciliorum Synopsis, Prideaux, 110
Confused Characters, Verax Philobasileus, 285
Consolation for all Christians, A Sermon of, Till, 327
Consolation for our Grammar Schools, A, Brinsley, 3, 212
Conspiracy, The, Killigrew, 216
Constantine, R., delivery, 50
Contemplations on the Hist. of the New Testament, Th. Hall, 261, 315
Contribution to the Hist. of the Eng. Commonwealth Drama, Rollin⸱ 4
Cook, ⸱⸱ of *About Winchester Co⸱⸱*, *The*,
science, The, ⸱ ⸱ Herford),

⸱⸱cessari-

⸱⸱⸱⸱06

⸱⸱ *for Charles*

⸱⸱., medicine, 200
⸱⸱., cited, 174; library,
⸱⸱; personality, 291
⸱⸱osmography*, Heylin, 168
Cotterell, Ch., 171
Cotton, E., Royal Society, 178
Cotton MSS., 140; library, 165
Courthope: *Hist. of English Poetry*, 232
Coward, Ch., music, 224
Cowley, A., 126, 131, 226, 266
Cox, L., rhetoric, 7
Craddick(-ock), W., sermon-dedication, 129
Cranmer, cited, 229
Cranwell, L., medicine, 198
Crashaw, R., cited, 111; ancient languages, 162; modern languages, 170; drawing, 218;

poetry, 225, 226, 229; epitaphs, 298; at Little Gidding, 246

Crawford, B. V.: *Questions and Objections*, 311

Creese (Creesh), Th., personality, 291

Creighton, R., cited, 24; popularity, 31; preaching, 40; delivery, 53, 57, 61; translations, 171; music, 221; court chaplain, 271

Crellius, 121

Cressey, Serenus de, antiquities, 139; on Earle, 288

Crew, N., chemistry, 154; music, 224

Cristina of Sweden, 179

Crofton, Z., his sermon advertised, 123; sermon-dedication, 135

Crofts, H., on Greatrakes, 200

Cromwell, Frances, 268

——, Henry, 102

——, Oliver, 30, 33, 40, 48, 58, 102, 114, 132, 164, 206, 220

Crosby, Th.: *Hist. of the English Baptists, The*, 67, 177, 229, 258, 268, 280

Crown and Glory of Christianity, The, Brooks, 128

Crowther, J., disputations, 10

Cruelty of the Spaniards, The, D'Avenant, 220

Crying Sin of England, The, Moore, 39

Cudworth, R., Hebrew, 163; teaching, 207

Cumberland, R., medicine, 201; math., 192; projected marriage, 192

Curriculum of English Schools in the 17th Century, The, Watson, 4, 5, 6, 7

Cyprianus Anglicus, Heylin, 100

Dalston, Sir George, 104

Danger of Greatness, The, Whitaker, 328

Davenant, E., memory, 76; library, 181; math., 192; his

daughters, 209; appearance, 300

D'Avenant, Sir Wm., 82, 121, 127, 220, 239, 273

Davies, J., Welsh, 167

Davila: *Hist. of the Civil Wars in France*, 171, 185

Davis, Anne, 131

——, Wm., farming, 257

Death's Alarum, Hardy, 99

Deaths Alarum, Whitefoote, 230

Death and the Grave, Spurstow, 94

De Coverley, Sir Roger, 205

Defence of Humane Learning in the Ministry, Thurman, 174

Degge, Sir Simon, 156

Delights of the Muses, Crashaw, 225

Dell, Wm., on education, 16, 17; on languages, 82

Demurrer, A Short, Prynne, 141

Denton, J., preaching, 97

De Quatuor Linguis Commentationis, Casaubon, 165

Description of the Use of the Carpenter's Rule, Newton, 193

D'Ewes, Sir Simonds, 9, 15, 76, 180, 228, 274, 296

Dialogues sur l'Eloquence, Fénelon, 34, 71, 75, 117

Dickinson, Chris., payment, 279

Dict. of the Booksellers and Printers, Plomer, 93

Dictionarium Brit.-Lat., Davies, 169

Dictionarium Saxonico-Lat.-Ang., Somner, 166

Didsbury, Mr., preacher, 23

Digby, 228

——, George and Kenelm: *Letters*, 311

Dircks, H.: *A Biog. Memoir of Hartlib*, 181

Discovery of a New World, A, Wilkins, 193

Discourse Concerning Prayer, A, Wilkins, 115

Discourse Concerning the Span-

ish Monarchy, A, Campanella,
170
*Discourse of Artificial Beauty,
A,* Gauden (?), 243
*Discourse of the Freedom of the
Will, A,* Sterry, 219, 223
*Discourse Made by the Bishop
of Rochester, A,* Sprat, 117
*Discourse on the Nature of
Friendship, A,* Taylor, 246
D'Israeli, I.: *Quarrels of Au-
thors,* 292
*Dissenting Academies in Eng-
land,* Parker, 322
Divine Arithmetic, Patrick, 99,
184
Dod, J., memory, 68; Hebrew,
159; love of flowers, 252
———, T., preaching, 36
Dolben, J., Thanksgiving Ser-
mon, 90
Donne, J., cited, 48; funeral
sermon by him, 107; sermon
copyright, 122; on painting
the face, 244; on fishing, 259
———, J. (the younger), 122
Downing, C., delivery, 61
Dowsing, Wm.: *Journal,* 312
Drope, F., horticulture, 254
Dry Rod Blooming, A, Hughes,
121, 122
Dryden, 60, 113, 126, 131, 137,
226, 227, 229, 245
DuBartas, cited, 186
Ducke, Mrs. Margaret, 99
Due Correction for Mr. Hobbes,
Wallis, 189
*Due Way of Composing the
Differences, The,* Thorndike,
41
Dugard, Th., poetry, 135
———, Wm., *Elementa Rhe-
torices,* 6
Duncon, J.: *Lady Falkland,*
271
Duport, Jas., examiner, 8;
Greek, 162; learning, 176;
popularity, 207
Duppa, B., tutor to Prince
Charles, 207; payment, 277

Durant, N., good birth, 261
Dury, J., librarian, 181

Eachard, J., sermon advertising,
123; on the position of the
clergy, 263, 266, 267; *Char-
acter*-writing, 285
Earle, J., cited, 24; popularity,
30, 288; Characters, 243, 282,
283; on universities, 265; per-
sonality, 288
Easter: Pell, 190
*Easy and Compendious History,
An,* Prideaux, M., 142
Ebenezer, Owen, 132
Ecles, N., preaching, 36
Ecclesiastes, Wilkins, 43, 45, 75,
86, 112
Edge, Th., cited, 38
Education, On, Milton, 162
Educational Charters, Leach,
4, 8
Edward VI, 71, 182, 189
Edwards, Th., controversy, 83;
on tolerance, 124; quoted, 273
Eighteen Sermons, Allestree, 305
Eighteen Sermons, Usher, 11,
179, 249
Eikon Basilike, 290
Elborough, R., plague sermon,
90; criticized by Pepys, 273
Elderfield, Chris., law, 155;
chaplain to Sir Wm. Goring,
155
Elementa Rhetorices, Vossius,
G. J., 6
Elford, Th., payment, 279
Elian: *Hist. of Animals,* 4
Eli Trembling before the Ark,
Calamy, 123
Elizabeth, Queen, 182
Ellis, Th., Welsh, 139
———, Wm., music, 224
Eloquentia Bipartita, Strada,
111
Elsynge, H., 118
Elyot, Sir Thomas, 10
Emblems, Divine and Moral,
Quarles, 219
Enderby, P., 139

English American, The, Gage, 243

English Gentleman, The, Braithwaite, 28

English Grammar Schools, The, Watson, 7, 65, 77, 158, 212, 220

English Printing, Plomer, 165

Enoch's Walk and Change, Jacombe, 99, 117, 205

Erasmus, comparison of preachers and actors, 63; on mannerisms, 64

Erminia, Flecknoe, 215

Essay concerning Preaching, An, Glanvill, 42, 46, 71, 75, 277

Essay on Dramatic Poetry, An, Dryden, 229

Essay toward a Real Character, An, Wilkins, 164, 167, 172, 254

Essays Ecclesiastical and Civil, Whitlocke, 181

Essays on Philosophy and Religion, Glanvill, 49, 82

Essex, Earl of, 102, 267

Etherege, Sir George, 126, 127

Evan, astrology, 147

Evelyn, 8, 10, 14, 24, 30, 54, 59, 61, 81, 102, 107, 126, 152, 161, 163, 172, 178, 180, 183, 192, 214, 218, 224, 249, 250, 274

Exact Collection of Farewell Sermons, An, 50, 92, 187

Examen Examinis, Th. Hall, 315

Exercitatio de motu cordis et sanguinis, Harvey, 194

Exhibiting the Doctrine of the Sphere, Newton, 193

Eyre, Adam: *Diurnall,* 22, 23, 116, 279

Fairclough, R., popularity, 31
——, S., memory, 68; antiquities, 139; poetry, 231; good birth, 262; personality, 298

Fairfax, J., delivery, 50; payment, 277

Fairfax, Lord, 37, 132, 234

Falkland, Lady Lettice, 271
—— Lord, 234, 246

Fanshawe, Lady: *Memoirs,* 98, 270, 271
——, Sir Richard, 270, 271, 282

Farnaby, Th.; *Index Rhetoricus,* 5, 6; teacher, 204

Farrington(don), A., aided by Hales, 182

Featley, D., disputant, 13; funeral sermon for him, 98; quoted, 111; learning, 176; preface by him, 215; appearance, 98, 300; quoted, 304

Fell, J., examiner, 8; executive, 10; delivery, 54; on Hammond, 67, 176, 298; collector of MSS., 140, 148; poetry, 229, 236; court chaplain, 271; controversies, 290, 292; personality, 292; appearance, 301

Feltham, O., 38, 63

Feminine Monarchie, The, Butler, 223

Fénelon, on popularity preachers, 34; on mannerisms, 59; on texts, 71; sermon-divisions, 75; sermon-borrowing, 117

Fermat, Pierre de, 189

Fermentum Pharisaeorum, Tombes, 120

Ferne, H., orientals, 164

Ferrar, N., paying churchgoers, 29; medicine, 201; on romances, 241; death, 246

Ferriby, J., sermon advertising, 123

Few Sighs from Hell, A, Bunyan, 74, 236

Firmin, G., medicine, 198

First Century of Scandalous, Malignant Priests, White, 41, 83

Fish, R., delivery, 54

Fisher, E., controversy, ix

Five Hundred Years of Chaucer Allusion, Spurgeon, 244

Five Sermons, Wright, 18, 233
Flavel, J., poetry. 236
Fléchier, E., preacher, 48; funeral sermons, 95
Flec(k)noe, R., *Character*-writing, 117; drama, 215; poetry, 227; private chaplain, 268
Fleming, D., 260
Flemings at Oxford, The, 12, 173, 250, 260
Fletcher, G., at Little Gidding, 246
——, P., drama, 215, 304; fishing, 259
Floating Island, The, Strode, 217
Flood, Wm., medicine, 198
Floyd, Mr., memory, 68
Forgotten Poet, A, Martin, 321
Formulae Oratoriae, Clarke, 7
Fowler, Chris., mannerisms, 58; chronology, 142
Fox, George, cited, vii; on education, 17; preaching, 114; medicine, 195; in a garden, 252; payment, 276; on retribution, 295
Fox, John: *Book of Martyrs*, 185
Fragmenta de Rebus Britannicis, Davies, 168
Frampton, R., popularity, 32; delivery, 50
Frankland, Th., medicine, 197
Free Grace Exalted, Sterry, 325
Freeman, J., sermon-title, 120
Fry, J., mannerisms, 55, 59, 64; payment, 96
Full Relation of Two Journies, A, Heylin, 243
Fuller, Th., cited, 26; popularity, 29; memory, 66; quoted, 111; learning, 178; read Chaucer, 244, 245; flowers, 253; birds, 255, 256; personality, 288; controversies, 73, 168, 290; poetry, 135, 298; recreation, 248; payment, 275; *Abel Redivivus*, 34; *Church

Hist., 35, 41, 100, 130, 131, 208, 252, 291, 304; *Hist. of the Univ. of Cambridge*, 161, 203, 260, 279; *Holy and Profane State*, 53, 66, 115, 135, 138, 149, 163, 188, 205, 210, 143, 275; *Romances*, 239, 242; *Worthies*, 32, 56, 96, 146, 172, 219, 221, 227, 277, 289, 297; *Character*-writing 243, 284; dedications, 130-131; essay-sermons, 88; prefaces, 111, 135
Fuller, Wm., law, 155; linguist, 159; *Polyglot Bible*, 163; teacher, 204; personality, 288
Fulman, Wm., antiquities, 139; chronology, 142
Funebria, Florae, Th. Hall, 215
Funeral Sermons by Eminent Eng. Divines, 282

Gage, Th., travels, 243
Gammer Gurton's Needle, 208
Gangraena, Edwards, 124, 273
Gardiner, cited, 229
——, S. R., *Hist. of the Commonwealth and Protectorate*, 30
Garthwaite, T., 123
Gataker, Ch., personality, 292
——, Th., astrology, 147, 148; orientals, 159; learning, 179; math., 192; funeral sermon for him, 205; payment, 277; cited, 149, 205, 299
Gauden, J., funeral sermon for Brownrig, 81, 98; for Rich, 84, 85, 94, 99, 105, 120; on painting the face, 244; private chaplain, 269; payment, 277; personality, 294; cited, 84, 147
Geastly, Mr., private chaplain, 270
Gell, R., astrology, 149
Genest, J., 60
Gentleman's Calling, The, 264

Genuines Remaines of Samuel Butler (*see* Butler, S.)

Genuine Remaines of Th. Barlow, The, 42

Geog. Description, A, Clark, *q. v.*

George, Mr., printed sermons, 119

Geree, J., astrology, 148

Gesner's Library, 4

Getsius, J. D., teacher, 200

Gibbons, E., music, 224

Gilbert, Th., learning, 175

Gill, Alex., cited, 204; whipped his pupils 212; subject of a ballad, 224

——, —— (the younger), teacher, 207; personality, 292

Gilpin, R., delivery, 51, 56; memory, 66; sermon structure, 71-72; medicine, 198; appearance, 301

Glanvill, J., on knowledge, 15; on religion, 26, 28; on preaching, 42, 46, 49; sermon structure, 71, 75, 82; on science, 251; payment, 277

Goad, J., math., 192

Goddard, G., *Journal,* 113

——, J., 178

——, R., funeral sermon for him, 133

God's Anger, Man's Comfort, Adams, 133

God's Doings, and Man's Duty, Peters, 61

Gods Fury, Englands Fire, Benbrigge, 306

Godwin, Th., teacher, 207

Gondibert, D'Avenant, 82, 121, 239, 273

Gonlartius, 4

Goring, Sir Wm., 155

Gouge, Th., paying churchgoers, 29; Welsh, 167

Gough, Wm., student moderator, 10; disputant, 12; sermon structure, 100; hard student, 177; good birth, 262; payment,

280; funeral sermon for him, 99; cited, 299

Grace Abounding, Bunyan, 34, 115

Grace, Love, 34, 74

Grammatica Arabica, Lamb, 160

Grammatica Lingua Anglicanae, Wallis, 167

Grand Cyrus, Le, 241

Graves, T. S.: *Puritanism and the Stage,* 215

Great Abnormals, Hyslop, 200

Greatrakes, V., 200

Greaves, J., 183, 191, 254

——, Th., Arabic, 51, 160; delivery, 51-52; *Polyglot Bible,* 164; math., 192

Greene, J., sermon-dedication, 129; appearance, 301

Gregory of Nyssa, 94

——, J., ancient languages, 159; modern languages, 170; learning, 174; hard student, 176; math., 192; good birth, 296

Greisley, H., poetry, 236

Grim the Collier, 208

Grounds of the Contempt of the Clergy, Eachard, 263, 266

Grotius, 121

Grundy, Th., math., 192

Guillim, J., 145

Gunning, P., preaching, 24; cited, 294

Gutch, J.: *Collectanea Curiosa,* 140

Hacket, J., cited, 24, 35, 170; quoted Chaucer, 245; quoted Jonson, 245

Hales, J., essay-sermon, 87; on funeral sermons, 97; sermon copyright, 122; learning, 179; generosity, 182; on book-borrowers, 186; tutor, 207; poet, 228; on Shakespeare, 245; at Great Tew, 246; of the Tribe of Ben, 246; personality, 288; appearance, 301

Halkett, Lady: *Journal,* 270

Hall, E., mannerism, 58

———, F. (*see* Linus, Franciscus)

———, G., sermon on the plague, 90

———, John, 12, 17, 154

———, Jos., imitated, 19; memory, 66; ques. and ans., 73; funeral sermon for him, 99, 230; heraldry, 145; math., 192; recreation, 224; read Chaucer, 244-245; Romance, 240; good birth, 261; *Character*-writing, 282-283

———, Th., on disputations, 13; Natural History, 84; sermon-help, 110; on astrology, 149; translations, 171; on learning, 174; drama, 215; on gentility in the Bible, 262; on educated clergy, 264; *Character*-writing, 285

Halliwell, J. O.: *Books of Characters,* 316

Halsey, J., good birth, 262

Hammond, H., disputations, 10; memory, 67; sermon structure, 75; hard student, 176; math., 188; personality, 298

Happiness of those who Sleep in Jesus, The, Calamy, 76

Hard Way to Heaven, The, Crofton, 135

Hardy, N., Natural History, 84; *conceit,* 85; November-fifth sermon, 89; London Fire sermon, 89, 242; a wedding sermon, 91; funeral sermon for him, 94, 106, 126; funeral sermon for Adams, 96, 99, 161; for Hewett, 124; sermon dedications, 132, 133; use of description, 242; court chaplain, 271

Harley, Lady Brilliana: *Letters,* 22

Harmar, J., Greek, 158; translations, 171; philologist, 172; appearance, 180; poetry, 236

Harrington, *Oceana,* 265

Harris, R., funeral sermon for Sir Thomas Lucy, 62, 165; sermon-dedication, 165; recreation, 248

Harrison, Chris., music, 224

———, Th., popularity, 33; memory, 67

Hartlib, S., 181

Harvey, Wm., 188, 194, 202

Haslitt, W. C.: *Schools and School-books,* 317

Hatton, Sir Chris., 252

Hatton Correspondence, The, 200, 291

Hawes, R., funeral sermon for him, 97

Hearne, Th.: *Reliquae Hearnae,* 14, 140, 141, 144, 163, 177, 223, 255, 300

Hearse of the Renowned, The, Vines, 267

Heath, R., orientals, 160; *Polyglot Bible,* 164

Help to English Hist., A., Heylin, 139

Henry VIII, 3, 71, 182, 208

Herbal of Divinity, The, Simpson, 73

Herbert of Cherbury, 107

———, Geo., law, 155; poetry, 176; *Character*-writing, 283; on mirth, 176

———, Th., poetry, 279

Herle, Ch., controversy, 290

Herrick, R., poetry, 225, 226, 229; at Little Gidding, 246; nature similes, 252; verse epitaphs, 298

Herring, Mr., hard student, 77

Hesperides, Herrick, 225

Hewett, J., funeral sermon for him, 123, 124; good birth, 297

Heylin, P., controversy, ix, 73, 164, 290; preaching, 24; memory, 67; ques. and ans., 73; on Laud, 100; antiquities,

139; heraldry, 145; on Hebrew, 164; Welsh, 168; drama, 215; poetry, 236; travelrecords, 243

Heyrick, R., sermon title, 317

Heywood, Wm., teacher, 208

Hickes, Gaspar, payment, 275
———, George, Anglo-Saxon, 166

Hierow, S., preaching, 35

Hildersham, A., on popularity, 34; serial sermons, 36; sermon-help, 112; marginal notes, 122; sermon-dedication, 127
———, S., good birth, 262

Hill, A., on poetry, 228
———, Th., law, 156

Hinde, J., on Laud, 100

Hindle, Chris., Hebrew, 162

Historical Collections, Rushworth, 30, 42, 93, 213

Historical Notices, Wellington, 98, 281

History of Cambria, Powell, 162

History of Cambridge (Univ. of), (*see* Fuller)

History of Civilization, Buckle, 295

History of the Commonwealth and Protectorate, Gardiner, 30

History of the Creation, Walker, 37

History of the Progress of Anglo-Saxon Lit. in England, Petheram, 166, 167

History of the Rebellion, Clarendon, *q. v.*

History of Sir Francis Drake, The, D'Avenant, 220

Histrio-Mastix, Th. Hall, 315

Histrio-Mastix, Prynne, 63, 64

Hobbes, Th., 7, 16, 64, 73, 189, 290, 292

Hodder, J., good birth, 262

Hodges, A., personality, 288

Holder, Wm., cited, 189; medicine, 200; taught the deaf and

dumb, 208; painting, 218; music, 221

Holdsworth, J., medicine, 199
———, R., popularity, 33; cited, 77; sermon-help, 112; on sermon-borrowing, 117; sermon title, 120; payment, 260

Holland, Th., good birth, 262

Holles (Denzil), Lord: *Memoirs,* 317

Holy and Profane State, The, Fuller, *q. v.*

Holyday, B., sermon-dedication, 132; drama, 216; poetry, 231, 236; translations, 216

Holy Dedication, Jacombe, 78, 80, 90

Holyoake, Th., medicine, 195

Hooke, R., 189

Hooker, R., cited, 103, 185, 229, 291

Hoole, C., rhetoric, 4, 5, 8; sermon notes, 65, 76; Hebrew, 158; text-book, 213; on poetry, 228

Hope and Fear, Hardy, 91

Horace, 6, 68, 216

Horne, T., rhetoric, 6

Horolog. Geometrica, Oughtred, 188

Hotham, Ch., astrology, 147; chemistry, 152

Houblon, J., Hebrew, 162; modern lang., 170

Houblon Family, The, 162, 170

House of Feasting, The, Taylor, 82, 87

House of Mourning, The, 107, 258

Howe, J., memory, 67; on funeral sermons, 94; preaching, 114; on Bates, 286

Howell, Jas., *Letters,* 242
———, Th., personality, 297

Hoyle, J., preaching, 27; sermon title, 124; personality, 37, 180

Hudibras, Butler, *q. v.*

Hughes, J., expanded sermons, 121, 122
——, S., delivery, 56; Welsh, 167
Hull, E.: *Text-book of Irish Lit., A,* 169
Hulse, E., medicine, 195
Humane Industry, Powell, 252
Humble Apologie, An, Water-house, 116
Humble Motion to the Parl., An., Hall, 13, 17, 154
Husbandmans Calling, The, Steele, 91
Hussey, Wm.: *A Plea for Christian Majestracie,* 318
Hutchinson, Lucy: *Memoirs,* 65, 76, 295
Hutton, M., music, 224
——, W. H.: *Hist. of the Eng. Church,* 246
Huygens, Mr., mechanics, 251
Hyde, Th., orientals, 160; *Polyglot Bible,* 164; on Creighton, 171; math., 192
Hyslop, T. B.: *The Great Abnormals,* 200

Ichabod, Anon., 43, 59, 160, 173, 174
Impresse of God, Hall, 145
Indago Astroloica, Childrey, 148
Index rhetoricus et orat., Farnaby, 6
Ingelo, N., astrology, 150; music, 224; Romance, 240
Inglet, R., medicine, 199
Inner Life of the Religious Soc. of the Commonwealth, The, Barclay, 276
In Praise of Folly, Erasmus, 63
Ireland, The Hist. of, Keating, 169
Ireton, H., 102
Irish Lit., A Text-book of, Hull, 169
Iter Boreale, Wild, 238
Itinerary thro Italy in 1646 and 1647, Bargrave, 243

Jackson, H., preaching, 24; collector of MSS. of Abélard, 140
Jacombe, S., funeral sermon for him, 99; his love of books, 184
——, Th., on literary style in sermons, 78, 80, 90; cited, 92; funeral sermon for Vines, 99, 119, 229; on teaching, 204
Janeway, J., math., 192
Jeanes, H., personality, 288, 290
Jeffreys, Judge, 262
Jehojadahs Justice, Hoyle, 124
Jenkyns, Sir Leolin, 267
——, Wm., funeral sermon for Gouge, 10; November-fifth sermon, 89; printed sermons, 92; poetry, 135; on Gouge's learning, 177; good birth, 262
Jephcot, J., math., 192
Jerome, on funeral sermons, 94; Hebrew, 163; astrology, 151; cited, 301
Jessey, H., memory, 67; orientals, 159; hard student, 177; library, 186; medicine, 199
Jewel, J., cited, 103
Jobson, Cirques, 181
Johnson, J., preaching, 22; Egyptian hieroglyphics, 159
——, Samuel, 79, 86
Jones, R., poetry, 236
Jonson, Ben, 245, 246
Jordan, Mr., preaching, 97
Joseph, Th., farming, 258
Josephus, 151
Josselin, R., church attendance, 23; payment, 97, 184; on playing chess, 249; on roses, 253; farming, 258; on Owen, 303
Joy Out-Joyed, Caryl, 309
Joynes, J.: *Christening Sermon,* 319
Judgment and Decree of the Univ. of Oxford, The, 89
Junius, Francis, 165, 177

Jusserand, J. J.: *A Lit. Hist. of the English People*, 282

Justice Triumphing, Hardy, 84, 124

Juxton, Wm., preaching, 32; on Charles I, 160; law, 155; *Polyglot Bible,* 163; enjoyed walking, 252; good birth, 261; personality, 289, 297

Keating, Geof., Irish antiquities and language, 169

Keene, S., funeral sermons, 98

Ken, Th., music, 224; poetry, 235, 236

Kennett, White: *Register,* 96, 171, 200

Kettle, R., teacher, 208, 209; executive, 210; singing, 221; appearance, 301

Killigrew, H., drama, 216

———, Th., 60

King, H., sermon copyright, 122; poetry, 227; preaching, 273; payment, 277

———, M., Irish language, 168

———, P., old Eng. literature, 140; poetry, 237

King Solomon's Directory, Riddington, 121

Kirby, J., poetry, 237

———, Joshua, Bible illustrations, 81

Knight, J., delivery, 52

Knott, E., controversy, ix

Krapp, G. P.: *The Rise of English Literary Prose,* 5

La Bruyère, 283

La Calprenède, 241

Lady Errant, The, Cartwright, 215

La Fontaine, 241, 242

Lamb, Jas., Arabic, 160

———, Ph., payment, 280

Lamentation, Mourning and Woe, Hardy, 89, 242

Langbaine, Ger., antiquities, 140; chronology, 141; read Chaucer, 244

Langley, J., antiquary, 140; coins, 144; teacher, 204, 209

Latimer, H., his boldness imitated, 40; one of his texts, 71; characteristic language, 78, 91

Laud, Wm., cited, 48; controversy, ix; last sermon, 100; coins, 144; his horoscope, 148; Arabic, 160; cited, 180, 229; library, 182, 183; math., 192; appearance, 301

Lauderdale, Earl of, 300

Launce, Mr., quoted, 186

Lawes, H., 217, 232

Lawful Preacher, The, Ferriby, sermon advertising, 123

Leach, A. F.: *Ed. Charters,* 4, 8

Lee, S., antiquary, 140; astrology, 147; medicine, 199

Legend of Captain Jones, The, Lloyd, 241

Leighton, R., personality, 289

Lemon, R.: *Collection of Printed Broadsides,* 273

Leo, Wm., funeral sermon for Featley, 98; on the short statue of the clergy, 300

L'Estrange, R., 21, 125, 131, 256, 284

Letsome, S.: *The Preacher's Assistant,* 320

Lever, H., good birth, 262

Leviathan, Hobbes, 16, 189

Lewes, Mr., delivery, 54

Lex Ignea, Sancroft, 90

Ley, J.: *A Monitor of Mortalitie,* 106

Life of Alleine, Baxter, 36

Life of Wm. Bedell, Burnet, 169

Life and Death of David, The, Hickes, 275

Life of Faith, The, Baxter, 72, 306

Life of Dr. Hammond, Fell, 10, 67, 176

Life of Henry More, 252

Life of John Shaw, 32, 40, 72, 278

Lightfoot, J., orientals, 160; cited, 206

Likeliest Means to Remove Hirelings out of the Church, Milton, 276

Lilly, Wm., 17, 18, 27, 37, 147, 148, 149, 160, 192, 249

Lily, Wm., 4, 212

Lines (Linus), Francis (Hall), math., 193; opticks, 251

Linguae Latinae Liber, Littleton, 173

Littleton, A., chronology, 142; philology, 172; poetry, 237; on romances, 241

Lives of Eminent Men, Wordsworth, 329

Lives of Sundry Eminent Persons, Clarke, *q. v.*

Llewellyn (Lluelyn), M., medicine, 109; poetry, 237

Lloyd, D., poetry, 237; narrative, 240

———, D. (the younger): *Memoirs,* 9, 13, 14, 32, 56, 62, 66, 67, 68, 96, 113, 139, 142, 156, 159, 165, 170, 174, 177, 181, 182, 186, 191, 192, 204, 207, 208, 209, 210, 211, 218, 224, 226, 237, 248, 249, 261, 279, 284, 286, 288, 289, 297, 300

———, Wm., chronology, 140, 142; Greek, 158

Lomax, J., memory, 68; learning, 174; medicine, 198

London's Calamity, Elborough, 90

London and the Country Carbonaded, Lupton, 268

Long, R., retribution, 294

Love, Chris., on religion, 26; on popularity, 34; sermon-wording, 74; funeral sermon for him, 102, 103; his published sermons, 133, 185

Love's Dominion, Flecknoe, 215

Lucas, Sir Henry, 189

Lucy, Sir Thomas, 106

———, ——— (the younger), 62, 105, 106

Ludlow, E.: *Memoirs,* 32, 243, 265, 271

Ludus Literarius, Brinsley, 3, 65, 76, 238

Lupton, D.: *London, etc.,* 268

Luther, Martin: *Thirtie Foure Sermons,* 112

Lydgate (Lydiat), Th., preaching, 37; delivery, 67; love of books, 187

Lye (Leigh), Th., cited, 92; teacher, 213

Lyly, John, 4

Lynch, S., payment, 277

Lyte, H. C. M.: *A Hist. of Eton College,* 300

Macham (im), J., medicine, 195

Maggot, Th., court chaplain, 271

Magia Adamica, Vaughan, 153

Maillard, O., delivery, 56

Mainwaring, R., delivery, 8; memory, 67

Malthurst, Mr., delivery, 52

Manassah ben Israel, languages, 159; medicine, 196

Manners, Lady Frances, 131

Man of Honour, The, Cheynell, 4, 40

Manship, J., medicine, 199

Manton, Th., cited, 24, 92, 113; popularity, 31; preaching, 32; funeral sermon for Love, 102; thanked by Commons for sermon, 118; sermon-dedication, 129; King's chaplain, 271; appearance, 302

Manuductio ad artem rhetoricam, Vicar, 6

Mariott, 122

Marriage of the Arts, The,
    Holyday, 216
Marrow of Ecclesiastical Hist.,
    The, Clarke, q. v.
Marsh, N., orientals, 160; Irish,
    169; bought Stillingfleet's li-
    brary, 183; music, 224
——, S., teacher, 209, 210
Marshall, Stephen, delivery, 60;
    marginal notes, 122; sermon-
    dedication, 129; on chem-
    istry, 153; Welsh, 167; per-
    sonality, 297; cited, 299
——, Th., Anglo-Saxon, 165
——, Wm., medicine, 199
Martin, E., library, 181
Martindale, A., math., 193
Martyrology, A General, Clarke,
    q. v.
Martyrs, A Book of, Fox, 185
Marvell, A., 285, 296
Mary, Queen, 182
Mason, H., delivery, 62
Masson, D.: Life of Milton, 122,
    160, 174, 196, 225
Master, Th., Latin poetry, 237
Mathematical Magic, Wilkins,
    250
Mathematics, A Hist. of, Cajori,
    188, 189
Mathematics, A Hist, of the
    Study of (at Cambridge),
    Ball, 188
Matthews, E., medicine, 199
Maxon, G., poetry, 237
May(i)ne, Jasper, cited, 19;
    translations, 171; drama, 216;
    court chaplain, 271; his cu-
    rate's salary, 278; personal-
    ity, 292
Mayor, J. E. B.: Nicholas Fer-
    rar, 29
Meade, Jos., teacher, 204
——, R., poetry, 237
Mediaeval Preachers, Neale, 71,
    259
Meggott, R., cited, 24, 273;
    funeral sermon for Hardy, 94,
    106; sermon-dedication, 125

Memento, A., L'Estrange, 21
Memorials, etc., Cary, 30, 58,
    76, 271
Mercury, Wilkins, 77
Mercy in her Beauty, Hardy,
    316
Microcosmographie, Earle, 283
Militius of Antioch, 94
Mills, D., Pepys's judgment of
    him, 79, 271, 272, 273
Milton, 12, 44, 73, 122, 124, 137,
    162, 194, 207, 263, 273, 275
Minnis, Sir John, 232
Mirrour for Saints and Sin-
    ners, A, Clarke, q. v.
Mollerus, J.: Allegoria pro-
    fano-sacra, etc., 110
Monitor of Mortalitie, A, Ley,
    106
Monk, George (Albermarle,
    Duke of), 39, 102, 128, 188,
    197
Monmouth, Geoffrey of, 140
Moore, E., law, 156
——, J., sermon on inclosures,
    39
More, H., ques. and ans., 73;
    controversy, 148; cited, 206;
    music, 221; poetry, 226;
    nature references, 252
——, Sir Jonas, 210
Morehouse, L., math., 193; pay-
    ment, 277
Moreland, M., terrae filius, 14
Moreton (Morton), C., math.,
    193
——, R., medicine, 199
Morley, Geo., preaching, 89;
    personality, 294; payment,
    277; laughed at, 274
Morton, J., cited, 229
——, Th., good birth, 261
Morus, A., delivery, 61
Mossum, R., delivery, 61
Moston, A., personality, 293
Motives to a Good Life, Holy-
    day, 317
Mountford, Jas., preaching, 41
Mullimger: Cambridge Char-

acteristics in the 17th Cent.,
29, 162, 207
Murray, J. O.: Serial Preach-
ing, 91
Murrey, Sir Robert, 201
Musarum Deliciae, 232
Music, A Hist. of, Burney, 200,
219, 220, 222
Mysterie of Rhetorique Un-
veil'd, The, Smith, 5, 7
Mystical Implantation, Of,
Brinsley, 122

Nalten, Jas., delivery, 56
Nason, A.: James Shirley,
Dramatist, 216
Naturall Mans Case Stated,
The, Love, 134
Neal, D.: Hist. of the Puritans,
96, 124, 159, 184, 199, 212
———, Sir Patrick, 250
Neale, J. M.: Mediaeval Preach-
ers, 71, 259
Nelson, R.: Life of Geo. Bull,
50, 66, 156, 192, 248, 291, 292
Newcastle, Duchess of, 69, 153,
171, 207, 227
———, Duke of, 153, 207
Newcome, H., on preaching,
23; serial sermons, 37; on the
farewell sermons, 92; on a
borrowed sermon, 115; chro-
nology, 142; Welsh, 168;
learning and personality, 175;
love of books, 184, 185; drama,
216; recreations, 247; tobacco,
248
Newcomes, M., funeral sermon
for Collins, 106
New Constellation, A, Bonhame, 81
New Discovery of the Art of
Teaching School, A, Hoole, 4,
76, 228
Newton, Lady Elizabeth, 131
———, Geo., good birth, 262
———, Isaac, 189
———, J., math., 193; text-
book, 213

Nicholas Ferrar, Carter, 246
Nichols, Mr., private chaplain,
270
Nicholl, F., preaching with
notes, 67
Nicholl's Literary Anecdotes,
206
Nicholls, P., payment, 280
Northam, R., delivery, 54
Nosegay of Rank-smelling
Flowers, A, Ricraft, 83
Notes and Queries, 225, 292
Nourse, T., coins, 144
Nye, Ph., imitated, 274; his
beard, 302

Oatus, Titus, 212
Of an Ague, Streater, 197
Ogden, S., chemistry, 152;
Greek, 158; orientals, 160;
math., 193; botany, 201;
music, 224; poetry, 237
Ogle, L., preaching, 79
Okley, Wm., payment for fu-
neral sermon, 97
Oldershaw, S., medicine, 199
Oldfield, J., math., 193; me-
chanics, 252
O'Mahony, J., 169
On Praying in the Spirit, Bun-
yan, 268
On the Serpent and the Dove,
Holyday, 132
On the Quadrant, Pell, 190
One Hund. and Eight Lect.
upon the Fourth of John,
Hildersham, 34, 37, 112, 122,
127
One Hund. and forty-five Sers.
upon the 17th chap. of John,
Burgess, 36
Oraisons Funèbres de Bossuet,
95-96
Original Records of Early Non-
conformity, Turner, 203
Origines Sacrae, Stillingfleet,
127, 166
Orinda, The Matchless, 76, 226,
246

sermon for Lady Anne Clifford, 114
Raleigh, Sir Walter, 162
Ralphson, Mr., popularity, 31
Rastick, J., coins, 144
Ravis, C., orientals, 160
Ray (Wray), J., botany, 254; ornithology, 255
Real Character, A, Wilkins, 164
Real Comforts, Howe, 94
Reconciler of the Bible, The, Thaddeus, 111
Record of the Royal Society, The, 178
Reeve, R., teacher, 204
——, Th., sermon title, 124; sermon-dedication, 128
Reformation and Desolation, Marshall, 153
Reformed Librarie-Keeper, The, Dury, 181
Reformed Pastor, The, Baxter, 46, 159, 264
Register, Eccles., and Civil, Kennett, 96, 171, 200
Register of the Visitors of the Univ. of Oxford, Burrows, 14, 265
Rehearsal, The, Buckingham, 216
Religious Refugees and Eng. Education, Watson, 179
Reliquae Hearnae, see Hearne, Th.
Resbury, R., medicine, 198
Resolves, Feltham, 64
Retrospective Review, 282
Reynell, Sir Th., 142
Reyner, J., Arabic, 160
——, R., medicine, 199
Reynolds, E., cited, 24; delivery, 53; sermon before East India Company, 93; before Parliament, 54; funeral sermon for Langley, 140, 174, 204; conformed, 257; court chaplain, 271; criticized by Baxter, 294

Reynolds, J., medicine, 198; disputation, 291, 292
——, Sir Joshua, 79
——, Wm., personality, 291-292
Rhetorica Sacra, Hall, 110
Rich, Jer.: *Charactery,* 77
——, Robert, 84, 85, 94, 99, 105, 120
Richardson, J., law, 155
Richmond, James Duke of, 130
Ricraft, J., sermon title, 83
Riddington, F., expanded sermon, 121
Ridley, cited, 229
Righteous Man's Weal, Watson, 92
Roberts, M., payment, 281
——, T., Hebrew, 162
Robinson, M., disputations, 10; paying churchgoers, 29; preaching when ill, 35; cited, 50; sermon structure, 72, 75; sermon length, 113; law, 156; Hebrew, 158; hard student, 176; medicine, 201; poetry, 237; hunting, 252; on the clergy, 264; *Character*-writing, 285
Rob-Roy, 145
Rochester, Earl of, 286
Roe, Sir Th., 131
Rollins: *Cavalier and Puritan,* 279; *English Commonwealth Drama,* 214
Rooke, L., 178
Rosicrucian, 85, 153, 154
Rous, J.: *Diary,* 280
Rowe, J., Greek, 158
Rowland, E., teaching, 211
——, Wm., medicine, 196; poetry, 237; personality, 289
Royal Common-Wealth Man, The, Hardy, 99, 161
Royal Slave, The, Cartwright, 215, 218
Royal Society, The Hist. of the, Sprat, 292
Rule, G., medicine, 196, 199

Rushworth: *Historical Coll.*, 30, 42, 93, 213
Russell, G. F. R.: *Mem. of Richard Busby*, 206
Rust, Geo., funeral sermon for Taylor, 104
Ryves, B., *Polyglot Bible*, 163

Sadler, J., personality, 296
Safest Convoy, The, Hardy, 93
Saintsbury: *Hist. of Eliz. Lit.*, 201
Saints Solemne Covenant, The, Brinsley, 73
Saints Triumph over Death, The, Manton, 102
Salmon, Th., music, 222
Saltmarsh, J., sermon title, 83
Samos, Archbishop of, 158
Sampson, H., medicine, 199
Samuel, Mr., printed sermons, 119
Sanchy, Mr., personality, 273
Sancroft, Wm., cited, 24; preaching, 57; memory, 76; sermon on the Fire, 90
Sanderson, R., cited, 24; memory, 68; on funeral sermons, 96, 97; sermon advertised, 123; sermon-dedication, 135; antiquities, 140; heraldry, 144; friend of Tombes, 175; music, 222; quoted Spenser, 245; recreations, 249; personality, 294
Sandys, Th., 185, 228, 246
Sarah and Hagar, Shute, 37, 78, 282
Satan the Leader, Baillie, 124
Scarborough, Sir Charles, 210, 303
Scepsis Scientifica, Glanvill, 251
Schlater, Mr., cited, 92
Scholae Academicæ, Wordsworth, 161
Scholasticae Theologiae Syntagma Mnemonicum, Prideaux, 324

Schools and School-Books, Hazlitt, 317
Scribe Instructed, The, South, 86, 116
Scudder, H., sermon-dedication, 129
Scudéry, Mlle. de, 241
Sculptura, Evelyn, 218
Seaman, L., orientals, 160; library, 182
Seasonable Caveat, A, Pierce, 80
Sedgwick, Jos., controversy, 17; Latin, 82
——, Wm., personality, 296
Selden, John, 21, 54, 64, 116, 151, 228, 242
Select Tracts, Maseres, 321
Seneca, 151
Seventeenth Cent. Life in the Country Parish, Trotter, 327
Shadwell, Th., 227
Shakespeare, 106, 133, 238, 244, 245
Shaking and Translating of Heaven and Earth, Owen, 322
Sharrock, R., law, 156; vegetables, 254
Shaw, J., popularity, 32; boldness, 40; cited, 72; payment, 278
——, S., on artificial tones, 51; plague sermon, 90; personality, 289; appearance, 303
Sheba's Head Cast over the Wall, Reeve, 124, 128
Sheffield, J., poetry, 237
Sheppard, S., drama, 216; poetry, 238
Sherlock, R., payment, 278
Shirley, Jas., 216
Short Discourse of the English Stage, A, Flecknoe, 215
Short Survey of Woodstocke, A, Widdowes, 141
Shorter Catechism, The, 197
Shute, J., serial sermons, 37; style, 78; cited, 282
Sibs (Sibbes), R., cited, 185

Thurloe, H., funeral sermon for Reynolds, 174; on math., 187

Tillotson, J., cited, 24, 31; sermon structure, 73; on Whichcote's poetry, 212; court chaplain, 271; personality, 293

Tipping, Wm., payment, 280

Titian, 219

Titus, Th., medicine, 198

Tombes, J., popularity, 34; sermon title, 120; Hebrew and Greek, 162; learning, 174; appearance, 304

Torner, J., personality, 295, 296

Towers, J., personality, 297

Tragi-comoedia Oxoniensis, Littleton, 234

Tregoss, Th., good birth, 262

Treasury of Similes, A, Cawdrey, 109

Treatise of the Roman Ports, Somner, 140

Triana, Fuller, 131, 239

Triplett, Th., ballad on Gill, 234

Tristram, A., medicine, 199

Trueman, J., memory, 68; law, 156

Tuckney, cited, 299

Tudor London, Besant, 71

Turner, F., chemistry, 154; personality, 296

——, G. L.: *Records of Early Nonconformity,* 203

Twi(y)ne, B., antiquities, 140, 142

Twisse, Wm., cited, 299

Two-edged Sword, A, Marshall, 122

Udall, E., preaching, 38

Udolpho, 242

Ulfilas, *Silver Codex of,* 165

Use of Humane Learning in the Ministry, Reynolds, 140

Usher, Jas., at a disputation, 11; cited, 24, 62, 142, 160, 161, 164, 230; popularity, 30; memory, 68; funeral sermon for him, 99, 104; chronology, 104, 141; how he learned to read, 104; antiquities, 140; coins, 144; on Eastern languages, 161; *Polyglot Bible,* 163; aided Junius, 165; Irish, 168; philology, 172; payment, 175; learning, 175, 179; aided scholars, 180; library, 182; recreations, 249

Uxley, Mr., cited, 23

Valle, Pet. de la, 243

Valley of Vision, The, Holdsworth, 117, 120

Van Dyke, 219

Vathek, 242

Vaughan, H., 152, 238, 246

——, Th., rosicrucian, 153; magic, 152; orientals, 160; poetry, 226, 238

Vaux, J., 97, 280

Verney, G., 97

——, Sir Ralph: *Memoirs,* 76, 77, 101, 107

Vicar: *Rhetoric,* 6

Vieryra, A., sermon to the fishes, 259

View of Univ. Hist., A, Tallents, 143

Villemain, funeral sermons, 95

Vincent, N., popularity, 33

Vindiciae Acad., Webster, 17, 148

Vindiciae, Lit., Hall, 174, 262

Vines, R., cited, 62, 118; funeral sermon for him, 99; his sermon for Essex, 102; aversion to print, 119; teacher, 204; punning on his name, 229; on chaplains, 267; cited, 299

Vinke, P., at a disputation, 11

Virgin's Pattern, The, Bacchiler, 76

Voice of one Crying, The, Shaw, 51, 90

Vossius, G. J., rhetoric, 6

——, I., library, 183; music, 234

Voyage to East India, A, Terry, 243

Vulgar Errors, Browne, 255

Walker, A., private chaplain, 269

————, G., serial preaching, 37

————, J.: *The Sufferings of the Clergy,* 30, 33, 57, 96, 145, 153, 156, 160, 162, 164, 172, 179, 180, 182, 192, 196, 206, 210, 236, 237, 238, 294

Wall, J., cited, 111; wrote a Preface, 135; personality, 292, 297

Wallis, J., memory, 68; chemistry, 154; Anglo-Saxon, 167; hard student, 177; Royal Soc., 178; math., 189; controversy with Holder, 200; medicine, 202; pupil of Oughtred's, 189, 210; music, 222, 223; read Chaucer, 244; astronomy, 251; conformed, 257; court chaplain, 271; controversy with Hobbes, 290

Walton, B.: *Polyglot Bible,* 163

————, Isaac, 68, 73, 97, 117, 123, 170, 226, 246, 259, 287, 294, 297

Ward, R.: *Life of Henry More,* 252

————, Sam'l, drawing (emblematist), 219

————, Seth, controversy on education, 17; sermon at Whitehall, 93; funeral sermon for Monk, 102; on astrology, 148; learning, 175; the Royal Soc., 178; math., 191; pupil of Oughtred's, 109, 209; athletics, 249; hunting, 252; cited, 193, 303

Warren, E., delivery, 54; medicine, 199

————, J., Latin, 157

Warwick, Earl of, 269

————, Mary, Countess of: *Autobiog.,* 269

Warwick, Sir Philip, 101, 304

Waterhouse, E., cited, 111; on borrowing sermons, 116; heraldry, 145; medicine, 199

Wat(t)s, G., translations, 171

Watson, Foster, 4, 5, 6, 7, 65, 77, 158, 179, 200, 212, 220

————, Th.: *A Pastor's Love,* 92, 185

Wavel, R., good birth, 262

Wayneflete, Mem. of Bishop, Heylin, 236

Weaver, Th., poetry, 233

Webster, J., controversy, 17; astrology, 149; music, 219

Weeks, Dr., personality, 289

Wellington, H.: *Hist. Notices,* 98, 281

Wesley, John: *Of a Wife's Duties,* 92

West, Mr., cited, 23

West Barbary, Addison, L., 243

Westfield, Th., delivery, 56, 57; memory, 68; sermon length, 113

Westley, B., medicine, 199; personality, 296

Westminster Confession, The, ix, 197

Westminster School, 8, 158, 206, 207

Wheatley, H. B.: *Samuel Pepys,* 60

Wheelock, A., Arabic, 161; *Polyglot Bible,* 164; Anglo-Saxon, 165; cited, 281

Whichcote, B., praised by Tillotson, 212

Whistler, Dr., on Kettle's Latin, 208

Whitaker, Wm., cited, 299

White, Gilbert, 252

————, Jer., private chaplain, 268

————, John: *First Century of Scandalous Priests,* 41, 83

————, John, poetry, 233; charm, 297

Whitefoot, J., on Jos. Hall's memory, 67; sermon title, 99; poetry, 230

Whitford, D., heraldry, 145

Whitlock, B.: *Essays,* 181

——, R., law., 156

Whitney, Parson, on math. and conjuring books, 189

Whole Duty of Man, The, Allestry (?), 291

Wickens, Wm., personality, 290

Wickleff, R., farming, 258

Widdowes, Th., antiquities, 141

Wild(e), Geo., drama, 217

——, Robt., bold preaching, 39; compared with Peters, 61; drama, 216; poetry, 229, 230, 238, 279; personality, 288, 290

Wilkins, John, examiner, 8; cited, 24, 43, 254; sermon structure, 45, 74, 77; shorthand, 77; on mystical divines, 85; sermon-help, 112; sermon borrowing, 115; origin of language, 164; Anglo-Saxon, 166; philology, 172; French, 170; Royal Soc., 178; math., 193; transfusion of blood, 202; pupil of Sylvester, 211; drawing, 219; music, 223; mechanics, 249, 251; conformed, 257; appearance, 304

——, J., delivery, 56

Willes, H., math., 194; law, 156

Williams, John, memory, 67; French, 170; recreation, 247; good birth, 261; personality, 293; appearance, 304

Williams, A Memoir of John, Hacket, 24, 35, 170, 245

Willoughby, F., 255

Wilson, J., medicine, 199

——, Th., memory, 67; sermon repetition, 75; recreation, 248; music, 224; cited, 298

Winchurst, J., math., 194

Winniffe, Th., *Polyglot Bible,* 164

Winstanley, R., 225

Wisdom of being Religious, The, Tillotson, 73

Wisdomes Character, Hardy, 133

Wisdomes Counterfeit, Hardy, 316

Wisdom's Folly, 171

Wither, Geo., 246

Wodenote, Theoph., teaching, 212

Wood, Anthony à: *Athenae Oxoniensis; Fasti Ox.,* 10, 30, 31, 37, 52, 57, 61, 67, 72, 96, 98, 139, 140, 141, 142, 143, 144, 145, 147, 148, 153, 154, 156, 158, 159, 160, 162, 165, 167, 170, 171, 172, 177, 179, 180, 181, 182, 183, 190, 191, 192, 194, 195, 196, 199, 200, 201, 202, 204, 236, 238, 243, 254, 255, 267, 280, 281, 284, 285, 288, 289, 290, 291, 292, 296, 304

——, E., poetry, 231

——, J., Greek and Latin, 175

Woodbridge, B., delivery, 51

Woodford, S., music, 224; poetry, 238

Woodroffe, B., chemistry, 154

——, T., library, 182; medicine, 195

Wordsworth, Ch.: *Scholae Acad.,* 161

Worthies of Eng., The (see Fuller)

Wotten, Sir Henry, 170

Wray, J., *see* Ray

Wren, Dr. Chris., Royal Soc., 178; math., 194; astronomy, 251; on frogs, 255

——, Sir Chris., 189, 192, 210, 250, 251

——, Sir Chris. (the younger); *Parentalia,* 42, 141, 145, 194, 225

——, M., impeached, 42; sermon-dedication to him, 128; antiquities, 141; heraldry, 145;

hard student, 177; Royal Soc., 178

Wren, Th., medicine, 196; music, 224

Wright, Abr., on preaching, 18-20; poetry, 233-234

Wyatt, R. B.: *William Harvey*, 188

Young(e), P., learning, 179; library-keeper, 180

——, S., personality, 293